Internetworking

Designing the
Right Architectures

Data Communications and Networks Series
Consulting Editor: Dr C. Smythe, University of Sheffield

Selected titles

NetWare Lite
  S. Broadhead

PC–Host Communications: Strategies for Implementation
  H.-G. Göhring and E. Jasper

Token Ring: Principles, Perspectives and Strategies
  H.-G. Göhring and F.-J. Kauffels

Ethernet: Building a Communications Infrastructure
  H.-G. Hegering and A. Läpple

Local Area Networks: Making the Right Choices
  P. Hunter

Network Management: Problems, Standards and Strategies
  F.-J. Kauffels

Distributed Systems Management
  A. Langsford and J.D. Moffett

Managing NetWare
  F. Nowshadi

X400 Message Handling: Standards, Interworking, Applications
  B. Plattner, C. Lanz, H. Lubich, M. Müller and T. Walter

Systems Network Architecture
  W. Schäfer and H. an de Meulen

Frame Relay: Principles and Applications
  P. Smith

Downsizing: Strategies for Success in the Modern Computer World
  D. Trimmer

TCP/IP: Running a Successful Network
  K. Washburn and J.T. Evans

Integrated Network and System Management
  H.-G. Hegering and S. Abeck

Network Operating Systems: Making the Right Choices
  P. Hunter

Internetworking

Designing the
Right Architectures

Colin Smythe

University of Sheffield
and
Dunelm Services Limited

ADDISON-WESLEY
PUBLISHING
COMPANY

Wokingham, England • Reading, Massachusetts • Menlo Park, California • New York
Don Mills, Ontario • Amsterdam • Bonn • Sydney • Singapore
Tokyo • Madrid • San Juan • Milan • Paris • Mexico City • Seoul • Taipei

The programs in this book have been included for their instructional value. They have been tested with care but are not guaranteed for any particular purpose. The publisher does not offer any warranties or representations, nor does it accept any liabilities with respect to the programs.

Many of the designations used by manufacturers and sellers to distinguish their products are claimed as trademarks. Addison-Wesley has made every attempt to supply trademark information about manufacturers and their products mentioned in this book. A list of the trademark designations and their owners appears on p. xxi.

Cover designed by Designers & Partners of Oxford
and printed by The Riverside Printing Co. (Reading) Ltd.
Typeset by the author using PageMaker™
Printed and bound in Great Britain at the University Press, Cambridge

First printed 1995. Reprinted 1995.

British Library Cataloguing in Publication Data
A catalogue record for this book is available from the British Library.

Library of Congress Cataloging in Publication Data

Smythe, Colin.
    Internetworking: designing the right architectures / Colin Smythe.
      p.   cm.
    Includes bibliographical references and index.
    ISBN 0–201–56536–6
    1. Local area networks. 2. Computer network architectures.
    3. Internetworking. I. Title.
    TK5105.7.S58 1994
    0004.6'8--dc20   94–23809
                                                  CIP

TO CHRIS, LUKE AND JENNIFER

Series Preface

For one reason or another, science and engineering books, and therefore their corresponding series, in the areas of computer communications and the ubiquitous information technology fall into one of two categories: academic (implying a deep fundamental analysis of the topic and so ideal for academics or those inclined towards the smallest of detail) or flexiware (implying a text which is an extension of the relevant technical manuals and covering much of what ought to be in said manuals).

This series is different. It is designed to cross the gap between the academic and flexiware approaches. The aim is to produce a series of books devoted to the field of computer communications for use by engineers, managers and, yes, even consultants, who earn their livelihood by making communications networks work. The books are neither detailed treatises on the theoretical operation of networks nor are they mere cookbooks on how to get the best from your network and its manuals. Instead this series brings the two fields together to explain how and why things are this or that way.

To ensure that this aim is achieved, the authors are drawn from people who are themselves actively engaged in fighting with their networks – and whether we like it or not much of the time it seems to be a fight in all senses of the word. One other trait of our authors is that not only are they practitioners of the art of networking – for art it is – but they have also been responsible for industrially based training of the new generation of network engineers. In other words this series is written by a group of professionals who have extensive experience as users, designers, maintainers and trainers in the art of communications networks.

It is our intention to address the full range of communications networking, including the future developments and their impact on current design considerations. Naturally this means that many of the texts are a product of their time and will reflect many of the immediate concerns of the networking community. The areas covered by the series include: internetworking both at the local and wide area scales, network management, low cost networking and internetworking, the design and maintenance of local area network systems, applications support including file transfer and electronic mail, and of course network operating systems, protocols and operational architectures.

I hope you get as much pleasure and understanding from reading these as our authors gained in writing them.

Colin Smythe
November 1994

Preface

Looking back over the past twenty years, there has been an incredible change in the way people work. One of the most significant contributors to that change has been the wholesale adoption of computers and the technology that enables them to be connected across short and long distances. Incredibly, but inevitably perhaps, the rate of development is slowly increasing. Many forces are responsible for this but it is the user who suffers the consequences. It almost goes without saying that the moment a new purchase is agreed then it becomes dated technology. Survival for a modern communications network is based upon flexibility; the ability to respond quickly and effectively to a change in user requirements, available technology and cost.

The internetworking of local area networks is one way of responding to these changes. Unfortunately, like all solutions, it is a double edged sword. What might have looked ideal can turn into a nightmare solution because of the simplest oversight. A common example of this is the prohibiting of 'one-stop' shopping to avoid being too dependent on a single supplier or manufacturer. Of course this is fine until the issue of network management is considered (normally the last issue addressed and usually once the network is actually operational) and then the strength of a single vendor solution becomes apparent – that is an integrated management system; something which is not yet available for the heterogeneous network architecture.

The aim of this book is to help you to avoid some of the less obvious pitfalls, but remember that mistakes will always be made. This book should help to:

- Clarify the terminology and jargon as it is used in the field of internetworking and so enable the reader to translate the current technological and marketing literature. It should also guide the reader in how to ask the manufacturers and suppliers the right questions.
- Describe the features and functions of the different internetworking relay elements and so provide an appreciation of the ways best suited to creating extended local area networks.
- To show the relationship between internetworking and the open systems interconnection reference model, thereby explaining the architectural considerations for future networks.

An underlying theme in this book is the use of the International Organization for Standardization's terminology adopted for the open systems interconnection seven-layer reference model (OSI/RM). This is not an attempt to advocate the OSI/RM in preference to any other protocol model but it is a reflection of the richness of the terminology available when using this approach. This use of the OSI/RM terminology as a common language is adopted by most suppliers and manufacturers and is a reflection of its capability to describe networks and protocols that do not conform to the formal standard itself.

This book was written in two distinct parts. The first introduces all of the networking terms used for the second part, which actually discusses the internetworking of local area networks. The emphasis is on the Ethernet and Token Ring local area networks because these account for the large majority of all installed local networks and this is unlikely to change in the next five years.

Chapter 1 establishes the case for internetworking. Internetworking is particularly important now that most organizations use different types of local area network and yet still require the seamless transfer of information across these. In fact, for many companies profitability is determined by the speed and accuracy by which this form of interconnection is supported.

Chapter 2 introduces the different types of network architecture commonly employed in the modern day network. One of the features of this discussion is the difficulty in categorically defining what is and is not a local area network. The formal definitions are not reflected in the ways in which such networks are really used and interconnected.

Chapter 3 discusses the fundamental aspects of protocols – that is the set of rules for governing data communications across a network. While there are several dozen different types of protocol, there are in fact only a few underlying principles which are true for all of them.

Chapter 4 formally introduces the open systems interconnection seven-layer reference model. While full adoption of this model is still a long way off it is the most effective reference for terminology and as such it has been completely adopted by manufacturers and suppliers in their sales literature.

Chapter 5 reviews the field of local area networks and describes all of the underlying principles and techniques used in this field. Although Ethernet and Token Ring local area networks dominate in the commercial world there are still many rival techniques which may slowly acquire more acceptance as technology improves and user demands change.

Chapter 6 describes the operation of Ethernet based local area networks. There is not just one Ethernet system or architecture. Instead there are several flavours of this carrier sensing system, each of which reflects different cabling systems and user applications.

Chapter 7 describes the operation of the Token Ring local area networks. The Token Ring is considerably less mature than its rival and so there is considerably more interpretation and debate by the manufacturers about the ways in which the corresponding standards should be specified and interpreted.

Chapter 8 reviews the myriad of proprietary systems currently in the marketplace. The present emphasis by the manufacturers may well be that towards standardization, however, there is a considerable investment in their own types of network operating systems, integrated architectures, closed protocols and local area networks.

Chapter 9 reviews the different types of internetworking relays and describes their relationship to the OSI. Each relay has its own particular role and so it is important to appreciate how each of them provides a part of the whole internetworking strategy. This chapter provides a synopsis of the information covered in the chapters on repeaters, bridges, routers and gateways, and as such is ideal for the reader who wants to acquire a quick overview of the technology used for internetworking.

Chapter 10 discusses both the Ethernet and the Token Ring repeaters, and shows how they are used to overcome the physical limitations imposed by the engineering of the network interface cards and the cabling structure.

Chapter 11 discusses bridges and describes how these are used to construct a single logical network from many linked physical networks. Again, both Ethernet and Token Ring bridges are discussed individually.

Chapter 12 describes how routers are used to create an integrated network by connecting different subnetworks, the only restriction on this connectivity being that each of the subnetworks support the same network layer protocol.

Chapter 13 addresses the problem of interconnecting completely different network architectures, in particular those from Digital and IBM. This requires the use of a gateway, which provides protocol translation between the two systems.

Chapter 14 discusses how network management can be imposed on multivendor architectures. While the aim of integrated network management across true heterogeneous architectures is still many years away the benefit of some form or another of network management cannot be overstated.

Chapter 15 draws together all of the issues concerning internetworking and discusses the ways in which the relay elements effect the design of a network. The usual aim is to provide immediate connectivity. However, the long-term survival of the network depends on its manageability and flexibility to adapt to new demands. The important feature of this chapter is that it draws together all of the discussions on the different technologies and attempts to construct a network design approach to help the network engineer to plan and implement LAN based network systems.

Chapter 16 attempts to put into perspective the potential effects that the enormous range of new developments in networking, particularly those concerning wide area connectivity, will have on current systems. The correct architecture today may ensure a flexible response to these new developments, but what is the 'correct architecture'?

Chapter 17 looks back at the topics discussed in the previous chapters and attempts to draw some conclusions on the ways in which the best possible use can be made of the current technology, how to exploit the technology now and in the future, and how best to avoid obsolescence.

The final section of the book contains all of the reference material necessary to supplement the main body of the book. This includes the list of references; a list of abbreviations; a glossary of terms which provides a brief, one paragraph, description of all of the important elements in internetworking; and lists of all of the relevant standards.

The field of communications is full of jargon and acronyms. The extensive list of abbreviations provided at the end of the book needs to be mastered, at some time or another. Unfortunately, in many instances jargon is used to hide understanding but is essential for the concise description of the functionality being described. Coupled with this all-pervasive jargon is an embarrassing absence of agreed graphical representation for the elements that make up a modern network. This book uses a symbol set to represent the different elements of a network and without advocating the use of this symbology, it is essential that each organization develop its own.

Colin Smythe
Sheffield, UK
November 1994

Acknowledgements

Writing a book is one of those activities that a sane person agrees to do about once every decade. It has taken over three years to write this book and so I'm looking forward to my seven-year rest. During the past three years several people have been instrumental in ensuring that this book was completed and so I would like to thank them all for their contribution.

Peter Jones and Steve Harmsworth have reviewed several drafts of the work and they, along with the Addison-Wesley referees, have done their best to keep me on the right track. I must, however, make it clear that any mistakes or misconceptions in the book are of my own doing. I would also like to thank Tim Pitts of Addison-Wesley who alternately played the good and bad guy, and Karen Mosman, also of Addison-Wesley, who ensured the book's completion.

Finally I would like to thank my wife for acting as secretary, proof-reader, page-setter and general dogsbody while still keeping two bouncy young children well under control. Perhaps writing books isn't so bad after all.

Contents

Trademark notice.

DEC, Digital Network Architecture (DNA), DECnet IV, PCSA, Pathworks, Advantage-networks, DECnet-DOS 3270 Terminal Emulator are trademarks of Digital Equipment Corporation.

AppleTalk, AppleShare, LocalTalk, Macintosh and MAC are trademarks of Apple Computer, Inc.

MS-DOS is a registered trademark of Microsoft Corporation.

Network File Service (NFS) is a trademark of Sun Microsystems, Inc.

HP LAN Manager, 4972A LAN manager, LANProbe, Open View are trademarks of the Hewlett-Packard Company.

IBM, Systems Network Architecture (SNA), OS/2, LANRES, OS/400, NetView, System View, Enterprise Management Architecture (EMA), VMS, Ultrix are trademarks of International Business Machines Corporation.

Switched Multi-megabit Data Service is a trademark of Bell Communications.

NetWare, NetWare Lite, NetWare 286, NetWare 386, NetWare 4 are trademarks of Novell Inc.

CO3, OSLAN, Information Processing Architecture are trademarks of ICL.

Xerox Network System (XNS), Ethernet (licensed by Xerox) are trademarks of Xerox.

Open Systems Cabling Architecture (OSCA), PSS+ are trademarks of BT Plc.

TOPS is a trademark of Sitka Inc.

3+, 3+ Open are trademarks of 3COM.

ARCnet is a trademark of Datapoint Corporation.

LANtastic is a trademark of Artisoft.

PowerLan is a trademark of Power Technology.

Burroughs Network Architecture is a trademark of Burroughs.

Distributed Systems Environment is a trademark of Honeywell.

Distributed Communications Architecture is a trademark of Sperry Univac.

Net/One LAN Manager is a trademark of UB.

LattisNet is a trademark of Synoptics.

LAN manager is a trademark of Microsoft Inc.

VINES is a trademark of Banyan Systems Inc.

UNIX, Premises Distribution System (PDS), Unified Network Management Architecture (UNMA) are trademarks of AT&T.

Symbol List

The following symbols are used throughout this text. Many organizations employ their own symbol set, however as yet there are no universally agreed symbols for each of the elements which go to make up a communications network.

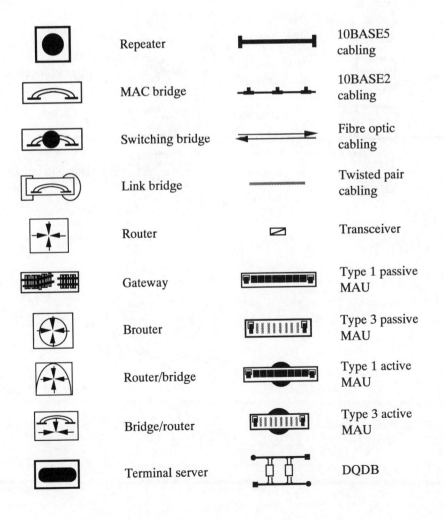

Repeater		10BASE5 cabling
MAC bridge		10BASE2 cabling
Switching bridge		Fibre optic cabling
Link bridge		Twisted pair cabling
Router		Transceiver
Gateway		Type 1 passive MAU
Brouter		Type 3 passive MAU
Router/bridge		Type 1 active MAU
Bridge/router		Type 3 active MAU
Terminal server		DQDB

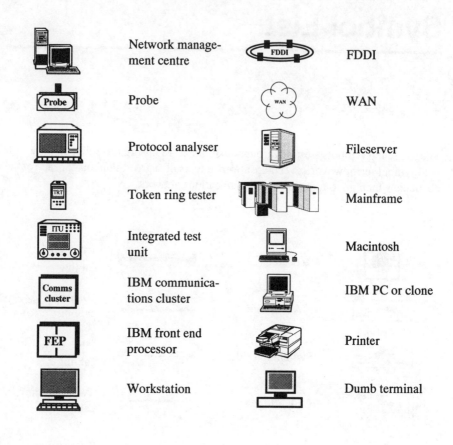

	Network management centre		FDDI
	Probe		WAN
	Protocol analyser		Fileserver
	Token ring tester		Mainframe
	Integrated test unit		Macintosh
	IBM communications cluster		IBM PC or clone
	IBM front end processor		Printer
	Workstation		Dumb terminal

1

Introduction

1.1 Communications networks

It is not an exaggeration to state that communications networks are an essential feature of everyday life. Whilst the telephone, radio and television networks are still the main services found in the home the same is not true at work. In most cases the work environment includes a fax machine and many organizations are now dependent on personal computers. The widespread use of the personal computer has revolutionized the way in which business operates and as a consequence we have had to rethink the ways in which electronic communication is exploited. In some cases the effectiveness of this exploitation now has a direct bearing on an organization's ability to compete in its chosen market-place, and so whereas the original revolution was 'technology-driven' it is now 'user-driven'. This change in driving force is accompanied by an increased wariness and scepticism from the user about what the new technology can provide: therein lies the problem. Users are only interested in what they understand and believe will deliver the necessary services whereas suppliers have to continually renovate their product line and introduce new technologies so that they can stay ahead of the competition. This conflict is further heightened by a communications community which is struggling to standardize untried technology, uses complex and changing jargon, has a history of proprietary and idiosyncratic systems, and which has no agreed single focus for research and development. Therefore, it is interesting to reflect on how we reached such a dubious position.

One of the first communication systems to use electrical methods was proposed by Charles Morrison, a Scottish surgeon, in 1753. He suggested a system in which each character of the alphabet was allocated a wire, and in which the receiver was constructed from pithballs and paper with preprinted characters on it. Also during the mid eighteenth century, a French monk, named Abbe Nollet, was demonstrating what was probably the first ring topology local area network. He connected together two hundred Carthusian monks with lengths of iron wire to form a circle approximately 1.5 km in diameter. To show that an electric signal travelled quickly around such a ring he then connected one of the lengths of wire to an electrostatic generator, promptly electrocuted all 200 monks and thus proved his point.

Throughout the rest of the eighteenth century development of the telegraph system was slow due to problems of charge storage and it was not until the invention of the battery by Galvani and Volta that electricity and not electrostatics was considered. The demand for a telegraph system was stimulated by the development and growth of railway systems (the first public railway opened in England in 1830) and by 1837 the first true telegraph systems were invented by Morse in America, and Cooke and Wheatstone in Britain. The first commercial telegraph was introduced in 1844 and this was further refined until the 1880s, at which time the telephone was introduced.

Bell, another Scotsman, invented the telephone in 1876 and this created the dominance of analogue signalling techniques over the digital methods – as used in telegraphy. In 1880 the Postmaster General obtained the rights to the telephone, after several lawsuits, which gave the Post Office licensing until 1911. Consequently, this stopped the North American companies, which had patented several telephone system designs, from producing any such system until 1912. From that time onwards the telephone has become the most important method of communication for people all over the world and its development has seen the introduction of digital switching techniques, satellite links, fibre optic cabling and, most recently, mobile telephones.

A development from the telegraph occurred in the 1890s when a telegraph operator, named F.G. Creed, became frustrated by the use of stick perforators in the production of morse coded paper tapes. Instead he connected a typewriter to a paper tape puncher and used it to generate the morse coded paper tapes. He later extended this system to receive morse signals and to automatically punch the equivalent received paper tape message. This was the embryo of the telex system. An important facet in the telex system is the automatic acknowledgement, by the receiver, of the request for start of transmission sent by the transmitter. This is necessary because a receiver can operate without human intervention and as such it was the precursor to the more sophisticated communication protocols used in computer systems.

The end of the nineteenth century also saw the development of the first radio systems, especially by Marconi, who by 1897 was transmitting atmospheric signals across a distance of nine miles. Transatlantic radio communication first occurred in 1901 between Cornwall and Newfoundland and by 1910 the first radio systems were installed on commercial ships. Marconi spent the rest of his life modifying radio techniques, and when he died in 1937 the world paid tribute to him with a two-minute total radio silence. Development of the radio produced the standard present-day modulation schemes such as amplitude modulation and frequency modulation.

During the 1950s two developments were to take place which would start a radical change in world communications. The first was the introduction of commercially available computers and the second was the launch of the first satellite Sputnik in 1957. The computers were digitally based, and, while they were not as compact as their present-day equivalents, they were based on semiconductor technology, for example the 1952 Gamma 3 which used germanium diodes and was built in West Germany. The American computers at that time were ENIAC, built in 1946, the EDVAC, built in 1949, and UNIVAC 1 which was built in 1952 and was the first commercially available computer. Transistorized computers were introduced in 1960 by Control Data Corporation with integrated circuits being first used in 1965. Digital technology was now well established and this encouraged the use of digital techniques in other systems which traditionally had been analogue based, for example the telephone.

In 1959 the first digital telephone switching system was proposed by the American Telephone and Telegraph Company and was named the 'experimental solid state exchange', or ESSEX. This provided the basis for all further work on digitally switched systems and in 1962 the first commercial system of this type, T1, was introduced by Bell Systems. By the end of that year 250 digital communication circuits had been installed and by 1976 that number exceeded three million installations.

After the shock of the Russian success with Sputnik, the Americans launched the first communications satellite in 1960, Echo I, and in 1964 this was joined by Echo II. Both of these were passive satellites and were used to reflect radio signals across the world, thereby solving the problems encountered with atmosphere reflection techniques (which had limited the range of point-to-point radio communications). Rapid development of active satellites followed and at the present time satellites must perform complex signal processing to efficiently share the available link bandwidth and time. Satellites now provide blanket coverage of the globe and enable the transmission of television signals and telephone conversations from one side of the globe to the other.

By the end of the 1960s the computer was firmly established as a major data processing tool but there was a growing need for a means to interconnect physically distributed computers so that they could share common data. The interconnection requirement for computers produced a large number of problems which had not arisen in radio and telephone networks because the computer had to be instructed on error correction and conversation protocols (derived from the experiences gained using the telex system), which a human performs naturally. The first full computer network was the US Department of Defense's (DoD) ARPANET, which used the existing telephone networks but which also implemented a packet switching protocol to provide both error control/recovery and a standard conversation protocol. These types of networks are now termed 'wide area networks' and would now be categorized as low data rate, high cost networks.

The 1970s was a period when large mainframe computers were slowly replaced by minicomputers and then microcomputers. The emphasis changed from the use of a large central processor to the use of individual workstations, which, although providing localized processing power, could not overcome the cost of providing specialized peripherals at each microprocessor. The solution is the local area network, or local network, which provides high data rate communications at a relatively low cost for a physically localized community of workstations. Figure 1.1 shows such a situation, where access to a laser printer for different types of personal computer is supported by a local area network. This network has then been extended using some form of relay element (labelled the 'Link') so that more users have access to the printer. The first commercially available local area network was ARCnet, which was introduced by Data Point in 1976. This was quickly followed by Ethernet, originally licensed by Xerox, and even though many other forms of local network are now commercially available, the Ethernet architecture is still the most widely used – Figure 1.1 shows two Ethernets linked together. The various standards agencies across the world are now attempting to define the protocols for networks in general and are currently providing the detailed specifications: the Institute of Electrical and Electronics Engineers 802 committees are responsible for the fine detail of local network architectures, with the International Organization for Standardization publishing the final standards.

Ironically, the trends in computer processing have also turned full circle and the requirement for coordinated processing power is implemented by using distributed systems which are interconnected with local area networks. Local area networks are also interconnected using repeaters, bridges, routers and gateways with wide area networks being used to connect the distributed local networks. Satellite links are also used in this interconnection, with project Universe being the original example in the UK. Current research and development interests for networking are concerned with the

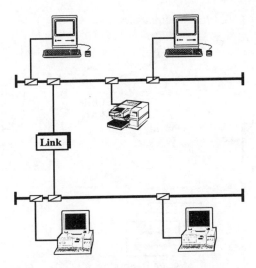

Figure 1.1   Initial local area network usage.

use of local networks to provide users with an integrated multi-services environment, including mixed voice/data access and the more generalized multimedia services. Unfortunately, the simplicity of the original local area networks architectures (which avoided the need for routing algorithms, error correction and recovery, packet protocols, and so on) has now been lost due to the more sophisticated needs of the users. It is these new demands from the user that have created the need for internetworking.

1.2 Internetworking

At present, internetworking is an important concern for all organizations that depend upon communications networks for any part of their welfare. Internetworking, like most new terms, can be interpreted in a number of ways but, strictly speaking, it refers to the linking of networks so that they retain their own status as a network, i.e. they are not merged into a single homogeneous network. It has long been realized that homogeneity is an impossible goal and is unnecessary provided that the appropriate internetworking devices are made available.

Internetworking as a concept has been superseded by the terms interoperability and interworking. While the origins of these three terms may be unclear, common usage has clarified their relationship. Internetworking is normally applied to the problems of physical connectivity between similar and different networks (including the use of wide area network bearers) whereas interworking is applied to the interconnection of similar applications and their supporting protocols (which in many cases do differ significantly). Interoperability between systems, that is, the ability for users to

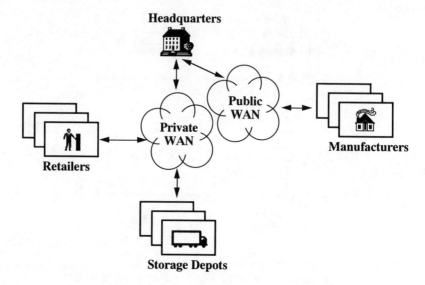

Figure 1.2 A typical corporate internetworking requirement.

transfer information between different communications systems irrespective of the ways in which these systems are supported, is usually dependent on both interworking and internetworking, as well as the issues of hardware and software compatibility within the host systems. This book will address many of the issues of interoperability and interworking but will concentrate upon internetworking, that is, the physical interconnection of local area networks.

As systems converge into networks, creating distributed systems, the term internetworking becomes wider and more far-reaching in its implications. It is no longer just about linking public networks, it is also about the provision of the services needed to provide effective sharing of resources across the networks. As a result, real internetworking is about delivering functions to end users, not simply installing cables and boxes to provide physical interfaces (important as this is). It is always humbling to remember that the network is there because of, and to support, the user, and not, as one might believe when witnessing the treatment of some users, the other way round.

The typical networking requirements for an organization are shown in Figure 1.2. In this example, the business structure consists of a headquarters, several retail outlets, several suppliers and several intermediate storage locations. In many cases such a network would make use of a privately owned network (which may or many not make use of leased lines from a telecommunications supplier) as well as accessing the public data networks. The former would be used for internal information whereas the latter would be necessary to interconnect with external organizations such as suppliers. A typical sequence of communications would involve the retailers requesting supplies from the local storage depots, the storage depots ordering more supplies from the manufacturers themselves (via the headquarters switching system) and the manufac- turers directly invoicing the headquarters. Unfortunately, this representation is too simplistic because it avoids the problems of linking the private and public networks,

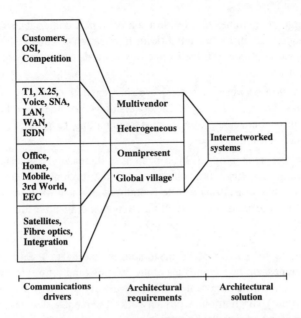

Figure 1.3 The demands on internetworked systems.

and applications, computer and network compatibility between the headquarters, storage depots, retailers and manufacturers.

In fact when the corporate structure becomes as dependent on the communications infrastructure as shown in Figure 1.2 then it is the quality of that infrastructure which determines whether or not the organization can compete effectively in its chosen market. This dependence on the communications infrastructure is also increasing because some organizations will only trade with other businesses if they can transfer information electronically. The effect of this approach is that the communications network is no longer just a small localized concern but is a fundamental contributor to the capability of the organization. This importance has been captured by the phrase 'enterprise networking', which is used to denote a network which encompasses all of the facilities, activities and relationships of the host business, and internetworking, interworking and interoperability are central features of such an infrastructure.

The internetworked system becomes characterized by the relationships shown in Figure 1.3, which shows how the available technology and the required architectures must be combined in an internetworked solution. Here the relationship between the enabling technologies and the user pressures which can be said to be forcing the development of internetworking are shown, and these can be summarized as:

- The development and acceptance of standards during the past few years has been dramatic and is now having a significant effect. In particular standards are swinging the purchasing arguments away from 'one-stop shopping' towards one in which the customer needs an 'open', or vendor independent solution.

- Technology continues to provide a source of new components functioning in new ways, with different networking implications. This is a long-term trend which will continue to drive technology towards a more heterogeneous environment.

- Competition between suppliers has sharpened significantly in the last few years and the spate of mergers and acquisitions continues to reflect the intense competition between those suppliers attempting to provide an 'umbrella' solution to customer needs.

- Information technology (IT) is becoming increasingly widespread both in terms of geographical and demographical distribution. Less developed countries are rapidly installing new telecommunications infrastructures to support their economic plans. This is fuelling a long-standing move towards the 'global village'.

The increasing sophistication of IT customers is leading to greater demands and enhanced awareness of the capabilities of the existing (and future) technologies, and as a result of some of the factors itemized above, very few organizations (even the 'Bluest of the Blue') have homogeneous networks. Frequently, devices are introduced from other vendors and new technologies brought to bear which remove the 'one-vendor' situation. The problem of internetworking at the highest level then becomes one of how to:

- Use a LAN as gateway into the mainframe networks, so that corporate data can be accessed from a single workstation which supports both departmental and corporate needs.

- Provide a common gateway between your main WAN (typically provided by the mainframe vendor – often IBM) and another WAN (perhaps provided by your favourite departmental supplier – often Digital, or perhaps a network belonging to a subsidiary).

- Link remote LANs so that one department which is split across multiple sites can function as if it was on the same LAN.

- Extend a LAN beyond the distance limitations of the cabling that you are using and link different media types onto the same LAN.

1.3 Internetworking: The business case

Most organizations now use LANs as their in-house electronic communications system but it wasn't until the mid to late 80s that their potential was fully appreciated. Since then the uptake of LAN systems has been widespread, so much so that it is claimed by various market researchers that 75% of the Fortune 500 Companies have both Ethernet and Token Ring LANs. In the USA, Ethernet has some 55% of the market for new installations, with Token Ring having most of the other 45%, whereas in the UK and Europe, Ethernet has some 70% of that market with Token Ring having most of the other 30%. The connection of Ethernet/Ethernet, Token Ring/Token Ring and Ethernet/Token Ring LANs is a problem of internetworking; if such systems are not interconnected then it is almost certain that time and money are being wasted in one way or another. If the normal trends are assumed then this problem will become more acute in the UK and Europe as the volume of sales of Token Ring rises in line with that of the USA.

Companies have become used to the real business benefits to be derived from networked PCs: many IT users see this as the paradigm for computing. The structured and hierarchical environment of the typical mainframe and its WAN does not meet all of today's computing needs. This is why the LAN market has seen (and continues to see) such rapid growth. An example of the classical communications architecture solution is shown in Figure 1.4. Here an X.25 network has been established to support:

- Remote user access to the corporate mainframe via dial-up modem facilities and native X.25 interfaces (the front end processor (FEP) for the mainframe must contain an X.25 interface).

- Dumb device access (typically asynchronous terminals) to the corporate network via packet assembler/disassembler devices (PADs).

- User/user communications via native X.25 interfaces.

- The use of X.75 trunk links to interconnect two X.25 packet switched data networks from different suppliers.

Such a system provides a highly reliable, readily available, but slow and expensive solution. Each user requires an X.25 interface for their workstation or PAD access for their terminal which typically supplies them with a 9.6 kbps point-to-point link, multiplexed across a 64 kbps carrier service. The modern equivalent is to replace the remote dumb devices and the native X.25 PCs with LAN based PCs. LAN/X.25 internetworking devices (routers or gateways) are then used to interconnect the LAN and WAN systems. The advantage of this approach is that the users can then use their PCs for local network access, for example to access the local file servers and print servers.

A natural result of the growing importance of LANs is that different depart-ments start to want to share their data and obtain access to the corporate data. The extended LAN is one vehicle to obtain this result. In some cases corporate architectures have always been based upon LANs, and have exploited whichever internetworking devices have been available to provide them with the required connectivity, without the heavy cost overheads of using mainframe resources (although such an approach is still rare). Within a corporate network, more commonly termed the 'enterprise network', the internetworked LANs are required to provide:

- Remote access – this function provides for an on-line session between one

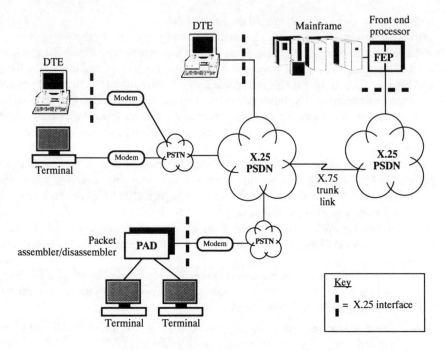

Figure 1.4 A classical X.25 networking solution.

network's terminal and another network's host. It primarily applies to the WAN domain, in which terminals have traditionally been dumb. This is variously described as 'terminal pass-through', 'virtual terminal' or TELNET capabilities, depending upon the technology and the way the function is achieved. As PCs become more widely used and the 'intelligent workstation' becomes a standard feature of office life, the capability to avoid fixed-function terminals is rapidly emerging, to be replaced by procedures to access multiple different server-networks. Frequently the best enabling technology for this sits within the LAN rather than the PC; however, this raises the issues of internetworking and the level of sophistication involved in internetworking is frequently greater than that involved with the more traditional access to remote hosts using a single network architecture.

- Resource sharing – access to expensive peripherals such as printers, image scanners, graphics devices etc. Figure 1.1 shows a system which supports shared access to a laser printer.

- Cooperative processing – in this situation, as part of a session between terminal user and their processor, there is a requirement for direct communication to another remote host in order to satisfy the requests of the user. Behind the scenes, the processor to which the user is attached generates an enquiry transaction to the remote host which traverses the linked networks, obtains a response, returns across the networks and, through the primary application,

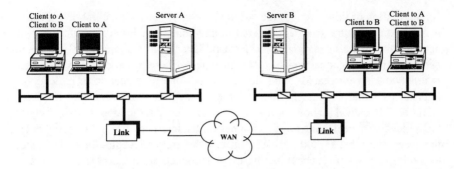

Figure 1.5 A client/server communications architecture.

returns a response to the user. This situation demands a complex set of interworking protocols to provide for the communications support demanded by the applications. Several vendors provide for such support, but it is only in recent years that such facilities have become seriously considered for frequent and mainstream use in heterogeneous, multivendor networks.

- Information transfer – to provide for these services (typically electronic mail or file transfers) it is usually necessary to interconnect several different types of networks if the service is to be effective. For this reason international standards in this area, such as X.400 electronic mail and electronic document interchange (EDI), have become widely adopted within a short period of their development;

- Client/server systems – this is one form of cooperative processing. Here the applications 'see' the network as a relatively simple application programming interface which they can use to distribute functions and procedures across the network. The local processing components are housed in a powerful low cost PC or UNIX box (delivering responsiveness to the user) and the remote processing component in a central database management system which functions as a repository of corporate data and common applications. This provides a central location which is secure and widely accessible through a powerful, structured and highly controlled WAN. However, underneath the application interface is a fairly complex set of internetworking products to provide for operation within the corporate wide area network as well as the LAN. The system shown in Figure 1.5 utilizes the LAN as the common access medium for client/server access. Each LAN has its own native server which the local clients can readily access (provided they have the appropriate client/server network operating system). The internetworking link also means that it is possible for users to have remote access to some servers, as is shown by two of the workstations, provided that the internetworking links permit the client/server protocol to cross them and that the clients also support that protocol.

In the early days of standardization it was assumed that in the long term the single 'open' network architecture would be based upon a single physical network. Any contemplation of this produces the question, 'Whose network will it be?'. Clearly it is not a question that can be answered in any commercially acceptable form – try debating this in the same room as a salesman. This means that the 'open' architecture demands the interconnection of different types of network and so the problem of internetworking is created. This demand is not one of academic or philosophical interest, as it may appear in some of the debates on standardization, but one of commercial survival for both the user and the supplier. It is the suppliers of networking equipment who are driving the development of the internetworking capability but it is the users who must exploit it. Unfortunately the users are caught in a whirlwind of technological expertise, a bewildering array of products and a wall of jargon. Commercial reality is not sympathetic to such obstructions and so it is time to unravel the field of internetworking.

2

Network Architectures

2.1 Introduction

Information systems comprise the users of the data and the network which interconnects them. The number of interconnected systems has significantly increased during
the past 25 years and the widespread proliferation of mobile and personal communications will cause an even greater number of new users to need extended connectivity.
This increase is in response to the huge demand for the rapid and reliable transfer of
many differing types of information between users separated by distances ranging from
just a few metres to thousands of kilometres.

Networks provide multiple access communications, that is, many users are
permitted access to a common communications channel, and it is the effective sharing
of this channel access that is provided by the protocols and architecture of the network.
In turn, these networks must conform to nationally and internationally agreed and
supported standards, otherwise cost effective internetworking based upon vendor
independence becomes almost impossible.

It is possible to categorize networks as one of three types: wide area networks,
metropolitan area networks and local area networks. In many cases it is not possible
to definitively categorize a network (even assuming that this is necessary in the first
place), particularly when several such networks become interconnected. However, it
is a useful exercise because it gives insight into the repercussions caused by uncontrolled and ill considered internetworking; it is important that the distinction should be
made according to the user's perception of the service and not on some arbitrary, and
permanently changing, technological basis.

2.2 The classification of networks

The first telephone system was established in the twentieth century and was based upon
analogue techniques. Bell's invention of the telephone in 1876 followed by Edison's
engineering work on it was the start of the discipline of communication networks. The
telephone system, now called the plain old telephone service (POTS), was the first
network to become available to households and in doing so became the original public
switched telephone network (PSTN).

The connection topology for telephones was, and still is, simple. Each
telephone is connected to a local switching exchange. The local switching exchanges
are linked to area switching exchanges, which in turn are linked to a national exchange,
and so on. A physical circuit must be established between the two telephones whenever
a conversation is required. This switching is termed circuit switching and the network
is called a circuit switched telephone network (CSTN). The circuit switching
nomenclature indicates the fact that all of the information flows along the same
physical telephone lines once the link is established and that no other information

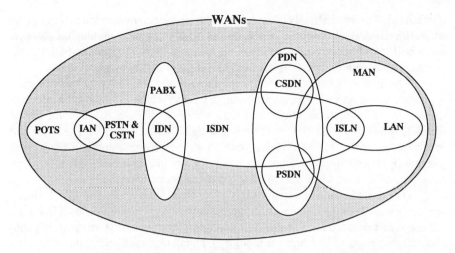

Figure 2.1 Relationships between network architectures.

makes concurrent use of that link. The use of analogue technology for voice communications and voice-like communications, such as modem links, gave rise to the term 'integrated analogue network' (IAN). The rapid introduction of digital switching exchanges during the 1970s (particularly in the USA) saw the IAN superseded by the integrated digital network (IDN).

The 1970s and 1980s also experienced an enormous expansion in the number of network architectures which became commercially available for the transfer of data as opposed to just voice. Human speech contains a lot of redundant information, so the telephone system does not have to accurately convey more than 40% of the original information for it to be understood. Computer systems, normally the end users of the public data networks (PDNs), are not so forgiving and so, in terms of reliability, a superior communication network is required. The end result is a myriad of network architectures, whose relationships are shown in the Venn diagram in Figure 2.1.

It can be argued that in principle all networks can be linked together, thereby forming the equivalent WAN with millions of users and covering thousands of kilometres. At the other extreme are geographically localized networks, or LANs, which may support just a few nodes and extend less than ten metres. Somewhere in between these two extremes lie the metropolitan area networks (MANs). MANs and LANs are predominantly data transfer orientated with throughputs in the millions of bits per second region and the number of errors being less than one every one thousand million bits. In contrast PDNs are, in general and at present, less demanding of their technology but they do require data transfer which is at least an order of magnitude faster and more reliable than for PSTNs. Circuit switching then becomes too slow and expensive, particularly when the data load characteristics of the users are considered, and so store and forward systems are used. In these systems the user information (which is either sent whole for message switching or is fragmented for packet switching) passes through each intermediate routing node until it reaches its final destination. The route actually taken by the data varies according to the loading of the network and the available capacity of each link. Unlike circuit switching the physical route will therefore vary on a message by message basis. PDNs use both packet switched data networks (PSDNs) and circuit switched data networks (CSDNs).

One of the primary aims of the telecommunications industry for this decade is to provide an integrated communications infrastructure which will enable the interconnection of all of these networks and their services. This is based upon digital technology and is called the integrated services digital network (ISDN). The ISDN will interconnect LANs, PDNs, PSTNs, MANs and the private automatic branch exchanges (PABXs) to produce a single communications infrastructure to provide voice, data, facsimile, telex, videotext, graphics, text and document transfer services

The classification of networks has so far emphasized their switching technology or their geographical coverage. A more detailed classification is shown in Figure 2.2 and is an expanded form of that introduced by Chou (1983). Here the tree is split according to physical structure (or topology), hierarchy, communications switching technology, control, multiplexing and protocols. The topologies are broken into two types: broadcast and point-to-point. The hierarchy refers to PSTN type architectures which use either a hierarchical or a monolithic approach. The control category addresses the classical distributed/centralization debate with the multiplexing category referring to the configurations which can be adapted by users accessing a network. The protocols element differentiates between the classical master/slave systems, the more modern transmitter/receiver equivalence of peer communications, the proprietary and the hybrid protocols. The communications/switching technologies category addresses the ways in which networks physically transfer data between their users. The basic elements show the switching techniques, the more commonly known multiple access methods and the ring switch/relay techniques, and as such list most of the commonly known communications techniques. The four internetworking elements, termed the repeater, bridge, router and gateway, will be discussed in later chapters.

The three super classes of network are local, metropolitan and wide area. The best way to decide the class of network is to use a composite metric, that is, one which combines all of the fundamental properties of data rate, maximum length, average message size and so on. Such a metric is the ratio of the propagation delay, or latency (across the channel), to the packet transmission time; τ is the end-to-end propagation delay across the channel, or latency of the channel, and T is the average packet transmission time (that is, its length in terms of transmission duration). The two parameters τ and T are represented by a the coupling ratio, α, which is defined as:

$$\alpha = \tau/T$$

α denotes how distributed the users appear to be relative to the average packet transmission time, that is,

- $\alpha \ll 1$ implies a LAN
- $\alpha \approx 1$ implies a MAN
- $\alpha \gg 1$ implies a WAN.

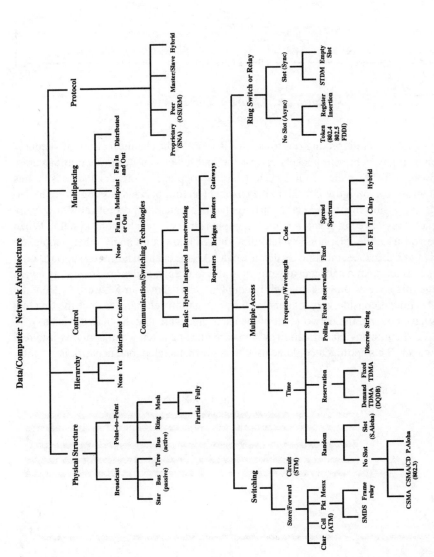

Figure 2.2   The computer/data networks family tree.

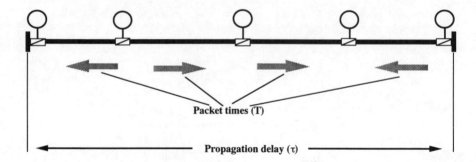

Figure 2.3   A loosely coupled network.

Another way of interpreting α is to say that in a WAN the channel can simultaneously support many complete packets and so the end nodes can never have an accurate knowledge of the state of the system (loosely coupled). Consider the passive bus system shown in Figure 2.3. Here the channel has four packets passing along it. No node knows how many packets are on the network because they do not know how many packets they have not seen! Another example is that of the telephone system. When a person uses the telephone system they do not know how many other people are making a call at the same time. In the case of a LAN the channel normally supports only a small fraction of a packet at any one time and so the end nodes are accurately aware of the true state of the system (tightly coupled), as is shown in Figure 2.4. Here the packet time is considerably longer than the propagation delay and so once the first few bits have covered the network, all of the users are aware that the network is busy.

As with any classification system care must be taken when applying it to real networks. This approach could be used to show that a telephone network is a tightly

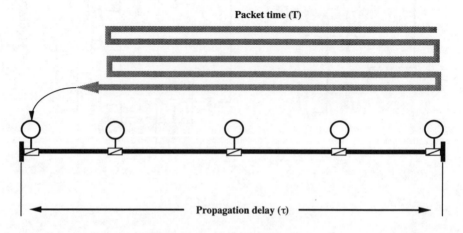

Figure 2.4   A tightly coupled network.

coupled system because the information transferred generally has a duration of many minutes with a worse case delay of only a few hundred milliseconds (it must be noted however that the system really transfers the data a few bits at a time and so the network can now be correctly categorized). This approach leads towards the consideration of the trade-off between latency and bandwidth, especially when considering high speed WAN environments. Kleinrock (1992) argued that for all such systems there is a set of conditions for which the delay is primarily dependent upon the latency (that is, the network is latency dependent) and that the addition of further bandwidth does not reduce the delay across the network. This means that a designer has to be aware of when the network becomes latency dependent so that bandwidth costs can be reduced. In a latency dependent network the bandwidth should be reduced as much as possible, thereby reducing the system cost, assuming that the latency itself cannot be reduced (this is unlikely because the latency is a direct consequence of physics in the real world and a large network has a large latency).

So, what is the importance of the LAN/MAN/WAN classification to network engineers? It means that care has to be taken when LANs are connected by a WAN backbone to ensure that the users' perceptions of the network are not altered. The users should feel that it is still their network. The WAN should provide high LAN connectivity with a minimal degradation in performance of the LANs and in a manner transparent to the end users: the end users should not be required to know, and should not even notice, whether or not their data crosses one or more networks.

2.3 Wide area networks

WANs are the networks most commonly used by individuals on a day-to-day basis. Most homes throughout the world have a telephone, whereas a telephone (or more likely PABX) plus a facsimile machine are considered essential for business use. The global network is a reality; this is shown by the speed with which the world's stock markets react with respect to each other and by the news services which report rapidly on events throughout the world. The new technology is going to make these services available at lower costs and so make them accessible to a wider range of people.

A WAN is typically characterized by the fact that it can readily support thousands, and in some cases millions, of users and can span thousands of kilometres. It is important therefore that WANs provide both an appropriate addressing system and a reliable and efficient information routing algorithm. The throughput rates for the data do not necessarily have to be that fast: a basic voice system requires a rate of only 64 kbps (current optical networks operate in the 100–1000s Mbps region). The addressing schemes must support almost unlimited expansion while ensuring that this expansion has no effect on the addresses of existing users (the proposed changes in the UK telephone code is a prime example of what will happen if this is no longer the case). In circuit switched systems the route through the network is fixed by the destination address; however, in message/packet switching systems the actual route to be taken may require the use of intermediate addresses. In such systems the route varies according to the time of transmission and so it is essential that the system, and not the users, determines these addresses. It is the efficiency of the routing algorithms which will determine the efficiency of a network and so it is important that each of its nodes is accurately aware of the true state of the whole network (finite propagation delays make it impossible for precise knowledge to be acquired).

Without doubt the field in which most rapid development will take place in the next five years is that of mobile and personal communication networks. The liberalization of the UK cellular radio telephone market has quickly established the UK as one of the leading users of mobile and cordless telephones. The aim over the next ten years is to establish the personal communications network, which will permit the use of mobile and cordless telephones from any place in the world.

The pressure placed upon WANs by the requirements of modern communications systems means that their capabilities, services and functionality must evolve so that they remain useful. This means that WANs must:

- Be designed and supported as the backbone infrastructure which they are becoming, as opposed to the primary service provider which they have been.

- Supply communication links which have a higher throughput and a lower access delay while still maintaining their level of reliability.

- Provide a wider range of services in an integrated manner and without any degradation in the efficiency of any of the individual services.

2.3.1   Switching techniques

There are a large number of different multiple access schemes and protocols, many of which are one form or another of time division multiple access (TDMA). The four basic schemes, as shown in Figure 2.5, are:

- Space – the information is transmitted along physically different routes depending on either the time of transmission or the location of the two communicating users, for example the telephone network.

- Code – this uses the concept of signal space (as termed by C.E. Shannon (1980) and the derivation of his channel capacity equation) and is the combination of time and frequency access, for example one of the latest digital cellular telephone systems undergoing trials.

- Time – each user sends their data at a separate moment in time. In the random access systems the transmission will collide, that is, there will be contentions, and a retry algorithm will act to move those transmissions apart, with respect to each other, in time, for example Ethernet.

- Frequency/wavelength – each transmission is assigned a particular frequency,

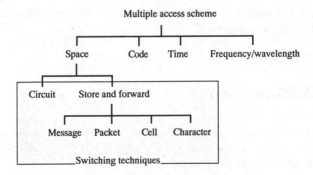

Figure 2.5 Switching techniques

used only by that link at that moment in time, for example radio and television. Wavelength schemes are identical to those of frequency but they have a far greater frequency (shorter wavelength) and are used in the context of fibre optic communications.

The space schemes fall into two categories: circuit and store/forward switching. The circuit switching techniques are used primarily in voice systems but can also be used for data transfer. Each exchange supports a limited number of lines and contains a switch matrix which can connect together all combinations of in-lines to out-lines. The two most important features of this system are:

- Each exchange can only support so many users. When the number of requests exceeds this number then some of these are blocked, that is, the exchange has no free lines available to support the required communications.

- Once a physical circuit link has been established between the users, it supports all of the information exchanged between them. Furthermore this link is dedicated to those users, that is, there is no multiplexing with data from other users.

In contrast, store/forward switching is the technique in which the user message can be broken into various types of fragments, such as packets, cells or characters, although in the case of message switching no fragmentation takes place. These fragments are then sent sequentially to the destination user. The store/forward route that each fragment takes between the users can differ on a per fragment basis, the individual routes being dependent upon the rest of the load on the network. In the case of a packet switching network, each packet is sent to the local packet switch exchange. Depending on the routing algorithm used by the network and the exchanges, that exchange then passes the packet onto one of its nearest neighbours, until eventually the packet arrives at its required destination.

In most systems, sequences of fragments can be transmitted before the acknowledgements for the others have been received. This means that any route differences can cause the fragments to arrive at the destination in an order different to that in which they were sent. Other problems include the duplication of fragments and fragment loss due to corruption.

2.3.2   X.25 networks

X.25 is the recommendation adopted by most organizations for the transfer of data across PDNs using packet switching (X.25 is specified by the International Telegraph and Telephone Consultative Committee, or CCITT). In the UK the primary PDN hosting X.25 is called the packet switched system (PSS) and is provided by BT. Both IBM's systems network architecture (SNA) and Digital's network architecture (DNA) support X.25 and some of the current open system interconnection (OSI) implementations use X.25 to provide the physical subnetwork access.

X.25 has been available since 1974 and consists of three hierarchically layered protocols: the packet, frame and physical layers (Deasington, 1986; Barnett, 1988). The usage of the term X.25 is confusing. The CCITT X.25 recommendation includes both the X.25 packet layer protocol (X.25 PLP for the packet layer) and the balanced link access protocol (LAPB for the frame layer). It states that the X.21 recommendation (among others) may be used for the physical layer. It is generally agreed, however, that X.25 refers to all the above three terms. The other terms normally used in describing X.25 systems are:

- The data terminal equipment (DTE) – this is the user node
- The data circuit-terminating equipment (DCE) – the network access interface
- The digital switching exchange (DSE) – this is the data switch.

Occasionally the term DXE is used to represent the fact that either the DTE or the DCE are being discussed. It is also common for the DSE to become the DCE-DSE-DCE equivalent to which the user DTEs are linked.

The problem with a packet switched network is that a user wishing to make use of it must support the full protocol – in this case X.25. There are some cases when this is not a cost effective option (remembering that the X.25 kit can cost thousands of pounds per user), for example when using asynchronous terminals. The solution is to use an interface box which takes the dumb device data and provides the X.25 protocol but which also supports many users, that is, it acts as a terminal concentrator as well as an X.25 interface. This lowers the per user cost. This device is called the packet assembler/disassembler (PAD) and it is defined by the following three CCITT recommendations, which are collectively known as the Triple-X:

- X.3 – the definition of the functions supported by the PAD.
- X.28 – the control flow specification between the dumb device and the PAD.
- X.29 – the PAD-to-PAD or PAD-to-DTE control exchange protocol.

The traditional use of PADs has been in the supply of relatively cheap remote terminal access to the data network. Sixteen-port asynchronous PADs cost only a few thousand pounds and so they were an essential element in providing mainframe access to a large number of users while ensuring that the bulk of the maintenance problems was restricted to the central facility, as opposed to being distributed across the network through the use of intelligent workstations. This network-centred concern has now, quite rightly, been superseded by user-centred concern and so the traditional X.25/ PAD approach is slowly being replaced by LAN based intelligent workstations which are linked to the mainframes using gateways and terminal emulation software.

The final element required in X.25 network architectures is the mechanism for interconnecting them. This is defined in the X.75 recommendation for signalling terminal exchanges (STEs). X.75 is virtually identical to the X.25 recommendation but it advocates the use of the G.703 (a 2.048 Mbps coaxial carrier link) to replace the X.21.

2.4 Local area networks

It was the widespread use of LANs in the mid 1980s which promoted rapid developments in the field of data and computer communications. The LAN provides a relatively cheap way to share expensive peripherals among users, fast reliable communications to support the development of distributed systems and a building block upon which larger and more complex networks and information systems can be built. In summary, a LAN is a network which can transfer data between users in a reliable, rapid and prompt manner (Flint, 1983).

Commercial opportunism and competition ensure that there will always be more than one type of LAN. Indeed, the demands made of LANs are such that it is improbable that any single version could be expected to support the range of applications presently in use or proposed. What has transpired is that the standards organizations and their collaborating agencies have been establishing many standards for LAN architectures and their interfaces (Cheong, 1987).

Ethernet is the predominant LAN architecture. It operates on a packet broadcast principle once the communications channel has been sensed and found idle. The finite propagation delay along the network produces contention problems, which are resolved by the collision detection algorithm; a contention occurs whenever two or more users simultaneously transmit data. In token passing LANs a user cannot transmit data until it has possession of the token; one or more tokens cycle around the nodes on the LAN in some predetermined or requested manner. The salient difference between a token bus and a Token Ring (IBM's implementation being the definitive reference) is that for a ring the physical topology matches the logical topology whereas for a bus the two are different. The original definition of a LAN was summarized as:

- Supporting no more than two hundred users – but it is not unusual for some LANs to have two or three thousand users linked together.

- Covering a distance of no greater than two kilometres – but what about the common situation where two LANs are integrated across the Atlantic?

- Supporting a point-to-point data rate in excess of 1 Mbps – this is a pedestrian data rate by common LAN standards and any high speed network is one which is commonly described as having a data rate in excess of 2 Mbps (this means that the ISDN is a high speed network).

- Providing a channel with fewer than one error every one thousand million bits (or about one error every 100 to 1000 seconds) – this has stayed very much the same.

There are several other criteria, but the point has already been made that those original ideas did not reflect the way in which LANs subsequently came to be used, and therefore did not anticipate the ways in which the product market was forced to evolve. Parametric definitions for a network are, as already discussed, unreliable and useless if we do not use them accordingly. What counts is how each and every user 'sees' the LAN, that is, as a high speed, low delay, reliable link which is dedicated to them.

A typical Ethernet supports a few tens of users and has average utilization in the order of 5–10% of its 10 Mbps channel. More importantly, there are some successfully operating LANs which violate many, or perhaps even all, of the generally accepted operating conditions, such as repeatered LANs with thousands of users. This demonstrates the fact that LANs are engineered systems whose standardization is not defined by a series of yes/no questions of whether an approach is correct or not. Instead there are always a multitude of acceptable network solutions for any one given requirement, and an acceptable solution in one environment should not, necessarily, be expected to work equally well in a different environment.

When either the functionality of a LAN is limited, or its performance becomes degraded, or its physical limitations are too restrictive then something needs to be done. All of these problems can be resolved by using the appropriate internetworking relay, whether it be a repeater to extend the physical connectivity of the LAN, a bridge to improve the performance profile, a router to provide WAN connectivity or a gateway to extend the functionality of the protocol system.

2.5 Metropolitan area networks

MANs are WANs which use LAN technology; that is, LANs with a fast circuit switching capability. This combination is best supported by optical technology and so much of the development and standardization for MANs is based upon fibre optic systems. One intention is to use a high speed backbone optical LAN to act as the switching centre for the linked LANs, consequently forming a MAN. The original development activity proposed the fibre distributed data interface (FDDI) as the backbone LAN with Ethernet and Token Ring LAN spurs. A full MAN would then be produced by interconnecting several FDDIs using either a synchronous optical network (SONET) carrier, a single mode fibre repeater extension or an intermediate network based upon the Bell Communications Research's switched multi-megabit data service (SMDS). SMDS is the original Bell proposal for a MAN solution and is now available in the UK as a 25 Mbps service from BT.

The original FDDI based MAN approach was superseded by the queued packet and synchronous switch architecture, which then gave rise to the distributed queue dual bus (DQDB) network. The DQDB is a dual optical bus configuration which utilizes a reservation algorithm called the distributed queuing system; the corresponding standards have not defined a particular carrier speed and so DQDB may be made available for a range of carrier speeds. This approach endows the DQDB with a slotted packet structure, so in principle it should be possible to integrate this architecture into the wide bandwidth ISDN systems. The DQDB is formally defined in the ratified ISO 8802/6 standard and as such is defined without a specific carrier rate. This means that the DQDB approach is advocated for a large range of carriers and consequently it is an ideal bearer protocol for the SONET services, which advocate transmissions ranging from 51 Mbps to 2.5 Gbps (Stallings, 1993).

In contrast, there are two versions of FDDI: the FDDI and FDDI II (Stallings, 1993). FDDI II includes an isochronous (or circuit switched) capability alongside the normal medium access control and so the carrier structure is similar to that advocated for the SONET services, which in turn means that the full range of FDDI II frames can be supported by SONET. The FDDI is a 100 Mbps LAN based upon a dual contra-rotating Token Ring protocol operating over an optical fibre medium; the contra-rotating rings endow the network with single failure resilience. A single FDDI network can support a maximum of 500 nodes over a perimeter distance of 100 km. The FDDI has been formally ratified but FDDI II is still undergoing development.

At present, the MAN market is confused with the FDDI and SMDS services being available and the DQDB products just becoming available. However, all of these may be being considered as stop-gap solutions until the cell relay products become available at reasonable prices. Until two or three years ago there was a firm belief that FDDI would be the way forward, particularly for LAN-to-LAN connectivity. However, the US communications devices manufacturers have now aligned themselves with cell relay and so the expected reduction in FDDI prices is unlikely given user uncertainty and the corresponding higher costs to compensate for the lower sales.

2.6 Internetworking

With hindsight, the problems which network designers, engineers and users now face were inevitable but avoidable. However, the important point is not to repeat those past failings but to learn from the mistakes and to anticipate similar sorts of problems in the future. The lessons which need to be learnt are:

- The world consists of many different networks and many competing manufacturers. There will never be a situation in which there is only one network or manufacturer. The best that can be hoped for is that different devices from different manufacturers can be based upon common interface specifications and the provision of a clearly defined and agreed minimum set of services.

- The established engineering wisdoms of 'divide and conquer' and 'provision of only what is immediately necessary' have produced a collection of networking solutions which, while effective for their original purposes, are difficult to interconnect with each other. The success of the 'divide and conquer' approach was always based upon interface specifications to which the separate sections would conform. In networking these interfaces were never agreed beforehand.

- The most technically proficient solution is not the one normally chosen. This applies to the standardization process as well as to network design. Political, commercial and cost interest are more important and so these must be considered as early as possible. A network has to be cost effective and has to be seen to be improving the cost efficiency of the organization it supports.

The previous overview of the current range of network architectures makes it clear that the increasing diversity of technology is going to mean that successful network design will be based upon the ease of internetworking. An organization's dependence on networking and the corresponding technology means that it is impossible to pretend that problems do not exist, instead the response should be to recognize that:

- The number of different networking and internetworking devices is going to continually expand and change due to both the needs of the users and the needs of the manufacturers to differentiate between themselves. Follow what the users need now, anticipate what they will need tomorrow and ensure that these needs support the organization in the most effective way.

- The number of standards is going to proliferate and, while well-intentioned, they will become increasingly meaningless and increase the complexity of internetworking. This is because the *de facto* standards, by definition, are more popular than their formal counterparts and manufacturers will always supply idiosyncratic 'add-ons' to ensure user 'loyalty'. In response, networks should be based upon well trusted technology from reliable suppliers with proven interconnection capability.

- The capabilities of the underlying network technology are going to be continually renovated and occasionally revolutionized. This means that, as is the case with computer systems purchase, network solutions are out-of-date in one way or another as soon as they are installed. Idea to market-place timescales for evolving products are in the order of twelve months, somewhat shorter than the design to installation and renovation timescales of networks. The corresponding response should be to create a network which works on known technology and does listen very critically to those who advocate continual state-of-the-art.

Table 2.1   LANs/MANs/WANs comparison.

Issue	WANs	MANs	LANs
Geographic size	1000s km	1–100 km	0–2 km
Number of nodes	10 000s	1–500	1–1000
Data rate	< 100 kbps	1–300 Mbps	1–100 Mbps
Error profile	1 in 1 Mbits	1 in 1 Gbits	1 in 1 Gbits
Transfer delay	100–1000 ms	10–100 ms	1–100 ms
Coupling coefficient	$\gg 1$	$0.1 < \alpha < 10$	$\ll 1$
Routing profile	Sophisticated	Simple	None
Internetworking	Gateways and routers	Routers/bridges	Routers/bridges/ repeaters

2.7 Summary

Table 2.1 provides a comparison of local, metropolitan and wide area networks according to their geographic size, number of supported nodes, and so on. Historically speaking, all networks were considered, by default, as wide area until the mid 1970s when the first local networks were introduced. The situation was further complicated when engineers started interconnecting LANs, thereby forming the early MANs. LANs, MANs and WANs are now clearly establishing their role with respect to each other, so much so that it is now possible to give a fairly clear, if not rigorous, definition of each of the three types of network.

A LAN is a network which is geographically localized. Typically it supports fewer than 200 nodes across a diameter of less than 2 km with the common configuration being much smaller. The performance capability of a LAN is characterized by its very high throughput and low delay supported by a low probability of error, that is, it is a fast and highly reliable communications link. The internetworking of LANs is primarily by repeaters, bridges and routers. A MAN is an integrated network capable of supporting a city or metropolis, but which uses LAN technology, that is, hundreds of interconnected LANs. The characteristic performance of a MAN is similar to that of a LAN but with relatively high delay times. Interconnection to, and between, MANs is by bridges and routers. A typical WAN supports thousands of users and crosses several thousands of kilometres; by implication all public networks are WANs. WANs have relatively low data rates and high bit error rates; however, they are highly reliable. Interconnection between WANs is generally supported by routers and gateways.

By definition, internetworking must be concerned with the connection of local, metropolitan and wide area networks to produce more highly connected local, metropolitan and wide area networks. From the design perspective the user requirements (where a user is defined as a person or device which needs to access a network for the reliable transfer of information) are paramount and so the construction of the network architecture must reflect that:

- There are hundreds, if not thousands, of different possible network architectures. Sound engineering practices advocate that a hierarchical design philosophy be adopted (divide and conquer) so that a flexible but functional network can be constructed to provide the users with what they want.

- Wide area networks are highly connected but loosely coupled systems in which many users access the network at any one time. Local area networks are closely coupled systems in which only one user accesses the network at any one time.

- Internetwork relay elements such as repeaters, bridges, routers and gateways are needed in the construction of large local networks to produce cost effective solutions which overcome the physical restrictions inherent in the operation of individual networks.

- Internetworking is about producing complex but robust and reliable network architectures by linking together local networks using backbone metropolitan and wide area networks.

3

Protocols

3.1 Introduction

3.2 Protocol standards and types

3.3 The functions of a protocol

3.4 Typical protocols

3.5 Internetworking responsibilities

3.6 Summary

3.1 Introduction

The operation of a communications network is controlled by the protocols which reside within the transmitters and receivers connected to it. A protocol is an agreed set of rules which must be followed when two users wish to communicate. The complexity of a protocol is dependent upon the errors introduced into the data by interference, distortion and the way in which the network is physically interconnected. All information transferred by a communications system suffers the injection of errors, so some mechanism must be provided to correct these.

When people physically talk to each other, they adopt a convention which lets all of the participants have the opportunity to speak and to hear what the others are saying. A network must provide such a convention for its users; in communications this convention is called a protocol. The human brain is particularly adept at understanding speech that has suffered considerable corruption – consider typical telephone lines – but more importantly it can adapt quickly to unforeseen events, for instance, the physical collapse of a speaker. The processors which house the protocols on networks are considerably less flexible and perceptive, so the correct response for each possible event, both known and unknown, must be predefined by the appropriate protocol.

Unfortunately, while a protocol can be used to remove the problem of corrupted data it is also the cause of considerable incompatibility problems. There is not just one protocol, but dozens of them, most of which are proprietary (owned by a particular supplier). It is not possible to get these different protocols to operate with each other unless some form of interfacing relay is supplied. It is this interfacing which is the core of internetworking. The different types of interfacing relay can be used to connect together different protocols, irrespective of their actual functional differences or the ways in which they are implemented.

3.2 Protocol standards and types

Naturally, there are many forces acting to produce the protocols we use today and those for tomorrow. The results of these forces can be distilled to:

- Proprietary protocols – protocols which were developed and are supported by particular suppliers/manufacturers for specific systems. Classic examples of these are Novell NetWare by Novell and SNA by IBM.

- Public protocols – protocols developed for free availability and whose usage does not infringe any licences. The American Department of Defense and their ARPANET work are responsible for the emergence of TCP/IP, which has established itself as one of the leading public protocols.

- *De facto* standards – proprietary or public protocols which through general acceptance and use have acquired the status of informal standards such as the TCP/IP protocols, which have established themselves as the *de facto* data communications standard for UNIX-based environments.

- *De jure* standards – these are the standards currently under development by the standardization organizations, such as the OSI/RM by the International Organization for Standardization, and it is against these that conformance testing and certification will be completed.

Clearly, it is impossible to expect industry and commerce to drop all of their established protocols and replace them by some standardized equivalent. Instead, the introduction of the appropriate internetworking relays is used to support mixed systems interconnection, migration to common protocols and eventually the full support of the appropriate formal standards.

3.2.1   Protocol standardization

The relationships between the formal telecommunication and information systems standardization bodies have slowly evolved, with much of their work relying upon the free and regular exchange of their own standards. One schematic representation of the current relationships between the standards organizations is shown in Figure 3.1 (Black, 1987). The ISO is the voluntary body responsible for coordinating the production of user standards for many walks of life. One of their committees is active in the field of information systems (Technical Committee – TC97), which is responsible for the OSI/RM, and many of the commonly adopted protocol standards.

TC97 is supported by the member states and by representation from the member state national standards organizations. In the UK this is the British Standards Institution (BSI). Other organizations also helping are the European Computer Manufacturers Association (ECMA), which specializes in certain parts of the standards effort.

The United Nations (UN) has a body called the International Telecommunications Union (ITU) within it. The ITU has several committees supporting their work, three of which are the International Radio Consultative Committee (CCIR), the CCITT and the World Administrative Radio Conference (WARC). The CCIR is responsible for the provision of mutually compatible telecommunications equipment between the suppliers, whereas the CCITT deals with recommendations concerning data communication networks, telephone switching, digital standards and terminals, and WARC maintains the world-wide radio spectrum allocation for communications services, thereby ensuring spectral compatibility between these.

The CCITT is composed of representatives from ISO (and vice versa), the national PDN providers such as the PTTs, and private companies such as AT&T. Supporting all of this effort is a myriad of smaller organizations which concentrate

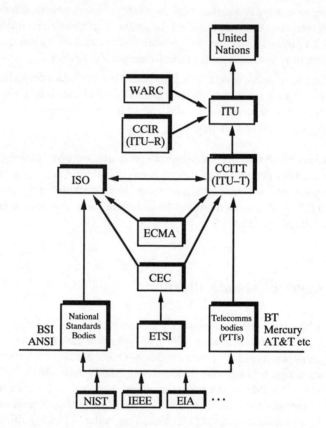

Figure 3.1 Standards organizations relationships.

upon particular areas of the communications discipline such as the IEEE and local area networks. In Europe, the Central European Commission (CEC) is becoming more prevalent in the unification of standards across Europe, hence the introduction of the CEN/CENELEC recommendations. Most of the detailed standardization research within Europe is provided by the European Telecommunications Standards Institute (ETSI), which supplies information to CEC and maintains an awareness of the activities of the other standards organizations in related fields of interest.

At a recent ITU forum, changes were announced concerning the naming and responsibilities of the CCITT and CCIR. While their areas of responsibility remain broadly what they were, the committees have been renamed; the CCITT is now called the ITU-T and the CCIR is the ITU-R. The four-year review procedure has also been replaced, so new recommendations will be released as and when they are completed.

In many instances the detailed analysis and design of standards is completed by small working groups composed of individuals working under the direction of a professional organization. Three of the most common participants in data communications are the Institute of Electrical and Electronics Engineers (IEEE) – LAN responsibility, the US National Institute of Standards and Technology (NIST) and the Electronic Industries Association (EIA) – responsible for RS-232. The findings of these organizations are usually presented to the formal standardization bodies as draft documents which are then released as draft international standards, thereby entering the formal ratification process.

3.2.2 Types of protocol

There are many different types of protocol and in general these can be classified according to their functional emphasis. The most common classifications are:

- Master/slave and peer-to-peer – the master/slave protocols require that one side of the communicating nodes acts as controller. This becomes responsible for controlling the communication link and data transfer between the nodes. The peer-to-peer protocols do not use any controller, so all communicating nodes can transmit information as and when they desire.

- Connectionless (datagram), connection oriented (virtual circuit), send-and-pray and remote procedural call (RPC) – these protocols reflect the ways in which information is transferred between the users and their differences correspond to varying degrees of reliability during that transfer.

- Synchronous and asynchronous – in asynchronous protocols the data is transferred one byte at a time, with varying time delays between each byte. In synchronous protocols the bit stream of a message is sent contiguously at the clocking rate of the network. In both systems the transmitters and receivers are asynchronous to each other because there is no common clock, so some form of data synchronization must be used.

- Layered and monolithic – modern protocol architectures use layering to construct the complete protocol system. Layering is the process where several protocols are stacked to achieve the common goal and different stacks are used to support different services. A monolithic approach is effectively a single layer in which all of the necessary functionality is supplied.

- Heavy and light – a protocol which provides a wide range of functions would normally be termed 'heavy' due to the high overhead in processing delay experienced in using that functionality. Conversely, 'light' protocols offer minimal functionality but incur low processing delays.

It is common for a protocol to be described by several of the above terms. Therefore, without reference to a particular protocol's name or its standard, there is no single terminology that can be used to uniquely describe a protocol.

3.2.3   Data transfer using protocols

Data will always be susceptible to corruption when physically transmitted. The number of errors per second will depend upon the quality of the channel and the ambient environment. Highly reliable networks, ones in which the bit error probability is about 10^{-9} or lower, normally make use of error detection systems followed by data retransmission algorithms, termed backward error correction (BEC). In the case where the error rate is high, greater than 10^{-5}, then some form of forward error correction (FEC) is used to correct the data without recourse to data retransmission. In fact even with FEC it is normal to have data retransmission once the number of errors has exceeded the FEC recovery threshold.

The protocol is responsible for data retransmission. Retransmission can be triggered either by the receipt of a negative acknowledgement (NAK) – that is, a data lost statement from the receiver or a timeout at the transmitter due to the absence of an expected acknowledgement. The protocols employed to retransmit the data vary depending upon the quality of the channel but are normally one of:

- Stop-and-wait – the retransmission of data upon receipt of a NAK or a transmitter timeout but where only one acknowledgement is outstanding at any one time.

- Go-back-n – the rapid transmission of many packets consecutively and the retransmission of all those from the point at which the loss occurred.

- Selective repeat – the retransmission of only those packets which become corrupted.

In the stop-and-wait protocol each packet is sent after the acknowledgement to the previous one has been received. If a NAK is sent by the respondent (due to data corruption) or a timeout occurs (due to data loss) then the initiator retransmits the previous packet and is not permitted to send other data until that message has been successfully acknowledged. Figure 3.2 shows the successful transmission of packets one and two. Packet three becomes corrupted and so the returned NAK forces the initiator to retransmit it. The second attempt is successfully received. Note that only one packet is unacknowledged at any one time, so the system operates at the speed of the slowest element (Halsall, 1992).

In the go-back-n protocol, which is a form of sliding window protocol (SWP), the initiator transmits all of the data that will fit into the available window width. The window width is the maximum number of messages that can be sent without there being a corresponding acknowledgement. Once the window is full, the initiator waits for an acknowledgement of one, or more, packets before sending further data. If some of the data becomes lost or corrupted then a NAK will cause all of the frames sent after and including the lost frame to be retransmitted. In Figure 3.3 the window size is four. Packets one to three are successfully received and acknowledged . The initiator then sends frames four, five, six and seven. Unfortunately, frame five is corrupted, so the returned NAK causes the retransmission of frames five, six and seven; this will occur

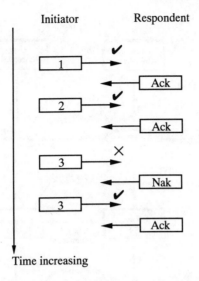

Figure 3.2 Stop-and-wait protocol.

irrespective of whether or not frames six and seven were received correctly during the first transmission attempt. The selective repeat protocol is a more refined version of the go-back-n and is also a form of SWP. In the case of selective repeat only the corrupted frame is retransmitted.

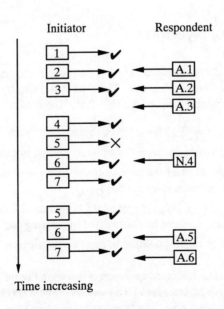

Figure 3.3 Go-back-n protocol.

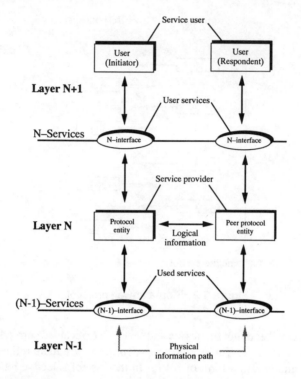

Figure 3.4   Service user and service provider relationships.

3.2.4   Protocol layering

The layering of protocols to produce a stack is the prevalent technique used in protocol architecture design and implementation. The X.25 system is a layered architecture and layering is the fundamental basis of the OSI/RM. The reasons for using the layered approach are:

- The individual components are simpler to design, implement and test.
- The interfaces between the protocols are more structured, so conformance testing can be completed more readily.
- The construction of different standard layers means that a wider range of protocol architectures can be constructed by 'mixing and matching' the layers.
- Protocols can be readily tailored to meet a specific user's requirements.

A model of the layered architecture approach is shown in Figure 3.4 (Knowles, 1987). This model shows three layers, (N+1), (N) and (N-1) with (N+1) being the top layer and (N-1) being the bottom one. The two communicating users (termed the initiator and respondent) are the 'service users' and are in layer (N+1). These two users have

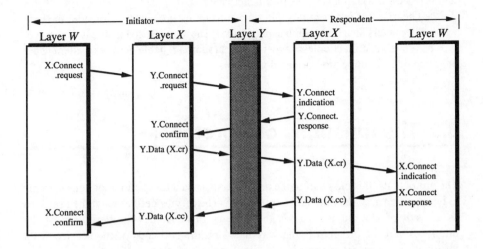

Figure 3.5 A timing graph for a layered protocol profile.

identical copies of the protocol stack and it is this stack which provides the communications system. They use the layer (N) services and access these via the N-interface (formally called the service access point). The protocol entities are in layer (N). These entities are the actual protocol implementations that provide the desired service to the user via the N-interface and, with respect to the higher layer, they are termed the 'service providers'. The protocol entities swap information via the services of the lower layers; that is, the protocol entities in layer (N) are the service users of the layer (N-1) services. This layering system can be applied to any number of layers, but at the very bottom must be the physical link – the actual physical network – which connects together the user stacks.

Peer-to-peer communications is the information that is swapped between the protocol entities in the same layer but which reside in different stacks. This is the logical communications path, but remember that the actual information goes down the initiator's stack and up the respondent's stack, passing through all of the layers. The appropriate protocol layer specific information is peeled off by the protocol entities as the data passes through each of the peer layers – this will be more clearly explained in Chapter 4.

The timing graph is another way of viewing the transfer of data between the stacks. A three-layer stack is shown in Figure 3.5. This figure shows a three-layer system (W, X, Y), in which layer W is using a connection oriented service (COS) from layer X and layer X is also using a COS from layer Y. Layer W issues an X.Connect.request primitive. This request causes layer X to establish a COS link across layer Y with its peer layer X. Once this has been achieved (again using the four primitive service system), layer X sends the connection request from layer W as data transfer across layer Y. The connection request is eventually passed up to the respondent's layer W, which confirms the request using the appropriate service primitives (once again the information is passed through layer *Y* as a data message).

Clearly, this is a complex and time consuming procedure. Consider the case when other layers also insist upon using a COS! The response to this 'heavy' protocol is to use several connectionless layers and to support a reliable network system using only one or two connection oriented protocols.

3.3 The functions of a protocol

The protocol itself is only half of the problem. It is usual for communications systems to be specified as a 'service' and a 'protocol'. The service defines what the user sees as a result of communicating via the system (this includes the definition of the interface) and the protocol is the way in which the two ends of the service swap information to support that service. A simple analogy is that of the railway timetable. The traveller's timetable gives the times for the arrival and departure of specific trains at the various stations – this is the service definition. The full timetable is however considerably more complex because this has to detail an efficient way of ensuring that the actual train movements across the rail network are sufficiently coordinated to supply all of the travellers' timetables – this is the protocol definition. The service definition limits the amount of information the user needs to understand so that they can use the system effectively and provides the supplier with some degree of flexibility in how they will provide the service.

3.3.1   Classes of service

If communications systems were built upon perfect physical networks then protocols would be considerably simpler. However, perfection is not available and so the protocol is responsible for establishing this perfection – that is, providing reliable and timely communications in a readily available form and equally accessible to all users. However, not all users need the same type of service, so there has to be some flexibility in the ways in which it is defined. There are four classes of service:

- COS or virtual circuit.
- Connectionless service (CLS), datagram or fire-and-forget.
- Acknowledged connectionless service (ALS).
- Unconfirmed connection oriented service (UOS) or send-and-pray.

A COS is similar in principle to a telephone conversation. Before data is transferred a link must be established. Once the data has been reliably transmitted then the link must be formally disengaged. In the case of the telephone the number must be dialled, the recipient must pick up the receiver and be willing to speak; if any clarification is required then one or other will ask for a point to be repeated or rephrased; at the end of the conversation both telephone handsets are returned to the telephone; end of conversation.

In the case of the connectionless service the equivalent analogy is the letter post. Here an envelope is addressed and sent containing the message. Normally the recipient will not know when, if at all, a letter is to be sent and so if it does become lost then only the sender can take the appropriate action. In fact if the letter is wrongly addressed then communication will never be possible. This means that in the case of the CLS the data must be totally self-sufficient, including error detection and correction if necessary.

The acknowledged connectionless service is a system used by the real-time communications fraternity. This is similar to the CLS but it also provides the initiator with an acknowledgement of the fact that the data has been delivered to the respondent. It should be recalled that this service is used in systems which, due to performance considerations and low noise channel characteristics, do not employ a connection oriented philosophy but which need some form of reliable data transfer.

The connection oriented equivalent to the ALS is the unconfirmed connection oriented service, or UOS. This was pioneered by IBM in the form of their send-and-pray protocol, which insisted that a link be established before data could be transferred. If such a technique is used then it means that the initiator provides the respondent with a warning of some intent that it will complete irrespective of the state of the respondent. Any subsequent failure recovery must be supported by the protocol or another higher level service.

Clearly a reliable communications system *always* needs at least one COS. If this were not the case then any corrupted or lost data would never be received or recovered. Once the service class has been agreed, the next step is to determine the type of protocol that will provide the service. Confusing as it may seem, the class of service does not dictate the type of protocol which is used in its provision. Hence a COS can, and in many cases is, supported by two datagram based protocols which are coordinated by the layer itself and in more extreme circumstances a CLS could be provided by a virtual circuit based protocol. In this instance, datagram is used to represent a connectionless protocol and virtual circuit, a connection oriented protocol. The coordinated datagram approach is more suitable for COS provision because it provides greater flexibility in supplying all of the COS services (Stallings, 1994).

3.3.2   Protocol responsibilities

The ways in which the service is supplied are the responsibility of the protocol. The more complex the service, the more complex the protocol; however, the inverse is not necessarily true. The functions typically supported by a protocol are:

- Data formatting – the convenient packing of the data and the information to control its handling at the destination.

- Address resolution – the mapping between different addressing systems and the provision of address consistency across the entire network.

- Synchronization – enabling the end systems to determine the location of the first bit, first byte, first fragment and first message.

- Error detection and correction – to enable the system to detect data corruptions, lost data, duplicated data and late data and then, if appropriate, to correct the error.

- Flow control – to ensure that the end systems do not overrun their partners and cause data loss due to buffer overflows etc.

- Routing – the construction and control of networks with multiple paths between the end systems, thereby producing high capacity and resilient networks.

- Segmentation and reconstitution – the breaking of messages into smaller fragments so that error recovery systems are more efficient and greater bandwidth utilization can be achieved.

- Congestion control – monitoring and control of the network load to ensure that its capacity threshold is not exceeded due to link failure or excessive usage.

- Access control – restricted access to the network to ensure that sensitive information or services are not compromised or used for irresponsible activities.

- Link management – the control of data transfer across the channel and control of the channel itself so that the information is reliably transferred.

- Quality of service support – negotiation and support of the level of service that the user needs.

It is not necessary for every protocol to support all of the above functions, but it is usual for all of these to be supported somewhere within a protocol profile. A protocol profile is the hierarchical layering of protocols so that the profile in its totality provides the services required by the user. Layering has been a principle of protocol design since the original implementation of IBM's SNA. This is because it allows the implementation to be managed in a more controlled fashion and provides flexibility for later additions and alterations. Naturally, there is a lot of debate concerning how a layer should be defined but there is general agreement that it should have a clearly defined function, reflect the data structures and processing for that function and minimize the amount of control information passed between adjacent layers.

Different profiles are constructed from different hierarchies of protocols. The only constraint on the hierarchy is that the total quality of service of the layers must satisfy the users' needs – this assumes that, if necessary, the profile can also make use of whatever physical network is mandated. Clearly, the quality of service could be provided by many different layer hierarchies, so the detailed internal interactions should not be of concern. Unfortunately, there is very little understanding of the complex interaction of layers in a profile, so it is not yet possible to design an integrated profile with a predicted, and hence guaranteed, quality of service. Once again, there is no substitute for experience and experimentation.

3.4 Typical protocols

There are, as has been discussed earlier, three sources of protocol: proprietary protocols such as Novell's NetWare, public protocols such as the Internet Profile and formal standards such as the OSI/RM protocols.

3.4.1 Proprietary systems

Many of the major computer system manufacturers have developed proprietary communications protocols. While many of these manufacturers are slowly embracing the formal standards it will be many years, if not decades, before these replace their proprietary protocols. Some of the most common proprietary protocol systems are:

- SNA – this is IBM's proprietary communications architecture which is used throughout their product range. This was one of the original protocol architectures and as such it does not map readily onto the OSI/RM structure.

- DECnet IV – Digital's Phase IV architecture is the last which differs from OSI (Phase V is fully conformant).

- ICL – until recently the ICL architecture did not conform to OSI but it has recently been revamped and is now fully conformant. The architecture is partially based upon C03 and the OSLAN product ranges.

- AppleTalk – the communications architecture used by all Apple products.

- Banyan VINES – the VINES approach is unusual in that it is a proprietary network operating system solution for use in Enterprise networks to support heterogeneous computer systems. It has an unusual architecture which makes it well suited to expanding network environments.

- Novell NetWare – this is the dominant PC based network operating system (claiming some 50–60% of the market). Several recent enhancements have extended its range of connectivity to include SNA and AppleTalk.

- Xerox Network System (XNS) – this is Xerox's communications architecture. Novell NetWare and VINES were derived from XNS.

3.4.2 Public and *de jure* protocols

The standardization organizations are continuing to work on the OSI/RM (this work started some seventeen years ago) – the details of this work will be discussed fully in Chapter 4. The OSI/RM stipulates no implementation specific requirements but it does define the service interfaces, the functions that must be supported by the protocols and the formats for exchanging information between the seven layers (plus the plethora of sublayers) in both layer-to-layer and peer-to-peer interactions. The question remains as to what happens until the OSI/RM is fully complete and adopted (if and when both of these occur), by the communications industry and the user community.

This is the point at which the public and *de facto* standards become important. The TCP/IP and its companion protocols such as the file transfer protocol (FTP) are being adopted by many manufacturers and users, and in the future these may act as the stepping stones towards full OSI/RM compliance. Migration towards a TCP/IP environment means that once the formal standards have been agreed and are fully available to the commercial user it is relatively simple to adopt them. This is because all of the hard work in protocol rationalization has been completed in the move to TCP/IP, so the move from TCP/IP is now concerned with replacing one common protocol architecture with another.

3.5 Internetworking responsibilities

Even when the formal standards have been completed, there will still be a need for internetworking devices – it must also be noted that there are standards for the services and protocols provided by each layer, further complicating the problem of network standardization. While the individual services, protocols and corresponding protocol stacks will have been standardized, the limitations of the technology used for the implementation and the need to overcome these limitations will demand the use of internetworking relays. The ways in which the internetworking boxes are, and will be, used include:

- Overcoming the cabling limitations introduced by the power constraints of the hardware network interface cards.
- Physically connecting together different types of networks which support almost identical protocol systems.
- Connecting together two OSI/RM conformant but different protocol stack systems. Commonality of the user application does not necessarily mean that identical stacks are needed or are available.
- Connecting together proprietary protocol systems with those that conform to the standards. This form of connectivity also includes those closed protocol stacks that are used for specific applications but which may need wider communications access.

In principle internetworking is about provision of an identified service across different networks which may or may not have different service criteria. In the case of networks that provide a common service internetworking is more concerned with protocol interconnection using encapsulation, whereas when there are also service differences there is normally a requirement for protocol conversion. The former is supplied using repeaters, bridges and routers whereas the latter can only be supplied by gateways.

3.6 Summary

Protocols are the elements that push the data around the network and thus contain the rules and instructions for data transfer in real environments. In fact, it is the wide range of different error conditions in these real systems that causes much of the complexity in a protocol. In summary:

- Protocols are the rules and regulations used by the transmitting and receiving elements to provide real communications in the applications environment.

- There is an important difference between protocols and services. Services are what the user uses for communications and protocols are what the system uses to provide the communications.

- It is impossible to create a communications system that is not subject to noise. Therefore a reliable system needs a protocol that is responsible for correcting the physical errors, thereby establishing an error-free link.

- There are two dominant connection services. These are the connectionless service, which is similar to the postal system, and the connection oriented service, which is similar to the telephone system.

- Most protocol architectures use hierarchical layering to provide the necessary functionality and service. This simplifies the construction of complex protocol systems and provides a wide range of protocol stacks to suit different users' needs.

- Communication between users requires that they use the same protocols or that they are linked by some internetworking relay which is responsible for interfacing the two different protocol systems to provide end-to-end communications for the users.

- Internetworking must be capable of linking together systems that are similar or that have differences in their service provision and protocol support. The interconnection of different services is normally achieved by adopting a compromise on common functionality, whereas for protocols the reconciliation can be more complete.

- The wide range of layers and protocols means that a large number of different communication architectures are available to support differing user applications. The selection between these architectures is being simplified by the registration of profiles which define layer groups for specific applications.

The final issue to be addressed is how does a protocol exist? Like most elements in communications, protocols can be realized as hardware, firmware, software or any combination of the three. A protocol profile will in most cases consist of all three realization forms, but one mainstream area of development is in the production of profiles that are fully implemented in dedicated hardware.

4

The OSI Reference Model

4.1 Introduction

Even the most superficial of surveys of the current range of networks and their services results in a substantial list and, needless to say, the proponents of each network consider theirs the best. Once a user has become acquainted with one particular network the next step is the need to communicate with other users on different networks; it is at this stage that even the most mundane of design decisions can render impossible the hope of total network compatibility and interconnection. In response to this the ISO has instigated the specification of a set of standards by which network services and protocols will be rationalized for the provision of a single 'open system', known as the OSI/RM.

In the context of this book an 'open system' is a communications network whose commonly agreed specification and standardization is vendor independent but whose implementation is supported by every vendor. Access to an open system requires the use of an interface which conforms to the OSI/RM and as such can be provided by any one of a number of vendors. It is *not* the intention of this book to advocate the adoption of the OSI/RM. The OSI/RM provides an extensive and useful language, or jargon, to describe most networks, irrespective of their size or complexity. To this end it is important to appreciate what the formal descriptions of the OSI/RM imply so that these can then be interpreted for different profiles, thereby providing a mechanism to compare and contrast different systems.

4.2 The fundamentals of the OSI/RM

Figure 4.1 shows the layered hierarchy of the OSI/RM; the seven layers are numbered in descending order (Tanenbaum, 1988). In the most simple case, each user of an 'open system' must use their own copy of the OSI/RM stack. The structure of the stack is based upon the layering of hierarchical protocols, a concept introduced by IBM for SNA. Its basic principle is the provision of the required network service by the accumulation of clearly defined subsets of that service. The actual service offered to the user can therefore be varied according to their particular needs; however, the OSI/RM states that a user must make use of every layer within the stack. This is the only way in which it can be guaranteed that there is a minimum level of service, thereby ensuring consistent user interconnection.

A layer is the mechanism for identifying a particular set of functional responsibilities and their associated data structures. The actual functions within a layer are provided by entities, so a layer may have more than one layer; for example, a protocol entity and a management entity. Therefore, peer-to-peer communication is between the equivalent entities in two or more separate stacks and a layer encompasses all of the entities in all the stacks. The entities provide services to their higher layer entities, make use of the services supplied by their lower layer entities and communicate with

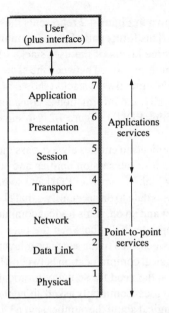

Figure 4.1 The seven layers of the OSI/RM.

their peer entities using the appropriate protocol. The services provided at each layer in the stack are:

- Application – direct provision of the services to the user. This includes services such as file manipulation and electronic mail.

- Presentation – the alteration of the structure of the data to increase efficiency, provide host independent data representation and ensure security and/or privacy of communication.

- Session – control of the communication between the users. This includes the grouping together of messages and the coordination of data transfer between grouped users.

- Transport – the management of the communications between the two end systems; that is, the point-to-point link. This maps the general user services (the top three layers) to the communications subnetwork (the bottom three layers).

- Network – the control of the communications network. This includes the routing of data, physical addressing, congestion and flow control, and bill management for the use of the network.

- Data link – attempts to ensure that errors in the received bit stream are not passed up into the rest of the stack. This requires the use of error detection and correction techniques (BEC and FEC).

- Physical – this includes the channel itself (optical, copper or wireless). The functional responsibilities are modulation, multiplexing and signal generation.

The central mini-stack shown in Figure 4.2 represents the network switching and the internetworking elements. This forms part of the communications subnetwork which encompasses the bottom three layers of the user stacks (the network, data link and physical layers). All information passed between the same layers in each stack (peer-to-peer communication) must traverse the stacks (shown in Figure 4.2 as the 'physical data flow'); however, logically, the information is considered to flow horizontally in the form of protocol data units (PDUs); Figure 4.2 also shows the naming of the PDUs for each of the layers.

In each stack the application entities always pass their data to the presentation entities, which in turn pass it to the session entities and so on. This means that the APDU becomes a PPDU, which becomes a SPDU and so on. However, from a single entity's point of view it passes data to its peer entity – that is, application to application, presentation to presentation and so on. This logical communication is represented by the swapping of the appropriate PDUs between the peer layers. Not only does the logical communication between each of the seven peer layer entities require a separate protocol but so does the physical communication between a layer entity and its adjacent layer entities. This explains the need for so many protocols and hence standards.

One of the questions most commonly asked about the OSI/RM is why are there seven layers? What is so magical about the number seven? The founding principles for the definition of the layers were established at the outset of the OSI/RM's specification. Some of these principles were that a layer should be established when (Knowles, 1987):

- The interaction between other layers could be minimized.
- It was possible to separate into different layers those functions that were very different in nature and purpose.
- Common or highly interrelated functions could be grouped together.
- There was a need to handle and process the data in a different manner.

In fact, there were some ten principles for layering with an extra three for the creation of sublayers. The difference between a layer and a sublayer is that in an 'open' system all seven layers must be present whereas sublayers may or may not be present in a stack (sublayers were created so that certain functionality in a layer could be made optional).

While the OSI/RM is to be the formal service and protocols standard, there are many applications environments that are not suited to it, such as real time systems. The strength of the OSI/RM is that it is a model of all of the services, functions and protocols which are needed to support any type of environment. The aim is to pick and choose those parts of it that benefit the application it is meant to support. Using this approach means that the OSI/RM can be the starting point for the creation of any 'closed' system – that is, one that does not conform to the principles of the OSI/RM. The OSI/RM is by no means complete but it has been, and still is, gradually evolving to address some very serious omissions:

- Network management
- Internetworking

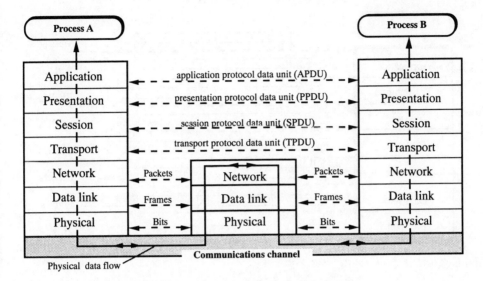

Figure 4.2   The full architecture of the OSI/RM.

- Secure communications
- Real-time communications systems.

So, the OSI/RM is not complete and perhaps never will be. This does not undermine its importance, because, if nothing else, it has provided a common language for the communications networking community.

4.2.1   Data transfer

The most important function of the OSI/RM is that it must transfer data between the users – the next step is for the transfer to become error-free. The user stacks complete a significant amount of processing of the data during its transfer, much of which is a consequence of the hierarchical nature of the stacks. Figure 4.3 shows one example of how the structure and content of the data changes as it traverses the stack. The user, or application process (AP), gives a message to the application layer. The application layer entity now adds to this data some peer specific information – information which will only be used by the destination application layer entity. This information is contained in a header which is inserted at the head of the user data – the formal name for this header is the protocol control information (PCI). The PCI plus the user data form the applications protocol data unit (APDU) which is sent to the remote applications layer entity (logically) but which is physically given to the presentation layer entity.

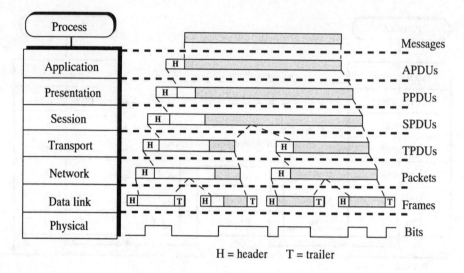

H = header   T = trailer

Figure 4.3   Data flow through the OSI/RM.

The presentation layer entity now adds its header (PPCI) to form the presentation protocol data unit (PPDU). This is passed to the session layer entity, which forms the SPDU, which is itself then passed onto the transport layer entity and so on. The effects of this repeated encapsulation are shown in Figure 4.3 by the decreasing proportion of the amount of information originating from the user (lightly shaded) to the total information carried in the PDUs.

Many of the layers have the option to fragment (also called segment) the data into smaller units, such as packets in the network layer. Each of these fragments has its own PCI, which must contain information for the receiving peer layer as to the order in which the fragments must be joined to reconstitute the original message. Fragmentation is used to improve the efficiency of the communications channel by reducing the processing demands made on each entity due to the effects of the physical structure of the network. Some layers append a trailer to the data units , for example the data link layer which uses a checksum or cyclic redundancy check to detect errors in the frames.

The result of all of this extra information is that the bandwidth efficiency of the protocol is lowered; in other words, some bandwidth is used to pass the control information. The aim is to minimize this overhead. The internal structure of an unframented frame is as shown in Figure 4.4 – in this diagram it has been assumed that the data link layer consists of the logical link control and medium access control sublayers used in LANs. Here it can be seen that the frame consists of the data link layer header, the network header, the transport header, the session header, the presentation header, the application header, the actual message and, finally, the frame check sequence and the end frame sequence.

The efficiency of the OSI is not degraded by the header and segmentation overheads only, but also by the functionality of the connection oriented and acknowledged services. Figure 4.5 shows one such scenario for a three-layered stack:

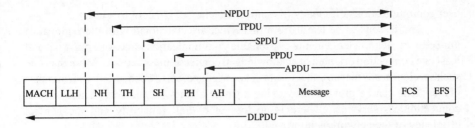

Figure 4.4   The internal frame structure at the data link layer.

- The user messages enter the system and require the use of a COS.

- The data is then sent and the link is closed down, or disengaged. Each of these activities requires transmitted information to be explicitly acknowledged.

- The second layer's COS must now establish a remote link also. Each of the higher layer transfers are treated as data elements by this layer, and each one must be explicitly acknowledged.

- The third layer's ACLS requires the acknowledgement of each PDU.

As can be seen, the entry of the messages at the top layer has a dramatic effect on the total amount of information generated at the lowest layer: the stack causes data avalanching (the acknowledgements come from the remote end of the link, which is why they are shown in a different shade and in a different direction). Clearly this data avalanching, data fragmentation and header addition all contribute to a significant processing and information overhead and consequently reduce the network's user-to-

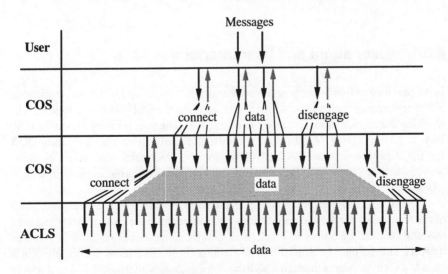

Figure 4.5   The data avalanching effect of the OSI/RM.

user communications efficiency (the only efficiency of concern to a user).

The lessons to be learnt from this effect are concerned with the removal of unnecessary acknowledgements. A reliable communications network must have at least one connection oriented or acknowledged connectionless service. More than one such service means that an unnecessary acknowledgement of acknowledgements takes place. This can be prevented by using a single acknowledged service and several connectionless services. There is no loss of overall reliability and the general efficiency of the network is improved.

4.3 The layer services

The seven layers of the OSI/RM can be categorized according to one of three primary services: user services, hosts services and communications subnetwork services (Rose, 1989). The user services are the pathway through which the user gains access to the network. The ease of use of the actual interface between a user, or user process, and the OSI/RM will dictate the rate at which the OSI/RM is adopted by users. It is essential that these interfaces be clean and simple and provide control over all of the user definable parameters. The communications subnetwork services are composed of the network, data link and physical layers. The subnetwork is the real network plus all of the protocols that are required to turn it into a logical network for use by the rest of the stack. The host services are responsible for mapping the user and communications subnetwork services together. They provide a point-to-point, or logical link, service across the physical subnetwork and map the end-to-end services onto this logical link.

4.3.1 User agent and user interface

In the past four or five years there has been a significant increase in the standardization effort concerning the ways in which a user accesses the OSI/RM environment. The resulting conceptual model is shown in Figure 4.6. The user is integrated to the OSI/RM via the user agent (UA); different applications require different UAs, such as DUA for the directory service UA and MUA for the electronic mail UA. In some implementations these UAs are also known as applications programming interfaces (APIs).

The UAs provide the users with an interface through which they can access all of the features of the desired applications environment. In the case of electronic mail this will include the ability to create mail groups, request confirmation of message delivery and so on. In some implementations these interfaces are supplied in a 'windows' environment through which the user interacts with the OSI/RM as if it were any other software system.

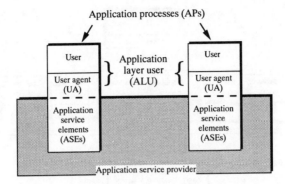

Figure 4.6 The user interface to the OSI/RM communications system.

4.3.2   Application layer

It is the users' responsibility to demand the appropriate service from the application layer entities. The services provided by the lower layers are derived from this original request. Originally the services offered to the user by the application layer were divided into two types known as the specific application service elements (SASEs) and the common application service elements (CASEs). However, this distinction has since lost favour and both types are now referred to as application service elements (ASEs) – the service supplied by the application layer consists of a variety of cooperating application entities in each stack. For the sake of clarity the original distinction will be maintained throughout this text. Some of the current SASEs, and their relationships to the CASEs, are shown in Figure 4.7. At present the most extensively standardized SASEs are:

- File transfer, access and management (FTAM) – this provides file manipulation and storage across a single or distributed file store.

- Message handling system (MHS) – this is the electronic mail standard whose OSI/RM implementation is called the message oriented transfer information system (MOTIS).

- Virtual terminal (VT) – this provides a standard terminal interface.

- Job transfer and manipulation (JTM) – this controls the distribution of a processing service among a series of servers, each of which completes a specific aspect of that service.

- Manufacturers message service (MMS) – this is an application service designed specifically for the control of industrial robots.

- Directory service (DS) – the address directory for the open system. This is the OSI/RM's equivalent of the telephone directory.

- Common management information service (CMIS) – this provides the network management information and is a system/network management facility.

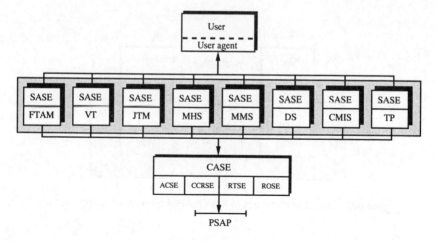

Figure 4.7 Some of the application services available in the OSI/RM.

- Transaction processing (TP) – for use in the financial and retail industries to support on-line and point of sale architectures.

Some of the other SASEs under development include:

- Office document architecture (ODA) – a definition for the structure and transfer of documents that contain different types of information , such as text, graphics and so on.
- Initial graphics exchange system (IGES) – this is the definition of the exchange formats for graphics information used with the graphics kernel system (GKS).
- System management application entity (SMAE) – this is the application used to help the network manager process the information supplied by the CMIS.
- Electronic data interchange (EDI) – to support the transfer of electronic documents between different companies. This builds upon the MHS services.

The number of SASEs will increase as the needs of particular user groups are identified, as exemplified by the MMS, EDI, TP, and so on. In contrast the generic ASEs, that is the CASEs (shown in Figure 4.7), will remain limited in number and will supply the commonly required functions, such as:

- Association control service element (ACSE), which is the connection establishment/disengagement service. This supplies the connection mode service for the application entities.
- Concurrency, commitment and recovery service element (CCRSE), which is the fault tolerant service for multilink systems. This provides the guaranteed consistency service for systems that require multiple copies of all information to be distributed across the communications architecture.

- Reliable transfer service element (RTSE), which is used to supply error free communications between the linked application entities.

- Remote operations service elements (ROSE), which is the support protocol for remote workstations. This mode of communication is more commonly referred to as the remote procedure call, or RPC.

One of the main reasons for the dropping of the SASE and CASE differentiation is that there is no simple hierarchical relationship between any of the application service elements. For instance, the MHS may support the EDI, the RTSE always uses the ACSE and in some cases the ACSE is replaced by the ROSE.

4.3.3   Presentation layer

The presentation layer is the least evolved of the seven layers and in many instances it is implemented as a 'null' layer; it acts as an interface pass-through without any form of data processing. The functional responsibility of the presentation layer entities concerns the representation of the data it receives from the application layer entities. This data is converted into some network convenient form upon which further processing is completed so that the appropriate user service can be supplied.

The network wide data representation is termed the 'concrete transfer syntax', which is the representation by which the data is transferred between peer presentation layer entities. In most systems the transfer syntax is defined in terms of octets and their relative position to each other. The local data form is defined in terms of the appropriate abstract syntax. The rules for generating an abstract syntax can vary but the most commonly adopted scheme is that termed the abstract syntax notation number one (ASN.1). Consider the analogy of a telephone conversation between the UK and France in which there are two translators, one in each country, who know only German as their common language. The three languages each have their own syntax; that is, their grammar and idiom usage. The German would, in this case, be referred to as the concrete syntax with both the English and French acting with local abstract syntaxes. Communication is now possible between the UK and France and, more importantly, it is possible between any other country provided that a translator to/from German and the native language can be found.

Once the data has been converted to the transfer syntax it is then possible to process it further. The sorts of processing that are appropriate at this layer are:

- Data encryption to support secure and/or private communications or to provide authentication via digital signatures.

- Data compression, so that the physical bandwidth requirements can be minimized.

In most cases the data encryption and compression techniques adopted will depend upon the types of data being transferred. For instance, very different compression algorithms are used when considering voice or video communications.

The presentation layer standards include both connection mode and connectionless definitions, with the services defined under ISO 8822 and 8822/1, respectively. The protocol definitions are given under ISO 8823 and 9576, respectively. As is the case with the session layer, it is the connection mode definitions that are adopted by the current system implementations.

4.3.4   Session layer

The session layer is responsible for providing a coherent communications link throughout the duration of the session. Consider the situation when editing a file. When an edit session is started, the file is opened, then edited and finally closed; all of these actions must take place for the successful completion of the session or else the file will be left in an unknown state. The session layer ensures that the session is consistent and provides the conversation management between multiple end users. There are in fact connection oriented and connectionless session services, ISO 8326 and 8326/3 respectively, but only the connection mode version is used by the established application systems. ISO 8327 defines the connection mode session protocols. The functions which are supported by a session protocol are:

- Connection management and basic link housekeeping.
- Full duplex data transfer.
- Negotiated release to provide an orderly tear-down of the link.
- Half duplex data transfer.
- Synchronization to coordinate data transfer between the users.
- Activity management to provide for the user the control of clearly defined activities within a session.
- Exception reporting to provide information concerning important events during the lifetime of the session.

These functions are available in five types of session layer. These types and their functionality are:

- Kernel – the most basic functionality which provides the basic connection management and full duplex data transfer.
- Basic combined subset (BCS) – including the kernel's and half duplex functionality.
- Basic synchronized subset (BSS) – including the synchronization and BCS functionality.

- Basic activity subset (BAS) – includes all of the functions except some of the extended synchronization features.
- Full – includes all of the available functions.

In most instances it is the 'kernel' which is adopted because of its simplicity and current availability. The BSS is intended for use in file or transaction processing environments, the BCS for terminal–host interaction and the BAS for highly structured communication systems such as electronic mail – that is, MHS. There should never be a need for the adoption of the full session as this is far too 'heavy' for all but the most idiosyncratic of applications.

4.3.5   Transport layer

The transport layer maps the user services onto the communications subnetwork and so maps the logical network onto the physical reality. The connection oriented transport service is defined in ISO 8072 with the corresponding transport protocols defined in ISO 8073; the connectionless transport service and protocol equivalents are defined in ISO 8072/1 and ISO 8602, respectively. The functions supported by a transport protocol are dependent upon the class of service supported (at the moment there are some seven different services available) but they would typically include some or all of the following:

- Connection management, which includes connection establishment and disengagement as well as normal housekeeping functions.
- Segmentation, or fragmentation, of the data into more manageable PDU sizes and, consequently, message reconstitution – the rebuilding of the messages at the receiver when they have undergone fragmentation at the transmitter.
- Flow control, including the use of a sliding window protocol, so that the receiver does not get overrun by the transmitter.
- Expedited data flow, which is another term for interrupt data transfer (the ability for some information to queue-jump). This provides the session layer with the ability to pre-empt data already queued within the lower layers of the communications architecture.
- Error detection and correction using BEC techniques, which is particularly important when using an unreliable network service. In some cases this will include the appropriate SWP.
- Multiplexing, the coordination of several real subnetworks for the transfer of data using one logical point-to-point link.

The transport service is the user of the network service and consequently it must be capable of compensating for any shortfall in the subnetwork's capabilities. The wide variation in the capabilities of subnetworks has necessitated the creation of several transport services, each of which is suited to a particular type of subnetwork. In total there are some seven transport services:

- Class 0 – this is supported by transport protocol zero (TP0) and supplies the basic data transfer and connection management facilities.

- Class 1 – which is supported by transport protocol one (TP1) and supplies error recovery on top of TP0's functionality.

- Class 2 – which is supported by transport protocol two (TP2) and supplies subnetwork multiplexing on top of TP0's functionality.

- Class 3 – this is a combination of TP1 and TP2 (error recovery and multiplexing alongside basic data delivery and connection management) to produce TP3.

- Class 4 – which is the most elaborate of the transport protocols (TP4) and which provides extensive error recovery and retransmission capabilities as well as full subnetwork multiplexing.

- Connectionless transport service (CLTS) – which is supported by the connectionless transport protocol (CLTP) and which provides basic data transmission and error detection capabilities.

- Express transfer protocol (XTP) – a hardware implementation of a combined transport and network protocol for use in high speed data delivery applications.

Classes 0 to 4, inclusive, are all forms of the connection oriented transport service (COTS) and as such must support connection establishment and disengagement as part of their intrinsic functionality. Given that there are seven transport protocols from which to choose it is important to consider the types of subnetwork they are intended to control. These subnetworks fall into one of three categories:

- Class A – subnetworks with an acceptable and known quality of service and which can reliably support that service. In this case TP0 or TP2 is used.

- Class B – subnetworks, such as X.25, which support an acceptable quality of service but which cannot be expected to supply that service reliably. In this case it is common to use TP1 or TP3.

- Class C – subnetworks which cannot be relied upon to provide an appropriate quality of service. Any form of connectionless network service (CLNS) could be deemed as unreliable, as is the case for most LAN environments. In this case TP4 would be used.

Originally the connection oriented philosophy of the OSI/RM ruled out the necessity for connectionless services; however, their relatively recent inclusion also requires that mixed connectionless/connection oriented services be considered. The typical combinations for the transport service would be for a COTS on top of a connection oriented network service (CONS), such as TP1 with X.25, or a CLTS with CLNS or, most common of all, the COTS with a CLNS.

4.3.6   Network layer

The network layer is responsible for controlling the topology and access to the network: the term subnetwork is used to reflect the presence of a real network such as a LAN, a PSDN, a CSDN or an ISDN. It maintains all of the routing tables alongside the address maps (to link the logical addresses to the physical addresses), manages the network data flow and access, and supports the user billing system.

The end-system network address, or network service access point (NSAP) address, is the address element that must be globally unique: the NSAP uniquely differentiates between all end-systems on all networks (some end-systems may have several unique NSAP addresses). It is essential, therefore, that the network layer possess the capability to be able to locate, and so send data, to any end-system on the network and to react to any change of address location. The protocols that support this address control are separate from those responsible for data transfer, so it is usual for the network layer to house many concurrently active protocols. Routers make extensive use of these protocols to support the addressing system and their differences are reflected in the dependence of the routers on the network layer protocol.

Once again, there are two basic types of service: the CONS and the CLNS. X.25 is the only recognized CONS and even this needs the appropriate sublayering support to conform to the OSI/RM. The CONS service specification is provided in the ISO 8348 standard but the network protocols (basically X.25) are defined elsewhere. The CLNS is supported by the connectionless network protocol (CLNP); these are defined in the ISO 8348/1 and 8473 standards, respectively.

4.3.7   Data link layer

The data link layer (also known as the link layer) is responsible for ensuring that no bit errors are passed from the communications channel to the higher layers; the LAN equivalent is called the logical link control. It is not necessarily responsible for the loss/ duplication/time re-ordering of data fragments produced by higher layers; in many cases this functionality is supported either in the transport or network layers. As in most error recovery schemes, the error detection and correction capability is based upon fragmenting the data into frames. Error detection then takes the form of a frame check sequence (FCS) or cyclic redundancy check (CRC). Unless some particular error correction capability is employed, such as forward error correction (FEC), the correction is solely dependent upon a BEC technique.

The data link layer's responsibility for data bit integrity means that its degree of functionality is very closely related to the type of subnetwork being supported. Each type of subnetwork tends to have its own specific data link layer but in most cases this is an appropriate subset of the high-level data link control (HDLC) protocol. The various subsets of HDLC are:

- Link access procedure (LAP) – the original master/slave access protocol which supported the initial X.25 systems.

- Balanced link access procedure (LAPB) – the peer-to-peer version of LAP. LAPB is normally used to support PSDNs.

- Modem link access procedure (LAPM) – this supports the error correction capability for use on modem links across PSTNs.

- Half duplex link access procedure (LAPX) – this supports teletex services.

- Designated link access procedure (LAPD) – access to narrowband ISDN based networks makes use of what is termed the 'D' channel. The access protocol for the full ISDN service is termed, therefore, LAPD.

- Link access procedure E (LAPE) – access to broadband ISDN networks based upon cell relay, for example asynchronous transfer mode.

- Logical link control (LLC) – this is the protocol used to support LANs.

The data link service specification is defined under ISO 8886. The HDLC protocol is defined by several ISO standards with each of the various subsets having their own standard. For example, ISO 3309 defines the HDLC frame structure whereas ISO 7776 defines the LAPB.

4.3.8   Physical layer

The physical layer is responsible for actually transmitting and receiving the data. This includes the coupling of the transmitters and receivers to the channel, the signalling of the information across the channel, and the modulation and multiplexing of the signals from the many transmitters. At this level the standards define signal qualities across the various channel types (leading onto a bit error rate), physical signalling across the channel and physical connectors to the channel. ISO 10022 defines the physical service whereas standards such as ISO 8482 define twisted pair multipoint interconnection and ISO 2110 defines the 25 pole DTE–DCE interface connector.

4.3.9   Security

The OSI/RM security architecture (ISO 7498-2) defines a set of security services, whose objectives are described in the associated standard ISO/IEC 10182-1. The security services are:

- Authentication – confirmation of the identity of the communicating partners, and of the source and integrity of the information.

- Access control – limitation of access to services according to the authorization level of the users.

- Non-repudiation – preventing users from wrongfully denying a particular action. This includes proof-of-origin and proof-of-delivery.

- Integrity – the prevention of loss or modification of information due to corruption or unauthorized access.

- Data confidentiality – the prevention of unauthorized access to information regardless of whether this is attempted during data storage or transmission.

- Audit framework – provision of an audit trail to enable user accountability and to demonstrate what, where and when events occurred.

- Key management – support for the distribution and maintenance of the keys used for the provision of the secure architecture.

These services are based on agreed objectives which themselves have been categorized as either primary or secondary. The primary objectives correspond to system threat such as disclosure, corruption or denial of service, whereas the secondary objectives are to support the primaries. The five primary objectives are data confidentiality, data integrity, data availability, authentication and non-repudiation, and the secondary objectives are access control, audit trail and security alarm. Techniques such as encryption are the basis for the provision of the non-repudiation and confidentiality services and as such are not services in their own right.

The allocation of responsibility for the secure services in the different layers is being studied but the intention is to provide a flexible framework within which further secure services can be provided easily; this is of particular importance to military applications. These extra services will take the form of new layer entities and new sublayers, and so the fundamental structure of the OSI/RM remains unchanged.

4.4 Internetworking and the OSI/RM

The OSI/RM defines a single physical network as a subnetwork, hence the 'open system' consists of many linked subnetworks. The interface between the transport and network layers must now be made common so that it is independent of the properties of the individual subnetworks. The interconnection of multiple subnetworks in the OSI/RM produces the architecture shown in Figure 4.8, in which the network layer has been split into three sublayers .

The three protocols for each of the sublayers are the subnetwork independent convergence protocol (SNICP or 3c), the subnetwork dependent convergence protocol (SNDCP or 3b) and the subnetwork access protocol (SNAcP or 3a). These three protocols are used to support two interconnection strategies employed by network layer relays: the hop-by-hop enhancement and the internet approaches. The hop-by-

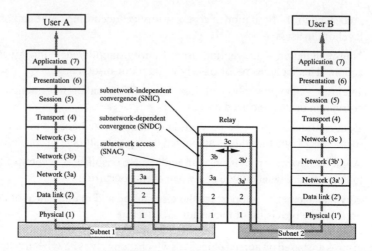

Figure 4.8   The internal structure of the network layer.

hop approach uses the sublayers 3a and 3b (3b is also known as the subnet enhancement layer) and the internet approach uses the sublayers 3a and 3c (3c is also known as the internet sublayer). The internet strategy requires the use of the same link protocol across all of the interconnected subnetworks – that is, using a router – whereas the hop-by-hop approach provides a gradual enhancement of the services as the linked subnetworks are traversed – a gateway. The hop-by-hop approach makes the most efficient use of a subnetwork's facilities whereas the internet approach requires the use of a single protocol, but at the expense of complexity and compromise of individual subnetwork facilities.

In some cases – and the use of the X.25PLP across a LAN is one such case – all three sublayers need to be present. The use of X.25 for the CONS across a WAN is shown in Figure 4.9. As can be seen in this diagram there is a subnetwork enhancement protocol (a SNDCP) which ensures that the X.25PLP can be accessed by the OSI/RM COTS. This sublayer, which has local significance only and so does not require peer-to-peer communications, is necessary because the X.25PLP does not provide a CONS interface and also because several optional facilities in the X.25 system have to be invoked before an OSI/RM type service can be supported. Figure 4.9 shows the ISO 8878 protocol acting only in the DTEs with the full X.25 network supplying the communications subnetwork.

When discussing the communications subnetwork, the role of the network layer included address table maintenance, which in turn required the introduction of protocols specifically to support this maintenance. The relationship of the address table protocols, and therefore routing table protocols to the OSI/RM is shown in Figure 4.10; the common network layer protocol means that the relay elements are routers. There are two important protocols used to support address maintenance across multiple subnetwork architectures:

- The end-system to intermediate system (ES-IS) protocol, which is used for

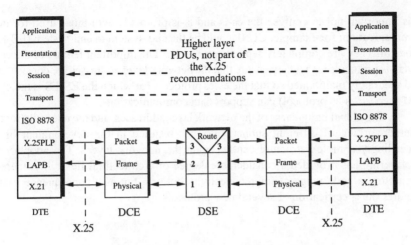

Figure 4.9 The use of the X.25 as a CONS.

communication between the end-systems and the routers. This protocol provides the local nodes with the knowledge of when and when not to send data to the router. In this text the term es-is will be used to denote a generic protocol whereas ES-IS will refer only to the specific OSI/RM protocol.

- The intermediate systems to intermediate system (IS-IS) protocol, which is used for router to router communications. This protocol provides the routers with the knowledge of when and when not to send data to the other routers. In this text the term is-is will be used to denote a generic protocol whereas IS-IS will refer only to the specific OSI/RM protocol.

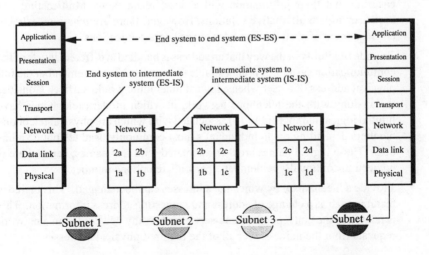

Figure 4.10 Internetworking protocols for the network layer.

It is important not to confuse the es-is and is-is protocols with those used for data communication; for example, CLNP could be the end-system to end-system (ES-ES) protocol. They are completely separate protocols. The important feature of the es-is and is-is protocols is that they ensure that the network layer addresses are consistently and accurately maintained so that the es-es protocols (of which the ES-ES is the OSI/RM specific es-es protocol) can support data communications.

The global uniqueness of the network layer addresses, and the necessity for the internetworking of different subnetworks has resulted in the development of an exceedingly complex structure centred upon the network layer. The adoption of sublayering has provided a considerable degree of architectural flexibility, thereby supporting a wide range of interconnectivity options, but as a consequence it also requires the specification of several new protocols.

4.5 Addressing

Addressing is a topic that is discreetly dropped in most discussions of communications systems. The reason for this is that it is an extremely complex area. However, it is the core feature for the correct operation of a network. Without some form of addressing system it is impossible to construct a communications system. The more complex the functionality of the network the more complex the addressing scheme needs to be to support the services (consider security and its implication on private/secure addressing). An addressing system must:

- Ensure that each user can be uniquely identified within the network, thereby ensuring that their information will at least reach them. Multicasting and broadcasting are alternative solutions. However, there are many undesirable consequences of such a scheme for normal communications.

- Provide flexibility in the way that an address is handled at different levels of the communication system. It is undesirable for a user to have to remember the full physical address of a user when a logical mnemonic would suffice. Consider the analogy with the telephone network, in which modern telephones have limited logical numbers (1 to 10) associated with which are physical telephone numbers depending on an individual's most commonly used telephone numbers. These logical names are then annotated with real names, hence there is no need to continually remember a person's telephone number.

- Provide a mechanism by which the addresses can be managed. This includes features such as a change of address and requesting address information. This is related to the concept of a name-server and so any newcomer on a network requests from the name-server all of the required physical addresses.

The standards for addressing are more concerned with ensuring the syntax of the addresses and the uniqueness of the NSAP addresses than with the ways in which the addresses are used. An address can be used in a variety of ways:

- As a physical and unique identifier for an end-system on the network. The number of addresses is therefore equal to the maximum number of possible users.

- As a functional identifier where the physical location is irrelevant and it is the responsibility of the receiver to watch for addresses which fall within its functional briefing. This form of addressing is used in network management, where the manager could consist of many functionally separated physical locations.

- A logical identifier, or selector, representing some internal mechanism or resource. This is commonly used in protocols where there are many user buffers and the different virtual circuits will be supported using different physical buffers.

The addressing system is a compromise between the globally maintained systems accessed via the PTTs, such as X.121, the proprietary systems such as Ethernet and Novell NetWare, the *de facto* systems such as TCP/IP and the locally maintained systems such as Token Ring. Addressing is normally considered as a local problem and only becomes an issue when WAN access becomes necessary. At this point the addresses have to be globally unique and unless a well maintained hierarchical system has been used from the outset it normally results in a complete reallocation of the NSAP addresses, at the very least.

Fortunately, the OSI/RM advocates the use of many different types of addresses – typically one scheme per layer. The aim then becomes one of deriving a system in which changes to that system are limited to one layer of the addressing schema – if this is not the case then it is a major problem for address reallocation. The OSI limits these types of changes by using a mix of physical, functional and logical addresses and collates all of these under the 'name'. The name is the title by which the end-system application process knows its communications partner. The address system now maps this name to the physical address of that user; data transfer can then begin.

An example of the different uses of addresses is shown in Figure 4.11. This shows two transport entities (one a COTS and the other a CLTS), two network entities and the connectionless LLC. At the bottom of the architecture is the subnetwork point of attachment (SNPA) address or, in this case, the LAN MAC address (08003446FEDC). Above this are three different LLC service access points (LSAPs) which denote different network layer services using the LLC; the IEEE register has assigned FE as the OSI network service, AA as the subnetwork access protocol (SNAP) service and 40 as the local management service. In this system communication is possible between A and E and B and E; these are the only two users that have a common set of SAPs: the COTS, CLNS and LLC (40). At the physical layer, communication between A/B and E requires the use of source and destination MAC addresses which must be uniquely assigned to NIAs.

The problem of addressing becomes more complex when two or more LANs

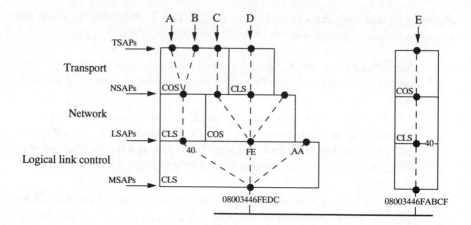

Figure 4.11 A four layer address structure.

are linked using an address sensitive internetworking device such as a bridge. A bridged network is shown in Figure 4.12 in which each user PC has a NIA with the MAC address as marked. The bridge has two ports, so its address table must assign each source MAC address to a port. When a frame is received by the bridge it compares the destination MAC address with those addresses in its tables and decides through which port the frame is to be transmitted – if the destination address is on the same port as the source port from which the data was received then the bridge discards the frame. It is not necessary to discuss how the bridge's address table are constructed to appreciate the importance of the MAC addresses in ensuring that the frames are received by the right users without unduly loading the rest of the network.

If a network was to remain static in terms of its users, their distribution across the network, the topology of the network and the application services offered by the network then there would be no need to provide an address management system once the initial address allocation had been conceived and installed. Such stability is totally unrealistic, so the network must be provided with an address management system that can distribute addresses when they are required. This is the purpose of the ISO's directory service (DS) or the CCITT's X.500 equivalent. The DS contains two classes of address maps: the logical application name and its corresponding SAP addresses; and the NSAP address and the corresponding SAP and physical addresses. The logical address map supports an application service itself; it takes some destination logical name and retrieves the associated set of SAPs, which is then used to establish the address fields in the various PDUs at each layer down to the network layer. At the network layer the DS, if necessary, is again interrogated to locate the associated physical address for the information – recall that the NSAP address is the only address that has to be unique across all of the subnetworks used throughout the world.

Two address maps are used to reflect the manner in which most networks operate, namely the communications subnetwork, whose address system reflects the operational state of the network, and the applications service, which reflects the manner

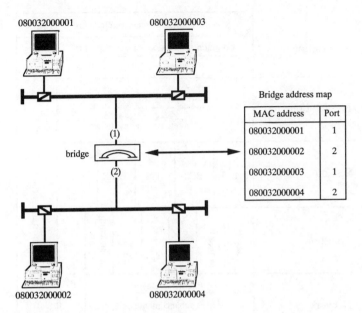

Figure 4.12   Internetworking devices and address consistency.

in which the network is used. This separation means that an alteration of the physical subnetwork will not necessarily cause an alteration in the higher address schemes and vice versa. Therefore, address management is simplified without compromising the user's requirements.

Two of the primary functional responsibilities of internetworking devices are to provide address consistency across the network and to ensure that changes to the network do not undermine the addressing system. This means that whenever possible and appropriate, the internetworking devices must automatically detect changes in the network and alter the address table maps accordingly. This need alone accounts for a lot of the complexity found in internetworking devices.

4.6 OSI/RM profiles

So far the discussion of the OSI/RM has followed a somewhat traditional approach in that it has concentrated upon each layer individually with only the occasional reflection on layer–layer interactions. It is, however, the combination of the seven layers that creates the OSI/RM communications environment. An abridged collation of the entities available in the seven layers of the ISO OSI/RM is shown in Figure 4.13. In summary this shows that:

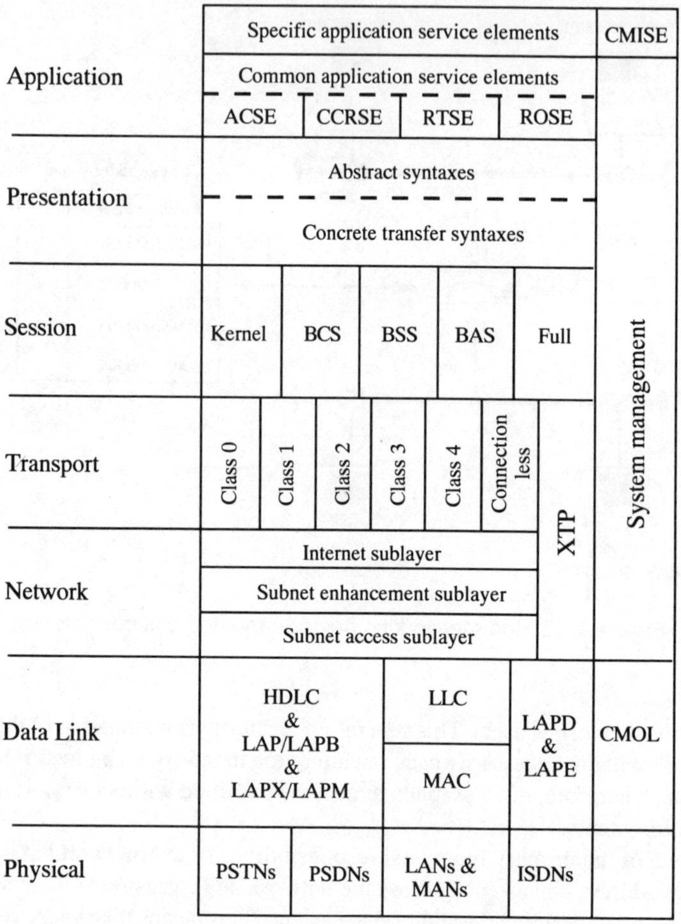

Application	Specific application service elements					CMISE	
	Common application service elements						
	ACSE	CCRSE		RTSE	ROSE		
Presentation	Abstract syntaxes						
	Concrete transfer syntaxes						
Session	Kernel	BCS	BSS	BAS	Full		System management
Transport		Class 0	Class 1	Class 2	Class 3	Class 4	Connection less	XTP	
Network	Internet sublayer						
	Subnet enhancement sublayer						
	Subnet access sublayer						
Data Link	HDLC & LAP/LAPB & LAPX/LAPM		LLC		LAPD & LAPE	CMOL	
			MAC				
Physical	PSTNs	PSDNs	LANs & MANs	ISDNs			

Figure 4.13   The ISO OSI/RM profile selection.

- The physical layer must support LANs, ISDNs, telephone switching (PSTNs) and data networks (PSDNs).

- The data link layer uses the LLC and media access control (MAC) for LANs, LAPD and LAPE for ISDNs and various forms of the HDLC for PSDNs and PSTNs.

- The network layer is broken into its three sublayers: the internet sublayer (3c), the subnet enhancement sublayer (3b) and the subnet access sublayer (3a). One, two or all three sublayers may be needed depending on the type of subnetwork being used.

- The transport layer has the 5 classes of COTS (class 0 being basic and class 4 being the most sophisticated). There is one CLTS and the express service, which is a high speed, hardware implementation of the combined transport and network layer services.

- The session layer supports five classes of protocol: the basic kernel, the basic combined subset, the basic synchronized subset, the basic activity subset and the full session.

- The presentation layer supports the abstract syntaxes, such as abstract syntax notation 1, with the concrete transfer syntaxes.

- The application layer is, conceptually, split into the specific application service elements and the common application service elements. The SASE consists of services such as the message handling system (electronic mail). CASE supports the connection management – that is, the application control service element, the reliable transfer service element, the concurrent and commitment recovery service element and the remote operations service element.

- Network management is supported by the common management information service element, which interacts with the individual layer management entities. The low level management protocols may also be controlled by the common management over link (CMOL) service, which interacts directly with CMISE to provide rapid and accurate management of high speed subnetworks.

The equivalent representation from the CCITT is shown in Figure 4.14, which is based upon the information given in the X.220 recommendation. It is interesting to see the difference in the amount of detail given to the lower layers compared with the higher ones. This is a reflection of the bottom-up design philosophy of the telecommunications discipline. There are considerably more ISO standards for the higher layers than in the CCITT counterpart. From the point of view of application services the CCITT are concentrating upon their X.400 electronic mail service with the X.500 directory service and a combined file transfer and document access system called the document transfer, access and management (DTAM) service. A recent addition is the network management application process (NMAP), or X.700.

The CCITT stack does not address LANs nor does it consider any connectionless services. CCITT protocols always support connection oriented services to such an extent that not even X.25 can supply a CLNS except by using an optional, truncated connection mode facility called the 'fast select with clear' service.

A profile is the name given to the description of the integrated stack in which the appropriate protocols are selected for each of the layers so that the user obtains the service to support their particular application needs. Clearly, even in the abridged forms discussed in this text, it is evident that there are a large number of different possible protocol combinations and hence profiles. The selection and configuration of the right profile is essential if the users are to be provided with a useful communications system.

The standards organizations have responded to this concern and have introduced the international standardized profiles (ISPs) register (MacKinnon, 1990). This register is a collection of OSI/RM function profiles which describe standard combinations of protocols and their implementation parameters, and states which elements are

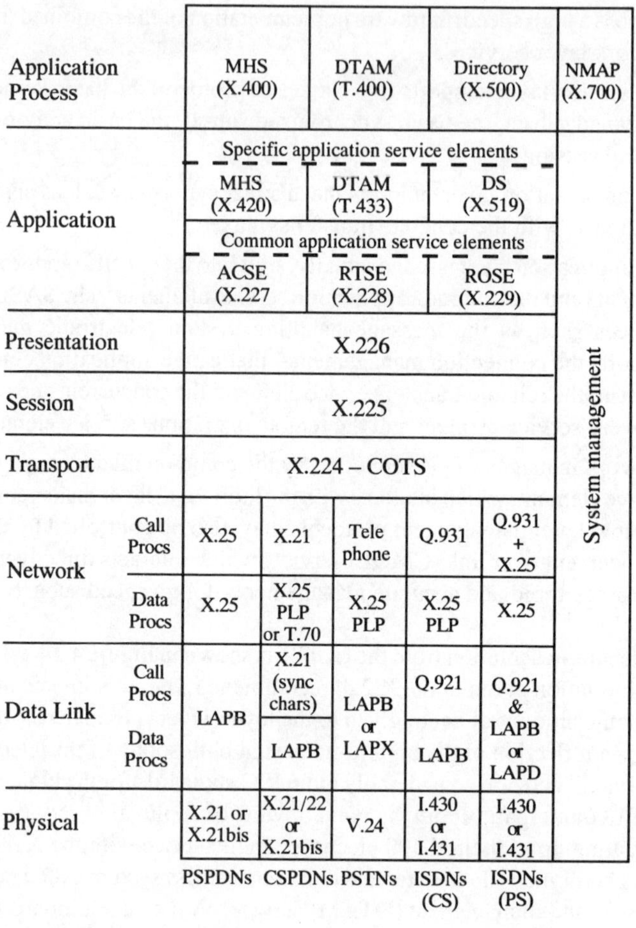

Application Process		MHS (X.400)	DTAM (T.400)	Directory (X.500)	NMAP (X.700)	
Application		Specific application service elements				
		MHS (X.420)	DTAM (T.433)	DS (X.519)		
		Common application service elements				
		ACSE (X.227	RTSE (X.228)	ROSE (X.229)		
Presentation		X.226				
Session		X.225				
Transport		X.224 – COTS				
Network	Call Procs	X.25	X.21	Tele phone	Q.931	Q.931 + X.25
	Data Procs	X.25	X.25 PLP or T.70	X.25 PLP	X.25 PLP	X.25
Data Link	Call Procs	LAPB	X.21 (sync chars)	LAPB or	Q.921	Q.921 & LAPB or LAPD
	Data Procs		LAPB	LAPX	LAPB	
Physical		X.21 or X.21bis	X.21/22 or X.21bis	V.24	I.430 or I.431	I.430 or I.431
		PSPDNs	CSPDNs	PSTNs	ISDNs (CS)	ISDNs (PS)

(Right-hand column, spanning all layers: **System management**)

Figure 4.14 The CCITT OSI/RM profile selection.

mandatory and which are optional. For instance there is the TA53 profile which defines the usage of a class 4 transport service with a connectionless network service across a Token Ring LAN (TP4, CLNP, LLC type 1 and 8802.5). Each protocol has an associated protocol implementation conformance statement (PICS) and so the profiles invoke the appropriate PICS, thereby ensuring that there is a clear relationship between the profile descriptions, the protocol and service standards, and the protocol implementation. An example of these registered profiles are the Government Open Systems Interconnection Profile (GOSIP), which has been defined for future networks that are to be used for public organization projects. Each government has its own GOSIP identifying the protocols and services that must be supplied for a particular communications environment.

The aim is for user organizations to adopt the appropriate functional profiles and thereby reduce the amount of effort required to determine the structure and configuration of their communications environment. The design exercise then becomes an investigation of the available profiles and a verification of the suitability of that profile to the user's own applications. As the number of established profiles increases this search and selection will become more complex and time consuming but three factors will always favour this approach:

- It will always be quicker to select from established profiles than to start from the range of raw protocols.

- There is considerably more likelihood of the profile actually working given that it has been registered and is almost certainly in use somewhere else.

- The internal organization of the register will itself be cross-referenced and reviewed so as to group together profiles that are more commonly used in specific market areas or where particular functionality is required.

4.7 Summary

The open system interconnection seven-layer reference model (OSI/RM) has now established itself as the model upon which all networks are defined and implemented. While it is not necessary or desirable that every network conform to the OSI/RM it is important to always consider it as the starting point when constructing even a 'closed network' or when discussing the required functionality of a network. The OSI/RM should be considered as the complete network specification, so individual 'closed networks' become non-conformant but useful subsets of it. In summary:

- The seven layers of the OSI/RM are, from top to bottom, the application (layer seven), presentation, session, transport, network, data link and physical (layer one) layers. An OSI/RM conformant system must support all seven layers, but currently very few do.

- The introduction of internetworking has produced a more complex network layer structure. This gives rise to the router (common end-system network layer protocols) and the gateway (different end-system network layer protocols).

- The OSI/RM is predominantly connection oriented but connectionless services are now available in several layers. In most real systems the higher layers are connection oriented while the lower layers tend to be based upon a connectionless service or the X.25 system.

- The more sophisticated the control in the stack the lower its efficiency. This is a natural consequence of the processing overheads incurred at each layer.

- The OSI/RM security framework has just been established. This framework describes the allocation of the responsibility for the primary and secondary security objectives with respect to the different layers.

- The range of applications supported by the OSI/RM will increase, particularly as more market specific requirements become clearly identified. The structure of the OSI/RM is such that these additions can be introduced easily and only in exceptional circumstances are alterations required in related protocol entities.

- Both IBM and Digital are committed to the OSI/RM, but the established user bases of their own proprietary systems mean that the migration path to full OSI/RM compatibility will be long and tortuous.

- The newly developing communications techniques such as frame and cell relay should be considered in terms of their relationship to the OSI/RM. Unfortunately, it is already known that some of the more long term system concepts are not compatible with the OSI/RM, so at some time in the long term its structure will have to be significantly revised.

5

Local Area Networks

5.1 Introduction

LANs provide a relatively cheap way to share peripheral access among a large number of users, fast reliable communications to support the development of distributed systems and a building block upon which larger and more complex networks and information systems can be built. By the mid 1980s there were approximately seventy different commercially available LAN architectures and this caused considerable confusion in the minds of the purchasers. Strange as it may seem, standardization was not introduced to lower this number but to ensure that network elements for identical systems from different manufacturers would operate together. Clearly, it would have been impossible to standardize on a single LAN architecture. In fact a single architecture is also technically undesirable because different LANs are better suited to different application environments; consider the different needs of industrial manufacturing and office support systems. The former requires real-time response of short messages in a potentially noisy (electrically) environment whereas the latter must support large message transfers (printing and file access) among a potentially large community of users.

5.2 LAN architectures

The classification schemes for LANs are almost as varied as the number of LANs. This is because almost every form of suitable architecture and technology has been used to implement one type or another of LAN. The most commonly used classifications are:

- Transmission techniques – the ways in which the actual signals are transmitted along the channel: baseband, broadband, wideband and carrierband.

- Channel – the types of channel used to support the LANs: copper based, fibre based and wireless.

- Topology – the different ways in which the users are connected together: broadcast or point-to-point connectivity.

- Access technique – how the users share access to the channel so that all of the users have equal access: token bus, slotted ring and so on.

It is common for a LAN to be generically identified according to its access technique, for example token bus. Different commercial implementations will then use some appropriately associated market-place name for the product. The most common example of this is the use of the name 'Ethernet' to describe all LANs based upon the carrier sensing multiple access with collision detection. 'Ethernet' is in fact the implementation trade name for the Digital, Xerox and Intel version of that LAN multiple access technique; however, its brevity and 'motherhood' nature have assured its adoption for common usage.

5.2.1   Transmission characterization

A signal, whether of electrical or other origin, can be considered in both its logical and physical forms. The logical, or symbolic, form consists of the data formats themselves – data 0, data 1 – plus some other control signals (used to establish synchronization). The data stream consists of a sequence of these 1s and 0s but this is not the form that is actually transmitted along the channel. The actual form of the signal depends upon the type of link through which it will pass and so this can be termed the physical form.

It is easiest to consider the physical signal as something varying in time – that is, at one moment representing logic '1' and at another logic '0' and so on. This time dependent signal can also be viewed as a series of frequencies that are simultaneously present on the channel. The sum of all of these frequencies creates the time domain equivalent; every signal can be described in both the time and frequency domains. One important qualitative relationship between the time and frequency domains is that as the time signals become shorter – that is, a higher data carrying rate – there are more higher frequency components. This means that high speed data systems use a greater bandwidth than low speed ones.

Unfortunately the channel distorts each of these frequencies in a slightly different way. This distortion consists of signal attenuation and variable propagation velocity. The signal becomes more attenuated as is passes through more of the channel; in general, the higher the frequency the greater the attenuation. The net result is that the signal may be lost entirely, becoming so attenuated that there is insufficient power for the receiver or being lost in the background noise. Each frequency component of the signal propagates along the channel at a different velocity; the higher the frequency the greater the velocity. This means the signal becomes slightly separated and reduces the receiver's effectiveness to identify it accurately. In engineering terms these channel effects dictate the maximum channel separation between the transmitters and the receivers, the power needed by the transmitter and the system's data rate.

Many signalling systems make use of baseband communications (Proakis, 1983). Here the signal is transmitted using its natural frequency components only, as shown by the left-most waveform in Figure 5.1. This signal consists of square wave pulses being transmitted at R_c bps; the actual internal detail of this power spectrum depends upon the signal modulation scheme. The problems with baseband are that if the channel is noisy in that frequency region then heavy data corruption and loss may occur, plus it is impossible to have more than one signal on the channel at any one time. Simultaneous signal transmission can be supported using a broadband system as shown by the right-hand waveform of Figure 5.1. Here the data signal is modulated by the carrier frequency, f_a. This carrier frequency is designed to ensure that no overlapping occurs with other signals on the channel, so that no information is lost due to mutual signal interference. This is exactly the type of system used by the television and radio

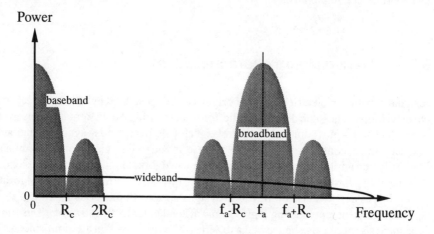

Figure 5.1 Transmission techniques power spectra.

networks (referred to as frequency division multiple access) so data reception requires that the receiver be tuned to the appropriate frequency carrier.

Carrierband, or single-channel broadband, communications is a combination of baseband and broadband techniques. This signalling system employs a single carrier frequency which is used for all data transfers. The advantage of this system is that it is possible to use the cheaper analogue systems without becoming involved in the frequency isolation problems normally encountered in broadband communications. One variant of the token bus LAN makes use of carrierband.

A further extension to these techniques is that of wideband communications. This system makes use of the fact that the signal to noise ratio (SNR) and bandwidth of a signal can be traded off with respect to each other. A very large bandwidth can compensate for a small SNR (Shannon, 1980). The power spectrum for such a system is shown by the flat waveform in Figure 5.1. The typical narrowband signal could be as shown by the baseband waveform. It is possible to send exactly the same information using the 'wideband version', which has a lower power level but wider bandwidth. The advantage in doing this is that it then becomes possible to have more than one signal on the channel at any one time both in the same frequency and time (broadband systems fragment the frequency domain among different users). There is considerable mutual interference from the simultaneous users (a SNR of considerably less than one!) but this is compensated for by excessive bandwidth utilization and a lowering of the point-to-point data rate. This technique is commonly termed 'spread spectrum', and it is one of the techniques being developed for wireless LAN architectures and mobile cellular systems.

The bandwidth allocation system is only the first step in ensuring an equally fair access scheme for all users. It is, however, essential that the most appropriate system

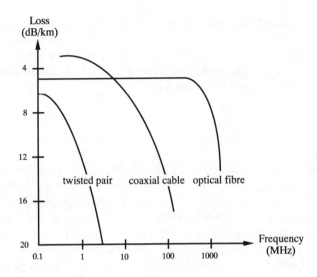

Figure 5.2 Attenuation coefficients for different types of channel.

is selected because any failures at this level will have significant repercussions for the protocols in the communications architecture and could ultimately result in the complete loss of communications.

5.2.2 Channel types

During the past ten years there has been a significant increase in the number of channel types used to support LAN communications and the latest area of interest is in the development of wireless links using either radiowave, microwave or infrared. One of the primary considerations in selecting a channel is the attenuation characteristic, as shown in Figure 5.2, which shows the variation of signal attenuation with signal frequency. Some channel types are better suited to high frequency communications than others, but the trade-off is between the frequency range and the length of channel through which the signal will pass: the higher the frequency, the greater the signal attenuation by the channel (per unit length). A quick inspection of the curves would imply that twisted pair cabling has comparatively high losses. However, this is compensated for by only using short cable lengths (no more than 100 m on average). A length of 100 m is normally sufficient for most installations and if not then a repeater can be used to extend the cabling system.

Coaxial cable

Coaxial cable (coax) is the classical channel type. There are several grades of coax, including twinax and triax, providing a wide range of signal propagation characteristics. Coax cable consists of a single conductor surrounded by a plastic dielectric coat and meshed shielding; television aerial cable is coaxial. The Ethernet and token bus LANs make extensive use of coax cabling.

Twisted pair

Two types of twisted pair are used in LAN cabling: shielded twisted pair (STP) and unshielded twisted pair (UTP). The basic structure of twisted pair is that two copper wires are twisted around each other. The signal is transmitted along both conductors, the actual signalling varying from system to system. At the receiver, the signals are subtracted from one another, thereby removing the noise and recovering the original signal. In the USA it is very common for communications systems to use UTP. This is because American UTP based telephone cabling is of data carrying quality and therefore can be used to provide a data carrying system. This is not the case in the UK and Europe, so a separate UTP wiring system must still be installed.

A recent addition to the twisted pair stable is intelligent twisted pair (ITP). This is twisted pair that provides a signalling quality equivalent to that of STP but at a fraction of the cost, and in only a slightly bigger cable than that used for UTP.

Multicore

Multicore cable is used in very high speed host-to-host communications across very short distances, typically less than 10 m. The advantage of this type of cable is that the data stream is not sent as a serial stream but as a parallel word. The bigger the word size, the greater the number of cores needed. Clearly this is a very expensive solution, so it is only used in specialized computer/computer communications environments.

Fibre

There is little doubt that in the long term fibre will replace all of the copper based backbone network systems. As can be seen from Figure 5.2, fibre is capable of sustaining longer distances for higher frequencies, so it is better suited to the very high speed data rates currently being proposed (in the gigabit range). Two grades of fibre are available for use in communications systems: multimode fibre and single mode fibre (SMF). A typical specification for multimode fibre (62.5 µm core) is a system supporting 100–500 Mbps across links of up to 2 km length, whereas for SMF (8 µm core) it would be 100–2000 Mbps across links of up to 60 km. SMF is considerably more expensive than the multimode fibre but in the next ten years this cost will drop, thereby enabling it to become the dominant carrier medium.

Wireless

The wireless systems currently in use for LANs are the radiowave, microwave, infrared and laser link systems. Indoor implementations rely upon low power utilization and have to contend with significant interference from objects such as hanging lights, potted plants and open/closed doors. The laser link systems are ideal for external use provided that line-of-sight communications is possible and that there will be no significant losses caused by weather effects. In many cases laser links are used as secondary systems for use in case of failure of the primary link.

Mainsborne

Mainsborne communications makes use of the electrical mains wiring system for data communication. The advantage of this system is that it uses wiring that is already installed and there is a readily available power source. Contrary to popular belief, the electricity mains is not a particularly noisy communications link provided that the data frequencies are up in the 100 kHz region. Several trial systems using mainsborne communications are undergoing evaluation in the UK and it is envisaged that at some time in the future these will be used, at the very least, to support the home utilities suppliers (gas, electricity and water) in remote meter reading.

5.2.3   LAN topologies

A further classification scheme is that of topology. The topology of a network falls into one of two categories: broadcast and point-to-point. Broadcast topologies are those in which the data ripples out across the network from the point of insertion. There is no active data regeneration by nodes, so data propagation is independent of the correct operation of these cards. Conversely, point-to-point communications makes use of the fact that each node actively regenerates the signal and passes it onto its nearest neighbours (Flint, 1983).

The typical structures adopted by broadcast systems are shown by the passive bus, tree and star topologies in Figure 5.3. In these topologies whenever a node transmits data the signal spreads out across the network until it reaches some termination point – that is, a matched impedance which absorbs the remaining power. The passive bus and tree topologies are classical architectures used by Ethernet.

The point-to-point topologies are shown by the active bus and ring systems, also in Figure 5.3. In these systems the signal is passed from node to node, undergoing

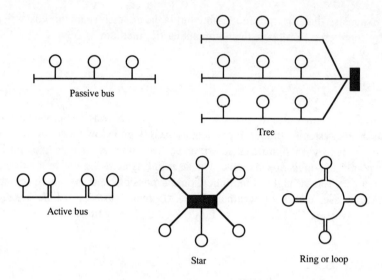

Figure 5.3   Network topologies.

regeneration at each hop. The primary concern of such systems is that a single node failure can cause the entire network to fail, so the actual implementations of such topologies are designed to compensate for such failures. The ring architecture is typical of that used by Token Ring, slotted ring and register insertion ring systems.

5.2.4   LAN access methods

The most common way to differentiate between LANs is by considering their multiple access scheme (Hutchison, 1988). The efficiency of the access scheme determines the limits of the performance capability of the LAN system, so it is essential to select the one that is best suited to the applications environment. In the late 1970s and the early 1980s it was very common to witness the creation of new access schemes whenever a new application system was under development. Fortunately, standardization has curtailed this proliferation.

Contention buses (Ethernet)

The Aloha network, one of the original computer communications protocols, operated on the basis that a node sent data whenever transmission was required. Sometimes this resulted in more than one node attempting to use the channel at the same time and so a data collision occurred. A feedback mechanism was compensated for this, whereby a transmitter had to listen to its own transmission to verify that it had been uncorrupted.

Several further developments of Aloha led to the concept of sensing the channel for other users before attempting to transmit and was called carrier sense multiple access; even in this system the finite propagation delays along the channel still cause contentions whenever two or more users attempted to send data at the same time. A later addition was collision detection (CD) to provide quick detection of the presence of more than one signal on the channel; this is the technique used by Ethernet. Several other contention system variants exist but the common theme is to stop or resolve the moments on the network when more than one node simultaneously accesses the link.

Token passing (Token Ring)

Token passing systems use the notion that a node can only send data when it is in possession of the token. This token is passed from node to node in a cyclic manner thereby enabling all of the nodes to gain access to the channel. Clearly such a system is dependent on the continued existence of the token, so it is essential that the token becomes neither lost nor trapped at a single node. Much of the complexity in token passing systems is concerned with maintaining the token's integrity and ensuring that it is regularly passed around the network. One important advantage of a token passing system is that it is possible to give prioritized access to the channel by providing nodes with the ability to bid for the next free token or by giving certain nodes more regular access to the token than that provided by a simple round robin approach.

Token passing is supported by both bus and ring topologies. Ring topologies require more sophisticated electronics to support the cable signalling (active repetition of the signals) and minimize jitter but they provide a natural cycle for token passing. Implementations of both bus and ring versions are commercially available, with IBM using the ring topology whereas General Motors have adopted the bus for their real-time manufacturing support network.

Slotted rings (Cambridge Ring)

One of the advantages of a ring topology is that it can be arranged for the data to cycle back to the originator. This feature can then be exploited to construct a rotating slot system. In slotted systems the bandwidth is partitioned in time, called slots, which travel around the ring. Nodes make use of empty slots to send data, and when this data has cycled back to them they mark the slot as empty, thereby permitting other users to use the slot. An example of this is the Cambridge Ring (Hopper, 1986).

Register insertion rings

Register insertion rings have a unique feature in that the propagation delay, or walk time, around the ring varies according to the load being supported by the network. This is because each node contains a data register, typically between 40 and 48 bits in size, which is switched into the ring when data is to be transmitted. This means that the data is broken down so that it can be sent one register fragment at a time. The advantage of this system is that it is now possible to efficiently send mixed types of data, such as data and voice. In fact it is the same method that has been adopted by the very high speed cell relay systems in which the bandwidth is broken down into cells that are only 53 bytes long.

Reservation systems

The slotted ring architecture is one form of reservation system. In reservation systems the time on the channel is divided into slots and in most cases the channel is actually a bus based system. Access to the slots is then provided by one of three schemes: static allocation, call allocation and dynamic allocation.

Static allocation systems are used when the traffic patterns are both constant and predictable. The time slots are then uniquely allocated to each node, so a node can only send data in one of its own slots. In call allocation a node requests access to the channel and this request is made to some link controller via a separate call access communications scheme. The controller then allocates some future number of slots to the requesting node. A further extension of this system is dynamic allocation. Here the slots are assigned and released more rapidly than in the call allocation method. The assignment follows the successful completion of some 'channel acquisition' protocol, which in many cases is based upon one form or another of CSMA.

Polling systems

In polling systems a controller is used to arbitrate on access demands to the network. The controller polls around the nodes and ascertains whether or not they require access to the channel. Each node which has data to send is then given access to the channel for some limited period after which the controller then provides access for another waiting node. The controller continually cycles around the nodes, providing them with access to the channel and controlling the order in which access is provided.

The problems with this type of system are that there is a considerable access delay at low loads and it is essential that the controller is always present. Failure of the controller would result in the failure of the entire LAN, so it is normal for dual redundant controllers to be active on the network.

Concurrent access systems

One of the more recent LAN access systems is based upon the spread spectrum multiple access technique. In this system it is possible for many nodes to transmit data across the channel simultaneously without incurring an access delay. A further advantage of this system is that the duration of the data transmission is unlimited, so each node can have unrestricted access to the channel. The disadvantage of these systems is that they are very bandwidth inefficient, typically down in the 1–5% region. These types of system are useful where bandwidth availability is not a problem; they allow each node to make use of the channel as and when it requires (Smythe, 1990).

5.3 LAN performance characterization

The realistic characterization of LAN performance is exceedingly difficult to achieve. Most quoted scientific performance figures are derived from either simple analytical models or computer simulations, and not from experimental or observed statistics. The main reason for this lack of empirical information is that it has not yet been possible for manufacturers to agree on a sound performance metric that is valid for the myriad of different LAN architectures, host implementations and user loading demands. The metrics used in the scientific literature are (Hammond, 1986):

- Data rate, which is the measure of the amount of data transferred point-to-point. This is the rate at which a transmitter sends the data once it has acquired access to the channel.

- Data throughput, which is a measure of the amount of information transferred by the network during the measurement period. The throughput is the aggregated sum of the individual data rates and can be used to determine the efficiency of the multiple access technique being used.

- Transfer delay, which is the measure of the amount of time taken between the system accepting a data transfer request and the data being delivered by the receiver to the recipient. This takes into account all of the accumulated delays due to channel access, propagation delay and the actual transmission time.

- Response time, which is the measure of the delay incurred between submitting a request for data transfer and receiving confirmation that the request has been successfully completed. The response time is dependent on the transfer delay, the types of host protocols supporting the system and the efficiency of the host protocol implementations.

5.3.1   Data throughputs

One of the most common representations for data throughput is its comparison to the offered load, as shown in Figure 5.4 (Hutchison, 1988). The offered load is the amount of information that the nodes attempt to transmit during a particular period, whereas the throughput is that part of the offered load which is successfully transmitted. For

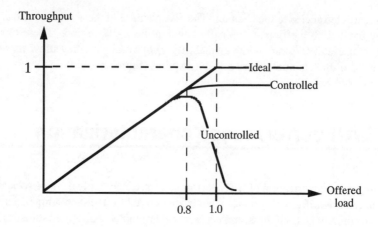

Figure 5.4 Throughput/offered load characterization.

any network it is always possible to attempt to send more information than the carrying capacity of the network – for example by increasing the total number of users – but the throughput is limited to the carrying capacity.

In Figure 5.4 the throughput has been normalized with respect to the carrying capacity of the network – that is, for a 10 Mbps Ethernet a throughput of 0.5 means 5 Mbps. The same normalization has been applied to the offered load. In an ideal network the throughput should increase linearly with the offered load until the offered load provides the maximum throughput – that is, 1. Any further increase in offered load cannot increase the throughput but, more importantly, it should not cause a decrease in throughput. A 'controlled network' closely follows the ideal performance curve and differs only by a few percentage points from the maximum throughput. This loss in throughput is due to the use of bandwidth for supporting the network access technique. In an 'uncontrolled network' the throughput actually decreases once an offered load threshold has been reached. This is because the network requires an ever increasing amount of bandwidth to support a fatally overloaded access system. Token passing systems are good examples of 'controlled' networks and CSMA/CD based ones always form 'uncontrolled' networks! The only system limitation for 'uncontrolled' networks is in designing the point at which the offered load threshold occurs.

5.3.2 Channel efficiency

It is not possible to determine the offered load of a network simply by observing it, so a more appealing measure is that of data throughput against the number of users – this plot is usually called the 'channel efficiency' curve (Stallings, 1993). Figure 5.5 shows the theoretical channel efficiencies for a variety of Token Ring and CSMA/CD LANs. In the case of CSMA/CD the efficiency can be characterized as:

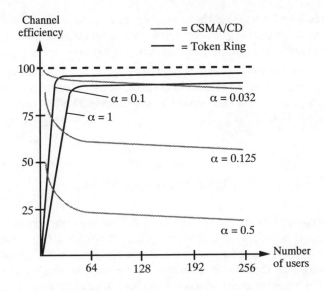

Figure 5.5 Channel efficiency characterization.

- A lowering of efficiency as the coupling coefficient (α) increases. This means keeping the network as small as possible and the frames as long as possible.
- Channel efficiency decreases as the number of users increases.
- Most of the bandwidth loss occurs in the first 64 active users on the network. After that there is very little bandwidth loss for large increases in the number of active users.

In the case of Token Ring the efficiency can be characterized by:

- As the number of active users increases the channel efficiency also increases. This is because less time is spent by the 'free' token cycling around the ring.
- As the coupling coefficient increases then the efficiency decreases. The effect in Token Ring is a lot less dramatic than that for CSMA/CD.
- Once again, the most significant change in efficiency occurs in the first 64 users, so it is important to have at least 64 active users on a Token Ring.

These curves clearly show that there are particular systems to which either CSMA/CD or Token Ring systems are well suited and those to which they are both equally badly suited. For instance:

- CSMA/CD LANs should be used with low numbers of active users, with small networks and large frames. In fact in the worst case CSMA/CD still gives a theoretical maximum efficiency of about 25% and this is well in excess of the typical levels of utilization seen on most real CSMA/CD networks of 5–15%.

- Token Ring LANs should be used when there are large numbers of users who require large amounts of bandwidth. In this environment the efficiency can approach 90–95%. At low loads the Token Ring system offers poor efficiency.

- When the number of users is between 32 and 64 then both systems have something to offer. The Token Ring should be used if there are some important time dependent activities, otherwise the CSMA/CD offers better support for large numbers of low load users.

5.3.3   Delay/throughput characteristics

Probably the most discussed comparison of LAN performance concerns the delay/ throughput characteristic, which is shown in Figure 5.6 (Bux, 1981). This shows the theoretical variation in transfer delay for a packet of information as a function of the network throughput. The delay is given in number of packets times – that is, the delay in seconds divided by the transmission time for a packet and the throughput is divided by the carrying capacity of the network. These normalizations make it possible to compare different network systems.

The problem with this characteristic is that the context for each of the curves is different so a great deal of care has to be taken when trying to establish realistic comparisons; the physical system definition assumes a 10 Mbps data carrier, with fifty nodes across a 2 km cable and with packets averaging 1000 bits (this makes the coupling coefficient equivalent to 0.1). The general trend is that as the network load increases, and therefore as the throughput increases, the delay increases until at some throughput it becomes asymptotic, that is, almost vertical. For each of the different systems the salient features are:

- For CSMA/CD systems the curve becomes asymptotic at about 60% of throughput. At very low loads the delay becomes the packet transmission time plus the propagation delay. The point of throughput saturation can be moved by altering the statistics of the average packet size. For minimum length packets (512 bits) the saturation occurs at about 40% whereas for fixed length frames at maximum size (1518 bytes) it saturates at about 90%. The other point to note is that for CSMA/CD the delay is statistical: for a given throughput there is a most likely delay but the actual delay could be greater or lesser depending on the load history of the network.

- In the case of Token Ring the delay at low throughput is much larger than that for CSMA/CD systems. This is because the token passing mechanism insists on each node releasing the token after the holding period, irrespective of whether or not any other node wishes to send data. At high throughput conditions the token passing system wastes very little bandwidth, making it possible to achieve a throughput capability of almost 100%. One other important feature of the Token Ring is that it is possible to calculate the worst

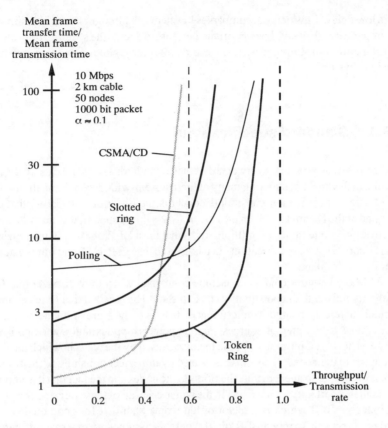

Figure 5.6 Delay/throughput characterization.

case delay for a particular throughput once the data has been queued at a node and this is essential when constructing real-time systems.

- The delay curves for the slotted rings and polling systems show that both of these systems incur a greater delay at low throughput conditions than the Token Ring or CSMA/CD systems. However, their high throughput performance falls between that of the CSMA/CD and Token Ring systems.

It must be remembered that the information shown in Figure 5.6 is derived from a theoretical analysis. However, it does show that there is a performance related consideration for choosing between CSMA/CD and Token Ring LANs. CSMA/CD systems, and the like, very rarely support average loads in excess of 10% and so the delay is always relatively low. Token Ring systems are better suited to very high loads and will supply a deterministic performance, and so they are ideal for heavily loaded applications.

The most important rule to be derived from Figure 5.6 is that when optimizing the performance of a LAN it is not possible to achieve both a high network throughput and a low delay. Low delay accompanies low network throughput and high throughput accompanies high delay. It is important therefore to decide the specification: low delay giving good point-to-point performance or high throughput providing a more cost effective system.

5.3.4 Standard specifications

While not advocating that every detail of these standards should be closely digested it is still worthwhile investigating many of their system-wide recommendations. One of the classical specification constraints concerns the bit error rate (BER) that can be tolerated at the channel level. In the case of LANs this is specified as no more than one bit error every one thousand million bits – that is, a BER of 10^{-9}. In many instances this is a conservative specification but it is used so that STP, UTP and fibre systems can be fully conformant.

Many network engineers become concerned when they discover that fibre is inherently noisier than good quality coax. It should be recalled that fibre channels are immune to electromagnetic interference; that is, they are immune to electrical interference from external sources such as power supplies and switching systems. They are, however, more susceptible to noise caused by the ways in which the channel is coupled to the nodes. This noise is caused by imperfect polishing of the fibre ends, the use of a bonding agent to glue the fibres to the nodes and the fact that it is impossible to establish a perfectly plane bond. In the worse case, all of these noise sources collude to produce a BER which is a factor of ten worse than that for good quality coaxial cabling; coax can supply a BER of 10^{-11} but this assumes no external interference.

The other important parameter specified in the standards is the mean time between failure (MTBF). This is specified as no more than one failure every 100,000 hours of operation. It is almost certainly true to say that no network exists which supports this reliability. Closer inspection of the standard shows that this reliability applies to all of the cabling, the internetworking relays and the network interface cards. So what has gone wrong? In most instances the failure of the LANs is due to one of two reasons: poor installation of the cabling system or switching off a powered device – both of which are human errors. It is very rare for a network failure to occur due to a failed network component.

5.4 IEEE 802 committees and LANs

The detailed specification and development of the standards for LANs has been given to the IEEE. Once they have completed and agreed their draft standard it is then adopted by the ISO committees and goes through the normal full ratification procedure.

The ISO 8802 committees are responsible for LAN standardization, hence the naming of the corresponding IEEE committee by dropping the first '8'. This standardization effort is concerned with the LAN reference model (LAN/RM) whose range of responsibility is for the bottom two layers of the OSI/RM, for LAN based networks (Stallings, 1990). The current scope of activities of the IEEE 802 is shown in Figure 5.7; once again, it is important to remember that the number of activities grow, as and when new areas are deemed necessary.

A key feature of the LAN reference model shown in Figure 5.7 is that the interface between the LLC and the media access control (MAC) sublayers is standard. This means that converting a LAN from one multiple access technique to another, for example Ethernet to Token Ring, requires the replacement of the interface card and a change of software driver. None of the higher layers of software have to be altered. Converting a PC from one network to another takes just a few minutes; this is a true reflection of the need and power of agreed and used standardization.

5.4.1   802.1 Internetworking

The IEEE 802.1 effort is directed towards establishing the overall LAN architecture, which includes management and internetworking. The current areas of interest are:

- IEEE 802.1 – Overview, architecture and addressing.
- IEEE 802.1B – LAN management.
- IEEE 802.1D – Local bridging.
- IEEE 802.1E – System load protocol.
- IEEE 802.1F – Guidelines for layer management standards.
- IEEE 802.1G – Remote MAC bridges.
- IEEE 802.1I – MAC bridges (FDDI supplement).

The two most active areas of the 802.1 effort are management and remote bridging. The network management aspects are related to the development of the heterogeneous LAN management (HLM) architecture whereas the remote bridging work is concerned with the connection of LANs via wide area point-to-point links.

5.4.2   802.2 Logical link control

The logical link control (LLC) is the interface between the network layer and the specific LAN environments, such as Token Ring. There are three types of LLC:

- Type 1 – the unacknowledged connectionless link service.

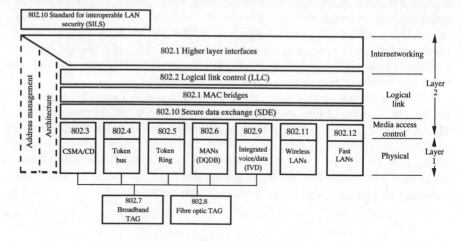

Figure 5.7 The IEEE 802 committees.

- Type 2 – the connection oriented link service, whose interface is very similar to that of LAPB and so is used to support X.25 based profiles.
- Type 3 – the acknowledged connectionless link service which provides data acknowledgement without requiring connection establishment/disengagement. This service is used in real-time applications such as manufacturing control.

5.4.3 802.3 CSMA/CD LANs

Carrier sense multiple access with collision detection (CSMA/CD) LANs are based upon the original Xerox Ethernet system – the two are similar but not identical. This system will be discussed in considerably more detail in Chapter 6. This committee is now addressing the development of the 100BASEX fast Ethernet.

5.4.4 802.4 Token bus LANs

Unlike the CSMA/CD systems, in which several users can be attempting to use the channel at the same time, the token bus imposes a rigid token passing mechanism along a passive bus topology. Only the station that holds the token can transmit data. After a maximum period the token must be released, thereby permitting other users access to the network. The token is passed logically around the network in a cyclic manner but each data frame is actually broadcast onto the passive bus. This is the classic example of physical topologies being used to support an inherently different logical topology.

5.4.5   802.5 Token Ring LANs

This LAN access technique is derived from the original IBM Token Ring system. Unlike the other access techniques, it also defines a bridging standard and so there are connectivity problems between bridges which conform to the 802.1 and 802.5 standards. Token Ring systems are discussed in Chapter 7.

5.4.6   802.6 Metropolitan area networks

The 802.6 work has been responsible for the development of the DQDB architecture, which was introduced in Chapter 2. This specification is carrier rate independent and as such it is expected to be used as the transport protocols for SONET systems in the MAN environment. The latest area of interest for this committee is that of cable television interconnection to support data transfer.

5.4.7   802.7 Broadband LANs technical advisory group

Some technologies are not specific to a particular LAN access technique and so it is important that the application of these to different systems is as consistent as possible. This consistency is the responsibility of the technical advisory groups (TAGs). The broadband TAG looks at the application of broadband signalling to the 802 medium access controls (MACs) such as 802.3, 802.4 and 802.5. The ISO 8802.7 committee is in fact concerned with the standardization of 'slotted rings' and so there is a discrepancy between the IEEE and ISO efforts in this area.

5.4.8   802.8 Fibre optic LANs technical advisory group

This committee is the fibre optic equivalent of the broadband TAG. One of its areas of interest is to maintain some form of physical compatibility with the FDDI and the SONET architectures and is leading to standardization on the single mode fibre work as well as the multimode fibre architectures.

5.4.9   802.9 Integrated voice/data LANs

Truly integrated multimedia systems require, as a minimum, the ability to transfer both voice and data across a common channel. Voice requires a slow but highly regular access to the channel for long duration (typically minutes) whereas data needs a high speed link, several megabits per second, for very short periods, typically milliseconds.

This committee has recently released an Isochronous Ethernet specification, IEEE 802.9a. This specification provides a 6.144 Mbps voice service (96 channels at 64 kbps) multiplexed with the 10 Mbps data service onto a single cabling infrastructure. This system is intended for multimedia based applications such as telemedicine.

5.4.10   802.10 Secure LANs

The original OSI/RM did not include security and it is only since 1990 that this has been considered in the LAN/RM. The current proposals include two approaches:

- The introduction of the secure data exchange (SDE) sublayer which sits between the LLC and the appropriate MAC. The SDE will provide a wide range of functions depending on the market demands: there will be a different SDE for military systems, as compared to medical systems for example.
- The introduction of the secure interoperable LAN system (SILS) architecture, which will define the system considerations for secure LAN communications.

5.4.11   802.11 Wireless LANs technical advisory group

One of the most recently instituted 802 committees is that responsible for the work on wireless LANs. The techniques of interest to this group include the use of spread spectrum signalling, indoor radio communications and infrared links. These systems will have limited application but in some environments, such as exhibition halls, and listed buildings, they will become essential for supporting the required connectivity.

5.4.12   802.12 Fast LANs

The latest committee is investigating the architecture for fast LAN systems. The aim is to produce a 100 Mbps data transport system capable of interconnecting to both Ethernet and Token Ring architectures. Hewlett Packard are responsible for guiding this specification which is based upon the 100VG AnyLAN architecture. 100VG

AnyLAN uses a demand priority MAC which can transport both Token Ring and Ethernet frames, as well as native data sources, at 100 Mbps across UTP cabling (categories 3, 4 and 5) – hence the VG qualifier. Originally Hewlett Packard proposed the similar 100BASEVG MAC as an alternative specification for the 100 Mbps Ethernet, 100BASEX, but since it did not use CSMA/CD it was incompatible with the rest of the IEEE 802.3 specification – this resulted in it being colloquially referred to as Ethernot. 100BASEVG has now been withdrawn leaving Hewlett Packard to concentrate upon the 100VG AnyLAN for the IEEE 802.12.

5.5 Local area internetworking

Once the characteristics of LANs have been established it becomes relatively easy to anticipate the types of devices that would be required to interconnect them. The reasons for internetworking devices are to:

- Link together LANs that use the same multiple access scheme but which use different types of cabling (Section 5.2.2).

- Overcome the effects of losses due to the attenuation of the cable. Signal regeneration and retiming is used at the junction point of two or more cables.

- Interconnect LANs with other categories of networks, either as an intermediate carrier or as the end-user's host network, including MANs and WANs.

- Link together LANs based upon different topologies and whether they are of a passive or active nature (Section 5.2.3).

- Link together LANs that use different multiple access schemes, for example token passing to contention buses (Section 5.2.4).

- Improve the performance of an individual LAN by reducing the number of nodes on any one LAN and so lowering the end-to-end delay (Section 5.3.3).

These criteria are based upon the characteristics of the LANs themselves and as such do not consider the problems encountered by higher levels of protocols and the types of applications supported by the network. These create further need for internetworking systems. Clearly, internetworking devices are a natural facet of LAN architectures.

5.6 Summary

LANs are an essential component in a modern communications system. They support a wide range of user services in a fast and highly reliable manner. In summary:

- The formal definition of a LAN is extremely vague and even the term 'local' is unjustified in many instances. The critical element is that each and every user of a LAN should feel that it is their network only.

- The two dominant LANs in the market place are the carrier sense multiple access with collision detection (CSMA/CD) and Token Ring systems. CSMA/CD is very similar to Ethernet, but, although they are similar, communication between them is only possible using an internetworking device.

- There is a wide range of available LAN architectures. These architectures can differ according to their multiple access scheme, physical topology, type of channel and bandwidth signalling scheme. It is, however, the selection of the multiple access scheme that has most effect on a network's performance.

- The performance capability of a LAN is characterized by its data throughput capability (several million bits per second), channel efficiency (as close to 100% as possible) and delay/throughput.

- LAN optimization is normally a trade-off between delay and network through-put. A low delay normally accompanies a low network throughput and a high network throughput with a high delay. It is not possible to have a low delay (good performance) with high network throughput (cost effective utilization).

- The IEEE 802 committees are responsible for the standardization of all LANs and related issues. This includes LAN management, repeaters, bridges and addressing systems.

- The standards state that there should be no more than one network failure every 100,000 hours. This specification covers the cabling system, the repeaters, the bridges and the network interface cards.

- Internetworking devices are an essential feature of LAN architectures because they provide a mechanism for overcoming the limitations produced by the physical world and cost effective engineering.

6

Ethernet LANs

6.1 Introduction

Ethernet was developed by the Xerox Corporation at its Palo Alto laboratories during the 1970s (Metcalfe, 1976). In 1980, Xerox along with Digital and Intel jointly published a LAN specification based on the Ethernet concepts, which became known as the Ethernet Blue Book 1 specification (ESPEC1; DIX). This was later superseded by a second version, the Ethernet Blue Book 2 specification or ESPEC2. In 1982 it was this version of the specification that was offered to the IEEE for standardization. In the middle of 1983, the IEEE 802.3 committee approved a basic specification for CSMA/CD based LANs, which was published by ISO in 1984 as ISO/DIS 8802/3. This full standard has been ratified but a series of amendments and systems innovations have been, and are being, made, thus demonstrating its evolutionary nature.

The result of this evolution is the existence of three different standards, ESPEC1, ESPEC2 and IEEE 802.3, the first two being known as Ethernet. Very little ESPEC1 equipment is currently in use and this standard can therefore be ignored. However, ESPEC2 equipment may still be in use, and potential incompatibility with IEEE exists. In many instances the name Ethernet is used generically for all CSMA/CD LANs. This is incorrect because they are two different systems. However, as a reflection of this common usage, the term 'ethernet' will be used to refer to IEEE 802.3 and 'Ethernet' for the DIX specification.

6.2 The multiple access mechanism

The relationship between LANs and the OSI/RM has already been discussed in general terms and now it is appropriate to look at more specific details. Figure 6.1 shows the relationship between the ethernet LANs and the OSI/RM. The ISO 8802/3 specification is concerned with all of the functionality below and including the MAC – that is, the network interface cards, the cabling and the repeaters (Hunter, 1993).

The actual physical connectivity to the cabling system is supported by the medium attachment units (MAUs) and the attachment unit interface (AUI) cable. These are controlled by the physical signalling interface, which is a part of a network interface card (NIC) or network interface adapter (NIA) – that is, the hardware board which is inserted into the host computer's backplane. The two basic structures for an ethernet based LAN are shown in Figure 6.2. The nodes are connected using either a passive bus arrangement (the left hand structure in Figure 6.2) or as an active star arrangement (the right hand structure in Figure 6.2). The passive bus architecture is based upon coax cabling whereas the star topology uses fibre optic and UTP cabling. In both cases more complex architectures can be constructed by adding more similar structures or by interconnecting the different structures. In all cases the nodes use the CSMA/CD technique to transmit the information across the network.

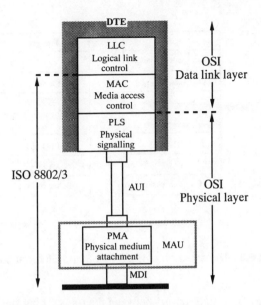

Figure 6.1   ISO 8802/3 and the OSI/RM relationship.

6.2.1   CSMA/CD operation

Each node constantly monitors the network and so is aware of the presence of traffic – in other words, each node is continually sensing the medium. If a node wishes to transmit data it will defer until no traffic is detected, denoted by the channel being sensed as 'idle'. Provided there is no traffic on the network, any node can transmit at any time. However, occasionally two, or more, nodes will start to transmit at the same time – the finite length of the network causing each node to perceive the network as

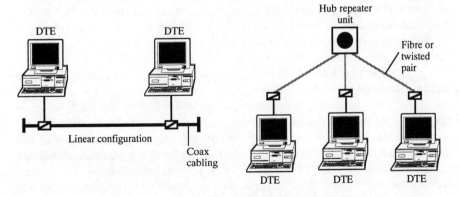

Figure 6.2   The basic structures for an ethernet LAN.

Octets

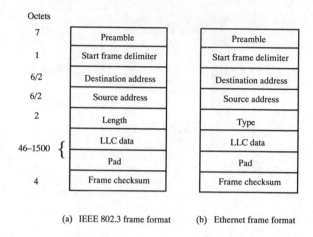

(a) IEEE 802.3 frame format   (b) Ethernet frame format

Figure 6.3 The structure of IEEE 802.3 and Ethernet packets.

'idle'. In this case a 'collision' occurs between the transmitting stations.

In ethernet a 20 MHz Manchester II encoded signal is used to provide a 10 Mbps data carrying capacity. The Manchester encoding provides the receiver with the clocking information as well as the data. Recall that the nodes operate asynchronously and therefore a receiver has to be able to acquire clock, and so bit, synchronization once the presence of a signal has been detected on the channel. The logical information – the collection of the bits – is grouped into data frames or, more formally termed, MAC PDUs; in many cases these frames are referred to as ethernet packets.

The MAC PDU structures as defined by the IEEE 802.3 and Blue Book 2 are shown in Figure 6.3; the only difference in the PDU structures is the use of a length field in IEEE 802.3 but which is a type field in ethernet. The frame is a minimum of 64 octets long and a maximum of 1518 octets (both of these figures ignore the length of the preamble and start delimiter). The first seven octets are a preamble. This is the sequence 10101010 repeated seven times and provides the digital circuitry with sufficient time to acquire clock and bit synchronization. The next octet is the start frame delimiter, which is the bit stream 10101011. This provides the system with octet alignment; the occurrence of the 11 sequence informs the receiver that the next bit is the first bit of the first octet of the frame.

The first data field is the destination address and this is followed by the source address. Both of these fields are either two or six octets long (most systems use six octet addressing) and their structure and content are controlled by the IEEE, which is responsible for ensuring that all NIAs are uniquely addressed. For IEEE 802.3 the next field is the length indicator, which is two octets long and is a number between 1 and 1500. If the data content is less than 46 octets then the frame has to be padded with data (normally all zeros) – this is essential if there is to be a clearly maintained minimum frame size and without this limitation it is impossible to construct a correctly functioning CSMA/CD system. For ethernet this field is a type indicator which is used to denote the immediate higher layer protocol. The values for the type indicator have

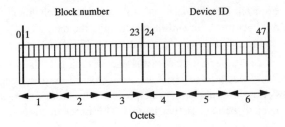

Figure 6.4 The address structure for an ethernet frame.

been arranged to start at a value greater than 1500. This means that IEEE 802.3 NIAs will reject ethernet packets as having an invalid length field (too long) and ethernet NIAs will reject IEEE 802.3 frames due to the unknown protocol types.

The final field is the frame check sequence (FCS) or checksum. This is four octets long and is used to determine whether or not the frame has been corrupted by the channel during transmission. The CRC algorithm for generating the FCS is defined in the IEEE 802.3 standard.

The address field structure in the MAC frames is shown in Figure 6.4. Each address is six octets long and is split into two three-octet blocks. The first three octets describe the block number to which the NIA belongs. The block number is the manufacturer's licence number: all NIAs manufactured by a company have this same number; for example, 02608C (hex) refers to NIAs produced by 3COM. The second three octets refer to the device identifier and each manufacturer is mandated by their production licence to allocate a unique device number to every ethernet card they produce. The combination of the block number and the device identifier create a unique IEEE 802.3 address scheme which can distinguish between 2^{48} users and so every ethernet NIA has its own unique address. There are three types of addressing mode:

- Broadcast – the destination address is set as FFFFFFFFFFFF hex. All nodes are expected to receive the information.

- Multicast – the first bit of the destination addresses is set to 1. This is used to provide group restricted communications, for example bridge to bridge.

- Point-to-point – here the first bit of the destination address is set to 0 and the rest of the address is set according to the target NIA.

The second bit of the address refers to the addressing administration adopted by the network – this is either local (1) or global (0).

Now that the physical and logical forms of the data have been established it is time to consider how data is transferred across a CSMA/CD LAN. When a node wishes to send data the following algorithm is used:

- The transmitter senses the channel (the sensing is in fact provided by the MAU, which is actually sending a channel status signal back to the NIA) to determine the presence of any other signals. If the channel is 'idle' – that is, no other user signals are present – then the data is transmitted. If the channel is busy, the NIA waits until it becomes idle and then transmits the data. This gives rise to the formal definition of this sensing technique as '1-Persistent CSMA'.

- While the node is transmitting data it is also 'listening' to its own transmissions. This 'listening' mechanism varies according to the type of cabling system being used. However, the underlying principle is to determine if more than one signal is simultaneously present on the channel. This procedure is collision detection.

- A contention will occur because several nodes may detect the channel becoming idle at the same time. Each node will then send its own data and eventually the transmitting nodes will detect the other signals. Each node detecting the contention sends a jam signal (to force all the other nodes to detect the contention) and then performs a back-off algorithm (formally called the truncated binary exponential back-off algorithm), which determines when the data retransmission attempt will occur.

- When the back-off time has expired the algorithm then returns to the first step in the transmission algorithm – that is, sensing the channel for other users.

Figure 6.5 shows how a contention is most likely to arise. In Figure 6.5a the central node C has successfully acquired the channel and is transmitting its data. Now assume that while node C is transmitting its data, nodes A and B attempt to send their data. Both A and B will detect that the channel is in use – their MAUs will 'sense' the presence of a signal and will defer transmission until the channel is 'idle'.

Once node C stops transmitting its information the channel will slowly return to the 'idle' state. Nodes A and B will independently detect this condition, and once they have waited for a mandatory 96 bits (to ensure an inter-frame gap period during which time the receivers can free-run and so prevent the possibility of two separate frames being treated as one single frame), they will both send their data. The situation is now that shown in Figure 6.5b. These two separate signals will cross at some point along the channel, causing a signal collision. At some brief moment later (about 1 ms if the channel is a 500 m thick coax cable) this collision will be detected by the nodes, which will then issue their jam signal and will fall into the retransmission algorithm.

From the receiver's point of view the situation is very different. Each node on the LAN is continually receiving data and deciding whether or not the information is intended for the local host. The actual algorithm is:

- The MAU senses the channel attempting to detect a frame preamble. The preamble is the 56 bit sequence 10101010 and so on. This bit stream allows the clock synchronization circuitry time to stabilize, thereby providing transmitter/ receiver bit synchronization. Octet synchronization is achieved by detecting the sequence 10101011 in positions 57–64 of the bit stream.

- Once bit and octet synchronization have been obtained the system strips away the full 64 bit preamble. The full frame is now stored internally until the MAU fails to detect a signal or a contention occurs.

- Once the complete frame has been received its internal structure is examined.

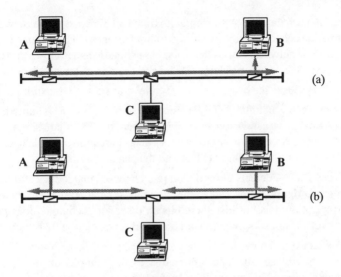

Figure 6.5 The most common cause of contention.

If the frame is too long or contains an incomplete octet then it is rejected. If the destination address is not for the node, its group or a broadcast then the frame is again rejected. Finally the local checksum is generated and compared with that received in the frame. If these are different then once again the frame is rejected, otherwise it is now accepted as a valid frame for this user.

- Any padding is removed and the data is passed up to the higher protocol.

The CSMA/CD standard does not support error correction. It provides error detection only. The error detection mechanism makes use of a checksum which has been generated by a CRC generator – that is, a shift register with feedback taps at various points across the register. The transmitter generates the checksum, which becomes part of the frame. Once the data has been received a second checksum is generated from it. The two checksums are now compared and if they are different then the data stream has been corrupted so the frame is rejected.

The source transmitter is not informed of the frame rejection; this means that the transmitter can not assume that the receiver has correctly received the data – in other words, the IEEE 802.3 standard is an unacknowledged connectionless service. The recovery of the lost information must be controlled by some higher level protocol such as the network layer and so a COS must be used somewhere in the higher layers.

6.2.2   Round trip delays

The reason for the minimum frame size (512 bits) is intrinsically related to the correct operation of the CSMA/CD scheme. Consider the situation shown in Figure 6.6:

- In Figure 6.6a DTE A transmits its frame. This crosses the network and no collision occurs until the frame is just about to reach DTE B, which is at the other end of the network – this is the worse case scenario and it shows the relationship between the round trip delay (RTD) and the size of the network.

- DTE B senses the channel, finds it 'idle' and starts to transmit its data.

- Within a few bit times, DTE B detects the frame collision. It immediately stops its own data transmission and sends, instead, the 32 bit jam signal. As shown in Figure 6.6b, this jam signal causes a data contention to ripple back across the network until it reaches DTE A and the channel terminator.

- When DTE A detects the collision (which means that it must still be transmitting its original frame and so the frame must be at least twice the end-to-end propagation delay or else the collision detection technique does not operate correctly), stops its own transmission and sends out the 32 bit jam signal.

- The jam signal now ripples back across the network as shown in Figure 6.6c. DTE B will be idle once more due to the completion of its jam signal transmission. This means that the system's vulnerable period is in fact three times the end-to-end propagation delay.

The prerequisite for a correctly operating CSMA/CD network is for the total propagation delay, there and back, across the network to be less than 576 bits; this is because there are 512 bits of data and 64 bits of preamble. If the network delay is greater than this then it is possible that for minimum length frames the nodes at either end of the network will not detect contentions caused by one another. If the contention is not detected the data will not be retransmitted by the NIAs and so some higher layer protocol will have to recover the lost data.

It is important to note that the receivers on an ethernet LAN do not detect contention; this is the transmitter's responsibility only. From the receiver's point of

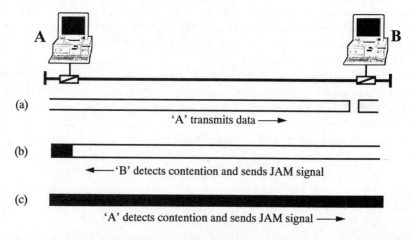

Figure 6.6 Contention and the jam signal.

view a contention will result in a frame that is either too short, non octet aligned or that has an invalid CRC. In each of these cases the frame is rejected by the NIA.

6.3 Ethernet components

One of the advantages of a stable and agreed standard is that over a period of time a substantial range of products becomes available – this is particularly important when considering the range of support devices such as terminal servers. In many cases a particular product can be purchased from several competing manufacturers, so it is possible to obtain a device that almost perfectly matches the requirement and at a reasonable price.

6.3.1   Network components

A typical ethernet LAN architecture, as shown in Figure 6.7, consists of the following physical components (Hegering, 1993):

- A transmission medium cable which acts as the communications channel. In general, Ethernet signals are carried by copper coaxial cable, twisted pair or fibre optic cable.
- Terminators, one at each end of the cable. Due to the signalling mechanism used on copper cables, ethernet cables must be terminated by 50 ohm terminators at both ends. If this is not done, signals reaching the end of the cable are not 'absorbed', but 'reflected' back along the cable. This would cause self-contention, making communications impossible.
- MAUs, also referred to as transceivers. This is the element of the network that supports the actual carrier sensing and the 'jabber protection' and 'signal quality error' (SQE) test functions. Jabber protection disables the transceiver should the NIA attempt to transmit more than 64, 000 consecutive bits (some 6.4 ms) whereas the SQE, or heart-beat, is used to confirm that the transceiver collision detection mechanism is operating correctly.
- Transceiver taps. In order to transmit and receive signals on the transmission media, a transceiver must be attached, or tapped, onto the cable. In the case of copper cables, these taps are made at points along the cable. The number of taps that can be made on a copper cable and their positions on the cable are specified by the standard. In the case of fibre optic and twisted pair cable, the transceivers are connected at the ends of the cable – that is, by point-to-point links only.
- AUI cables to link the NIAs and the transceivers. One advantage in separating

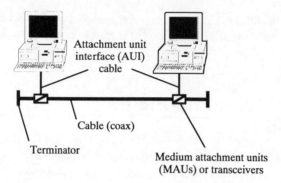

Figure 6.7 The 10BASE5 system architecture.

the DTE from the transceiver, is that it allows the same physical interface – the AUI cable – to provide connection to different network media, such as fibre or twisted pair, without changing the NIC itself.

- Ethernet NIAs. Some of the NIAs have internal transceivers, so it is unnecessary to use an external transceiver and AUI cable. The latest NIAs are available in the form of personal computer memory card interface adapters (PCMCIAs).

In the case of thick coax based ethernet systems (ones which use the thick yellow or orange coax cable), it is important that one of the cables is correctly earthed. Only one cable per physical system should be earthed or else earth loops can be created if the earths have not been bonded together. It should be noted that in some installations there is upwards of a 20 V ground potential, which means that multiple but non-bonded earths would cause a 20 V signal to pass along the cable shielding.

6.3.2   Support components

The range of support products is critical in promoting the rapid adoption of any system. Ethernet LANs are well served in this area, which has undoubtedly helped to maintain its installation lead over Token Ring. The support components available include:

- Fan-out boxes – where there is a high density of DTEs, it may not be possible to provide a separate tap for each device. In this case a fan-out unit can be used. This device sits between several DTEs and a single transceiver and enables the DTEs to use the network via the same transceiver. Note that the DTEs have the same access to the channel as if they were connected separately.

- Terminal servers – which are a convenient way of connecting dumb devices to ethernet. Terminal servers provide an ethernet NIA which supports a number of synchronous and asynchronous serial lines, to which dumb devices are connected. These devices can then use ethernet on a cost effective basis because the cost of the NIA is shared among several host systems.

- Repeaters – many networks need to connect two sets of DTEs together which cannot, because of their physical locations, all tap onto the same segment, even with the use of fan out units. If this is the case, a repeater can be used to link two separate segments. The repeater appears as a signal regenerator on both segments, but it 'repeats' signals transmitted on one segment to the other. This allows devices on one segment to communicate with devices on the other.

- Hubs – repeaters which are used to wire together UTP or fibre optic systems. Each of the spokes of the hub supports a single NIA so it is possible to provide management and extra functionality associated with a particular spoke, for example individual NIA partitioning or transmission security but broadcast prevention. The most recent advances are stackable hubs so that expanding numbers of users can be easily supported.

- Concentrators – unintelligent hubs which are used as wiring concentrators for either UTP or fibre optic cabling systems. Concentrators are low cost devices and, unlike hubs, they do not need a power supply.

- Bridges – transparent bridges are used to improve the performance and reliability of ethernet LANs. Reliability is improved by providing multiple links between the LAN segments whereas performance is improved by distributing the users on either side of the bridge.

- Switches – these fast bridges (reduced latency across the bridge itself) can provide fast switching, simultaneously between many pairs of segments. Performance is further improved by providing a full duplex facility.

The current trend is towards the adoption of hub architectures in which all of the interface devices, except the user workstations and their NIAs, are centrally located. The wiring system is then designed to flood out from these hubs to the user workstations. This is one reason why 'structured cabling' is growing in popularity.

6.4 Ethernet architectures

The standards organizations have developed a nomenclature for the concise description of different ethernet configurations. The convention is *X Type Y* where:

(a) *X* refers to the carrying capacity of the network in Mbps
(b) *Type* refers to the type of transmission system: baseband or broadband
(c) *Y* refers to the maximum segment length in hundreds of metres.

This means that the 10BASE5 specification refers to an ethernet system which transfers data at 10 Mbps using a baseband signalling technique across a cable segment whose length must be less than or equal to 500 m. The systems which have been, or are undergoing specification at the current time are:

- 10BASE5 – also known as 'thick ether', and based on coaxial cabling
- 10BASE2 – also known as 'thin ether' or 'Cheapernet' and based on coax
- 10BASET – the star topology ethernet based upon UTP cabling
- 10BASEF – the fibre optic equivalent of 10BASET
- 10BROAD36 – the broadband equivalent of the 10BASE*Y* systems
- 1BASE5 – known as 'Starlan', which is a low speed UTP ethernet version
- 100BASEX – the proposed 100 Mbps ethernet, or 'fast ethernet', architecture. 100BASET is the UTP cabling version
- Isochronous ethernet – the integrated voice/data ethernet which supplies a 10 Mbps data link with a 6.144 Mbps voice service (96 channels, each at 64 kbps)
- Full duplex ethernet – in which different data streams are simultaneously received and transmitted between the hub and NIA.

6.4.1   10BASE5 architectures

Figure 6.7 shows all of the components for the thick ether architectures. The limitations on the connectivity for this type of system are:

- Each segment must be less than 500 m in length. This ensures that the signal power does not become too attenuated for accurate data reception.
- There must be no more than 100 transceiver taps on each segment. Each segment could support up to 200 transceiver taps; however, this would lead to an erosion of the interframe gap which in turn causes false synchronization.
- The distance between each transceiver must be at least 2.5 m and must be multiples of 2.5 m. This separation distance equates to null wavepoint positions, which means that the signal reflections from the taps cancel each other out at these places, thereby minimizing self noise.
- There must be a single earth, the cable must have a 50 ohm impedance and must have a minimum bend radius of 25.4 cm. Too tight a cable bend will cause severe signal reflections, causing self contention, and in the worse case a breaking of the internal conductor.

The coax cable normally used in thick ether systems is either a yellow plastic or orange Teflon. The latter is preferable because in the case of fire it will not emit poisonous fumes. In both cases the cable is marked at 2.5 m intervals, thereby simplifying the task of accurately locating the transceiver tap positions.

6.4.2   10BASE2 architectures

The thin ether architectures are based upon a lower grade of coaxial cable, to which workstations are normally directly linked via a BNC T-piece. The daisy chain architecture, which is typical of thin ether, is shown in Figure 6.8. The connectivity limitations for these types of system are:

- The cable segment must be less than or equal to 185 m (note, not 200 m!)
- There must be no more than 30 transceivers connected to each segment
- Each transceiver must be separated by at least 0.5 m, but there is no further restriction upon the distribution of the transceivers
- The cable must be of a 50 ohm impedance, it does not need to be explicitly earthed and its minimum bend radius is 5 cm.

Connection to a thin ether system is via BNC connectors, which means that for a daisy chained architecture the NIAs can support an internal or external transceiver. Once again, the cabling system must be terminated with 50 ohm terminators.

6.4.3   10BASET architectures

The 10BASET system format is predominantly used in structured cabling environments. Here each user is supported by a single spoke which feeds back to a local hub, or multiport repeater set. These repeaters are then linked together, thereby forming one large hub-like network. Figure 6.9 shows a typical twisted pair architecture.

Each hub must be capable of supporting a segment of 100 m, giving a total separation along the spokes of at least 200 m. It is this approach which forms the basis of 'flood wiring', in which a building is wired with excessive numbers of connection points. The connection points are a part of the star topology with the hub wiring centres linking these together as appropriate. An added advantage of this approach is that an intelligent hub can then be given the functionality to decide which spurs should, or should not, receive the information, thereby improving the security of the network.

6.4.4   10BASEF architectures

The 10BASEF standard is again based upon a hub structure. Unfortunately the development effort on the FDDI (the 100 Mbps data carrier system) and the need for using a fibre optic inter-repeater link (FOIRL) has caused a serious delay in this standard and it is only recently that the full standard has been ratified. This standard has three proposed architectures:

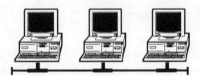

Figure 6.8 A typical 10BASE2 architecture.

- 10BASEFL – defines the structure and operation of a fibre link segment and is a 2 km upgrade to the current FOIRL standard. This will be more fully discussed in Chapter 10.

- 10BASEFP – defines a star topology network based upon the use of a passive fibre optic star coupler. Up to 33 ports are accommodated per star and each segment can be a maximum of 500 m.

- 10BASEFB – defines a link segment in which data is transmitted synchronously thereby reducing the time to transfer a frame across the repeater hub. The maximum link length is 2 km.

An example of a 10BASEF architecture is shown in Figure 6.10. In this architecture, two synchronous hubs are used to interconnect a passive hub with the rest of the network. The passive hub can support up to 33 users using link segments of less than 500 m but it is available to fibre cables only – its passive nature means that there is no power source to support an AUI interface or transceiver. The passive hubs are suited to electronically noisy environments and secure applications. In these systems the optical fibre is limited to a maximum length of 2000 m. The fibre cores are commonly pulled at 62.5 μm with an outer clad diameter of 125 μm but you are advised to install, if possible, the SMF links which are only 8 μm. The 8 μm fibre is more expensive but will enable you to upgrade the system to the full FDDI II or cell relay architectures without installing new cabling.

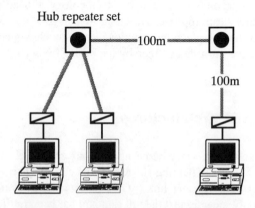

Figure 6.9 A typical 10BASET architecture.

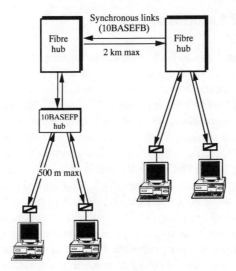

Figure 6.10   A typical 10BASEF architecture.

6.4.5   10BROAD36 architectures

This is the only ethernet broadband architecture currently available. Its structure is shown in Figure 6.11, in which the data is transmitted along either a single or dual 75 ohm coax configuration. The 'head-end' is responsible for the frequency translation between the transmit and receive frequency bandwidths. Each transceiver transmits on one frequency but receives on a separate one and each of the receive and transmit data streams requires a 14 MHz bandwidth plus a 4 MHz collision enforcement channel. This means that the total bandwidth requirement for a broadband system is 36 MHz; either 18 MHz on two cables or 36 MHz on a single cable.

    Some manufacturers recommend that no more than six transceivers be connected to a broadband system and that the linking together of two or more broadband systems requires the use of a special repeater, called a 'buffered repeater'. The cable is limited to 1800 m because each signal must traverse the channel twice and so the worse case distance is 3600 m, hence the 10BROAD36 specification.

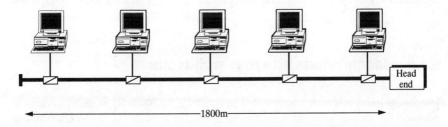

Figure 6.11   A typical 10BROAD36 architecture.

6.4.6   1BASE5 architectures

The 1BASE5 system is fundamentally different from the others due to the fact that it supports only a 1 Mbps data rate, and not the more usual 10 Mbps. This means that it cannot be used in conjunction with the other systems without making use of a bridge.

Again, it is a hub system, as shown in Figure 6.12, but with two types of hub; the header and the intermediate. The intermediate hubs pass either any single signal or the collision present signal upwards. The header hub is responsible for taking all the received signals and for transmitting them back down the tree structure. Each segment is limited to a 250 m length and with a maximum of five levels of hubs this produces a total network span of 2500 m – there-and-back. The 'special link' is a higher quality twisted pair cable which is up to four times as long as the other cables. The number and location of these special links is dependent on the delay budget across the network.

The cabling is again based upon UTP. However, the lower signalling rate means that greater cable distances can be supported. This structure is ideally suited to flood wiring in that each floor has its own intermediate hub (thereby permitting simple expansion) with the header conveniently based in the network management centre. Originally, due to its use of UTP, this technique was the low cost ethernet version. However, the adoption of the 10BASET architecture means that there are very few new installations now based on this scheme.

6.4.7   Fast ethernet architectures

The two most prominent proposals were the 3COM solution of 100BASEX and the Hewlett Packard proposal of 100BASEVG. The 100BASEX approach, termed 100BASET for UTP category 3, 4 and 5 implementations, supported by the IEEE 802.3 committee, extends the capability of the CSMA/CD approach and is applicable to all of the cabling systems. The 100BASEVG solution was intended for use on voice grade UTP wiring and, while it could have been considered as a natural upgrade to 10BASET, it used a different MAC mechanism called demand priority frame switching. The Hewlett Packard suggestion has since moved to the IEEE 802.12 committee and as such is termed 100VG AnyLAN and will eventually support 100 Mbps communications across UTP and will eventually transport ethernet, Token Ring and CDDI frames.

6.4.8   Isochronous ethernet architectures

The isochronous ethernet, trademarked as isoENET by National Semiconductors, is intended for applications which need an integrated voice/data/video communications infrastructure. This system provides the original 10 Mbps data service with an

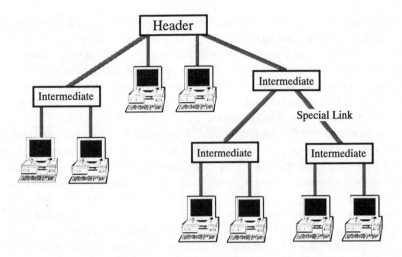

Figure 6.12 A typical 1BASE5 architecture.

isochronous service of 6.144 Mbps, across a UTP cabling infrastructure; the full duplex of the latter actually supplying an isochronous transfer capacity of over 12 Mbps. The 96– 64 kbps isochronous channels can be assigned in any number of ways with a typical configuration being one channel for voice and six for video (384 kbps) with the actual application data being supported by the traditional ethernet MAC. The architecture for this system is identical to that shown in Figure 6.9 with the proviso that the hub supplies the isochronous switch capability and the NIAs have the IEEE 802.9a MAC NIAs. It is possible to interconnect isochronous and non-isochronous hubs for the traditional ethernet 10 Mbps data service.

6.4.9   Full duplex ethernet architectures

Full duplex ethernet is based upon modified NIA and specialized hub adapters across UTP cabling infrastructures. The actual architecture is identical to that shown in Figure 6.9 – the only differences are in how the information is transferred along the UTP cabling. Full duplex communication provides simultaneous data stream transmission and reception between the hub and the user, thereby increasing the available throughput to 20 Mbps between the two of them. Not all of the ports in the hub have to be full duplex and so at present, due to cost, only essential hosts are normally provided with this capability, for example file servers.

6.4.10 Cabling guidelines

The different media available for use in ethernet networks reflect the different physical and technical requirements that different operating environments pose (Kauffels, 1989). To highlight these, consider connections to the 'desk'. Initial requirements may be for a few PCs to be networked within a single room or upon a single floor. This will need the network to be flexible to allow the re-siting, and addition of PCs, as the network grows. Connections should therefore be easy to 'make-and-break', preferably without interrupting the rest of the network.

Historically, the first suggested solution to this environment was the 10BASE2 specification. This has gained a considerable installed base in the UK and Europe. It lends itself to star topologies, with segments fanning out from a multiport repeater housed in the corner of the room or floor. Each segment can support up to 30 devices via T-piece connections. This allows for a high density of devices to be supported from one repeater device. While individual cable costs are low, the bus topology provides little resilience to a failure of the cable and for the devices attached directly to that cable.

More recently, products that provide 10 Mbps ethernet over twisted pair cables have become widespread. These have been fuelled by the 'flood wiring' of data-grade twisted pair cables by the American PTTs. Although standard BT telephone UTP cables are not suitable for ethernet, the cost advantages of such an approach have led to an increasing demand for these products in the UK and Europe. The hub architecture allows large numbers of dedicated cables to be laid, one or more to every desk in the building, centred at distribution panels mounted on a floor or within each room. These distribution panels are usually in the form of patch panels and allow devices to be moved, or added, to the network by a simple re-patching of cables. The use of UTP cables in this way is at the heart of a structured wiring system; for example, the premises distribution system (PDS) from AT&T, or the open systems cabling architecture (OSCA) from BT. Both of these advocate the use of UTP cables (among other options) for cabling to the desk. For new installations, where the advantages of increased resilience and flexibility are important, UTP is the ideal medium for use to the desk.

The use of fibre to the desk provides many of the advantages outlined above for UTP. Cable costs are greater, however, and connecting equipment at both the PC and hub ends is significantly more expensive. Therefore, fibre tends to be used only where additional benefits are required which only fibre can offer. These include security through the difficulties associated with tapping fibre, immunity to external noise sources and increased bandwidth allowing the use of 100 Mbps systems without the need to re-cable. In practice, therefore, few sites require fibre to the desk.

Between floors, and ends of buildings, the distances involved may be greater than UTP or 10BASE2 cables can span. In this case, either 10BASE5 cable or fibre is necessary. Again, the choice between these depends on cost, future expansion and the structured wiring options available for the system that has been selected. Clearly, distribution boxes at the base of a building, linking to the distribution boxes on each floor, provide a neat solution. The use of fibre is recommended between buildings due, at the very least, to their electrical isolation effect. These fibres interlink the building distribution boxes and are themselves best run from a central site distribution box.

6.5 Performance characterization

The characterization of LAN performance was discussed in Chapter 5. This characterization is further refined for ethernet LANs by the three graphs shown here in Figures 6.13 and 6.15. Figures 6.14 and 6.15 are derived from measurements made by Digital Western Research Laboratory on their in-house Ethernet system (Boggs, 1988). The three graphs show:

- The throughput versus offered load shown in Figure 6.13 displays the way in which the network throughput varies as the amount of data required for transmission approaches the network maximum.
- The average delay versus numbers of active users shown in Figure 6.14 demonstrates the average delay for a frame between the time when it is submitted to the network by one user and the time when it is received by the other user. This displays the efficiency of the switching/multiple access scheme for various frame lengths.
- The utilization versus number of active users shown in Figure 6.15 shows the total throughput of the network against the number of active users, for varying average frame lengths.

The points to note from the throughput curve (Figure 6.13) are:

- In typical networks the throughput drops once the 80% threshold is reached. This is because the network is using the rest of its bandwidth in arranging when information should be transmitted.

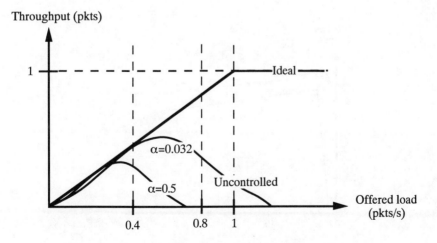

Figure 6.13 Measured throughput versus offered load.

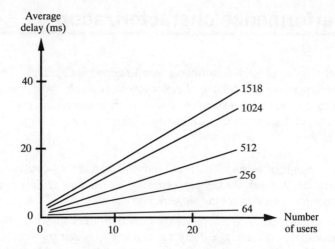

Figure 6.14 Measured average delay versus number of users.

- The relative throughput decreases as the value of the coupling coefficient α increases. The lower limit is encountered when the frames are minimum length, whereupon the maximum achievable throughput is only 37%.

In the case of the average delay graph (Figure 6.14) it was found that:

- For about 25 users the average delay for packets of length 1518 octets was about 40 ms – the standard deviation was about 9 ms and so some 75% of the users experienced an average delay of 22–58 ms. The transmission time for a 1518 octet frame is 1.2 ms and so the rest of the delay is due to the CSMA/CD scheme.

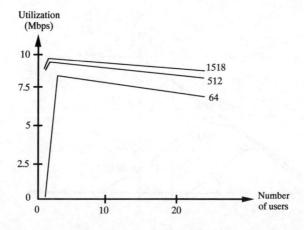

Figure 6.15 Measured channel utilization versus number of users.

- The average delay decreases as the frame size decreases. The probability of contention is independent of the frame size but longer frames increase the size of the waiting backlog. This means that the number of contentions experienced by a frame increases the longer the frame, hence the increase in average delay.

Figure 6.15 shows that the utilization decreases as the number of users increases and as the message size decreases. These curves confirm the theoretical curve shown in Figure 5.8, with the exception of the very low utilization point for only two or three users. This 'low' is due to the fact that it was impossible to get this number of workstations to physically load the network to its capacity – the internal protocol system was the bottleneck and not the network; this effect is very common in many real applications environments, particularly when network operating systems are supporting the network access.

The throughput/delay trade-off is clearly demonstrated when considering Figures 6.14 and 6.15. For a fixed number of users the average delay decreases as the message length decreases but the network utilization also decreases. An improved network utilization requires the transfer of long frames but these incur significantly increased delays.

6.6 Summary

The ISO 8802/3 carrier sense multiple access with collision detection (CSMA/CD) technique is the most firmly established and standardized LAN system. It currently consists of six integrated but different signalling schemes; a comparison of their differences and similarities is shown in Table 6.1. This table compares the segment lengths, data rate, number of transceivers permitted on each segment, the minimum distance between the transceivers, the minimum bend radius of the cable permitted to avoid damaging the cable, the cable diameters, the cable impedance, the velocity of propagation factor of the signal along the cable (the fraction of the speed of light in a vacuum), the signalling technique and the earthing requirement. Each of these six systems supports the CSMA/CD system across a particular physical cabling architecture, with each type being suited to a particular installation environment and for a certain cost effectiveness. In summary:

- The ISO 8802/3 system is based upon the CSMA/CD technique in which the nodes continually sense the channel while transmitting information.
- The frames must always be greater than or equal to 64 octets and less than or equal to 1518 octets. The minimum length ensures that the CSMA/CD system operates correctly and is one of the main reasons for the size limitation in the topology of ethernet-like LANs.
- At present there are six established ISO 8802/3 CSMA/CD LAN architectures:

Table 6.1   A comparison of the six types of ethernet system.

Criteria	10BASE5	10BASE2	10BASEF	10BASET	10BROAD36	1BASE5
Segment length (m)	Max of 500	Max of 185	Max of 2000	Max 100	Max of 1800	Max of 250
Segment type	Coax	Coax	Fibre	UTP	Coax	UTP
Data rate (Mbps)	10	10	10	10	10	1
Transceiver number	100	30	2	2	6	2
Transceiver spacing (m)	2.5	0.5	—	—	2.5	—
Minimum bend radius (cm)	25.4	5	10	N/A	25.4	N/A
Cable diameter (mm)	10	5	0.125	0.45	10	0.45
Impedance (ohm)	50	50	N/A	N/A	75	N/A
Velocity of propagation	0.77–0.83	0.67–0.77	0.65–0.67	0.59–0.63	0.77–0.83	0.59–0.63
Signalling technique	Baseband Manchester II	Baseband Manchester II	—	Baseband Manchester II	Broadband DPSK	Baseband Manchester II
Earthing	One only	Maybe	No	No	One only	No

thick ether (10BASE5), thin ether (10BASE2), the fibre (10BASEF) and twisted pair (10BASET) architectures, the broadband architecture (10BROAD36) and the original low speed UTP system, Starlan (1BASE5).

- 100 Mbps ethernet systems are under development based upon the 100BASEX specification. Other new systems just becoming available are isochronous (IEEE 802.9a) and full duplex ethernet and the 100VG AnyLAN transport.

- The smaller the average frame size the lower the average delay but the lower the network utilization. The average delay for a system that supports 25 active users each sending 1518 octet length frames is between 22 and 58 ms.

- Ethernet (Blue book 2, ESPEC 2 or DIX) is not the same as the ISO 8802/3 CSMA/CD standard. They are very similar but direct communication between the two is not possible due to the slight, but significant, differences.

- The latest ethernet NIAs are provided with a network management task facility (this is similar in concept to the Token Ring management facility). This enables the NIAs to communicate directly with a network management system.

7

Token Ring LANs

7.1 Introduction

During the 1970s a research team at MIT investigated the possibility of using token passing for use in communications systems. This work had started in the late 1960s and was later adopted by the IBM Zurich Research Laboratories, culminating in a 1 Mbps Token Ring demonstration system (Bux, 1983). The name Token Ring is applied to LANs that support a multiple access system using a token passing scheme across a ring topology. The IBM demonstrator became a fully fledged product in 1983 and by 1987 it had been upgraded to a 4 Mbps system. The aim of the IBM Token Ring was to supply a LAN which operated efficiently at very high user loads, something which is almost impossible to supply with ethernet (Hunter, 1993).

In 1985 IBM submitted the specification of their Token Ring to the then newly established IEEE 802.5 committee. This committee was charged with providing a standard for token passing rings equivalent to the CSMA/CD standard for ethernet. The Token Ring is still under development. It has not yet had the time to stabilize as a coherent product and unfortunately it is undergoing standardization before having achieved any fully engineered internetworking stability. Ethernet was given this time due to the fact that it was developed over many years by a small development team who were under relatively little commercial pressure. This means that we can expect several subtle changes to the Token Ring in the coming years, particularly as the other standardization efforts are completed, including system management, the usage of bridges and routers, the full OSI/RM, and so on.

7.2 Token passing rings

The more recent development of the Token Ring system has resulted in it adopting a layered architecture which is similar to that of the CSMA/CD LANs. The relationship between Token Ring and the OSI/RM is shown in Figure 7.1. When this architecture is compared to the ethernet equivalent (Figure 6.1), the only major architectural difference is the inclusion of a station management task. This task is essential for the correct operation of Token Ring and so its inclusion is for reasons other than network management. At present the ISO standard is still in its draft stage, hence the ISO/DIS 8802/5 identification.

The general architecture for a simple Token Ring system is shown in Figure 7.2 (Göhring, 1992). Here, the three wiring hubs, called multistation access units (MAUs or MSAUs) – not to be confused with transceivers – are daisy chained together, using STP cabling for the main ring, in a fault redundant manner – in other words, all of the ring in (RIN) and ring out (ROUT) ports are connected to their corresponding opposites. The individual nodes, DTEs, are also connected to the MAUs using STP lobe cables. The MAUs themselves contain the basic ring wiring structure, employed

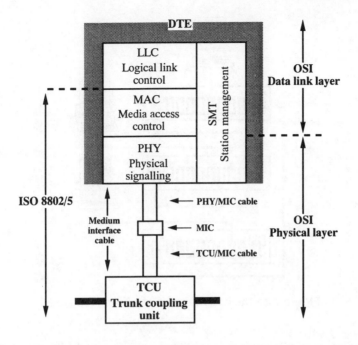

Figure 7.1   ISO 8802/5 and the OSI/RM relationship.

to construct a design which is robust and reliable, and this leads to the architectural description of Token Ring as a 'starred-ring'.

It is not essential that a token passing network be of a ring topology. The token bus technique (defined under IEEE 802.4) uses a token passing scheme but makes use of a broadcast bus topology. The advantage of a ring is that a transmitting station is not only the node to send the data but is also the last to receive it. This means that there is a very fast feedback response which it can use to provide a very low level acknowledged protocol. In fact this type of information cannot be used to derive information about the state of the end-to-end data transfer (the use of bridges causes a distortion in the validity of this local ring information), and so in general it is only used to support the network management functions.

7.2.1   Token passing

A time division multiplexing system is the most efficient sharing scheme for applications which produce high and evenly distributed loads. The Token Ring LAN architecture was specified to provide a time based access mechanism that was efficient at high loads but that was also well suited to the typical office environment. The other main criteria was that it should be totally decentralized: there should be no central clock

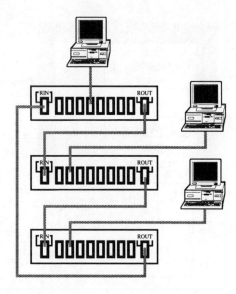

Figure 7.2　The basic structure of a Token Ring LAN.

or central monitor. The solution is to use token passing in which a station can only transmit data when it possesses the token. The token cycles around the stations, along the active ring topology (a series of point-to-point links culminating in a single closed path across the stations), thereby giving each station equal opportunity to access the channel. Multiple access to the channel is provided by restricting the time for which a station can keep the token.

The signals are encoded using a differential Manchester II encoding system which is similar to Manchester II but polarity independent; that is, it is insensitive to which way round positive and negative are connected. The use of this encoding means that the signal rate is 8 Mbps for a 4 Mbps data system and 32 Mbps for a 16 Mbps one. Once again this encoding is employed so that the receivers can synchronize with the transmitter's clock without recourse to some centralized global clock. The logical information is grouped into the IEEE 802.5 data PDUs, which are similar in structure to those for the CSMA/CD systems.

The data PDU and token structures, as defined by the IEEE 802.5, are shown in Figure 7.3. The token is a three octet frame which contains the start delimiter, the access control and the end delimiter. This three octet structure cycles around the network until a node seizes it and converts it into a data frame, whereupon the data is transferred. Once the entire data frame has cycled back to its originator a new token is released onto the network and this again cycles until it is seized by a node wishing to send data.

The data frame is a minimum of 22 octets long. The first octet is the start delimiter (SD); this is the sequence *JK0JK000*. The *JK* bits are differential Manchester II encoding signal violations which permit the receiver to detect them and so begin the process of clock and bit synchronization. The access control (AC) contains the three

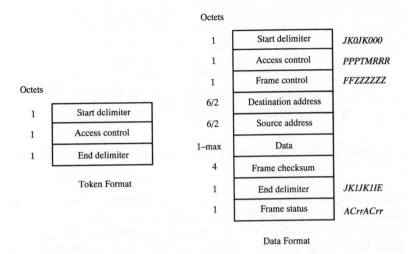

Figure 7.3 The basic structure of a Token Ring frame and token.

priority (*P*) bits, the reservation (*R*) bits, the token (*T*) bit and the monitor (*M*) bit. The token bit distinguishes between a token, 0, and a data frame 1. The monitor bit is used by the monitor to inspect continually rotating frames – when a transmitter fails to remove its own frame. The priority (*P*) and reservation (*R*) bits are used to decide which stations can acquire the token and to bid for the priority of the next token generated.

The first data field is the frame control (FC). An FC of 00 denotes a MAC PDU and a 01 an LLC frame. A MAC PDU is used by the Token Ring station management to transfer information to other station management entities and to interact with a network manager. The LLC frames are used to transfer actual data across the network. If it is an LLC frame the *ZZZZZZ* is split into the *rrrYYY* field in which the *YYY* field contains the LLC service call priority value, equal to the *PPP* value. This is followed by the destination and source addresses, both of which are either two or six octets long.

The FCS or checksum is four octets long and is used to determine whether or not the PDU has been corrupted by the channel during transmission. The CRC algorithm for generating the FCS is defined in the IEEE 802.3 standard. The end delimiter (ED) contains more *JK* bits, the intermediate bit (*I*) and the error bit (*E*). The *I* bit is used to denote whether or not the node currently holding the token will send other frames before releasing the token. The *E* bit is set by any station that detects an error, such as FCS violation or non-data signals, as the frame cycles around the ring. The frame status (FS) is not covered by the FCS, hence the duplication of the nibbles. The address (*A*) bits denote whether or not the address has been recognized by a receiver and the copied (*C*) bits indicate if the frame has been copied by a receiver. The SD and AC fields constitute the start-of-frame sequence (SFS) and the ED and FS fields constitute the end-of-frame sequence (EFS).

The address field structure in the frames conforms to one of two basic structures: universal or local addressing. In both schemes bit 0 is used to denote the

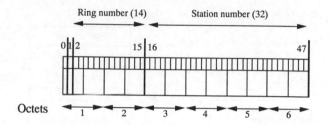

Figure 7.4 The local addressing mode structure for Token Ring frames.

individual/group address (note that in the case of the source address this bit is used to denote the use of routing in bridged multi-ring architectures) and bit 1 is used to denote universal/local address administration. The universal mode is similar to that used by the IEEE 802.3 system, as shown in Figure 6.4. The local mode structure is shown in Figure 7.4 and is based upon a ring number (14 bits) and a station number (32 bits). It should be noted that for Token Ring, bit zero is the most significant bit whereas in ethernet it is the least significant. There are three types of addressing mode (all of the codes are shown in hex):

- Broadcast – the destination address is set as FFFFFFFFFFFF for all nodes on all rings, or C000FFFFFFFF for all nodes on the local ring.
- Multicast – in universal addressing the first bit in the destination address is set to 1. The situation for local addressing is still under discussion.
- Point-to-point – the first bit in the destination address is set to 0 and the rest of the address is set according to the target NIA.

The transmission of data in token passing systems requires that the transmitting station has possession of the token. Data transmission is then permitted until the holding period has expired, at which point a new token must be generated and sent onto the network so that another station can transmit data. Given this basic concept the algorithm for data transmission is:

- When the station has data to transmit it waits until it detects a token. The token would be cycling around the network as shown in the schematic Token Ring in Figure 7.5.
- The token priority is inspected and if it is less than or equal to that of the station's data then it is changed to a start of frame sequence (set the token bit to 1). The data frame is transmitted synchronously after the start sequence.
- The frame is transmitted. If the token holding time (THT, which is the period allotted to each station for data transmission each time it acquires the token) has not expired and more data is queued for transmission and if this transmission will not exceed the THT, then this can also be sent. The standard is inconsistent in this area and many implementations do not support this capability.

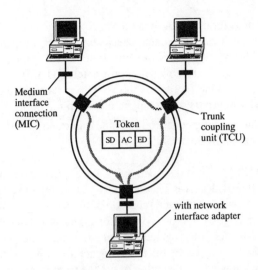

Figure 7.5   A schematic representation of the operation of a Token Ring.

- Once all of the data has been transmitted the station checks to see if the frame start sequence has returned to it – that is, the frame has started to complete its rotation of the channel. If the frame has not been detected then the channel is filled with stuffed data until the THT expires or the frame is detected.

- Once the frame has returned it is inspected (via the A, C and E bits to ascertain if the destination received the data and whether or not the data was received without error. The new token is now generated and placed onto the channel.

The above description is somewhat simplified – it does not include scenarios such as when a transmitter detects a frame and not a token, and so is permitted to bid for the priority of the next token, and so on (Stallings, 1994). The receivers in each of the stations are continually receiving data frames or tokens – remember that a ring is an active network and all information is passed on from live node to live node. When receiving data:

- The stations inspect each start of frame sequence to determine whether or not the frame contains data. It must be stressed that each station injects only a one bit latency in the propagation delay – that is, it takes the station one bit time to record and inspect its contents. This is possible because each station makes a copy of the passing frame and the order of the MAC PDU bit stream is designed to facilitate this copying. The bit is then sent out onto the main ring cable and the copy is kept for internal manipulation.

- If it is a data frame then the destination address is inspected and the station determines whether or not the data is for that node – that is, whether it has the appropriate individual, group or broadcast address.

- If the frame is for that NIA then the frame is copied until the end delimiter is detected. The locally generated checksum is then compared with that of the frame and the appropriate error status is appended to the rotating frame. The two flags A and C are now set appropriately (11 if the data is successfully received or 01 if the receiver is too busy to receive the data) and the source transmitter will use these to confirm the reception of the data.

- The data must now be unpacked from the frame and passed either to the station management or the next level of protocol.

As with the CSMA/CD system the IEEE 802.5 Token Ring standard does not support error correction. It provides error detection only and operates in exactly the same way as the CSMA/CD version. The cyclic rotation of the frame in a Token Ring provides one important advantage over its bus competitors. This is that the transmitter receives its transmitted frame after it has cycled through all of the nodes. This means that the use of a low level error flag set by the receiving station provides the transmitter with almost immediate knowledge of whether or not the frame was received error free. If an error occurred then the data could be retransmitted without too much delay between error detection and retransmission. It must be stressed, however, that the MAC standards are connectionless. The use of the frame rotation provides an acknowledged connectionless service in which the status flags may or may not be acted upon by the higher layers of protocol.

7.2.2   Token Ring monitor

The principle of decentralization causes many implementation problems. For instance, what is responsible for regenerating the token if it becomes lost or corrupted? Also, the absence of a central clock means that the individual node clocks will drift with respect to each other and so cause synchronization jitter. The solution is to provide a distributed monitoring system which elects a single monitor from the live nodes. It is therefore essential that every token domain have one and only one monitor. The first NIA to become active on the network becomes the monitor. If this NIA is then switched off another NIA becomes elected as the monitor – during this election and recovery period (which in theory should last seconds but which in practice can take one or two minutes) no data can be transferred across the network. The responsibilities of the monitor are:

- Creating the original token and ensuring that either a frame or a token is cycling around the network.

- To compensate for the accumulated ring synchronization jitter. The latency buffer compensates for these jitter effects by providing a shift register whose size grows and shrinks according to the jitter effects on the network.

- Storing one whole token. Each NIA has a one bit latency and so at least 24 stations would have to be active before a ring could hold the token; if this buffer was not supplied it would mean that each active node would need a 24 bit buffer to hold the token as it is passed out around the network, thereby significantly increasing the propagation delay. The monitor becomes responsible for holding a complete token and so it supplies a 24 bit token buffer.

- To remove unwanted frames and to ensure that a frame cycles only once around the ring. If a NIA failed while transmitting data, this would result in the continual circulation of the frame and the permanent loss of the token. The monitor inspects each frame and marks it, using the monitor bit, as it passes through the monitor. Should the monitor detect a previously marked frame then it removes this and regenerates the token (each frame should pass around the network once only).

- To establish the nearest neighbour order around the network thereby promoting the operation of the 'beaconing' fault detection mechanism – beaconing is the transmission of beacon MAC PDUs which are used to signal the location of a cabling fault.

So, one of the important features of the monitor is its latency buffer. This shift register is used to ensure that the ring can always contain a token and to compensate for ring jitter. Therefore the latency buffer must be at least 24 bits long – the size of a single token. A single physical ring is limited to 260 stations and repeaters. The data signalling rate is specified to be within ±0.01% of the 4 or 16 Mbps. The accumulated jitter for a 4 Mbps maximum sized ring will therefore be ±3 bits, and for a 16 Mbps maximum sized ring ±16 bits. Therefore the latency buffer has a maximum size of 30 bits for a 4 Mbps and 56 bits for a 16 Mbps system. The buffer length is initialized as 27 bits and 40 bits, respectively, so that the actual latency can grow or shrink depending on the number of live stations on the network.

The monitor issues an active monitor present (AMP) frame on a periodic basis, every seven seconds. If, after a predefined period, a station fails to receive this frame then it attempts to claim monitor responsibility. The first station detecting the absence transmits a claim token. The propagation delay around the network means that other stations may also detect the failure and so there may be more than one claim token cycling around the network. If any station receives a foreign claim token with a source address higher than its own then it relinquishes its claim and moves into standby mode. The same is true of an active monitor should it detect the claim token: it is possible to pre-empt the monitor allocation scheme by forced issuing of a claim token upon station initialization. This means that the station with the highest address that is participating in the claiming process becomes the new monitor.

The first station to receive the AMP then issues a standby monitor present (SMP) frame. This frame is received by the nearest downstream node, which can then use the associated source address to determine its nearest upstream neighbour. In response this node then issues its own SMP frame, which its nearest downstream neighbour can detect. This SMP ripple (the AMP/SMP combination is also known as the 'ring poll') enables all of the nodes to determine the address of their nearest upstream neighbour (used for beaconing) and to enable a network management centre to construct a map of the location of the nodes on the network.

Beaconing occurs whenever the claim token process fails – that is, if the transmitting station never receives back its transmitted claim. This implies that the network has failed at some point, for example because of a cable break, a MAU failure or a station failure. The beaconing process starts with the loss of reception of the AMP. The claim token is not returned (or the election process is not resolved) and so the detecting station transmits its own beacon frame. This frame contains the address of its upstream station: the problem lies between that node and the current node.

For this technique to operate correctly, each station must know the address of its upstream neighbour. This 'neighbour notification' process is started by the monitor. It transmits an AMP frame and the first station receiving this copies the source address into its upstream neighbour address (UNA) field and sets the A and C bits. Other stations receiving the AMP now know not to copy this address into their UNA. The station which copied the monitor as its UNA issues, as soon as possible, a standby monitor present (SMP) frame. The first station to receive this copies the source address into its UNA and sets the A and C bits, thereby stopping other stations from copying this address. This SMP and UNA process is repeated in a daisy chain until all stations know the address of their upstream neighbour. The process stops when the monitor receives an unused SMP, indicating that the source of that frame is its own UNA.

7.2.3   Ring 'walk-time'

The 'walk-time' is the time that it takes a signal to travel one circuit of the ring; this is normally quoted in bit times. In a Token Ring the walk-time, as shown in Figure 7.6, consists of:

- The station latencies – 1 bit for every NIA and repeater on the ring.
- The monitor latency buffer delay – 30 bits for 4 Mbps systems and 56 bits for 16 Mbps ones.
- The cable delay around the longest path of the ring.

In a maximally sized 4 Mbps ring with 260 users, the walk-time is given by:

$$\text{walk-time} \quad = \quad (260 \times 1) + 30 + \text{cable delay}$$

$$= \quad 290 + \text{cable delay}.$$

The cable delay can be determined only if the length, type and quality of cable is known. As the walk-time increases so the average delay increases. This leads to problems in very large 16 Mbps networks where the cable delay could be a few hundred bits long. In an attempt to overcome the long delays produced by this propagation delay and the frame transmission time the 16 Mbps systems employ an 'early token release' scheme

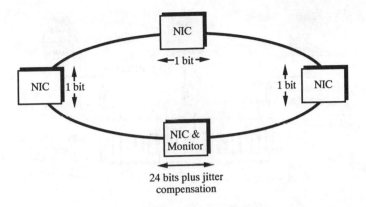

Figure 7.6 The walk-time around a Token Ring.

in which the new token is generated and released as soon as the transmission of the original frame has been completed. In the 4 Mbps systems the leading edge of the original frame has to be received before the new token can be released. Therefore, in large networks it is now possible for several data frames to exist on the channel at the same time.

The Token Ring walk-time is equivalent to the ethernet propagation delay. Its value is therefore used in the calculation of the coupling coefficient and so it has a bearing on the channel efficiency of the Token Ring, as discussed in Chapter 5.

7.3 Token Ring components

Many Token Ring architectures are based upon the starred hub configuration, as shown in Figure 7.7. The MAU contains the actual ring wiring, lobe connection points (part of the trunk coupling unit or TCU) for the stations, and RIN and ROUT connections. The RIN and ROUT ports are used to connect together MAUs in a cable daisy chain but still forming one physical ring. The MAU only opens the ring for the stations when:

- The station is physically connected to the MAU – that is, the TCU is complete.
- The station is powered on, resulting in the provision of a DC voltage applied across the TCU. This is termed the 'phantom' voltage because it does not get transmitted along the channel and has no effect on the data signals.

The medium interface cable (the TCU/MIC and PHY/MIC) must provide two twisted pairs: one for station transmission and one for station reception. The actual MIC is normally a wall socket connected to a patch board. This permits the use of a structured cabling layout within a building, thereby restricting access to the MAUs themselves but

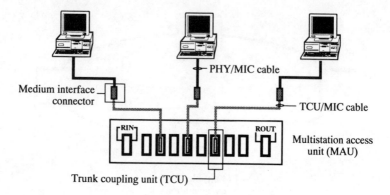

Figure 7.7 The Token Ring.

providing flexibility in station location.

At initialization the station/MAU moves from the bypass mode into insertion initialization, to full operational initialization and finally data transmission standby mode. When a station is first plugged into the MAU the mechanical bypass is disabled, however, the station is still not a part of the ring. The station must now be powered: the 'phantom' signal must open the electronic relay (causing an audible click as the relay opens).

All of the internal timers are reset and the latency buffer is deleted. The standby monitor timer is now started and the station attempts to acquire clock synchronization with the current ring monitor. This is achieved by waiting to receive an AMP or purge (PRG) token; these are the only two frames that are always sourced by the current monitor. If no AMP is detected then the station attempts to claim the role of monitor by issuing a claim token. If this is successful it now operates as the ring monitor.

If an AMP or PRG is received the station now attempts to detect a duplicate address. This is implemented by transmitting a duplicate address test (DAT) frame. This frame cycles around the ring with a destination address equal to that of the transmitting station. If another station has the same address, it will recognize the address, copy the frame and set the A and C bits. The originating station will eventually receive its frame. If the A and C bits are zero then there is no other station with that address and the station moves to data transmission standby mode. If not – that is, if a station with that address is already active – then the station returns to the bypass mode and the 'phantom' signal is removed.

7.3.1   Network components

The basic Token Ring architecture consists of MAUs, NIAs and the cabling system. Although the price of the basic components is slowly dropping, the cost of the Token Ring NIAs is still considerably higher than the ethernet equivalents.

Multistation access units

Originally, MAUs were passive devices; they required no power source. The necessity for network management and the capability of driving signals across greater lengths of cable has resulted in the introduction of the increasingly popular active MAU – a MAU plugged into the mains. Each MAU has two types of port:

- The workstation port. This is the port that the MAU uses to communicate with a NIA via a lobe cable. Two types of port are available: the STP universal data connector port (UDC, also known as the hermaphrodite connector) and the UTP RJ45 or RJ11 connector port.
- The RIN and ROUT ports. These are used to link together MAUs, thereby increasing the number of users connected to a single ring.

MAUs are available with a range of user port numbers: 4, 8, 12, 16, and so on. A 32 user ring could therefore be supported by two 16-port MAUs, four 8-port MAUs, two 12-port MAUs and an 8-port MAU and so on. The classification of MAUs is:

- Passive – standalone devices into which the node lobe cables are connected. It is not possible to directly manage such devices.
- Active – which are powered devices and which fall into three further classes:
  - Powered, in which the individual node ports act as repeaters and so can support fully extended lobe lengths
  - Intelligent, in which a network management facility is supplied so that the MAU port states can be remotely controlled and reported
  - Fault tolerant, in which the failure of RIN/ROUT ports on connected MAUs can be detected, thereby forcing the ring into automatic wrap-around and thus supporting continual operation.

It is possible to use MAUs of different cable type and to get a cable adapter to connect the two types together. However, this is not to be recommended because it severely distorts the network design rules and these are already complex enough. The only other difficulties that occur when linking passive and active MAUs together are concerned with the automatic wrap-around facilities in the active MAUs. These must be disabled, or else the active MAU will partition off the passive MAU, thereby breaking the network.

Controlled access units and lobe attachment modules

One of the original Token Ring hubs was developed by IBM and called the controlled access unit (CAU). The CAU is a large wiring hub centre capable of supporting tens of users (typically 80 ports). The CAU supports 4 or 16 Mbps NIAs on both STP and

UTP cabling by making use of lobe attachment modules (LAMs). The LAMs sit inside the CAU chassis and provide the lobe interface; different cabling systems use different types of LAM. The CAU consists of several LAMs plus repeater ports for connectivity to other CAUs or to remote MAUs.

A typical CAU architecture is shown in Figure 7.8, in which a CAU supports two remote MAUs. The CAU consists of one UTP and one STP LAM plus a repeater card – this provides access for 32 users. An important feature of the CAU is that it provides an automatic wrap-around facility for each of the LAMs by using fault tolerant cross-links on its backplane. The advantage of this approach is that it provides a rugged wiring centre without having to physically stack and cross-link individual MAUs on top of each other.

Network interface adapters

The NIA is the hardware board which is the actual implementation of the IEEE 802.5 multiple access system. The most important features are the two external connectors:

- The 9 pin D connector used for the standard MIC cable connection to the NIA. This is used in the STP wired networks.
- The RJ45 connector for use in the UTP wired networks. On many NIAs the UTP filter is supplied on-board, thus removing the necessity of having a clumsy external filter box on the MIC.

In PC based NIAs a set of memory and I/O jumpers are used to configure the operation of the board so that it is consistent with the rest of the host operating environment. These jumpers must be set so that they are consistent with the system generation options used to configure the NIA driver software. It is also possible to buy external NIAs, which are housed outside the workstation but make use of the parallel interface. The disadvantages for Token Ring NIAs are that different data rates need to be supported and their inherent complexity makes them more expensive than ethernet NIAs. The problem of dual data rate support is solved by providing self switching NIAs which, when activated, automatically sense the carrier rate on the network and operate accordingly. The cost differential will probably exist for several years, by which time a different LAN architecture will have superseded both ethernet and Token Ring. This difference is reflected in the costs of the Token Ring PCMCIAs which are 50% more expensive than their ethernet equivalents.

Network cabling

The IBM cabling system is used as the standard for Token Ring wiring guidelines; the IEEE is establishing the definitive standard but this is still under development. The guidelines devised by IBM for Token Ring cabling are available in the appropriate IBM

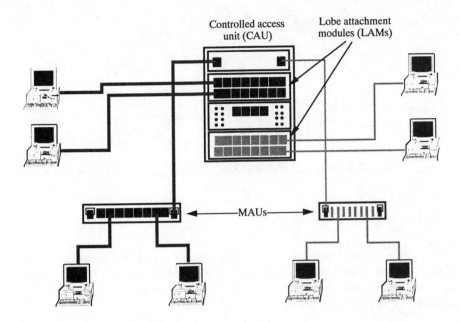

Figure 7.8 A controlled access module based Token Ring architecture.

cabling and installation guides. Each cabling system is given a type number and the types relevant to Token Ring are:

- Type 1 – data grade STP using solid copper and providing two pairs. This is used for the main ring and lobe cables.

- Type 2 – voice/data grade STP using solid copper and providing two data pairs and four voice pairs. This is used for the main ring and lobe cables.

- Type 3 – UTP data grade telephone cable using solid copper. This is used for the main ring and lobe cables.

- Type 5 – fibre optic cable. This should be avoided because it recommends the use of 100 µm fibre whereas the preferred core diameter is 62.5 µm.

- Type 6 – twisted pair data cable for use as patch cables using stranded copper.

- Type 8 – data cable using solid copper which is shielded but not twisted and is flat so that it is suitable for installation under carpets.

- Type 9 – low cost STP data cable with solid or stranded copper for use in short-run main ring and lobe cables.

Care must be taken when considering telephone cabling because this generally refers to US grade telephone wire which is of a better grade than that in the UK. UK telephone wire should not be used for data applications.

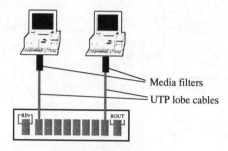

Figure 7.9 The use of media filters for UTP based Token Rings.

7.3.2   Support components

The number of manufacturers of Token Ring support devices is considerably fewer than that for ethernet. This is reflected in devices such as terminal servers where there are only two or three manufacturers. The extra devices that have been produced to extend the connectivity of a Token Ring include:

- MAU extension units – these come in two types: the lobe extension devices and the miniMAU units. The lobe extension units permit two NIAs to be supported off one lobe cable and the units can themselves be cascaded to support further NIAs. The miniMAUs (or satellite wire centres) act as true MAU extensions and several of these can be daisy chained one after the other.

- Media filters – these are required whenever UTP cabling is employed. The filters are placed between the NIA and the MAU, as shown in Figure 7.9, and are used to convert the UTP signal into a form that is compatible with the NIA interface (this includes the filtering of some of the extraneous noise picked up by the UTP). Different filters are required for the 4 and 16 Mbps systems.

- Line drivers – these are available for both copper and fibre systems and can be used to convert from copper to fibre and vice versa. Drivers are a low cost repeater that provide signal re-amplification but not full regeneration. The typical uses of line drivers are shown in Figure 7.10, in which both copper and fibre drivers and their distance limitations are displayed.

- Terminal servers – these are a recent addition to the product range and provide the same functionality as their ethernet counterparts.

- Repeaters – again these are similar to their ethernet counterparts. The repeaters are sources of jitter and so count in the maximum number of nodes total. A repeatered architecture is a single token domain; there is only one monitor and token on the whole architecture.

- Bridges – either source routing, transparent or source routing transparent bridges are available for Token Ring architectures. Each of these can be used to improve the performance and reliability of the network.

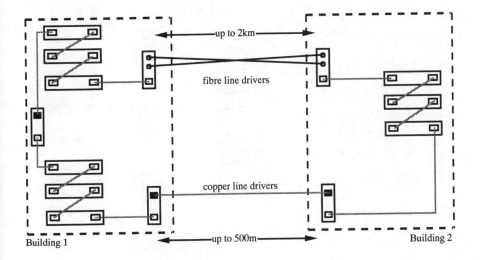

up to 2km

fibre line drivers

copper line drivers

Building 1   Building 2

up to 500m

Figure 7.10 The use of copper and fibre line drivers.

- Switches – these are low latency bridges which can forward the Token Ring frames without waiting for the full reception of the frame beforehand.

7.4 Token Ring architectures

The core architecture for a Token Ring system is shown in Figure 7.11. The MAUs are stored in a single wiring closet, stacked on top of each other, and are interconnected using the 2.5 m patch cables. The MAUs are also linked to a punch down block using 2.5 m length patch cables. The cables linking the punch down block to the wall sockets are commonly termed lobe cables but the full length of the lobe should really include the two patch cables. The design of a Token Ring network is concerned with establishing whether or not the available lobe length is sufficient to support the required distance. The wall socket to NIAs (inside the PCs) use 2.5 m patch cables which end in either a 9 pin D-connector or a RJ11/RJ45 connector. This gives the MIC a total length of 105 m (this may consist of different grades of cable). The extended version of the Token Ring layout with multiple wiring closets is shown in Figure 7.12. Here three closets hold the 12 MAUs and are connected with intercloset cables which constitute part of the main ring. The patch cables and rack cables are normally of different length but of the same type.

There are in effect four separate types of Token Ring system that must be considered when establishing the cabling design rules (Bird, 1994):

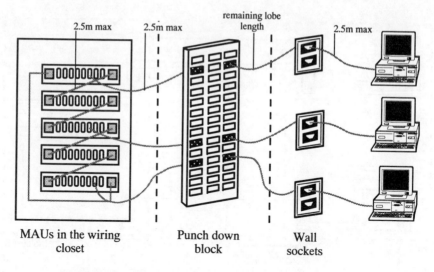

Figure 7.11 The basic physical architecture for Token Ring.

- 4 Mbps data rate over STP
- 4 Mbps data rate over UTP
- 16 Mbps data rate over STP
- 16 Mbps data rate over UTP.

It is not possible to mix the 4 and 16 Mbps NIAs without using bridges, at which point the cabling rules do not have to be considered across the bridge (the bridge creates two separate token domains). It is possible to mix STP and UTP; however, as mentioned before, this should be avoided.

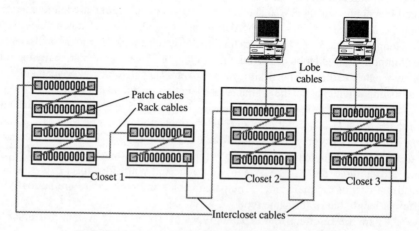

Figure 7.12 A complex architecture for Token Ring.

Two recent innovations for Token Ring are switched communications and fast Token Ring. Fast Token Ring is in fact FDDI, or more appropriately CDDI, under another name and as such is the 100 Mbps equivalent of the fast ethernet. Switched Token Ring is fast bridging in which the bridge begins to forward the frames onto the target ring before the frame has been fully received from the source ring. The reduces the bridge latency considerably and also means that a switch can be forwarding several simultaneous data streams across different pairs of rings.

7.4.1   4 Mbps systems

The underlying rules in the 4 Mbps systems are that the number of users must not exceed 260 and that each NIA must be able to drive a signal along 700-800 m of type 1 cable or 135–180 m of type 3 cable.

4 Mbps systems across STP

The simple design rules for STP 4 Mbps systems based upon 8-port passive MAUs are:

- The number of NIAs is limited to 260. This limit defines the amount of jitter that can be incurred in the round trip journey and so defines the length of the latency buffer required in the monitor station.

- Assuming that there are 260 users and that each MAU supports 8 users, then 33 MAUs are sufficient. Fewer, larger MAUs are acceptable; however, more MAUs should not be used because this will require more patch cables.

- Type 6 cable should be used for all short length connections such as MAU/ MAU in the same closet and should be no longer than 2.5 m. Rack to rack connectivity in the same closet is limited to 10 m cable lengths (Figure 7.12).

- Type 1 cable should be used for the lobe and closet/closet connection. The lobe cable has to be traversed twice for every single main ring cable propagation, thus the maximum lobe length should be 100 m and the main ring 200 m for wire closet connectivity. If active MAUs are used then the lobe cable can be the maximum specified by the manufacturer, typically 300 m (Figure 7.12).

4 Mbps systems across UTP

The simple design rules for UTP 4 Mbps systems based upon 8-port passive MAUs are:

- The number of NIAs is limited to 72. This limit defines the amount of jitter that can be incurred in the round trip journey and so defines the length of the latency buffer required in the monitor station.

- Assuming that there are 72 users and that each MAU supports 8 users, then 9 MAUs are sufficient. Fewer larger MAUs are acceptable; however, more MAUs should not be used.

- Type 6 cable should be used for all short length connections such as MAU/MAU in the same closet. These cables should be no longer than 2.5 m. Rack to rack connectivity in the same closet is limited to 10 m cable lengths.

- Type 1 cable should be used for the main ring connection. There should be no mixing of type 1 and type 3 cables in the ring or as lobes. The maximum distance between closets is limited to 120 m.

- The type 3 lobe cable should be less than 45 m (this equates to the 100 m for the type 1 cable). In the cases where a single closet is supported then the lobe can be up to 100 m in length. Media filters must be used on all type 3 lobe cables to ensure that the signals conform to the NIA input criteria.

In the case of active MAUs the cables can be up to 120 m long. In most type 3 systems the entire cabling is based upon UTP (including the patch cables) and so the general equivalence of 100 m type 1 = 65 m type 6 = 45 m type 3 should be used.

7.4.2   16 Mbps systems

The 16 Mbps Token Ring design guidelines are still vague and vary significantly from vendor to vendor. The trade-off is always between the number of NIAs on a single ring and the maximum lobe length. Until recently there was just the STP and UTP wiring systems for Token Ring. These have recently been joined by the intelligent twisted pair (ITP) system, championed by a UK cabling company, which costs almost the same as UTP, is less bulky than STP and provides superior performance to both STP and UTP.

Up until the very last months of 1991, IBM insisted that it was not appropriate to use UTP for 16 Mbps systems. This attitude was consistently challenged by companies such as Proteon and StarTek, who have championed the UTP approach. IBM and Synoptics are now producing the 16 Mbps UTP standard and their proposals appear to be contrary to some of the established products. Naturally this will create confusion in the market place and could even lead to serious NIA and MAU incompatibilities between vendors. In a recent development, a rival 16 Mbps UTP standard is now challenging the IBM/Synoptics proposal. This new proposal, from a consortium including StarTek and Proteon, is recommending that the jitter compensation system be placed in each port as opposed to a global compensation circuit in the MAU as a whole. The formal rules for Token Ring design for 16 Mbps on STP and UTP are still being standardized and so at present the techniques that the standard will adopt are still subject to alteration; the specific cabling guidelines from IBM and other manufacturers should still be used.

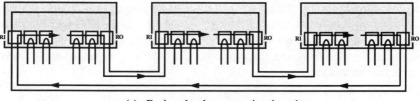

(a)   Fault redundant operational mode

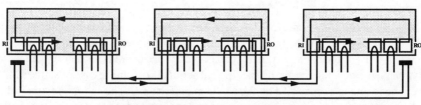

(b)   Non-redundant operational mode

Figure 7.13   Redundant and non-redundant MAU connectivity.

7.4.3   Redundant/non-redundant ring connectivity

When multiple MAUs are linked together using RIN and ROUT ports the ring topology can adopt one of two forms. If only a single cable is used between each MAU the topology is as shown in the non-redundant mode in Figure 7.13b; note that the data signal flows along all of the twisted pair cables. Each MAU–MAU cable consists of two twisted pairs – one for data in and one for data out – so correct operation of the ring does *not* need the two end RIN/ROUT ports to be connected. If any of the main ring cables become split then some MAUs have the capability to automatically partition off that port, causing the ring to become split. Each operational MAU will then carry on supporting its own local workstations.

When each MAU has two MAU–MAU cable connections then the topology and signal flow is as shown in the fault redundant mode of Figure 7.13a. Here the data signal propagates down only one pair of the main ring cable. The original IBM and similar passive type 1 MAUs do not support automatic fault tolerant topology and so, if the MAUs are wired as shown in Figure 7.13a, a cable failure will not cause wrap-around. This only occurs when the two ends are physically disconnected so that the UDC roll bar closes, forming a complete circuit.

The automatic wrap-around, supported in some active systems and nearly always available on type 3 MAUs, is provided by supplying a 'phantom' signal between the RIN and ROUT ports. If the RIN/ROUT ports do not detect this 'phantom' signal then they wrap-around and do not allow the signal onto the failed cable.

The use of this phantom signal highlights a very important problem with connectivity between type 3 MAUs. At present there is no agreed connector standard for use in type 3 systems. This omission has resulted in different manufacturers using both RJ45 and RJ11 connectors, using four, six and eight of the RJ45 wires and using straight through and crossed connectivity. The result of this confusion is that it is impossible for users to assume that type 3 active MAUs from separate vendors can be readily internetworked.

7.4.4   Cabling guidelines

The maximum lobe length (MLL) for a Token Ring network is dependent on the maximum transmission distance (MTD) of the network cards and the adjusted ring length (ARL) of the cabling system. In passive MAUs the MTD is determined by the station NIA card and is normally specified at about 800 m. In the case of active MAUs the lobe length is as specified by the MAU manufacturer. The cabling design is then followed to ensure that the rest of the topology does not produce an effective lobe length of zero, or less, metres (Bird, 1994).

The worse case situation for the redundant ring is if it is operating in the non-redundant mode. The ARL is defined as the total main ring length minus the smallest cable length – so the worse case operational scenario is when the shortest link fails. The active main ring length then becomes twice this ARL. The maximum lobe length is not just the difference between the MTD and twice the ARL. The signal must pass up two lobe lengths (assuming a passive MAU system) and so in the failed state with no other station the maximum permitted lobe length is in fact only one half of the difference between MTD and 2ARL.

The RIN and ROUT power levels are usually expected to support 200 m of type 1 cable or 120 m of type 3. If type 6 cable is used then this must be restricted to about 160 m. It is important to note that the real length calculations should take into account the attenuation effects of different types of cable. However, it is poor engineering to design to the extreme limits of cable lengths; leave a margin of error of at least 20%.

The more modern approach is to use hubs or active MAUs to provide signal regeneration and hence support full lobe lengths. This approach is also adopted by the CAU/LAM combination in which the powered LAMs can support several full length lobe cables. Not only do hierarchical architectures support the full lobe lengths; they also provide the network with layered fault tolerance. The automated ring-wrap capability at all powered wiring centres (MAUs, CAUs and hubs) means that the network can protect itself at the lowest possible scale, thereby ensuring that as few nodes as possible are disconnected from the network. This fault tolerance and the addition of remote management means that the hub and active device based architectures provide several important advantages when compared with those produced by the classic passive devices. The overall effect of using an active architecture is that the network is more reliable, manageable and flexible but is subject to problems related to power supplies, which can be alleviated by using an uninterruptable power supply (UPS). Cost permitting, an active device approach should be adopted whenever possible.

7.5 Summary

The ISO/DIS 8802/5 Token Ring multiple access technique for LANs has clearly established itself as an alternative to the ethernet LAN. It was predicted that the number of new Token Ring based installations within the UK and Europe would, as has occurred in the US, equal that for ethernet. Recent market surveys have implied that this may not now be the case. As yet, the cause for this change is still unclear but it may be due to the new fast ethernet proposals and the availability of cell relay products. The Token Ring standardization effort is still very immature and so, in many cases, it is not possible to reliably interconnect equipment from different manufacturers without taking great care. One example of this problem is the interconnection of active MAUs using UTP for the main ring segment, where there is no agreement on the standard connector or the wiring system used within the connector. In summary:

- The ISO/DIS 8802/5 technique is based upon the passing of a token around a ring topology network. The transmission of data is only permitted when a node possesses the token and the token must be released within a predefined period (usually 10 ms).

- The maximum frame size in Token Ring is limited by the token holding period. This is usually sufficient to permit a maximum frame size of 4472 octets. The minimum frame size is 22 octets, which consists of 1 octet of data plus the 21 octets of MAC header and trailer.

- The multistation access unit (MAU or MSAU) is the network component that houses the actual ring; note, this is not the same as the ethernet MAU or transceiver. The MAU is the wiring hub to which the workstation lobe cables are connected and so is the basic building block for Token Ring connectivity.

- The MAUs are provided in passive and active forms. The passive systems operate without a power source whereas the active ones need a power supply. The active MAUs supply a combination of full lobe signal regeneration, intelligence in the form of port management and fault resilience due to automatic wrap-around in the failure of a linked cable or MAU.

- Hub architectures and active MAUs is the recommended architectural construction. The controlled access unit (CAU) and lobe access module (LAM) combination is particularly well suited to the construction of large star based topologies using a structured cabling infrastructure.

- At the present time there are four distinct Token Ring systems: 4 Mbps across shielded twisted pair (STP), 4 Mbps across unshielded twisted pair (UTP), 16 Mbps across STP and 16 Mbps across UTP. The 4 Mbps and 16 Mbps network interface cards cannot be used on the same Token Ring architecture. This is only permitted in bridged architectures.

- Two innovations under development are fast Token Ring which is 100 Mbps system based upon FDDI/CDDI, and switched Token Ring in which a fast bridge is used to provide concurrent frame switching between pairs of rings.

- The basic design aim when considering the architecture of a Token Ring system is to establish whether or not the desired maximum length of lobe cable can be provided by the designed topology. If this is not the case then repeaters must be appropriately located and used to regenerate the signal.

- The performance of Token Ring systems is relatively insensitive to the value of the coupling coefficient. The maximum number of nodes per token domain is limited to 260 and, in reality, is usually no more than 100.

8

Established Networks

8.1 Introduction

While the international standardization effort is becoming increasingly fundamental to guiding the product development of many manufacturers, there is still a very large and significant product base that precedes all of the results of this activity. Most of the major computer system manufacturers use proprietary communication protocols to support their own systems, such as IBM and SNA, Digital and the DNA (Bartee, 1989). More importantly, in many cases it was the experience gained from these which guided, and still guides, the developing standards. The interconnectivity of mixed proprietary systems can be supported using one of two basic approaches:

- The use of a common backbone network to which all of the other systems are linked using an appropriate gateway. This is the solution preferred by the standards organizations, provided that the backbone is an OSI/RM based network, as shown in Figure 8.1.

- The use of specific relays to form individual network-to-network point links, as shown in Figure 8.2. In this situation each network pair uses their own gateway and so a form of hop-by-hop enhancement is employed. Traditionally this has been the favoured approach but the proliferation in the number of different networks is making this a commercially non-viable proposition.

The user community as a whole is still not convinced of the efficacy of the OSI/RM. However, it is agreed that some form of 'open' connectivity is essential. It is at this point that the *de facto* standards become particularly helpful in that they are seen as useful migration milestones towards some future *de jure* standard. One area where this approach is being particularly successful is in the case of TCP/IP. Many manufacturers

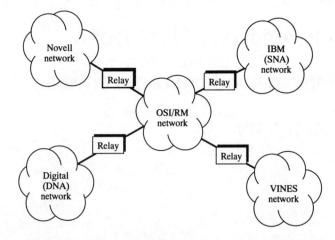

Figure 8.1   Interconnectivity using a common backbone.

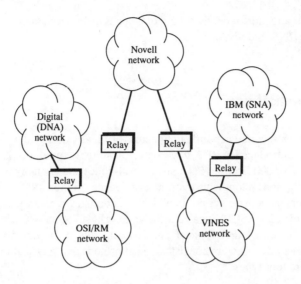

Figure 8.2   Interconnectivity using a network hopping technique.

now support one form or another of TCP/IP connectivity and so by using this it is now possible, in principle, to interconnect different systems, that is, use the approach shown in Figure 8.1 but replacing the OSI/RM with TCP/IP. The user community has also recognized TCP/IP as a convenient interconnectivity technique and so they too are advocating its adoption; together, the manufacturers and users have established TCP/IP as a *de facto* networking standard.

There are considerable long-term benefits in this migration towards TCP/IP. Whether or not TCP/IP remains the standard is not as important as the fact that any further migration is simplified. If interoperability is already supported by a common protocol then any change to a different protocol requires a single migration path and not the myriad caused by the current range of protocols and network operating systems.

8.2 Proprietary architectures

Large data networks have traditionally developed around mainframe and minicomputer installations so that distributed access to some central processing capability is readily available. Digital and IBM have been pre-eminent in establishing proprietary integrated computer/networking infrastructures. Typically, many organizations have used Digital processors for process engineering and systems support, and IBM mainframes for task intensive transaction and accounting systems. In turn, this has generated a large demand for products to provide connectivity between both networks and processors, and more recently for interconnectivity between their two proprietary architectures: DNA and SNA.

8.2.1   The IBM way

SNA is a highly structured network architecture originally designed to operate across leased circuits. Introduced in 1973, it is a mature, feature rich product with a significant user base (over 20 000 licensed SNA sites world-wide) and arguably it has been one of IBM's strongest developments over the last decade (Meijer, 1987). SNA is based upon a hierarchical domain system in which each domain is controlled by a systems services control point (SSCP), located in the domain host. The SSCP is responsible for the management of all the physical and logical units in its domain. The SNA communications infrastructure consists of a set of nodes, or physical units (PUs), of which there are four types:

- Terminal (PU type 1) – which is a dumb workstation.
- Cluster controller (PU type 2) – which controls terminals and other peripheral devices (PU 1 nodes).
- Communications controller (PU type 4) – front end processors (FEPs) which pre-process all communications aspects before passing the data onto the host.
- Host (PU type 5) – the hosts themselves, such as mainframe computers.

A typical SNA architecture, as shown in Figure 8.3, has the mainframe acting as the domain SSCP for a variety of PUs hosted on Token Ring LANs (Schäfer, 1992). The FEP is responsible for pre-processing all of the host related communications and the gateways act as IEEE 802.5/SNA adapters. In this system the PCs host the appropriate terminal emulation software, assuming that they require access to the mainframe. While the physical architecture of the network is its collection of PUs its functional capabilities are defined in terms of logical units (LUs) and LU types. The range of LU types is intimately related to the protocol layering within SNA and the relationships between these layers. The SNA layering is shown in Figure 8.4 and consists of:

- Physical – the physical connectivity, including the appropriate NIAs.
- Data link control – which uses the synchronous data link control (SDLC) protocol which is similar, but by no means identical, to HDLC.
- Path control (PC) – which creates the logical channel links across the network. Later versions of SNA use the virtual route control, explicit route control and transmission group control protocols for route selection and control.
- Transmission control (TC) – which is responsible for ensuring that end-to-end session transmission is reliable and orderly.
- Data flow control (DFC) – which is responsible for controlling the ways in

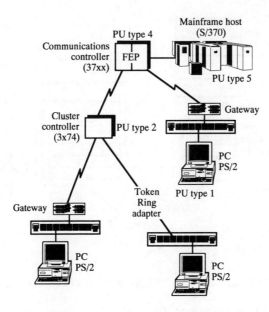

Figure 8.3   A typical SNA network.

which the two end systems can communicate with each other, such as full
duplex, half duplex and so on.

- Network addressable units (NAUs) services manager – which supports the user
  with presentation services such as data compression, and the session services
  such as end user communications management.
- Function management data services (FMDS) – which support the mapping
  between the end user applications, such as file access, and the appropriate NAU
  services manager.

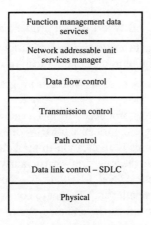

Figure 8.4   SNA layers.

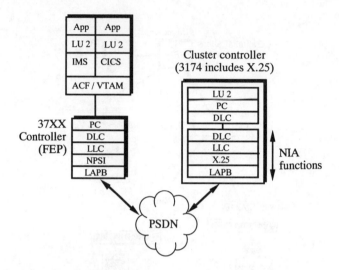

Figure 8.5 X.25 PSDN connectivity in SNA.

The bottom three layers (physical, DLC and PC) constitute the transport network whereas the LU types are based upon different combinations of the upper four layers (transmission control to NAU services manager). NAUs are the source and destination entities between which information is exchanged, and so a NAU can be identified as a PU, LU, SSCP or a central manager. The six LU types and their relationship to the SNA layering are (Kauffels, 1989):

- LU type 0 – sessions which use the TC and DFC but not the FMDS.

- LU type 1 – for communications between applications programs and data processing terminals.

- LU type 2 – for use between sessions that support an application program and a single terminal.

- LU type 3 – similar to LU type 2 but for printer access.

- LU type 4 – for terminal to terminal communications and for sessions that need one to many application/terminal communications.

- LU type 6 – for applications to applications program communications.

All of the new communications products will in fact now be LU 6 based devices, denoted as LU 6.2. The strategic significance for IBM of the LU 6.2 is based upon the recognition that communications is application-to-application oriented and that full peer-to-peer access is needed in the long term – particularly if OSI/RM migration is to be supported. On a more practical level, LU6.2 devices do not need SSCP support so their associated networks are smaller and cheaper to construct while providing added functionality such as dynamic directories and message re-routing.

Figure 8.5 shows the relationship between the LU and PU for access to an X.25 network. The FEP hosts the full X.25 interface using the network control packet switch

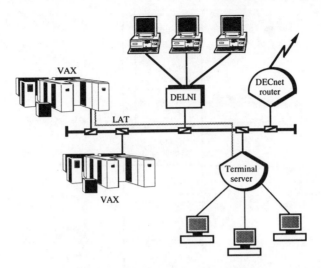

Figure 8.6 A typical DECnet architecture.

interface (NPSI) with the LU supporting the host mainframe applications. The cluster controller is an X.25 PAD and consists of the X.25 network interface adapter (X.25 NIA) plus the terminal support software – that is, an LU 2. The FEP, host and cluster controller are separate PUs.

8.2.2   The Digital way

DECnet is the name given to the Digital family of networking products and the DNA is the term used to describe the protocols housed within that family. Unlike IBM, Digital was firmly committed to LAN technology at the very beginning, being one of the original Ethernet founders, and has always been committed to a truly layered architecture. One of the reasons for this more 'open' approach is that in comparison to IBM, Digital is the newcomer and so was not encumbered by historical precedent or a commitment to established product lines which could strongly restrict any new technological development.

The classical Digital architecture is shown in Figure 8.6, in which a VAX host is supporting both intelligent and dumb remote terminals (Kauffels, 1989). The preferred CSMA/CD access is always via the appropriate DECnet device such as a CSMA/CD concentrator (DELNI), repeater (DEMPRA), bridge, router, gateway or terminal server, with only the hosts having direct access. The local area transport (LAT) protocol supports the host/terminal server access and this uses the CSMA/CD bus as its transport bearer. The DELNI supported devices supply their own CSMA/CD cards but use of the concentrator requires only one tap on the cabling system.

The DNA is an evolutionary layer profile whose product form is released as a

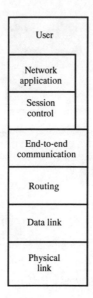

Figure 8.7 The protocol layers for the Digital network architecture.

series of phases. The Phase IV profile is shown in Figure 8.7. The Phase V development, now renamed Advantage-networks and which has been promised for the last two or three years, will fully conform to the OSI/RM, including the full adoption of the accepted layer name convention. The layers in Phase IV are responsible for:

- Physical – supporting the host drivers and the communications hardware.
- Data link – supplying the classical error free communications environment. This includes the use of the byte oriented Digital data communications message protocol (DDCMP).
- Routing – selecting and maintaining the route allocation for all packets across the network. This also includes congestion control.
- End communication – supplying point-to-point communications control including fragmentation and reassembly.
- Session control – the system dependent elements of interprocess communication, including the mapping between logical names and physical addresses.
- Network application – supplying the general network services including file access and transfer, and remote terminal access.
- User – the user programs and user level services plus the network management functions for an integrated network management facility.

The use of this profile is demonstrated by the X.25 access system shown in Figure 8.8; the network application is the X.25 gateway (Bartee, 1989). This network supports DNA/X.25 connectivity via a gateway and the two end systems host their network appropriate protocols plus the appropriate user layer software which is configured to

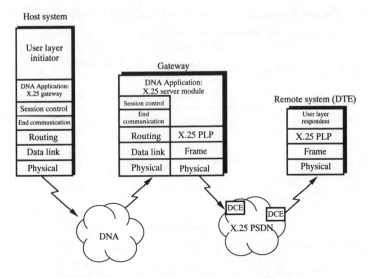

Figure 8.8 X.25 PSDN connectivity in DECnet.

access X.25. At the DNA host the network application supports the local X.25 and the gateway converts the DNA profile to its equivalent X.25 form by stripping away the DNA encapsulation and then by wrapping it in X.25.

8.2.3   A comparison of architectures

A comparison between the proprietary protocol profiles to the OSI/RM is a simplistic measure of their architectural similarity. However, it is a useful way of visualizing their approximate equivalence. Table 8.1 compares SNA, DNA and the OSI/RM, and at first sight, apart from names, there appears to be very little difference between them. Unfortunately, whereas the DNA profile maps elegantly onto the OSI/RM, the SNA architecture does not easily confine itself to the OSI/RM layering schema and so several layers find their functionality spreading into more than one layer.

A more subtle difference between SNA and DNA is the manner in which they treat interconnectivity. The SNA approach is similar to that of the OSI/RM and is based upon a common backbone (see Figure 8.1), the major difference being that IBM believe that SNA should act as the backbone with OSI/RM conformant networks being treated as any other communications system. Digital prefer the hop-by-hop enhancement method, as shown by a comparison of Figures 8.2 and 8.8.

IBM also support the hop-by-hop enhancement method, as shown in Figure 8.5. However, they supply a very limited set of gateways, namely TCP/IP, OSI/RM and X.25. It is noticeable that IBM are reluctant to develop gateways to other proprietary systems, so the availability of such interconnectivity is left for the other manufacturers to develop, such as Digital and their SNA gateways.

Table 8.1 A comparison of the SNA, DNA and OSI/RM layers.

Protocol	Systems Network Architecture (SNA)	Digital Network Architecture (DNA)
Application	Function management data services (FMDS)	User interface
Presentation	NAU service manager	Network application
Session	Data flow control	Session control
Transport	Transmission control	End communication
Network	Path control (PC)	Routing
Data link	Data link control– SDLC	Data link
Physical	Physical	Physical link

8.3 Established protocols

There are a few non-proprietary profiles which have established themselves as important interconnectivity protocols. These protocols include X.25 for PSDNs, the Internet's TCP/IP architecture, and the manufacturing automation protocol (MAP) and technical & office protocol (TOP) for use in specific LAN environments.

8.3.1 X.25 systems

X.25 is the most widely used protocol implementation for PSDNs, as a result of its recommendation by the CCITT. Most computer manufacturers supply X.25 interfaces for their proprietary architectures and many companies use these for supporting remote mainframe access. The 'heavy' and slow nature of X.25 is not suited to LANs and so only in very few cases is it used to support LAN based communications.

Reference to the X.25 protocol takes many different forms, so when discussing these systems it is important to establish exactly what is being discussed. The CCITT X.25 recommendation details the layer two and layer three protocols; the balanced link access procedure (LAPB) and the X.25 packet layer protocol (X.25PLP), respectively (Deasington, 1986). The CCITT recommends that either X.21 or X.21bis – digital and analogue interfaces, respectively – be used, although this is not mandatory. In the most formal sense X.25 refers to the DTE/DCE layer two and three interfaces only. Many companies refer to other informal configurations as X.25 including the X.25PLP, LAPB and X.21 combination while others refer only to the X.25PLP. Under the ISO, the X.25PLP and the LAPB are defined in different standards – LAPB is defined as a particular subset of the generic HDLC protocols.

The layered architecture of an X.25 based architecture is shown in Figure 8.9. This consists of four layer abstractions; the network layer represented by X.25PLP, the data link layer as denoted by LAPB, the physical layer in the guise of X.21 and an intermediate sublayer for multilink systems. The multilink procedure (MLP) sublayer is used as distinct from single link procedure (SLP) systems. An SLP system consists of a single LAPB whereas the MLP maps several LAPB interfaces to a single X.25PLP. The MLP is used to construct fault resilient and load balancing X.25 systems and allows the X.25PLP to transparently access several LAPB interface ports.

The default X.25 data units consist of 128 octet sized packets with both the packet and frame layers using a sliding window size of two. In the most extreme case this service can be negotiated to support packet sizes of 4095 octets and a window size of 127. A total of 4096 logical links can be concurrently supported. The standards concerning the performance of PSDNs stipulate that:

- 95% of all packets (assumed to be 128 octets) must reach their destination within 650 ms of being submitted to the source DTE, assuming a 9.6 kbps carrier (X.135).
- 95% of all packets (assumed to be 128 octets) should have a measured throughput of 2.4 kbps, assuming a 9.6 kbps carrier (X.135).
- The packet layer residual error rate is 2.10^{-10} (X.136).
- The service availability is 99.5% – that is, a mean time between service outage (MTBSO) of 1200 hours and a mean time to service restoration (MTTSR) of 6 hours (X.137).

X.25PLP is defined as a set of standard functions plus a series of optional facilities. The availability of these facilities is dependent on the supplier and the version that they are supporting. The most common X.25 systems are the X.25(80) and X.25(84) releases (the bracketed number denoting the year the standard was released). Compatibility between these is normally guaranteed and in many cases optional facilities in earlier versions form part of the core standards in later releases, for example the MLP. Conformance to OSI/RM and its CONS is not supported in X.25(88); however, many

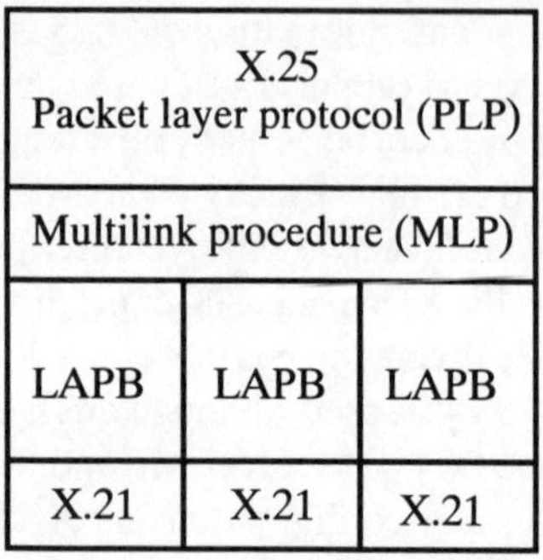

X.25 Packet layer protocol (PLP)		
Multilink procedure (MLP)		
LAPB	LAPB	LAPB
X.21	X.21	X.21

Figure 8.9 The X.25 protocol profile.

of its omissions will be supplied as facilities in the X.25(92) release. This means that it will be possible to support the CONS using X.25 provided the telecommunications supplier supports the required optional facilities.

Both public and private X.25 systems are in use. Public X.25 systems are supplied by the PTTs with users paying connection, rental and utilization charges. The basic infrastructure of a public PSDN, such as BT's PSS+ service, is available to the full user community and so there may be problems with access but there is no maintenance responsibility on the users for the network. Conversely, in a private X.25 system the network is dedicated to the funding organization but this is also responsible for the maintenance of the network. Normally, the actual X.25 lines are leased from the PTT but the switching exchanges and other equipment will be owned by the user. Private X.25 networks are normally assumed to be more cost efficient if they are used for at least 35% of the time, otherwise public connectivity is recommended, and so it is essential to know the volumes of traffic that need to be supported on a daily basis.

8.3.2   TCP/IP based systems

The term TCP/IP refers to the layer four and three protocols, respectively, of the Internet protocol suite. However, the Internet profile supports a considerably wider range of protocols, many of which have established themselves as the *de facto* international standard for their appropriate role (Lynch, 1993). This pre-eminence in acceptability is precedented on two factors: in many cases the protocols were the first to be formally specified for general access and implementation; they are non-proprietary and so are freely available. The non-proprietary nature of these protocols has resulted in many computer systems manufacturers (particularly in the UNIX world) adopting them for their own networking implementations, thereby rapidly promoting their world-wide acceptance.

A subset of the current Internet Protocol Suite (IPS) is shown in Figure 8.10 (Washburn, 1993). Within this profile is a microcosm of the many protocols required

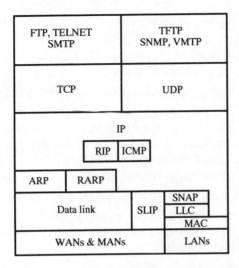

Figure 8.10   A selection of the Internet Protocol Suite (IPS).

for the successful support of a world-wide network, which is hosted by many different platforms and which is operational on almost every conceivable type of network. There are at present approximately thirty protocols associated with the Internet system. However, those that are most commonly employed for data communications are:

- Reliable applications services, which make use of the connection oriented transport service (TCP). The actual applications using this service are:
  - File transfer protocol (FTP), which is responsible for file transfers from one machine to another. The ISO equivalent is FTAM
  - Simple mail transfer protocol (SMTP), which is responsible for trans-ferring electronic mail messages between machines. The ISO and CCITT equivalents are MOTIS and X.400, respectively
  - TELNET, the remote terminal connection service. This provides remote terminal access to a host processor. The ISO equivalent is VT.
- Application services, which do not use the reliable transport service but which make use of its connectionless partner (UDP) are:
  - Simple network management protocol (SNMP), which is the Internet network management protocol. The ISO and CCITT equivalents are CMIP and X.700, respectively
  - Trivial file transfer protocol (TFTP), which is the connectionless version of FTP. Its restricted capabilities are ideal for supporting memory limited systems such as diskless workstations
  - Versatile message transaction protocol (VMTP), which provides a reliable end-to-end datagram delivery service without dependence on TCP. This can then be used in a variety of message transfer systems.

- The transport services, which support both a connectionless and connection oriented service. These protocols are:

  – Transmission control protocol (TCP), which is the connection oriented transport service and supplies a reliable, full duplex byte stream service

  – User datagram protocol (UDP), which is the connectionless transport service.

- The network services, which are responsible for data transfer plus all of the associated control, services such as routing and dialogue control. It should be noted that both RIP and ICMP are encapsulated by the IP whereas ARP and RARP directly access the data link. The responsibilities of these protocols are:

  – Internet protocol (IP), which is the connectionless delivery service

  – Address resolution protocol (ARP), which is responsible for establishing the address relationships between the physical subnetwork address and the IP address

  – Reverse address resolution protocol (RARP), which is a protocol for requesting the allocation of an IP address. This is used by constrained systems such as diskless workstations

  – Routing information protocol (RIP), which is used in the UNIX community for the exchange of routing table information. This is also used by Internet routers

  – Internet control message protocol (ICMP), which is an integral part of IP and supplies the control, and error handling functions.

- The data link services protocols, which are responsible for mapping the network layer protocols (namely IP, ARP and RARP) onto the physical network. The protocols responsible for this are:

  – The serial line internet protocol (SLIP), which is the data link protocol for systems that use IP across a serial link

  – Subnetwork access protocol (SNAP), which is used to map the IP address system onto the IEEE 802 LLC frame system. This is optional and is not required when using direct Ethernet support

  – LLC/MAC combination, which is the common LAN support protocol.

A thorough description and appreciation of the range and depth of the Internet protocols is beyond the scope of this text. However, its significance to the networking community cannot be overstated. It could be argued that it is the success of the Internet protocols which has precipitated the interest in internetworking and which has finally halted the increasing dependence on closed proprietary protocol systems. In fact the success of Internet during the past three years has created a crisis in address allocation. The available address space is almost fully allocated so several proposals are being studied for its extension. The basis of deciding which scheme will be adopted is considering the problem of backwards compatibility and it is to be hoped that the new scheme will not require all of the existing IP addresses to be changed.

8.3.3   MAP and TOP

In 1982, General Motors (GM) introduced the manufacturing automation protocol (MAP) architecture in an attempt to promote the rapid standardization, and subsequent development, of computer and communications equipment for use in computer integrated manufacturing (CIM). GM's own primary interest was, and still is, concerned with cost effective automated car manufacture but they needed the computer systems manufacturers to develop open systems that they could then integrate to construct their facilities.

At about the same time, the aircraft manufacturer Boeing began work on an equivalent type of paper documentation system called the technical & office protocol (TOP). The design and construction of aircraft is extremely paper intensive, both in terms of design and quality assurance, and Boeing required a fully computerized equivalent to their manual system. In basic outline and architecture MAP and TOP are very similar. However, there is one very important difference between them: MAP supports a real-time environment and TOP does not (Jones, 1988).

The resulting MAP architecture, as shown in Figure 8.11, consists of the MAP profile, the enhanced performance architecture (EPA) profile and the MiniMap profile. MAP is used to supply the network control facilities and to act as the network overlord. Communications between the controller and the remote sensors and actuators is supported by the EPA/MiniMap communications. The MiniMap profiles are the communications elements supported within the remote units whereas the EPA is the equivalent profile in the controlling unit – in other words, MAP uses the EPA to control the remote MiniMap based devices.

The MAP profile is based upon a connectionless communications subnetwork which supports the sophisticated transport protocol class four (TP4) with the session kernel and null presentation layers. The communications subnetwork consists of the connectionless network protocol (CLNP), the class one LLC and the token bus LAN (IEEE 802.4). The EPA/MiniMap profile consists of just three layers, with the manufacturing messaging system (MMS) sitting atop the acknowledged connectionless

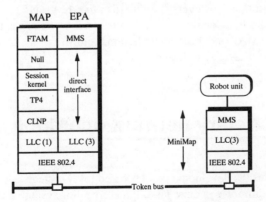

Figure 8.11   The manufacturing automation protocol (MAP) architecture.

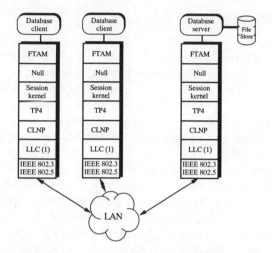

Figure 8.12   The technical & office protocol (TOP) architecture.

LLC(3) and the token bus; a closed system approach is necessary for real-time support.

As can be seen in Figure 8.12, the TOP profile is very similar to MAP; the only difference is the use of either CSMA/CD or Token Ring to replace the token bus. The paper processing nature of TOP's intended environment places a heavy emphasis on file processing (FTAM) and associated applications such as electronic mail (MOTIS).

8.3.4   A comparison of established protocols

Table 8.2 compares the protocol profiles of X.25, TCP/IP, MAP and TOP, and shows their relationship to the OSI/RM. As can be seen, X.25 is defined only for the bottom three layers – it is the communications subnetwork definition for PSDNs. TCP/IP has a full profile definition; However, it is primarily a five-layer suite, with the applications also providing the functionality normally attributed to the presentation and session layer protocols. MAP and TOP are both formal profiles of the OSI/RM and as such have the full seven-layer specification.

8.4 Proprietary network operating systems

In historical terms the development of PC based LAN systems is very similar to that of networked mainframe systems. The original operating systems were stand alone and when distributed access was required the solution was to augment the host operating system with access to the network, creating a network operating system (NOS).

Table 8.2   A comparison of the X.25, TCP/IP, MAP and TOP profiles.

Protocol	X.25 PSDN	Internet	Manufacturing Automation Protocol	Technical & Office Protocol
Application		Simple mail transfer protocol, TELNET	FTAM, MMS	FTAM, MOTIS
Presentation		Simple network management protocol	Null	Null
Session	Undefined	File transfer protocol, TFTP, VMTP	Kernel	Kernel
Transport		Transmission control protocol, UDP	Transport protocol 4	Transport protocol 4
Network	X.25 Packet layer protocol, MLP	Internet protocol (ARP, RARP, RIP, ICMP, OSPF, IGRP)	Connectionless network protocol	Connectionless network protocol
Data link	Balanced link access procedure	SNAP, LLC, MAC, SLIP, HDLC	LLC(1), LLC(3), IEEE 802.4	LLC(1), IEEE 802.3, IEEE 802.5
Physical	X.21	LAN, MAN, WAN	Broadband IEEE 802.4	IEEE 802.3, IEEE 802.5

8.4.1   Operating systems across LANs

The classical NOS is based upon the client/server architecture in which a dedicated file server is responsible for maintaining and supporting access to the user data files. The users, who are distributed across the LAN, are supported by the client access software, hosted on their own workstations/PCs. This software communicates with its file server based counterpart and provides the user with access to the file server as if it were just another local hard disk. The typical architecture for a client/server system is shown in Figure 8.13, in which a CSMA/CD LAN supports two separate file stores. The Novell NetWare and SUN Microsystems network file service (NFS) file stores are accessible only to their client counterparts but readily share the common LAN bus. In essence this is a remodelled version of the master/slave communications architecture with the mainframe replaced by a file server and the remote terminals by PCs.

In contrast, the peer-to-peer system, as shown in Figure 8.14, has no dedicated file server. Instead, each workstation has access to the local file stores of all the other similarly supported workstations. The total storage capacity of the network is then determined by the individual capacities of the workstations as opposed to that of a central file server. The peer-to-peer system is very common in NOSs that are aimed at supporting low cost solutions, such as AppleTalk and Sitka's TOPS, and this has resulted in the client/server systems attempting to supply low cost versions, for example Novell with NetWare Lite.

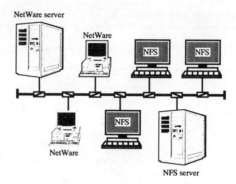

Figure 8.13 The client server network operating system architecture.

An important distinction between client/server and peer-to-peer systems is that in the former, all communications between clients must be actioned through the server, for example by electronic mail, whereas in the latter communication between the end systems is direct. In both systems the major attraction is that once the basic communications protocols have been specified and a common communications medium established then it is relatively simple to provide implementations that can be hosted on just about any processor. In fact it is the range of host environments that are supported by a NOS that will have a significant bearing on its acceptability for a particular environment. Given the current spread of workstations used in the workplace it is important for a NOS to support at least the PC, PS/2, Macintosh and UNIX boxes.

8.4.2 Commercially available NOS

A series of recent market surveys have found that about 50% of PCs are networked. One of the reasons for this is the number of different NOSs that are now available to support networked PCs, including systems from many of the major computer systems

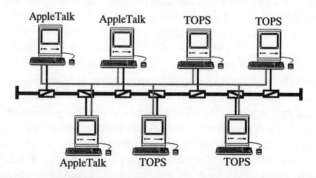

Figure 8.14 The peer-to-peer network operating system architecture.

suppliers and specialist manufacturers. A list of the dominant NOSs includes:

- AppleShare from Apple
- HP LAN Manager from Hewlett-Packard
- LAN Manager from Microsoft
- Windows NT and Windows for Workgroups from Microsoft
- NetWare 286, 386 and version 4 from Novell
- PCSA and Pathworks from Digital
- OS/2 LAN server, LANRES and OS/400 from IBM
- 3+ and 3+ Open from 3COM (no longer supported)
- Net/One LAN Manager from UB
- VINES from Banyan
- Xerox network systems (XNS) from Xerox
- Network file system (NFS) from SUN.

Novell NetWare accounts for about 50% of all PC/LAN NOS installations and so it is the clear market leader, but XNS from Xerox was the first commercially available NOS (Nowshadi, 1994). The limited market of XNS is due to its excessive price in comparison with other systems but its technical excellence is reflected by the fact that its development team was later responsible for the production of many rival systems, such as NetWare. In fact the similarity of several of the current NOSs betrays their origins and demonstrates that while interconnectivity between these systems is not simple they are in fact all supplying the same basic functionality.

Microsoft's success with Windows forced many organizations to come to terms with networking PCs hosting Windows – Windows was never intended for this type of environment. This was possible, but difficult and temperamental, especially where printing across the network was concerned. The introduction of the network 'savvy' Windows for Workgroups for peer-to-peer communications and Windows NT for client/server architectures has improved Windows networking considerably.

The basic protocol profiles for XNS, NetWare, VINES, NFS and AppleTalk are shown in Figures 8.15, 8.16, 8.17, 8.18 and 8.19, respectively. A closer examination of the XNS, NetWare and VINES profiles shows that their network and transport layer protocol systems are very similar. XNS uses the internet datagram protocol (IDP) and the sequenced packet protocol (SPP) for layers three and four, respectively, whereas peer-to-peer NetWare uses the internetwork packet exchange (IPX) and sequence packet exchange protocols (SPX). The IPX/SPX protocols are very similar to IDP/SPP. The courier protocol in XNS is subtitled the remote procedural control (RPC) and is responsible for end system transmission control – RPC is also used by NFS.

The client/server architecture for NetWare is based upon the network core protocol (NCP) which, when supported by the service advertisement protocol (SAP), ensures that the client workstations can access the file server. RIP is used to support the NCP and SAP protocols routers are used.

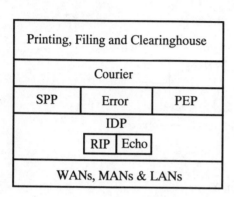

Figure 8.15   The XNS protocol profile.

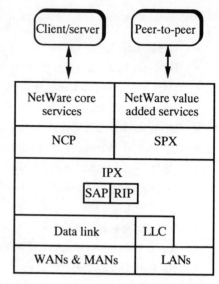

Figure 8.16   The Novell NetWare
protocol profile.

The VINES architecture is a combination of proprietary and Internet based protocols. This has produced VIP and IP, VARP and ARP, VINES routing update protocol (VRUP) and RIP, and VINES internet control protocol (VICP) and ICMP. The VINES transport service is supplied by their interprocess communications protocol (IPC) and their sequenced packet protocol (SPP) which offer a range of connectionless, acknowledged connectionless and connection oriented services. The session and presentation layer type services are supplied by NetRPC (cf. XNS Courier and NFS RPC) and the VINES API. This most important feature of the VINES approach is that it is provided within an integrated physical framework which is capable of supporting all sizes of network from the smallest single segment to a full blown enterprise network. It is therefore a very powerful 'one-stop' LAN solution.

The protocol profile of NFS, shown in Figure 8.18, is a perfect example of the method by which Internet acceptance has grown. SUN Microsystems adopted the Internet protocols as the core for their own UNIX based NFS and later released its full specification as an attempt to establish it as the *de facto* UNIX based NOS. As can be seen, NFS is based upon the IP and UDP protocols supported by the appropriate LAN access system. The actual file service protocol is supported by the RPC and external data representation (XDR) combination which minimizes the amount of traffic which needs to cross the network.

In contrast to SUN's attempts at standardization, the Apple approach to its product development has been shown to be somewhat idiosyncratic and isolationist. It is only very recently that the Apple has acknowledged that its new systems will be architecturally different so that an open systems can be supported. The AppleTalk architecture is shown in Figure 8.19. A detailed discussion of the finer points in its

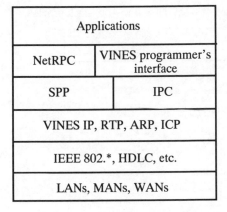

Applications	
NetRPC	VINES programmer's interface
SPP	IPC
VINES IP, RTP, ARP, ICP	
IEEE 802.*, HDLC, etc.	
LANs, MANs, WANs	

NFS file system
RPC/XDR
UDP
IP
IEEE 802.* (LLC & MAC)
LAN

Figure 8.17 The Banyan VINES protocol profile.

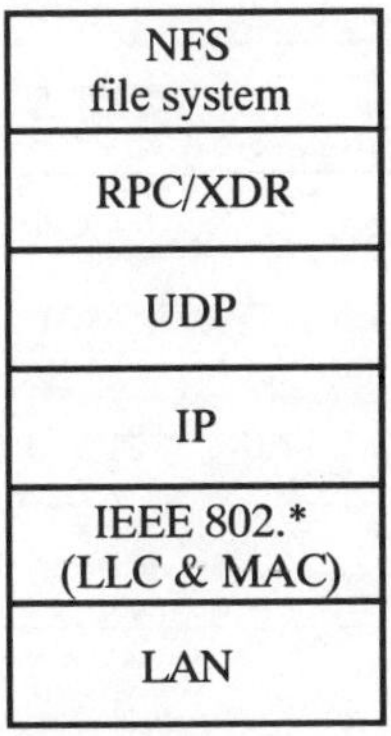

Figure 8.18 The network file system (NFS) protocol profile.

design is once again beyond the scope of this text. However, its basic principles are clear and the classical layering approach is yet again evident.

A comparison of the XNS, NetWare, VINES, NFS and AppleTalk systems with respect to the OSI/RM is shown in Table 8.3 (Miller, 1990). With the exception of AppleTalk the profiles are very similar at the lower layers (physical to transport) and only at the applications service layers do the significant functional and architectural differences appear. Again with the exception of AppleTalk, these systems are client/

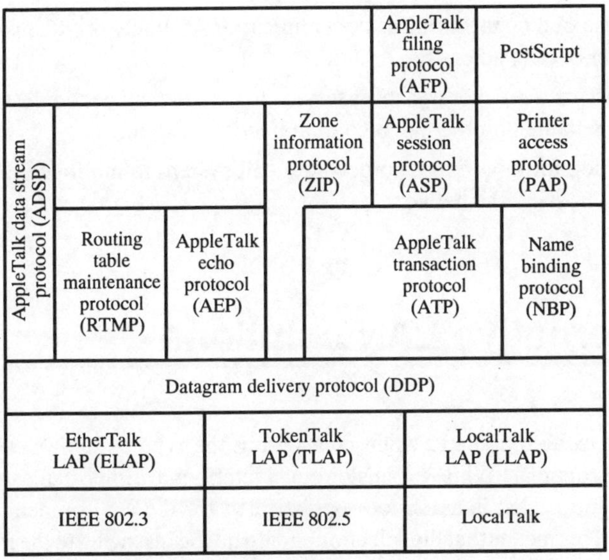

AppleTalk data stream protocol (ADSP)				AppleTalk filing protocol (AFP)	PostScript
			Zone information protocol (ZIP)	AppleTalk session protocol (ASP)	Printer access protocol (PAP)
	Routing table maintenance protocol (RTMP)	AppleTalk echo protocol (AEP)		AppleTalk transaction protocol (ATP)	Name binding protocol (NBP)
Datagram delivery protocol (DDP)					
EtherTalk LAP (ELAP)		TokenTalk LAP (TLAP)		LocalTalk LAP (LLAP)	
IEEE 802.3		IEEE 802.5		LocalTalk	

Figure 8.19 The AppleTalk protocol profile.

Table 8.3   A comparison of XNS, NetWare, VINES, NFS and AppleTalk profiles.

Protocol	Xerox network service (XNS)	Novell NetWare	Banyan VINES	NFS	AppleTalk
Application	Printing, filing, clearinghouse	NetWare core services	Application (LOGIN etc.)	NFS file system	AFP and PostScript
Presentation			NetRPC, VINES programmer's interface		
Session	Courier			Remote procedure call (RPC), external data representation (XDR)	ADSP, ZIP, ASP, PAP
Transport	Sequence packet protocol (SPP), error, packet exchange protocol (PEP)	Sequence packet exchange (SPX),	Sequence packet protocol (SPP), interprocess communications protocol (IPC)	User datagram protocol (UDP)	RTMP, AEP, ATP, NBP
Network	Internet datagram protocol (IDP), RIP, Echo	Internet packet exchange (IPX), RIP, SAP	VINES IP, RTP, ARP, ICP	IP	Datagram delivery protocol (DDP)
Data link	Ethernet	IEEE 802.*	IEEE 802.*, HDLC	IEEE 802.*, (LLC & * MAC)	ELAP, TLAP, LLAP
Physical	Ethernet	LANs	LANs, MANs & WANs	IEEE LANs	IEEE LANs, LocalTalk

server architectures and so the applications services protocols are asymmetric with respect to the server and client hosts. From these profiles it is clear that certain design guidelines have been adopted by the NOS manufacturers:

- The use of a connectionless communications subnetwork to ensure the rapid transfer of data across the LANs.
- The use of a reliable transport service to turn the connectionless subnetwork into a reliable point-to-point communications system.
- The adoption of a remote procedural call system to minimize the amount of traffic crossing the network.

8.5 Alternative LAN solutions

It is essential to be pragmatic when considering the type of LAN best suited to a particular environment. While expansion considerations are important it is all too easy to install a solution that is much too sophisticated for the environment, even in the longest term. This means that the selection should not be restricted to the more obvious full scale CSMA/CD and Token Ring solutions but should perhaps consider the cheaper options such as Arcnet and some of the low cost entry level solutions.

8.5.1   Token passing bus systems

Arcnet was developed by Datapoint Corporation in 1977 and currently claims about 5–10% of the USA's PC based LAN connectivity market. Its multiple access scheme is based upon token passing but unlike the Token Ring systems its capability is not dominated by its architectural shape.

The pre-eminence of the Token Ring as 'the' token passing LAN architecture has somewhat overshadowed what could be considered a more reliable topology, that of the bus (active and/or passive). Token passing bus systems use a similar scheme to that of the Token Ring: the token being cycled around the node community; possession of the token denoting the right to transmit data; a distributed token recovery system should the token become lost or corrupted. The only differences are that the data is broadcast to the users (as opposed to point-to-point cycling) and the logical token cycle is defined by the address order and not by the physical order on the network.

The attached resource computer network, or Arcnet as it is more commonly known, is a 2.5 Mbps token passing network, whose topology is normally a distributed star architecture. Several different system configurations are available using both shielded and unshielded twisted pair and coax, and Figure 8.20 shows the three topologies normally used for Arcnet: the hub structure (Figure 8.20a) where further network extensions are possible using hub-to-hub connectivity; the passive bus topology (Figure 8.20b) where the NIAs use T-pieces for coax connectivity; and the active bus topology (Figure 8.20c) where twisted pair cabling is used. The Arcnet Trade Association is responsible for developing Arcnet and one of their proposed enhancements is a data rate increase to 5–10 Mbps, thereby extending its appeal.

While Arcnet is a commercially successful token passing system, it is not formally standardized and so it is unlikely to significantly increase its market share. The token passing bus standard is the IEEE 802.4. Figure 8.21 shows the recommended token bus architecture, which is similar in topology to the CSMA/CD networks and similar in operation to the Token Ring networks. The token is passed from NIA to NIA according to the address order (this may be pre-empted by the relative priority of the data frames held by the NIAs), high to low. Both the tokens and the data are broadcast and so the order of reception is independent of the logical order on the network. The token bus is capable of supporting 1, 5 and 10 Mbps data rates, and is available as broadband, carrierband and fibre optic systems. Ironically, while it enjoys standardized status its total market share is less than that for Arcnet and without the manufacturing automation protocol work its relevance is difficult to explain.

8.5.2   IBM LANs

Many people assume that IBM's commitment to the Token Ring precludes any involvement with rival LAN architectures. IBM is a commercial organization, it needs to make money, and as such it has an interest in any potentially lucrative market. It

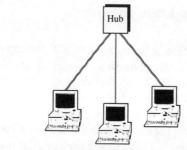

(a) Twisted pair hub architecture for Arcnet

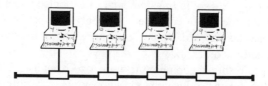

(b) Coax based t-piece junction architecture for Arcnet

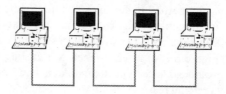

(c) Twisted pair daisy chained architecture for Arcnet

Figure 8.20   The architectures used for Arcnet LANs.

should therefore come as no surprise to find that it is has four different LAN product
ranges: the Token Ring, an industrial token bus LAN and two CSMA/CD systems
(Schwaderer, 1989). Each of these systems is engineered for a particular market; a
reflection that no one LAN is ideally suited to all possible applications.

The two CSMA/CD LANs are the baseband and broadband PC network
systems. The broadband version supports a 2 Mbps data rate within two 6 MHz
bandwidths. The network is formally termed a passive midsplit broadband system
using the 47.75–53.75 MHz and 216–222 MHz bandwidths for return and forward
communications, respectively. Unlike the broadband system, the baseband version is
based upon twisted pair cabling and once again supports a data rate of 2 Mbps. While
both systems support a lower data rate, in other respects they conform to the IEEE 802.3
standard, but interconnection between the IBM and standard versions requires a bridge.

The relationship between the IBM LANs is shown in Figure 8.22. The four
LAN systems are supported by adapters for the full PC and PS/2 computer range. These
hardware environments are then hosted by the umbrella of the IBM LAN support
program which consists of three separate protocol interfaces:

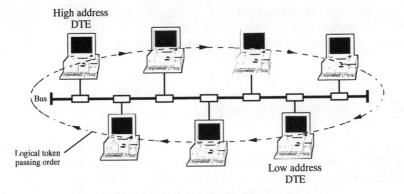

Figure 8.21   The IEEE 802.4 token bus architecture.

- Network basic input/output system (NetBIOS) – which is the standard applications programming interface for network based services.

- Advanced program to program communications interface (APPC) – which supports cross network communications, such as Token Ring to SNA.

- IEEE 802.2 (LLC) – which is the standard data link interface for LANs.

The original IBM PC network is derived from the Sytek LocalNet/PC architecture. This is now housed within the network protocol driver (IBM PC NPD) and is called the PC network layer architecture (PC/NLA). The PC/NLA is tailored for distributed communications across broadband PCX networks and consists of five layers: physical layer, which is CSMA/CD; link layer, normally LAP; network layer, which supports a CONS (send-and-pray) and a CLNS; transport layer, which has a datagram and reliable byte stream service; and session layer, which has four management and data transfer protocols.

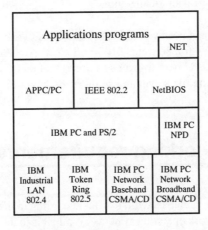

Figure 8.22   The IBM range of LANs.

Clearly, IBM are committed to LAN technology, but while they are supportive of the standardization efforts they are still maintaining an active development of SNA, particularly with respect to its LAN interconnectivity.

8.5.3   Low cost solutions

The gradual reduction in the cost of LAN specific ICs has meant that it is now possible to purchase some NIAs for under £100 (the latest single chip CSMA/CD is reputed to cost under £20 when purchased in bulk) – Token Ring NIAs are still considerably more expensive than their CSMA/CD counterparts. This dramatic reduction in the hardware costs has now been accompanied by a lowering of NOS costs. The results of this are threefold: the more idiosyncratic low cost solutions have seen a reduction in their market, network downsizing is possible on the smallest scale and cost effective networking is now possible for the smallest of systems (Bridges, 1986). Four of the more popular low cost LAN solutions are:

- LANtastic – this is supplied by Artisoft and supports its own peer-to-peer CSMA/CD type network (2 Mbps data rates) as well as the IEEE 802.3 version.
- NetWare Lite – which is the entry level NetWare solution. Its two most significant advantages are that if necessary it is possible to upgrade to the full NetWare and the full range of interfaces are available.
- TOPS – which is produced by the SUN Microsystems offshoot, Sitka. TOPS is a peer-to-peer system which supports all of the major CSMA/CD and LocalTalk NIA manufacturers.
- PowerLan 10 – is supplied by Power Technology and is compatible with NetBIOS and many of the major CSMA/CD NIAs. It supports both client/server and peer-to-peer architectures.

Using the above systems it is now possible to install a network systems including the NIAs, cabling and NOS for between £100 and £200 per node. The further cost advantage of the entry level peer-to-peer systems is that there is no requirement for a dedicated PC to act as the file server and so there are fewer hidden costs.

8.6 Internetworking requirements

No two networks are the same. Networks differ according to their architectures, their protocols and their network operating systems. While it is in the interest of the user to have compatibility between systems it is important for manufacturers to be able to differentiate their products from those of their competitors. This leads to problems when trying to internetwork these different systems, such as:

- Most computer systems were developed with proprietary architectures and included proprietary network interfaces. This is further compounded by the need to ensure that new developments do not isolate the established user community and so a system's history is carried into its future.

- Manufacturers interpret standards differently and in many cases each interpretation is valid – this is a reflection of the difficulty of producing a clear and unambiguous standard without over-specification. Even without different interpretations problems are still caused by the evolution of the standards themselves – consider the situation regarding the different versions of X.25.

- The speed of development for new products means that, in many instances, once a network has been installed it is based upon old technology. This makes designers and planners conservative and uncertain of how to plan for the future. In turn this makes it difficult to justify continual renovation, which means that compatibility problems become accentuated.

- New manufacturers are continually entering the networking device product market and they need products that are different from those of their competitors. This causes a proliferation in the jargon used to describe identical products but also means that new functionality is regularly introduced.

- The current 'management thrust' is for integrated systems and services. Although this is fine in principle it is currently impossible to provide. Such requests are becoming more common and whilst the use of devices that conform to standards does simplify the problem, in many cases it is still impossible.

Given that internetworking is such a difficult task, in all but the simplest of networks, what requirements need to be considered when approaching such a task? The types of requirements that should be considered are:

- What is the range of computers and computer devices which have to be interconnected? Who are the device manufacturers and what is the relationship between their proprietary systems, other proprietary systems and the standardization efforts? This information will provide some insight into which and when new computer systems should be purchased, and the order of device retirement.

- What is the range of protocols, network operating systems and applications used? Who are the manufacturers of these systems and what are their future integration plans with regard to their other products and competitors' products? This will dictate the type of interworking devices required.

- What is the current distribution of users across the physical network and is this a reflection of how they are expected to work? New network services will almost certainly mean different user practices, so it is important to consider other changes, such as the physical locations of users. It is important to make sure that the network is not designed or altered for working practices which by definition will change anyway.

- What form of integration is needed? Identify which systems need to be interconnected now and assume that the others will follow some time in the future. It should not be an intention to force all interconnected systems to be identical, simply that they need to be able to swap information. The interconnection mechanism should be as flexible as possible, to permit further interconnection. In contrast, the user systems should be focused on user needs to ensure the appropriate level of service. The user needs must not be compromised for the sake of interconnectivity.

8.7 Summary

The development of open systems is dependent upon manufacturers. It is their experience of, and willingness to release, the details of their proprietary systems which is used to develop the new standards. The success of a new protocol architecture is no longer that important because the impetus of the standardization effort has focused a significant amount of attention on the problems of internetworking. The next step is to consider the internetworking of proprietary systems.

Table 8.4 collates the principal manufacturers and their products for three product categories: systems architecture, network operating systems and network interface adapters. Both IBM and Digital, the major system suppliers, have product ranges of great depth and breadth and although they were originally aligned to different LAN architectures, Token Ring and ethernet respectively, this is no longer the case. The major network operating system supplier is Novell, with some 50% of the PC LAN market. IBM and Proteon are the major suppliers of Token Ring adapters with 3COM the leading supplier of CSMA/CD adapters.

In the USA the ratio of CSMA/CD to Token Ring installations is approximately 55/45, respectively, whereas in Europe it is 60/40. The initial general market trends implied that within Europe there would be a gradual increase in the number of Token Ring installations as compared to CSMA/CD, becoming similar to that in the USA. However, the latest market survey suggests that this may not now be the case. The most significant growth is expected in the area of NOSs with a projected 50% increase in the number of networked PCs during the next five years. It is important to be aware that:

- Irrespective of the future success of OSI/RM, or its successors, there will always be a significant proprietary network market presence. Companies like Digital and IBM have too large an established clientele dependent on their proprietary systems for these to be 'dropped'. The only possible solution is the support of open interconnectivity or long-term migration.

- The Internet Protocol Suite (IPS) has an extremely important role to play in the

Table 8.4 The major manufacturers for networking products.

Product category	Manufacturer	Product name
System architectures	Banyan	VINES
	Burroughs	Burroughs network architecture
	Digital	Digital network architecture Advantage-networks (DECnet phase V)
	Honeywell	Distributed systems environment
	IBM	System network architecture
	ICL	Information processing architecture
	NCR	Distribued network architecture
	Sperry Univac	Distributed communications architecture
Network operating system	Apple	AppleTalk and AppleShare
	Banyan	VINES
	Digital	PCSA, Pathworks
	Hewlett Packard	HP LAN Manager
	IBM	LAN server, LANRES, OS/400
	Microsoft	LAN Manager, Windows for Workgroups, Windows NT
	Novell	NetWare and NetWare Lite
	Sitka	TOPS
	SUN	Network file system
	UB	Net/One LAN Manager
	Xerox	Xerox network system (XNS)
Network interface adapters	Apple	LocalTalk
	BICC	IEEE 802.3
	IBM	IEEE 802.5, CSMA/CD and IEEE 802.4
	3COM	IEEE 802.3
	Cabletron	IEEE 802.3, IEEE 802.5
	Hewlett Packard	IEEE 802.3
	Intel	IEEE 802,3, IEEE 802.5
	Madge	IEEE 802.5
	National Semiconductor	IEEE 802.3
	Olicom	IEEE 802.5
	Proteon	IEEE 802.5
	RAD	IEEE 802.5
	StarTek	IEEE 802.5

establishment of open systems. The Internet protocols have already been recognized as *de facto* standards in a number of areas, including network management. Migration to these protocols will greatly simplify a further migration (to say OSI/RM) and, more importantly, they provide a cost effective method for rationalizing a networking infrastructure.

- There are two basic approaches to NOS support: client/server and peer-to-peer. The client/server approach uses a centralized file server whereas the peer system makes all users equal and provides them with direct access to each other local disk storage.

- The Xerox network system was the first NOS designed specifically for the LAN environment. The protocols developed for this were then used as sources for NetWare and VINES. A combination of these plus the Internet suite accounts for most of the protocols used to support the physical, data link, network and transport layer services in most of the proprietary NOSs.

- While the CSMA/CD and Token Ring techniques dominate the LAN market (accounting for some 75% of all installations) there are several other commercially available and successful systems. Both Arcnet and the IEEE token bus have firmly established niche markets and many specialist systems are designed for proprietary environments, such as AppleTalk for Apple computers.

- One of the current trends is in 'downsizing' or moving to smaller systems more suited to the task in hand. From the point of view of networking this is reflected in the increasing popularity of entry level systems such as Artisoft and LANtastic, which supply a complete networking solution (NOS, network adapters and cabling) for as little as £100 per node.

- There is no doubt that the relationship between manufacturers in the field of networking is undergoing, and will continue to do so, a rationalization. Many of the successful start up companies of the 1970s and 1980s are either being absorbed by the larger more established giants such as Digital and IBM or are establishing very close trading links. It has been predicted that by the end of the decade only five or six distinct network manufacturers will exist and that in the main these will be conglomerations of those that exist at the present time. Perhaps one-stop shopping will once again become inevitable.

- Internetworking is a very difficult problem. The problems for internetworking are caused by commercial competition between rival manufacturers, the wide range of different products all providing similar functions but idiosyncratic capabilities and the problems in producing concise and effective standards. Network integration will be a major problem for many years to come.

9

Network Relays

9.1 Introduction

Internetworking can be interpreted in a number of ways. Strictly speaking, it refers to the linking of networks to create an integrated infrastructure within which the original network components retain their own status – that is, they are not merged into a single homogeneous network. Unfortunately, it is often difficult to readily create an integrated network because of inherent incompatibilities: LANs do not simply 'plug-into' a WAN.

As systems converge into networks, creating distributed systems, the term internetworking becomes wider and more far-reaching in its implications; it is no longer just about linking two public X.25 networks, it is about all of the services that need to be provided in order to allow effective sharing of resources across networks. As a result, real internetworking is about delivering functions to end users, not just installing cables and boxes to provide physical interfaces. In fact, it is becoming more usual for the term 'internetworking' to refer to physical connectivity and the term 'interworking' to be applied to the protocols, management and applications needed to support the user. Therefore, the integrated network is concerned with both internetworking and interworking, or more succinctly, interoperability.

It is common practice among the networking community to dismiss the OSI/RM as unwieldy, unavailable, irrelevant to modern communications systems and, with particular reference to internetworking, part of the cause of the problem. All of these criticisms are true but in most cases overstated. The intention here is to use the rich and exhaustive set of ideas, structures and principles of the OSI/RM as a common language to describe all networks based upon similar principles. This is what manufacturers do, and in some cases it is in response to pressure from the standardization committees, which makes it even more important to be able to compare what is claimed with reality.

9.2 Relays and the OSI/RM

The layered nature of the OSI/RM means that networks can be interlinked at different levels: layer 1, layer 2 and so on. This gives rise to the four basic types of relay, commonly referred to as the repeater, the bridge, the router and the gateway (Miller, 1991). The secondary types of relay are the switch, bridge/router, router/bridge, the brouter and the transport bridge. Each of these relays provides a functionally different class of network connectivity, which means that in most real networks there is more than one type of relay in use.

Figure 9.1 shows the relationship between the four basic relays and the well known 'eight' layer OSI/RM; the data link layer has been split into its two constituent sublayers for LANs. The connectivity supplied by each of these relays can be summarized as (Held, 1993):

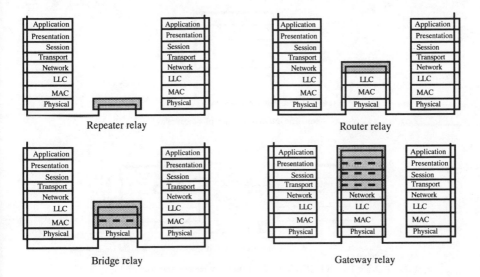

Figure 9.1 The four basic internetworking relays.

- Repeaters are the simplest form of relay and are used to link networks at the physical layer. They are used to overcome the restrictions caused by single segment usage such as the number of users, cable length and so on. Repeaters construct a single physical network (or extended LAN) which is accessed using one type of LAN MAC only. This means that whatever happens on one segment will ripple across on all of the other linked segments. It is also possible to connect together LANs of a similar type but which use different media; for example, a repeater could be used to link together a 10BASE5 (coax) and a 10BASEF (fibre) pair of LANs, in a fully transparent manner.

- Bridges are used to create a logical network and in many cases they are used to interconnect networks that have already been extended using repeaters. The bridge can be considered as an intelligent repeater because it is capable of deciding whether or not to forward frames. This technique is used to link LANs which may be many kilometres apart and/or where the user load is too high for a single physical network.

- Routers are used to interconnect different subnetworks to provide a well connected and reliable network. They are also capable of routing traffic so that the network load is evenly distributed, thereby reducing the likelihood of congestion. Routers can interconnect different types of LAN provided the end-systems use a common network layer protocol, such as IP, and so they provide subnetwork transparent connectivity.

- Gateways are used to connect end-systems whose host protocols have varying degrees of difference. At the simplest level this is a translation between different transport layer protocols whereas a more sophisticated translation is needed between different proprietary protocols, such as SNA and DNA. This

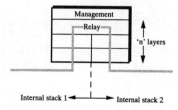

(a) The internal structure of a local relay

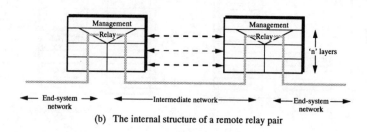

(b) The internal structure of a remote relay pair

Figure 9.2 The general internal structure of a relay.

means that gateways operate at levels four, five, six and seven of the OSI/RM but the application layers must have a common intention: it is not possible to convert an electronic mail service to a terminal emulation service, for example.

The internal structure of the relays will be discussed in considerably more detail in the following chapter. However, it is appropriate to briefly describe their general architecture. Relays support one of two architectures depending on their intended connectivity: local and remote. A local relay provides back-to-back LAN connectivity whereas a remote relay makes use of at least one intermediate network (Figures 9.2a and 9.2b, respectively). The implication in Figure 9.2b is that some form of routing is taking place (this is the appropriate form of address mapping between the local and the intermediate network) as well as the conversion process from one environment to another; the diagonal lines are used by the standards organizations to denote the presence of routing. In both cases the relay supports a management function as well as the basic relay entity. The management function permits the network management centres to interact with the relay as well as enabling relay-to-relay management communications such as routing table updates. Each relay consists of at least two stacks (one for each physical network supported) with the number of layers in each stack depending on the type of relay and intermediate link.

Unfortunately, as is the case in many instances within the field of networking, the standardization bodies use a more formal set of terms when describing network relays; 'gateway' is the generic term used in the OSI/RM for a 'relay', but industry uses this term to describe a particular type of relay used for protocol conversion. Their first distinction is to classify internetworking relays into one of two categories (as presented in the draft version of IEEE 802.1):

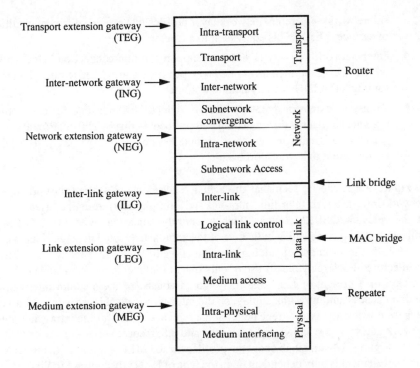

Figure 9.3 The formal OSI/RM categorization for gateways/relays.

- Intra-network gateway, which is concerned with the interconnection of similar LAN segments to create a single extended LAN.

- Inter-network gateway, which is concerned with the interconnection of LANs with MANs and WANs to form an integrated network.

The adoption of this classification leads to a further refinement in the definition of internetworking relays which reflects the principle of layering within the OSI/RM – this refinement is shown in Figure 9.3 (Stallings, 1990a). The four lower layers of the OSI/RM and their associate sublayers creates six separate relay definitions:

- Medium extension gateway (MEG) – to support the extension of the basic LAN segments to overcome the limitations imposed by cost effective engineering. The MEG is equivalent to a 'repeater'.

- Link extension gateway (LEG) – to support the interconnection of similar LANs to establish an intelligent repeater function. The LEG is equivalent to a 'MAC bridge'.

- Inter-link gateway (ILG) – to support the interconnection of similar and different LANs but using static routing relationships. The ILG is equivalent to a 'Link bridge'.

- Network extension gateway (NEG) – the interconnection of asymmetric subnetworks – different network layer profiles that provide different qualities of service. The NEG is equivalent to a 'router'.

- Inter-network gateway (ING) – to support the interconnection of networks which use a common network layer protocol and which require dynamic routing. The ING is equivalent to a 'router'.

- Transport extension gateway (TEG) – which is responsible for connecting together similar but different transport protocols – that is, TP0 to TP4 and so on. This was originally termed the distributed system gateway (DSG). The TEG is equivalent to a 'transport bridge'.

In Figure 9.3 it can be seen that the actual relay elements (Intra-transport, Inter-network, Intra-network, Inter-link, Intra-link and Intra-physical) are defined as sublayers of the relevant OSI/RM layer. This is entirely consistent with the OSI/RM's philosophy of layering and is indicative of the approach adopted in networking when faced with the problem of adding new functionality into an already established architecture. Each relay makes use of only one of the internetworking sublayers. In the case of a bridge, or LEG, the relay would consist of the medium interfacing, medium access and intra-link sublayers: the intra-physical sublayer is inappropriate because this is only used in repeaters. Some typical profiles for the intra- and inter-network gateways are shown in Figures 9.4 and 9.5, respectively.

Figures 9.4a and 9.4b show the profiles for the MEG and LEG. In both cases the relay element is only dependent upon the type of LAN. By contrast, in Figure 9.4c the relay is dependent on the subnetwork access protocol (SNAP), which provides mixed LAN connectivity by defining a fixed global addressing scheme to which the individual LAN addressing systems are mapped.

All of the inter-network gateways are protocol dependent. The NEG and ING profiles, shown in Figures 9.5a and 9.5b, respectively, are subtly different and reflect the fact that the network layer is composed of three sublayers within which are several different but valid combinations. The NEG supports an asymmetric system in which the LAN access profile must be enhanced to support the WAN access capability. In this example the ISO 8881 and 8878 protocols are of local significance only and are used to ensure that the X.25 PLP can be used in the OSI/RM and LAN based architecture; this is necessary because in its native form the X.25 PLP does not support the OSI/RM CONS. Figure 9.5c shows the TEG profile which is being used to support the TP4 and TP2 connectivity, but which, more subtly, is also being used for connectionless to connection oriented subnetwork interconnection. From the point of view of the transport service, TP2 and TP4 are symmetric but the full profiles are asymmetric and so the transport service is being used to provide a common platform.

The OSI/RM definitions for the different relays have been introduced for completeness and to ensure that at least some familiarity with the formal terms is provided. In most environments the common usage names for the relays are used and the responsibilities of each of these four basic relays can be loosely summarized as:

- Repeaters interconnect similar LAN segments to form a single extended LAN

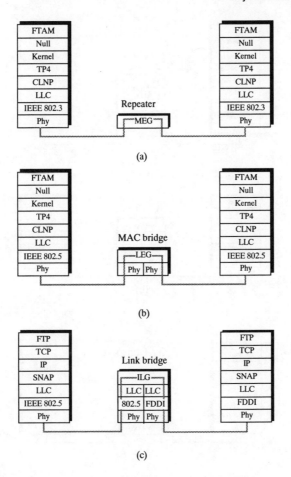

Figure 9.4 Typical protocol profiles for intra-link gateways.

- Bridges interconnect similar LANs to form a single subnetwork
- Routers interconnect subnetworks to form a single network
- Gateways interconnect different networks to form an integrated network.

9.3 Repeaters

The most basic relay is the repeater. This provides physical interconnectivity between like LANs, wherein the only permitted difference between them is their type of channel. A schematic representation of the internal architecture of local and remote repeaters is shown in Figure 9.6. The profile for the local repeater (Figure 9.6a) shows

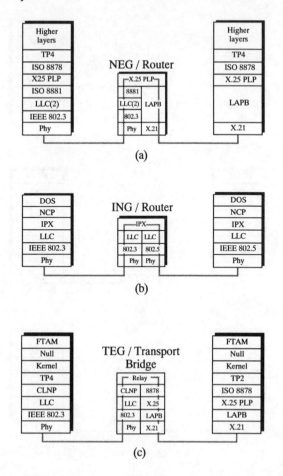

Figure 9.5 Typical protocol profiles for inter-link gateways.

the common management facility and the physical layer above the actual media interfaces whereas in the case of the remote repeater (Figure 9.6b) there is an intermediate network interface supported by an appropriate physical layer. The local profile supports back-to-back connectivity whereas the remote profile provides connectivity across a few kilometres.

9.3.1 Repeater usage and functionality

The repeater provides the network designer with the capability to exceed the engineering limitations imposed by the original requirement for cost effective product engineering. By definition the resulting networks are more complex and therefore more unreliable, so some of the most important features of a repeater are concerned with

(a)   The internal structure of a local repeater

(b)   The internal structure of a remote repeater pair

Figure 9.6   The internal profile architecture for a repeater.

limiting the effects of fault conditions; paradoxically it is the basic functionality of the repeater itself which threatens the reliability of the whole network. The most important functions required of a repeater are:

- Full signal restoration – the full regeneration of the signal to its original structure. This is not simply the reamplification of the signal but usually includes some interpretation of the received signal.

- Full preamble restoration – in the case of the CSMA/CD LANs it is essential that the preamble does not become excessively eroded when passing through a repeater. In modern repeaters the full preamble is regenerated; however, this algorithm also causes it to exceed the original size and so this causes inter-packet gap shrinkage. The result of both problems is that only a limited number of repeaters can be used in an end-to-end link.

- Faulty cable isolation – this is needed to ensure that the effects of a fault on one of the segments do not ripple across the full network architecture and cause a complete failure. Repeaters continually monitor each of their segments and are therefore able to detect and isolate (by partitioning) the faulty segments.

- Mixed cable support – each of the LAN standards supports a range of different cabling media and so the repeater is designed to provide interconnectivity between these. It is particularly important to support cabling mixes between UTP, STP and fibre optic for Token Ring, and coaxial, UTP and fibre optic for CSMA/CD networks.

- Management interface – integrated network management demands that the repeaters themselves be manageable devices. This provides functionality such as remote partitioning of segments and in some cases the capability to limit the transfer of data between identified segments.

Repeaters are bit sensitive devices and so they operate independently of the frame structures. Conversely, it is impossible, in principle, for a repeater to operate according to information contained within a frame, so intelligent frame switching is beyond its capability. However, some of the more recent functional innovations for repeaters enable them to read frame addresses and to supply services such as data privacy.

9.3.2   Types of repeater

The term repeater is used generically to describe a series of similar devices, each of which support the same functionality but which must be used in different architectures. The different types of repeater are used in the following situations:

- Local repeaters are used when the two LANs are in very close proximity – that is, back-to-back connection of typically no more that 100 m separation.

- Remote repeaters allow the linkage of LANs that are up to 2000 m apart. Each LAN has its own half repeater with the two halves typically being connected by a fibre optic cable.

- Buffered repeaters are used if very long distances must be crossed to link CSMA/CD LANs. These repeaters store the full data frame and forward it when the forward channel is clear. Buffered repeaters are non-discriminating bridges.

- Multiport repeaters are used to interconnect LANs whose architecture is based upon linear cabling – that is, passive bus systems. These are commonly used in CSMA/CD based LANs, such as for 10BASE2 and 10BASE5 connectivity.

- Hub repeaters are the multiport equivalent for UTP, STP and fibre optic based cabling systems. In these systems the users are supported as point-to-point links fanning out from the central hub. For installations where the hub is a standalone device – it cannot be interconnected to other hubs – then it is commonly termed a concentrator.

- Modular rack repeaters are used when a connection centre is required to act as a single point of repeater interconnection. Each module in the rack acts as either a multiport or hub repeater and in the latest generation of racks they can support mixed LANs (cross traffic is not permitted).

- Stackable hub repeaters are hub repeaters which can be stacked to any depth. In most cases the stack functions as a single logical and physical network, irrespective of the distance between the stack components (they do not have to be stacked on top of each other). Stackable hubs are the latest, cheaper alternative to modular rack repeaters.

Excluding the use of the third generation modular rack system, the repeater based Token Ring and CSMA/CD systems are treated as separate architectures and are commonly structured as shown in Figure 9.7. Figure 9.7a shows both local and remote

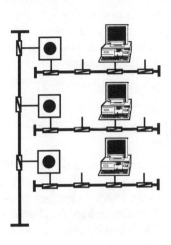

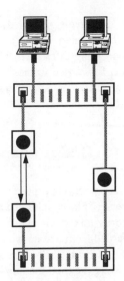

(a) Ethernet repeater architecture   (b) Token Ring repeater architecture

Figure 9.7 Typical repeater based network architectures.

repeaters supporting four 10BASE5 segments and using the classical backbone approach. A more compact version of this architecture would make use of a single hub repeater to replace the backbone (Hegering, 1993).

Figure 9.7b shows the use of local and remote repeaters in a Token Ring based system (Bird, 1994). Unlike the CSMA/CD systems, Token Ring networks are designed to employ repeater loops, thereby augmenting the reliability of the LAN. Another difference between repeater based CSMA/CD and Token Ring networks is that the Token Ring has no added restrictions on the number of repeaters that can be connected end-to-end and so it is possible to create very large networks; in CSMA/CD networks the maximum end-to-end distance, according to the original cabling guidelines, that can be supported by repeaters is approximately 3 km.

9.4 Bridges

In their most simple form bridges are intelligent repeaters. A bridge inspects the destination address of a frame and decides whether or not that frame has to be forwarded onto another of the connected LANs; normally a bridge is a two-port device but this is not always the case. Bridges are layer two relays, so they are dependent on the MAC and LLC sublayers only (repeaters are layer one relays). This dependence on two sublayers gives rise to two different types of bridge: the MAC bridge, which is used to interconnect similar LANs (cf. repeaters), and the link bridge, which is capable of connecting different LANs. Switches are the latest form of MAC bridge. They subject forwarded frames to the lowest possible bridge latency and as such they are similar in concept and operation to a traditional circuit switch exchange.

9.4.1   Bridge usage and functionality

The fundamental purpose of a bridge is to improve the performance capability of the network. This is achieved by breaking the network into two physically separate networks linked via the bridge. The bridge then decides which frames are to be forwarded from one network to another. Network performance is improved because without a bridge all of the users would be connected to a single segment, thereby increasing the total load on that segment instead of spreading it across two.

A performance comparison of repeater based and bridge based networks is shown in Figure 9.8. The lower curve shows how the network throughput would vary with offered load in a bridge free network. The performance for the same user population but this time distributed across a bridged network is shown by the upper curve. These two curves show that for a given offered load on the full network the throughput is greater for bridged architectures. This is to be expected because, for example, in the case of a 4 Mbps Token Ring network the non-bridged system has a full capacity of only 4 Mbps whereas in the bridged case this will be up to 8 Mbps (two bridged Token Ring LANs). The increase in throughput is therefore no surprise. The general functions that are required of a bridge are (Perlman, 1992):

- Data forwarding from one LAN to the other at the speed of the target LAN. In remote bridges the intermediate network carrier rate is normally considerably less than that of the LAN, so a severe bottleneck can be created. Further limitations are introduced because the target LAN has its own local data and so the forwarded information must compete for the bandwidth with this local information.

- Frame filtering determines which frames are to be forwarded and which are to be discarded. In the more sophisticated bridges this filtering process can be augmented to support user defined filters, which is a useful mechanism for establishing restricted zones.

- It is helpful if the bridges can learn the topology of the network and so establish a default filtering system. An alternative to this is to employ static tables which must be manually updated if the user distribution is altered. Another alternative is to make the end-systems responsible for determining the distribution of users across the network, for example by source routing.

- In the case of remote LANs the intermediate link should support a variety of links, such as kilostream (64 kbps) and megastream (2.048 Mbps), plus the

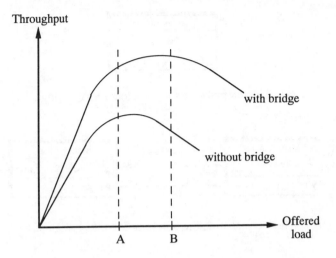

Figure 9.8   Bridged and non-bridged network throughput performance.

protocols to transfer the information reliably across the link.

• Interaction with a network management system is important but this is dependent on such an interface being within the bridge's firmware.

• Network resilience by using several bridges to provide multiple routes and loops across the network is important. While connectivity loops are important for fault resilience it is essential that data looping is avoided or else the network will become congested by duplicated frames.

9.4.2   MAC bridges

The MAC bridge provides connectivity between Token Ring and Token Ring or CSMA/CD and CSMA/CD. MAC bridges can compensate for a difference in carrying capacity and channel type. However, the interconnected LANs must support the same multiple access technique. The schematic internal architectures for local and remote MAC bridges are shown in Figures 9.9a and Figure 9.9b, respectively. The local bridge connects LANs in a back-to-back manner whereas the remote bridges make use of an intermediate network, cf. repeaters.

CSMA/CD LANs employ the transparent bridge only; these use the algorithms proposed by the IEEE 802.1 committees for the interconnection of locally and remotely bridged LANs. For historical reasons transparent bridges are also known as spanning tree bridges (STBs) even though the spanning tree algorithm is also used by source routing bridges in Token Ring LANs. The role of the spanning tree algorithm is to construct a single path between any two users and to ensure that if the physical topology

Management	
MAC	
Phy 1	Phy 2

(a)   The internal structure of a local MAC bridge

(b)   The internal structure of a remote MAC bridge pair

Figure 9.9   The internal protocol profile for a bridge.

of the network becomes altered, for example the failure of a bridge, then appropriate new pathways will be created. One of the advantages of the spanning tree algorithm is that bridges use self learning algorithms and configure themselves to the appropriate tree structure independently of the end-systems and so the presence of bridging is fully transparent to the users.

An example of a network architecture that uses transparent bridges is shown in Figure 9.10. The physical connectivity of the bridges is shown by Figure 9.10a, in which bridges 3 and 4 are connected to the same two LANs, as are bridges 1 and 5; this means that a failure of bridges 4 and 5, or 3 and 5, or 1 and 3 will not cause the network to become physically disconnected. The spanning tree algorithm configures the logical connectivity of Figure 9.10a as shown in Figure 9.10b; the manner in which the algorithm selects this bridge configuration is not relevant here. Once the physical architecture of the networks has been established and the bridges switched on, they do the rest. The resulting bridge configuration ensures that only one copy of the data frame is delivered – so that duplication and data looping do not occur.

In contrast, the internetworking of multiple IEEE 802.5 LANs has only been adopted relatively recently. There are three basic approaches:

- Source routing – in which a route searching technique is used by the stations to determine the best route across the structure. When the best route has been determined, the frame is sent across that route via the bridges whose addresses were identified using the route search.
- Transparent bridging – which follows the work being developed in the IEEE 802.1 standards. IBM systems do not support this as a standalone form.
- Mixed bridges – which will eventually become available to link 802.5 LAN groups which support different routing domains such as transparent and source

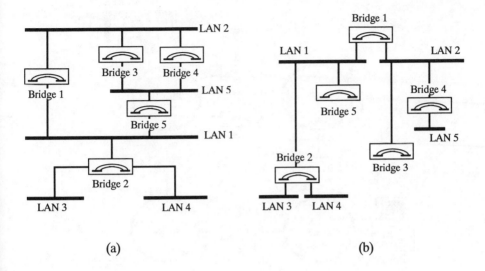

(a)   (b)

Figure 9.10 The operation of the spanning tree protocol.

routing. The current proposal is for the use of source routing transparent (SRT) bridges, thereby providing full freedom and vendor independence.

Source routing is the predominant bridging technique currently in use by Token Ring LANs. A typical schematic source routing architecture is shown in Figure 9.11, in which the four separate ring systems are interconnected by five bridges, thus creating three possible routes between any two users. In this system the initiating host must first ascertain the best route for communicating with the respondent. Using one of a variety of techniques (as discussed in Chapter 11) it obtains the best route through the bridges for communication between itself and its desired destination. This routing information (defined by a series of bridge and ring identity numbers) is now inserted in the data frame, which is then transmitted across the network. The bridges then make use of the frame's routing field to ensure that the data reaches its desired destination (Stallings, 1993).

Unlike the transparent bridge environment, in source routing there is no difference between the physical and logical connectivity of the network. The fundamental difference between the two techniques is described by the responsibility for route identification. In transparent bridging the end system NIAs do not need to consider whether they are operating in a bridged or non-bridged domain. The bridges are responsible for all frame forwarding. By contrast, in source routing the bridges are passive elements in the forwarding process and it is the end system NIAs that determine which bridges will forward the frames. The bridges merely act upon the routing field information.

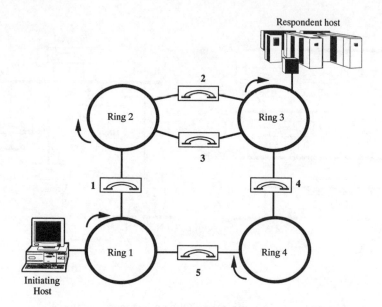

Figure 9.11 A Token Ring system using source routing bridges.

9.4.3 Switches

The latest innovation for bridges is that of switching. Switches or switch bridges are bridges which have minimal latency. This reduction in latency is achieved by having the switch forward the frames before they have been received in their entirety. Normal bridges are store-and-forward devices which receive a frame, evaluate the frame and, when necessary, forward the frame; all of this processing waits until the whole frame has been received. Switches on the other hand wait until the destination address part of the frame has been received, whereupon the frame is immediately submitted for forwarding. This means that the frame can be forwarded onto the target LAN before it has been completely received by the switch itself. In the case of an ethernet LAN this means that the minimum latency for a maximum length frame is reduced from 1.2 ms to 5 μs and that in many cases this lower latency is true for every frame, that is, the latency is now independent of the frame length.

9.4.4 Link and mixed bridges

Unlike the MAC bridge the link bridge is capable of interconnecting mixed LANs. The first bridge capable of such interconnectivity was IBM's 8209 device, which was actually named the 'mixed bridge'. In essence there are two types of link bridge:

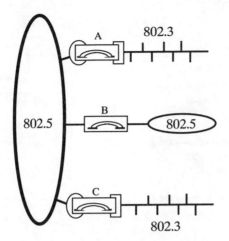

Figure 9.12 A link bridge in a mixed LAN architecture.

- Encapsulational bridge – which is used where the two end-system LANs are the same type but where the intermediate LAN is different (this is similar to remote bridges making use of a LAN as their intermediate link). Encapsulational bridges wrap the end-system frames in their intermediate system frames.

- Translational bridge – which supports true mixed LAN interconnectivity in that the frame structures are actually changed from one format to the other. Translational bridges must therefore be used if the communicating end systems are supported by different LANs.

A typical link bridge based architecture is shown in Figure 9.12. In this network there are two link bridges (A and C) and one MAC bridge (B). If communication between the LANs is to be limited to like-with-like then the two link bridges could be encapsulational – on other words, they would be supporting CSMA/CD-to-CSMA/CD communication across the Token Ring backbone. If, on the other hand, mixed end-system communication is required then the bridges must be translational.

9.4.5   Types of bridge

The term bridge is used generically to refer to a series of similar devices, each of which supports the same functionality but which must be used in different architectures. The different bridges are used in the following situations:

- Local bridges are used when the two LANs are in very close proximity – that is, for back-to-back connection of typically no more than 100 m separation.

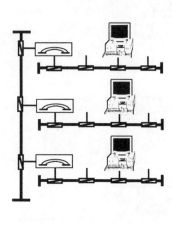 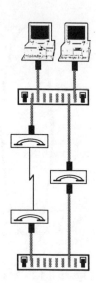

(a) Ethernet bridge architecture   (b) Token Ring bridge architecture

Figure 9.13 Typical CSMA/CD and Token Ring bridged network architectures.

- Remote bridges allow the linkage of LANs that can be hundreds of kilometres apart. Each LAN has its own half bridge with the two halves typically being connected by serial links.

- Multiport bridge is the term applied to a bridge that has more than just two ports. Unlike the definition for repeaters, there is no reference to the cabling type. The number and type of ports is variable to suit the architectural needs. However, it is common for there to be a mix between LAN and WAN access interfaces.

- Switching bridges are high speed multiport bridges which make use of a high speed circuit switched backplane to forward frames between the relevant segments. These bridges can begin forwarding the frame, when possible, before it has been fully received and so considerably reduce the bridge latency.

- Modular rack bridges, or bridge hubs (brubs) are used when a connection centre is required to act as a single point of bridge interconnection. Each module in the rack acts as a multiport bridge in its own right. Mixed rack architectures for CSMA/CD and Token Ring support are also available but cross-communication is not possible unless a link bridge is used.

Figure 9.13 shows typical CSMA/CD and Token Ring bridged networks. From the architectural point of view the CSMA/CD bridged networks are identical to their repeater counterparts. In the case of Token Ring the bridges are connected to the lobe ports of the MAUs whereas the repeaters are linked to the main ring segment ports, RIN and ROUT. In both the CSMA/CD and the Token Ring networks the presence of the bridges limits the flow of information across the network, thereby improving the network-wide performance. In the examples for the CSMA/CD network there are four separate carrier sensing domains and in the Token Ring network there are two token passing domains. Each domain is its own network and the bridges provide a means for the transfer of information from one network to another.

9.5 Routers

Repeaters and bridges, with the exception of the forthcoming link bridge, are technology dependent devices and are used for intra-LAN connectivity. The router is the lowest level inter-LAN connectivity device and as such is the current standard approach for connecting different LANs. The technology independence is achieved at the expense of using a common network layer protocol, whose addressing scheme is responsible for threading the data from the originator through the router system and finally delivering it to the correct destination.

The internal protocol organization of a full and half router (both of which are referred to as routers) is shown in Figure 9.14. In both Figures 9.14a and 9.14b the network layer protocols are common on both sides of the profile whereas the lower layers may be different depending on the type of network being supported. The router is capable of connecting different subnetworks and relies upon the natural process of encapsulation through the layering system to provide this capability.

Management	
Network	
LLC 1	LLC 2
MAC 1	MAC 2
Phy 1	Phy 2

(a)   The internal structure of a full router

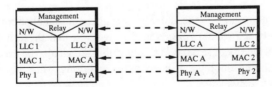

(b)   The internal structure of a half router pair

Figure 9.14   The internal protocol profile for a router.

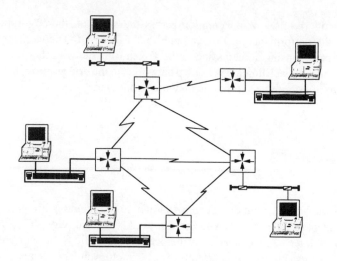

Figure 9.15 Highly connected networks based upon routers.

9.5.1   Router usage and functionality

The primary function of a router is to provide a highly reliable store-and-forward packet switching environment to support mixed subnetwork connectivity. Routers provide this reliability by establishing a highly connected network which, whenever possible, offers the routers two or more paths between any two subnetworks. A typical router based network architecture is shown in Figure 9.15, in which five routers are used to interconnect five mixed LANs. The routers make use of six wide area links and, with the exception of one Token Ring network, there are several different routes between any two subnetworks; for most of the network the failure of a single link will not cause the network to become disconnected.

The highly connected nature of a router based system creates problems for maintaining the availability of the network, for optimizing access to it and for ensuring an evenly distributed load across it. The functionality required of routers to provide these capabilities includes (Perlman, 1992):

- Routing algorithms – these are responsible for establishing the appropriate routes between subnetworks and for ensuring that these routes support the necessary quality of service. The algorithms must also be capable of responding to changing topological and loading conditions so that the optimal routes are always made available.

- Wide area connectivity – this defines the range of interfaces available to support the interfaces to the WAN. The interface options normally supported include kilostream, megastream, FDDI, ISDN, frame relay, synchronous lines, point-to-point fibre optic, microwave and more recently cell relay.

- End-system protocol – which is the support of the user data delivery protocol and which may support either a CONS or CLNS. In many applications the actual network layer protocol is dependent on the type of physical network; for example, for LANs it is common to use a CLNS.

- Intermediate system protocols – which are responsible for maintaining the address mapping tables on a host-to-router and router-to-router basis. These tables are populated according to routes selected by the routing algorithm and normally at least first and second choice selections are available.

- Tunnelling – the process by which a router makes use of a second network layer protocol to encapsulate the end-system network layer protocol. This is particularly necessary if the WAN is relatively unreliable as compared with the LAN. In this case the LAN would typically support a CLNS but the WAN would require a CONS and so the WAN's protocol is used to encapsulate the LAN's protocol, thereby forming a tunnel for the LAN information across the WAN backbone. This means that routers can act as tunnels for protocols which they cannot route.

- Data handling – once the user data leaves the 'safety' of the LAN then it becomes exposed to a more hostile and expensive environment. The routers therefore supply a range of data oriented services that are used to protect the data and to reduce the WAN access cost. These services include: data encryption and compression, data filtering and prioritization, information multiplexing and, most important of all, flow control.

- Management facilities – these are essential if the router is to be part of an integrated network management environment. The router's sensitivity to packets and the unique nature of network layer addressing mean that invaluable information is available to the router; it is essential that this information can be reported to the appropriate management centre.

9.5.2   Types of router

The classification of a router is comparatively simple (cf. the range of bridges) and is based upon three principles: the separation of the subnetworks for interconnection, the number of network layer protocols to be supported by the router and the number of local area and wide area access interfaces to be provided by the router. The environments for each of the types of router are:

- Routers allow the linkage of LANs that can be back-to-back or hundreds of kilometres apart (routers were originally LAN/WAN interface devices and it was only later that they were used for LAN/LAN connectivity). Back-to-back LAN connectivity makes use of the normal LAN cabling infrastructure whereas the more common access routing uses an intermediate network such as kilostream or megastream.

- Single protocol routers are devices that support a single network layer user data protocol. There will be other network layer protocols responsible for address support between the host systems and the routers, such as Novell's routing information protocol.

- Multiprotocol routers are devices that are capable of concurrently supporting many network layer user data protocols. Once again there will be many other support protocols also active within the router. While the router is capable of supporting many protocols there is no translation between them.

- Modular routers, or router hubs (rubs) are devices that support more than two ports, as is the case with most of them. This term is also applied to routers which may be inserted into modular rack systems, alongside repeater and bridge interfaces, to create a complete wiring centre solution.

- Boundary routers are the central switching agents for a star topology router network in which the devices at the spoke-ends are either remote bridges, brouters or low cost two-port routers. The spoke-end relays provide the WAN interface to the hub router, which switches the information onto the appropriate output spoke.

- Access routers are functionally reduced versions of modular routers. An access router normally has just three or four LAN and WAN interfaces and support for a reduced number of network layer protocols. The typical configuration of an access router is an ethernet or Token Ring LAN interface, megastream and ISDN WAN interfaces and two or three network layer protocols (including IP). This specification is considerably cheaper than the modular router alternative but unlike the boundary router it is still a full router in its own right.

A range of the physical options for a router is shown in Figure 9.16. Router (1) is being used to support back-to-back Token Ring and CSMA/CD connectivity while router (2) is used to link a CSMA/CD LAN with the wide area routing backbone. The modular router (3) shows the typical range of connectivity required to support several local area and wide area access links. If the users supported by all of these routers needed to communicate with each other then there must be a common network layer protocol used by those users and by all of the routers. When other network layer protocols are required for part of the network a multiprotocol router would be needed.

9.6 Mixed bridges and routers

It would appear from the brief descriptions of the relays that the categorization between repeaters, bridges and routers was distinct, even if the process of deciding when to bridge or route is not simple. Unfortunately, commercial pressures on the bridge and router manufacturers have meant that they have both further developed the capabilities of their respective products. Growth in the bridge market has reached a plateau and so

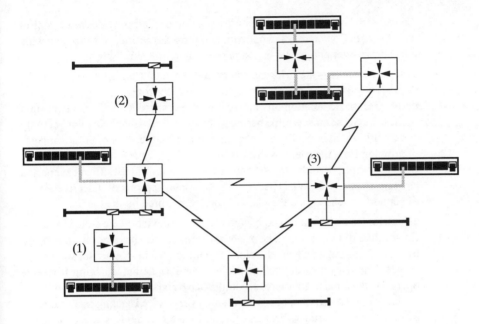

Figure 9.16 Typical router based network architectures.

these manufacturers are providing some routing capabilities more typically found in routers. Similarly, the router manufacturers have been limited in their capability to support the SNA (SDLC) and DECnet (LAT) markets. SDLC and LAT do not have network layer protocols and so cannot be routed. In response the routers have been provided with bridging functionality for profiles that do not possess a network layer.

The confusion in the market has been further compounded by a poor selection of terminology concerning the old and new product ranges. This has given rise to the bridge/router, router/bridge, routing bridge, bridging router and the ubiquitous brouter. Apart from the terms applied to the same device, the differences between these devices are subtle and based on their development roots. In may cases there is very little functional difference between them and selection is more concerned with the nature of the installed network devices and the suppliers normally used by the purchaser.

In all three cases the device is normally employed to provide wide area access, even though back-to-back LAN connectivity is also possible. The reason for this is that these hybrid devices are usually more expensive than their router equivalent, so they are usually employed to provide a more sophisticated connection capability. The three most common mixed bridge and router devices are:

- Routing bridges – the routing bridge and the bridge/router are one and the same. They are devices produced, primarily, by bridge manufacturers and derive their basic functionality and philosophy from bridges. In many cases bridge/routers support only one type of LAN (depending on the types of bridge) but support the network layer dependence features of a router. This provides more control over the data flow across the network and provides resilience across the wide area access over and above that supported by remote bridging.

- Bridging routers – the bridging router and the router/bridge are one and the same. They are devices produced, primarily, by router manufacturers and derive their basic functionality and philosophy from routers. The router origin of these devices is discernible because of their mixed subnetwork connectivity capability, which is usually a central marketing feature. One of the advantages of growing from the router is that the bridging links can be supported either by dedicated links, or multiplexed bandwidth with non-bridge traffic or supported as a tunnel across the WAN backbone network layer protocol. Clearly the type of support depends upon the class of service required by the LANs.

- Brouters – the original mixed bridge and router devices were called brouters, irrespective of their roots. The use of the term brouter has since been adopted by manufacturers who have developed an integrated bridge, router and hybrid device. The particular advantage of these devices is that changing from one operational format to another is accomplished by changing the device software: the hardware environment is fixed whether the device is acting as a bridge, as a router or as a true hybrid. By definition, these devices are capable of supporting multiple local and wide area access interfaces, and the actual configuration is normally selected to fit the particular environment. At present most brouters have proprietary interfaces and so they can only be connected to other identical devices, but in many cases open interfaces to standard bridges and routers are under development.

9.7 Protocol converters

The term 'protocol converter' is generally applied to any device which converts from one protocol to another via their common service feature. This transformation is performed on an intimate basis, so different protocol converters are needed for each transformation. The networking industry refers to such devices as gateways, whereas the standards organizations the term gateway as the generic name for an internetworking device; the term 'relay' has been used here to act as this generic name.

9.7.1 Gateways

Gateways are used when there are significant differences between the user network architectures, therefore the most common usage of gateways is interconnecting two proprietary protocol systems such as SNA and DNA. Irrespective of the differences between the protocol profiles they must both be used for similar purposes, for example file transfer, electronic mail and so on. This means that it is inappropriate to use a gateway to provide interconnectivity between an electronic mail system and a file access system because there is no common purpose between these two types of application. The typical uses of a gateway are:

- LAN-to-host (remote access) connectivity – where the LAN based PCs require seamless access to the host file server. One example of this, as shown in Figure 9.17a, is where a Novell NetWare file server is located on an IBM mainframe and the users are located on a LAN. The gateway provides LAN-to-SNA connectivity across which the NetWare operating system is now transported (Göhring, 1993).

- LAN-to-LAN connectivity – is required where the application systems are linked on common or different LANs but where their protocols are incompatible. Electronic mail is a typical example, as shown in Figure 9.17b, where different LAN NOSs support a proprietary mail system. A gateway would be responsible for seamlessly linking the different mail systems, thereby providing each user with the apparent view that their particular mail system is used by all of the hosts.

- LAN-to-WAN connectivity – is necessary when dealing with networks which have steadily grown and evolved from a traditional PSDN environment, for example in the financial sector. The newer LAN technology has to be interfaced to the WAN, as in the case of X.25 and ethernet connectivity, and so a gateway has to translate between the connectionless LAN and the connection oriented WAN.

Originally the LAN-to-host connectivity was a simple extension of the remote terminal access system but recent advances have developed a more peer-to-peer type of interface. The LAN-to-LAN connectivity is a refinement of the foreign server-to-foreign server access where the latter is used to support mainframe interconnectivity. In all three situations the gateway consists of three basic elements:

- A copy of the application profile used by the first of the end systems, including the appropriate subnetwork access hardware.

- A copy of the application profile used by the second end system, including the appropriate subnetwork access hardware.

- A piece of system software which sits on top of both applications (making use of their application programming interfaces – API) and translates between the two of them.

A gateway can be supplied in two basic architectural forms: the half and full gateway, both of which are referred to as gateways (cf. the router). A typical half gateway based architecture is shown in Figure 9.18. In this network each half gateway houses two protocol profiles: the application profile associated with its local end system and the

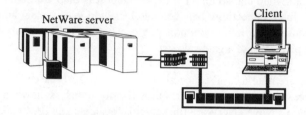

(a) LAN-to-host gateway connectivity.

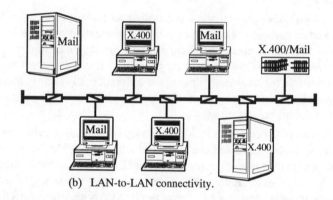

(b) LAN-to-LAN connectivity.

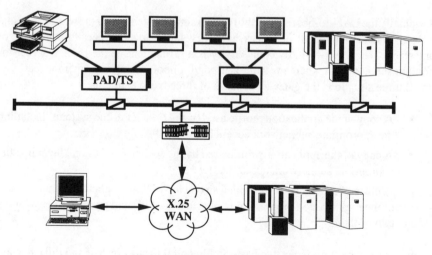

(c) LAN-to-WAN connectivity.

Figure 9.17 The basic uses of a gateway.

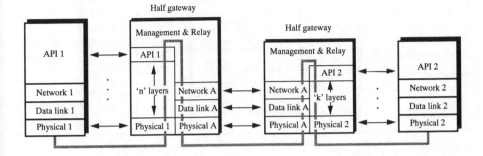

Figure 9.18 The internal architecture of a gateway system.

intermediate system profile which supports the gateway-to-gateway connectivity. The aspects which need to be considered when selecting a gateway are:

- The type of network architectures that are to be connected. It is important to establish the exact applications which need to be linked and the subnetworks being used, and to determine what types of host, PC, remote terminal and LANs need be connected.

- Whether or not an intermediate network is required. Politically, an intermediate network will ease maintenance problems because faults will be located in one of three areas (either side of the gateway or on the intermediate link) as opposed to somewhere in one amorphous mass.

- The number of hosts and remote devices that need to be supported. This number manifests itself in terms of the number of concurrent sessions needed and the buffering capability required in the gateway.

- The protocol translation will normally result in only the common services being supported. This means that, in general, there is a loss of functionality across a gateway and so any idiosyncratic functions of a particular network will not be available on a wider scale.

In many cases there is a significant mismatch in the raw data rate of the LAN and the networks on the opposite side of the gateway. Normally this is not of too great a concern because the amounts of data being transferred are very small, and even when this is not the case the data is normally segmented into packets of no more than 1000 octets at any one time. The only situations when this can become a problem are when the gateways are themselves very slow and/or they have a very large number of concurrently active sessions (over about one hundred sessions). In this case the user must either suffer the slow response or the number of open sessions must be firmly restricted.

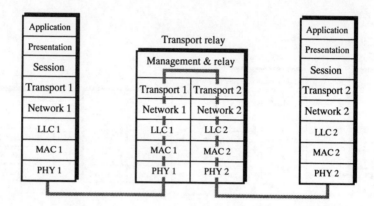

Figure 9.19   The internal protocol profile of a transport relay.

9.7.2   Transport bridges and gateways

A transport gateway is the relay that provides translation between two transport protocols. A transport bridge is a type of transport gateway but it is one in which the two transport protocols are based upon OSI/RM or related standards (Rose, 1990). The gateway performs full protocol translation whereas the transport bridge simply copies the messages from one transport protocol, filters and then forwards the appropriate ones to the other transport protocol. Naturally, this is only possible if the two protocols are similar and operate upon identical message structures.

The general architecture for the transport bridge/gateway is shown in Figure 9.19. In the case of the transport bridge the two protocols could be most combinations of the OSI/RM protocols (TP0, TP1, TP2, TP3, TP4) and Internet's TCP. There is no restriction on the protocols that can be translated by the transport gateway. The advantage of the transport bridge is that a single device is capable of supporting many protocol translations whereas a transport gateway is fixed for pairs of protocols only.

The transport bridge/gateway is normally supplied as an integrated unit, as opposed to using an intermediate network (cf. the full gateway). The functionality which should be considered when selecting a transport gateway includes:

- Protocol translation – the transport protocols must be interconnected. The form of the underlying services is also important; that is, the use of COTS or CLTS and, if necessary, the ability to translate between them.

- Concurrent sessions – the maximum number of point-to-point sessions that can be supported at any one time. While the gateway performs translation between only two transport protocols, there may be many different user pairs wishing to actively communicate across the gateway.

- Physical interfaces – the types of LAN that must be supported.

Ironically, there are very few transport bridges and gateways available for OSI/RM and

TCP interconnectivity. Most of the commercially available transport gateways are used for SNA/remote terminal connectivity where the remote terminals are normally PC based systems but which operate in a predominantly IBM based environment. A full gateway must be used for remote terminal access when the PCs are supported by non-IBM and IBM related systems.

9.8 Hub architectures

The hub has become a key device for interconnecting the internetworking devices themselves. Throughout the past few years, the architectures of the hubs themselves have become more sophisticated and a diverse range of hubs has been introduced to the marketplace so that it is now possible to purchase a hub which exactly fits the required specification. The fundamental feature of a hub is that it is the central switching element in a star topology network with the switching taking place on either a store-and-forward or on-the-fly basis. This central switching role exposes the network to the problem of single point of failure and so a key development during the past few years has been that of fault tolerance within the hub for reliability.

Originally, the zeroth generation hubs were no more than concentrators or wiring centres in the form of 10BASET repeaters and Token Ring MAUs. First generation hubs were the modular repeaters which supported the interconnection of many tens of LAN segments and which introduced the use of the collapsed backbone. Second generation hubs, or intelligent hubs, introduced dual redundancy and management whereas the third generation hubs now support repeater, bridge and router interfaces which are interconnected using one or more collapsed backbone switches. The next generation of hubs will use a common backbone switching architecture, based upon cell relay, that will enable the hubs to be linked using a cell relay switching network.

The latest innovation has been the introduction of low cost stackable hub repeaters. In principle, an almost unlimited number of hubs can be interconnected by stacking one on top of the other to create a single logical repeater. This means that the number of ports can be fixed to that required and this number can be readily expanded or contracted by adding or removing one or more of the stacked hubs. The range of functions currently available in hubs includes:

- Mixed interface interconnection – the support of repeater, bridge (transparent, source routing and source routing transparent) and router interfaces. Only the router interfaces provide mixed LAN interconnection.
- Dial-up remote access so that users can be linked to the system either through the traditional PSTN or via the cellular telephone network.
- Fault tolerance – dual redundant interfaces, ports and power supplies which are automatically switched when a failure is detected.

- Port switching – fixed segment switching so that user groups can be configured, thereby controlling the distribution of traffic on the network.

- Management – remote and local management of the entire hub itself. This normally includes hierarchical management of other hubs in the architecture and full control over each port in the hubs.

The advantage of using a hub-based architecture is that the network is easier to manage and maintain, the network can be easily extended and the traffic distribution across the network can be closely controlled by permitting or prohibiting different types of information to and from certain parts of the network. The issue of reliability has been addressed by providing fault tolerance in the hub itself, including dual redundant power supplies, as well as improvement in the build quality of the devices themselves.

The major criticism of the third and later generation hubs is that their collapsed backbone infrastructure makes them relatively slow when compared to networks based upon dedicated standalone devices. The introduction of cell relay based backbones operating in the gigabit region should ameliorate some of this problem but performance will always be a problem given that all of the traffic in the hub is supported using a single switching infrastructure. One of the fundamental aims of internetworking devices was to break the network into several independent but connected LANs so that the performance can be improved, whereas the hub is doing the reverse, albeit in a limited domain.

Hubs are an essential feature of any modern LAN infrastructure and their performance capability can be improved by limiting the number of ports and by using several interconnected hubs. This approach also removes the problems of a single point failure causing the collapse of the entire network.

9.9 Summary

The aim of internetworking is to provide an integrated network within which the individual subnetworks retain their own autonomy while still providing external access to their users. In the larger networks it is common for all four of the primary types of relay to be used, resulting in a structure similar to that shown in Figure 9.20. In this network the repeaters and bridges supply the intra-LAN connectivity in which the remote bridges make use of the backbone WAN. The backbone would normally consist of several different types of link, each of which would be supplied independently of the others, and so interconnection would have to be supplied by the relays themselves.

The routers and gateways provide the inter-LAN connectivity, both of which would make use of the backbone WAN. The gateways support remote PC access to the mainframe whereas the routers are used for mixed LAN connectivity. Clearly many

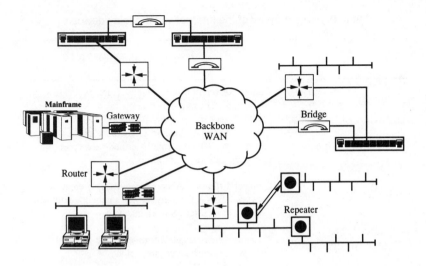

Figure 9.20   An example of the use of the four basic internetworking relays.

other network devices could be added to this system, such as terminal server/router combinations to provide added remote terminal access. The long-term concern for this network is the capability to manage it effectively (this topic is discussed in Chapter 14). This will be particularly difficult if the relays are purchased from different suppliers, each of which has its proprietary network management system.

The range of internetworking relays currently available is listed in Table 9.1. Their order in the list is also indicative of their relationship to each other and to the OSI/ RM. Generally speaking, the functional demands placed upon the relay increase the higher its position in the table, as do the unit costs. The cost of a repeater could be as little as £400 whereas for a gateway the cost could be as high as £75 000. In summary:

- The common usage names for the four primary relays are repeater, bridge, router and gateway. Further refinement of these relays gives rise to the MAC bridge, switch, link bridge, brouter, bridge/router, router/bridge and transport bridge. Manufacturer devices such as the trouter (terminal server/router hybrid) are also available but these are vendor specific.

- The selection between repeaters and bridges is clear cut. The only concern for selecting a bridge is when considering Token Ring networks and the problems of source routing and transparent bridge compatibility.

- The selection between bridges and routes is very complex, particularly if the brouter, bridge/router and router/bridge devices are also considered. In general the final choice is significantly influenced by the currently installed architecture and the manufacturing emphasis of the preferred suppliers, as well as functional considerations.

Table 9.1 A summary of the internetworking relay devices.

Relay	Function summary
Gateway	Connect different protocol architectures to create a single applications environment.
Transport bridge	Connect different transport protocols to create a single end system. This is formally termed a transport extension gateway.
Router	Connect different LANs (subnetworks) to create a network. This is formally termed a network extension gateway or an inter-network gateway.
Router / bridge	A router which bridges information that does not possess a network layer protocol.
Brouter	A true combined bridge and router but which relies upon proprietary inter-link protocols.
Bridge / router	A bridge which creates separate subnetworks by operating on the network layer protocol.
Link bridge	Connect LANs to create a single subnetwork. This is formally termed an inter-link gateway.
MAC bridge / switch	Connect similar LANs only, to create a single subnetwork. This is also called a link extension gateway.
Repeater	Connect similar LANs to create a single physical network. This is formally termed a medium extension gateway.

- Gateways are primarily used in the LAN/WAN internetworking arena and usually for remote terminal access. The choice of gateway is limited to the specific protocols requiring interconnection, so the only considerations are those such as the maximum number of supported concurrent sessions.

- In many of the areas concerning internetworking the OSI/RM standards are still vague and complex. Token Ring source route bridging and the general remote bridging standards are undeveloped, the suitability of the transport bridge is hotly debated, gateways (protocol converters) have not yet been formally considered and the internal structure and operation of the network layer are too complex for simple consideration.

10

Repeaters

10.1   Introduction

One of the important design features of an NIA is its power budget; that is, the power provided for the transmission of a signal and the amount of power required by a receiver for the successful reception of data. This power budget determines the maximum length of cable that can be supported by the network. From an engineering point of view it is possible to design NIAs that produce any required power capabilities. However, increased transmission power and receiver sensitivity is always accompanied by a higher production cost; it is the classical cost versus capability trade-off.

A repeater is the internetworking relay element that is used to overcome these power limitations (Miller, 1991). The use of a repeater means that the cost of improving the capability of each NIA is limited to the cost of a single repeater. The repeater was the first internetworking element to become established and, since its introduction, it has been gradually enhanced to provide a range of features designed to improve the overall reliability of the network as well as increasing its connectivity.

10.2   Functions of a repeater

The intrinsic relationship of the repeater to the cabling and multiple access systems means that different types of repeater are required for different types of LAN NIA. While the primary function of a repeater is concerned with signal regeneration it must also supply a certain amount of fault resilience. If this resilience were not provided then the very nature of the repeater would mean that its inclusion would make the network more susceptible to catastrophic failure (any failure on the network being repeated to all parts of the network).

10.2.1 Signal and preamble regeneration

In both the ethernet and Token Ring system the data is encoded in one form or another of Manchester II coding. This uses a signalling frequency twice that of the desired data rate, thereby providing the receiver with clocking information about the data signal. At a receiver the electronics is continually sampling the channel and attempting to detect changes in signal level. When signals are detected they are converted into their data equivalents of 0s, 1s and coding violations. If there is electronic noise then it is possible that the signal will not be detected or that its real value will be changed to some valid but incorrect value, such as a 0 to 1 conversion or vice-versa. This form of error is always possible but its likelihood increases the greater the attenuation of the signal – that is, the longer the network.

A repeater is responsible for restoring the signal to its original structure for the information being transmitted. A repeater does not simply reamplify the signal (this is the function of a line driver) but actually creates a new signal according to the data. Using this technique it is possible to repeat the data more reliably and to minimize the signal distortion caused by a repeater. It is also true, therefore, that repeaters must repeat and regenerate noise. If a data value becomes corrupted then that corruption will be faithfully repeated across the rest of the network. Also, if rubbish is put onto the network then this too will be repeated. This is particularly a problem in ethernet where it is important to ensure that the SQE function is disabled for all transceivers that are connected to a repeater. If this is not the case then the SQE signal is detected as transient data (data which is under some minimum length) and causes the repeater to issue a 96 bit jam signal. Clearly, an SQE causes significant noise on such a network.

A final function of the signal regeneration is ensuring that the preambles do not become eroded. The synchronization period for a receiver or repeater is typically two or three bit times – in other words, the first two or three bits of the signal are lost. This means that every device which has to actively regenerate the signal (not transceivers) causes loss of data. A preamble is prepended to the frame so that user information is not lost: the preamble is a sacrificial lamb. Of course, in a network with a large number of repeaters the preamble itself can become completely lost and so networks are strictly limited in the number of repeaters in any one end-to-end run.

For ethernet, all but the oldest of repeaters ensure that the preamble is itself fully regenerated. This regeneration is simply the automatic addition of a few bits (two to six) which means that the preamble now has a tendency to grow. This growth causes erosion of the interframe gap, which leads to consecutive frames being interpreted as one frame only. The number of repeaters must therefore be limited once again.

In the case of Token Ring the situation is somewhat different. The continual rotation of the token means that the NIAs maintain relatively good clock synchronization and so the preamble only needs to be a few bits long so that octet alignment can be provided. In fact the Token Ring repeaters do not cause preamble erosion or extension and so the number of repeaters is limited only by the total jitter (aggregated clock misalignment around the network) caused by them and the NIAs.

10.2.2 Fault isolation

Repeaters connect together identical LAN access schemes to create one physical network. This leads to the construction of relatively large LAN architectures with, in some cases, several hundred users. In such an architecture the failure of a single NIA could cause the failure of the entire network: an undesirable situation. To overcome this the repeaters are provided with the capability to partition faulty cable segments.

Before the repeaters can partition a segment they must first detect the fault. In ethernet systems this detection entails counting the number of consecutive contentions. If this number exceeds a threshold (typically sixteen) the segment is partitioned. This is because that number of consecutive contentions (equivalent to the number of attempted frame transmissions) implies that self contention is occurring, perhaps due to a fractured cable or failed terminator. In the early repeaters once a segment had become partitioned it had to be manually reintroduced by resetting the repeater. In their modern counterparts this reintroduction is now automatic and occurs as soon as 512 bits of valid data have been detected on the isolated segment.

In Token Ring systems, cable faults can only be detected by the loss of the phantom voltage on the main ring segments. Both MAUs and repeaters must provide the phantom signal to the main ring segments (as opposed to the NIAs and the lobe cables) and so active MAUs are needed. The absence of the phantom signal causes the partitioning and its reappearance causes the reintroduction of the segment.

10.2.3 Mixed cable support

It is essential that the repeaters can provide mixed cable support. In the most extreme case this entails the conversion of the signal from an electrical form into an optical one. The forms of conversion that must be supported are:

- Coax to twisted pair and vice versa.
- Coax to fibre and vice versa.
- STP to UTP and vice versa.
- Twisted pair to fibre and vice versa.

The connectivity between the different cabling systems is not just a matter of converting the signals from one physical form to another. In some instances there must be some logical consideration given to the operation of the system. For instance, in ethernet the jam signal has to be supported in a different way on fibre cabling to that on the copper cabling. In fibre a different frequency has to be allocated to the jam signal whereas in the copper architectures a random stream of data is sufficient to ensure that all of the transmitting nodes detect the contention.

One of the primary reasons for the current architecture of LAN systems is so that it is simple and relatively cheap to change from one cabling infrastructure to another. All of the cabling considerations are located external to the NIAs but make use of firmly established interfaces to the NIAs. The task of changing the cabling architecture then becomes that of laying in the new cable and changing the MAUs (either type).

10.2.4 Status display

One pressing problem in networking is the identification of failed devices. This difficulty is further compounded when the devices themselves do not provide status displays or, even more frustrating, have displays that are impossible to view when the element is *in situ*. The types of information which LEDs display include:

- Receiving and/or forwarding information along the segment
- Segment is active or partitioned.

This form of visual display is the minimum requirement for management support; while most repeaters offer the same operational characteristics, it is this sort of value added element that should be used to discern between competing suppliers' solutions.

10.2.5 Security

One of the growing areas of concern in LANs is that of security. In an ethernet or ethernet-like environment the information is broadcast to all of the NIAs, which then decide whether or not the information is addressed to them. This means that the transmitter cannot dictate which nodes will or will not physically receive the information, irrespective of whether or not the information itself is encrypted.

One of the latest features provided by ethernet hub repeaters is the capability to transmit information to only those nodes addressed in the frame. This function is now supplied in intelligent hub repeaters which learn the address of the node supported on each spoke. The repeater then examines the destination address of the frame and ensures that this frame is forwarded down the appropriate link only. The other links have random information transmitted down them to ensure that the CSMA/CD algorithm still functions correctly. This approach makes it impossible for the wrong node to receive the information and so improves the security of the network by masking the destination of information.

10.2.6 Management facilities

One of the more recent trends in repeater design is the inclusion of management facilities, both locally and via remote access. The management of repeaters usually entails the use of a PC or workstation connected to the repeater via a serial interface (part of an out-of-band management facility). The management software is normally supplied for the host workstation but in some cases it is located within the repeater itself. If this is the case then the PC/workstation merely needs to support some terminal emulation software or a terminal is connected directly to the repeater. The management control and information available via a repeater is limited to:

- Enabling or disabling specific ports on the repeater
- Enabling or disabling the entire repeater

- Password protection for access control to the repeater
- Remote access to other repeaters on the network
- Collation of the number of failure and recovery events on each segment.

Repeaters are not capable of interpreting the frame information which passes through them and so they cannot be used as a source for performance statistics – this is left to the bridges. The management facilities are limited to controlling the repeater environment and therefore to limiting the physical topology of the network.

10.3   Types of repeater

It is now possible to purchase a repeater which provides the exact connectivity required and for a reasonable price. This flexibility is provided because the connectivity requirements of different organizations vary considerably and so it is essential that the external architecture of a repeater can readily support a wide range of different configurations (Held, 1993).

10.3.1 Local repeater

The local repeater is responsible for connecting together two identical LANs, back-to-back; it is a two-port device only. This means that there is no intermediate network or cabling and so the maximum separation between the LANs is limited to the native cabling distances on either side of the repeater.

Figure 10.1 shows an ethernet architecture supported by a local repeater. In this figure the two 10BASE5 systems are linked by AUI cables to the repeater, which means that the two LANs must be within 100 m of each other (two AUI cables each of 50 m length). The equivalent architecture for Token Ring is shown in Figure 10.2. Here the two type 1 passive MAUs are linked to the repeater using an STP main ring segment cable. The maximum length of this cable is defined by the architectures on either side of the repeater, but according to the IBM guidelines this length must not be greater than 200 m (the maximum unrepeatered distance permitted between two wiring closets).

In both the ethernet and Token Ring situations the local repeater is acting as a simple cable extension in a local environment, for example on the same floor of a building, where all of the users are close to each other. The local repeater will cost between £400 and £800 depending on the type of cabling supported by the two ports, fibre interfaces costing the most.

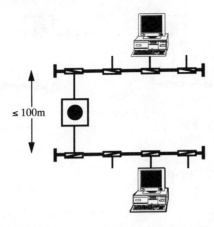

Figure 10.1   CSMA/CD local repeater network architecture.

10.3.2 Remote repeater

Remote repeaters are two-port devices used to link LANs which are less than 2000 m apart. These sort of links are nearly always based upon fibre optic channels but the linked LANs do not have to be fibre based because the repeater is responsible for the conversion. This type of repeater must be used in pairs for each repeater link – that is, half repeaters – and it is important that the two ends use the same repeater/repeater signalling scheme. This 'openness' is not a problem in ethernet; however, many Token Ring systems need the two remote repeaters to be supplied by the same manufacturer; special care is needed when considering fault tolerant architectures.

Figure 10.3 shows the remote repeater architecture for ethernet.. This produces a maximum LAN separation of 2100 m (including the AUI cables and the appropriate 10BASEF device). The equivalent Token Ring network is shown in Figure 10.4.

Once again the cost for the repeaters is in the £400 to £800 region. However, two are required (one at each end) and so the total cost is between £800 and £1600.

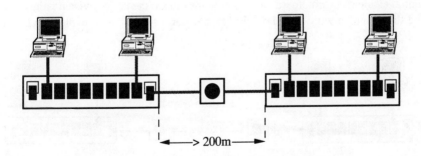

Figure 10.2   Token Ring local repeater network architecture.

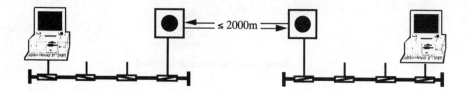

Figure 10.3 CSMA/CD remote repeater network architecture.

10.3.3 Multiport repeater

Multiport repeater is the term given to an ethernet repeater which supports three or more linear bus segments – that is, three or more 10BASE2 or 10BASE5 segments. In almost every instance such a repeater supplies at least one AUI port and so this can be used to support any type of cabling system once the appropriate transceiver is used. Figure 10.5 shows a typical multiport repeater architecture with two AUI and three BNC ports (used for the 10BASE2 systems). Multiport repeaters are used to create extended linear bus systems and until the introduction of twisted pair systems this was the best way to construct a structured cabling system.

Typical multiport configurations include the 2 AUI and 6 BNC ports, 1 AUI, 1 fibre and 6 BNC ports or 1 AUI and 14 BNC ports. The fibre ports are commonly used to provide repeater/repeater connectivity. The cost of such a repeater ranges from £900 to about £2000 depending on the number and type of the ports.

10.3.4 Hub repeater

Hub repeaters, or just hubs, are the equivalent of the multiport repeaters except they refer to the fibre optic and twisted pair point-to-point cabling systems. Again, the number of ports supported by each hub depends on the manufacturer but, typically, both ethernet and Token Ring hubs support eight or twelve ports. Hubs are one of the central elements in structured cabling systems (due to the use of twisted pair cabling) and this, coupled with the relatively low per port cost of a hub, explains why such

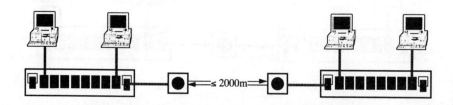

Figure 10.4 Token Ring remote repeater network architecture.

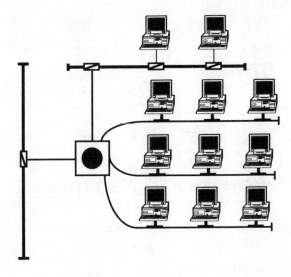

Figure 10.5 CSMA/CD multiport repeater network architecture.

structures are becoming more and more popular.

Figure 10.6 shows a 10BASET hub. The fibre optic equivalent has fibre replacing the twisted pair. The typical costs for a 10BASET hub are between £50 and £100 per port whereas the fibre equivalents are more in the region of £200 to £300 per port. The Token Ring hub equivalent is shown in Figure 10.7. Here the fault tolerant architecture is supported by the hub, so each MAU uses two of the hub's ports. In many Token Ring hubs it is possible to alter the port connectivity by changing its internal wiring. This is particularly useful if a single hub is to be used to support more than one type of cabling. Again, the cost is between £300 and £400 per port.

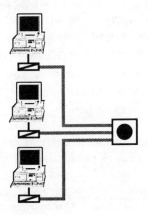

Figure 10.6 CSMA/CD hub repeater network architecture.

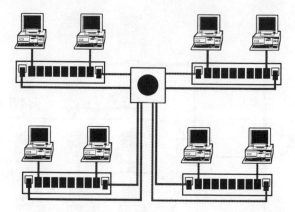

Figure 10.7   Token Ring hub repeater network architecture.

10.3.5 Modular repeater

Modular repeaters have become established as a central feature of large networks. A modular repeater is a collection of multiport and hub repeaters all linked via a single common backplane. It is also possible in the latest modular systems to support both Token Ring and ethernet systems using a single rack system but it must be stressed that no form of connectivity between the two systems is provided.

The hubs are normally available in many user selectable sizes and configurations. The range of interface slots available include:

- The hub management interface to control the entire hub architecture. This may also support dual card redundancy, with a 'hot swap' capability, to prevent the failure of a single card causing loss of network connectivity.
- Supplementary power supplies, which are required whenever extended hubs are used – each power supply can usually support up to four other cards. Extra power supplies can also be supplied as part of the rack's fault resilience features.
- Fibre interfaces for ethernet or Token Ring – typically up to eight of them.
- Twisted pair ports for either ethernet or Token Ring systems – typically between eight and sixteen of them.
- BNC and AUI connectors for ethernet – typically between two and eight ports.

Figure 10.8 shows an ethernet modular repeater system. This network is using four modular hubs, each of which has its power card and appropriate network interface ports. The two larger rack systems each support a management facility and this would provide local rack management. The general cost of a rack system is split into two sections: the cost of the shell itself, including the power supply unit, of between £1500 and £2500, and the interface port cards, which cost between £1000 and £2000 depending on their functionality. This means that for an 8 card modular repeater the cost could be in the region of £15 000, but this would interconnect dozens of users in

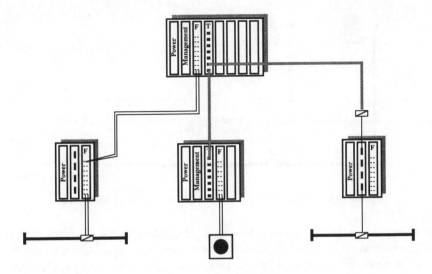

Figure 10.8 Modular repeater network architecture.

a robust, reliable and flexible architecture.

The CAU/LAM approach for Token Ring (see Figure 7.8) is IBM's modular repeater architecture for Token Ring networks. The CAU wiring centre is capable of supporting many users using different cabling systems via the LAMs. The management capability and fault resilience is supplied through the CAU's backplane.

The primary concern with these types of architectures is that should the power supply unit for the rack fail then the whole network becomes disconnected. However, if this does occur then at least it is easy to locate the failure, and restoring the network simply requires the replacement of the faulty card.

10.3.6 Buffered repeater

Buffered repeaters are similar in some respects to bridges. A buffered repeater does not forward a frame until the other LAN channel is idle – buffered repeaters are ethernet based systems. This means that the CSMA/CD mechanism is not propagated across the LANs and so the lower number of contentions permits more nodes to be supported by the network. Because the repeater does not filter information, all frames are passed across the link, thereby maintaining the broadcast nature of the system.

It is common to use this type of system when LANs must be linked across very long distances, for example in broadband systems, where the frame undergoes frequency translation and so on. The propagation characteristics are very different for broadband systems, so this type of repeater is necessary when linking baseband/broadband CSMA/CD systems. Figure 10.9 shows the typical architecture supported by buffered repeaters. The backbone broadband system supports the other three

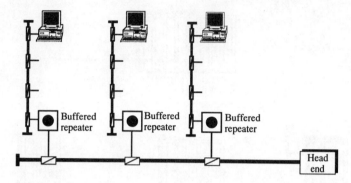

Figure 10.9 CSMA/CD buffered repeater network architecture.

baseband systems, thereby creating four separate CSMA/CD domains. The typical environment where this type of system is used is when broadband cabling is used for mixed services, for example voice and data. The CSMA/CD system can use this backbone cabling to provide data connectivity between its disparate baseband systems.

10.3.7 Repeater type comparison

The historic development of the repeater is reflected by the types of repeater that are now commercially available. The original two-port local and remote repeaters were well suited to simple architectures but extended systems needed multiport repeaters to provide simple connectivity for many hundreds of users. The introduction of the twisted pair systems and the gradual use of fibre optic as the backbone medium promoted the use of hub repeaters, and these were the final step before the introduction of modular rack architectures as integrated solutions.

The current trend is towards further integration and so the third generation rack systems (the first generation supported single LAN systems and the second supported separate Token Ring and CSMA/CD repeater systems in the same shell) house repeater, bridge and router devices in a common rack and on a collapsed backbone. Only the routers support the CSMA/CD and Token Ring translation whereas the other devices provide separate LAN domains using the common network infrastructure.

10.4 CSMA/CD repeater architectures

Given that there is a wide range of repeaters to choose from, and it thus being possible to purchase the exact box required, when, how and where should they be used in a CSMA/CD network?

10.4.1 Uses of a repeater

One of the most common uses of a repeater is to interconnect different types of cabling. Such an architecture is shown in Figure 10.10 where the multiport and hub repeaters are linked via the 10BASE5 backbone. This architecture supports the interconnectivity of three different cabling systems, all of which provide a single carrier sense domain and a 10 Mbps data carrying capability. In the case of CSMA/CD, the repeater itself is capable of detecting a contention and can issue the jam signal. This speeds up the process by which the detection of a contention is announced across the network. The jam signal issued by a repeater is 96 bits long, some three times longer than that issued by the NIAs, and so the worst case delay budget must consider the situation for a repeater detecting the contention and not that of a host's transceiver.

It is important to note that when the 10BASE5 and 10BASE2 systems are used the cables have to be terminated with 50 ohm impedances. When the cabling is connected directly to a repeater – that is, no external transceiver is used – then the cable may or may not have to be terminated, depending on the internal configuration of the repeater. Some repeaters supply internally terminated coaxial interfaces, some do not and some are user selectable. When internal termination is not used the cable is normally connected to the repeater using a T-piece which has either further cabling or the terminator attached to it.

Another typical usage of a repeater is when the limit on the maximum number of users per segment or the separation between them, must be exceeded – this typically occurs in 10BASE2 and 10BASE5 systems. Such a situation is shown in Figure 10.11, where two 10BASE5 systems each support their limit of 100 nodes and are separated by a distance greater than 100 m. The remote repeater pair is ideal for such a link.

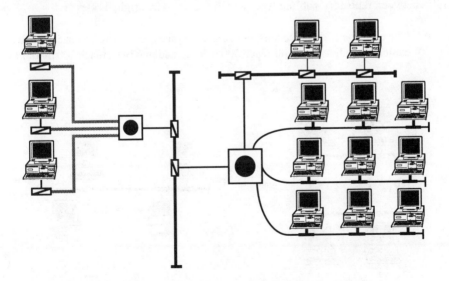

Figure 10.10 CSMA/CD mixed cabling architecture.

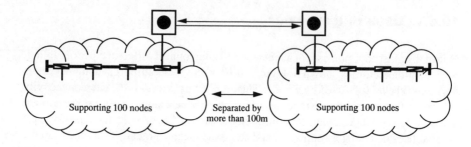

Figure 10.11 CSMA/CD extended network architecture.

Figure 10.12 shows the equivalence in performance for two different CSMA/CD architectures. The actual use of repeaters themselves, in most instances, causes very little degradation in the effective performance of the network. In the diagram the two architectures provide exactly the same performance capability but the advantage of the repeater based solution is that a failure of part of the cabling system will not disrupt the whole network.

10.4.2 Cabling design rules with repeaters

Throughout the discussion of the CSMA/CD operation, with and without repeaters, the existence of a design guideline has been implied. This guideline, from the appropriate IEEE 802.3 standards and which has been updated recently, defines the connectivity rules between repeaters, cabling types and the users. The original rules are:

- The end-to-end distance must not be greater than 3 km. This is ten 50 m AUI cables, three live segments (each 500 m long) and two IRLs (each 500 m long).

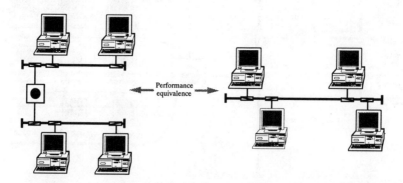

Figure 10.12 Performance equivalence of CSMA/CD architectures.

- Of the five segments which are used in a maximum length system only three may be active. An active segment is one which supports more than two transceivers. Therefore an IRL, or link segment, is a passive segment.

- Only four repeaters may be used in any one end-to-end run. A remote repeater set counts as TWO repeaters. The limit on the number of repeaters is determined by the total delay each set inserts in the delay budget calculation and the limit on the erosion of the interframe gap.

- The total IRL distance should not be greater than 1 km. The exception is for some 10BASEFA architectures where the limit is 2 km.

Figure 10.13 shows a maximal length ethernet configuration. There are two IRLs, each of 500 m (denoted by P for passive segment), with the four repeaters connecting these to the active segments. The network is structured around a central active segment (all the active segments are denoted by A), with the other active segments either connected to it via a local repeater or via the IRLs; this old-fashioned approach has been superseded by the use of hubs which are based upon a collapsed backbone. If any two nodes are chosen, then the paths between them obey the following rules:

- No more than four repeaters are crossed.

- There are no more than three active segments in the chain.

- There are no more than two passive segments in the chain, and these have a combined maximum distance of 1 km.

- There are no more than five segments in a chain.

It can be seen that the network follows all of the design rules. The design rules do not

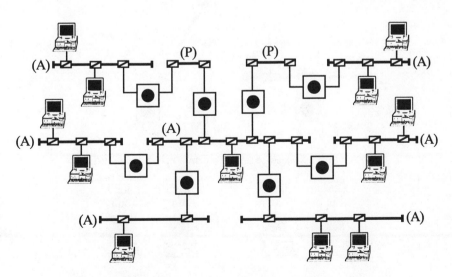

Figure 10.13 Maximally sized CSMA/CD network architecture.

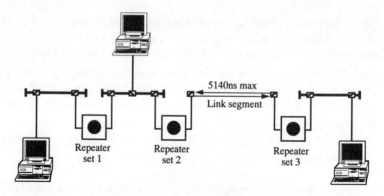

Figure 10.14 Three active segment CSMA/CD network architecture.

therefore limit the total number of segments or repeaters in a network, only their number in any one end-to-end chain, and so some very large networks can be constructed from these very simple design rules.

In the large link system shown in Figure 10.14 it can be seen that the IRL has been lumped into one physical segment of 1 km. This is permitted if only three active segments are to be used in the network, as in the configuration shown, and that no other IRLs will be used in the network. In effect, the two passive segments are linked end-to-end without the use of a repeater – a single run of cable. The total delay along this cable is 5140 ns (for a 10 Mbps system) or 51.4 bit times – if this was a fibre link then the delay would be only 50 bit times.

The hybrid system shown in Figure 10.15 consists of 10BASEF FOIRL,

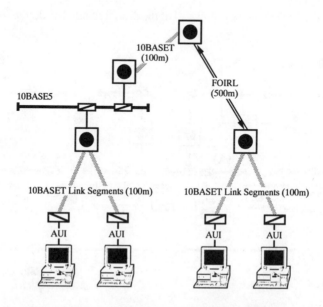

Figure 10.15 CSMA/CD mixed cabling architecture.

10BASET and 10BASE5 segments connected using four repeater sets. Each UTP link segment is limited to 100 m and so the maximum separation between two DTEs in a single hub is 300 m (two 50 m AUI cables). The RTD calculation of 512 bits must still apply. If the central repeater set was a multiport repeater then it could also support some 10BASE2 segments, thereby creating a 10 Mbps architecture with all of the permitted media types. In fact the architecture shown is typical of that used in flood wired buildings in that the 10BASET hubs are used to support the individual DTE points and these hubs are connected together using the appropriate backbone architecture.

10.4.3 Typical architectures

Two architectures are commonly adopted by CSMA/CD network designers, both of which rely upon one form or another of backbone link. Figure 10.16 shows the bus backbone where a 10BASE5 cable is run the length of the building (top to bottom) and the multiport repeaters are placed at the appropriate positions along this bus. This architecture is capable of supporting thousands of users, so it is very easy to exceed the recommended limitation of just 1024 users (if this is significantly exceeded then under extremely heavy loading conditions the network may undergo what is termed 'melt-down' causing the loss of the network for several minutes). The reason why this architecture can support many users is that it does not violate any of the design guidelines, so there can be 100 multiport repeaters connected to the backbone. If each repeater has seven BNC and one AUI ports then each repeater can support 210 users, leading to a total user population of 210 by 100, or 21 000 users!

The hub backbone configuration is shown in Figure 10.17 and is a reflection of structured cabling based architectures. In this configuration the backbone consists of a hub which is linked to the multiport repeaters using fibre optic cabling. It is also possible to modify this approach and replace the multiport repeaters with 10BASET

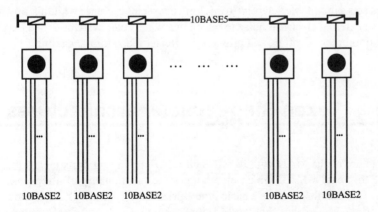

Figure 10.16 A linear backbone CSMA/CD network architecture.

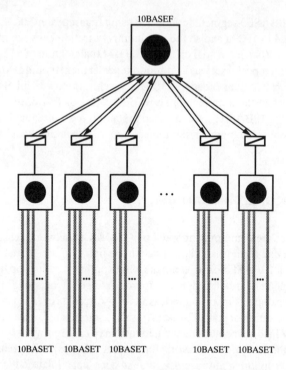

Figure 10.17   A hub backbone CSMA/CD network architecture.

hubs and to have a single link segment supporting each user. In fact in some environments, even when such an approach is adopted, multiport repeaters are used with each port supporting one user only: the RJ45 connectors for 10BASET are identical to the telephone connectors, so users feel quite happy to disconnect their workstations, move them and reconnect elsewhere without confirming that their desired network connectivity support is still available. The use of BNC connectors and T-pieces acts as a suitable deterrent to this form of user interference while also avoiding excessive external electrical noise to which the twisted pair systems are susceptible, such as fluorescent lighting, and providing a greater reach for the cabling.

10.5   Token Ring repeater architectures

The structure of the MAU with its RIN and ROUT main ring ports means that it is possible to create a MAU which incorporates the functionality of a repeater. For instance, it is possible to have a basic type 1 passive MAU but with fibre optic RIN/ROUT ports. This means that the MAU must be powered (and therefore active by definition) and that the two main ring ports are in fact acting as remote repeaters. This does not mean that repeaters are irrelevant in the Token Ring context (consider networks in which only passive MAUs are installed), rather they are not the only available solution, especially when faced with a 'green-fields' situation.

10.5.1 Uses of a repeater

Unlike CSMA/CD systems, Token Ring repeaters do not provide extended user connectivity: the limitation on the number of users is independent of the use of repeaters. However, they are still important for providing Token Ring architectures with support for mixed cabling, a greater area of coverage and fault resilient cabling.

Consider the architecture shown in Figure 10.18. In this network there are three sets of MAUs, situated in two buildings and configured in the fault redundant mode. Without the use of repeaters the two buildings would have to be within 200 m of each other (assuming the use of STP). The STP remote repeaters provide a connectivity of up to 750 m and the fibre optic ones 2000 m. The use of a copper link across the two buildings is not to be recommended because this assumes that the two earths are bonded together. This is almost certainly not the case and in locations where there is a significant ground potential then there will be a signal propagating along the earth shielding! Another reason for avoiding this is that if there is an electrical failure or a lightning strike then its effects will cross from one building to another. Fibre optic links avoid these sorts of problems.

The fault tolerant architecture means that the signal actually travels across all of the cabling. If the remote repeaters support the automatic wrap feature (repeater/ repeater and repeater/MAU), then as soon as a failure is detected (loss of the main ring phantom signal) the repeaters wrap the signal back onto the previously unused twisted

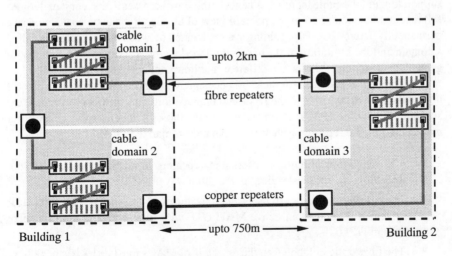

Figure 10.18 An extended Token Ring network architecture.

pair in each of the cables (each cable consists of at least two twisted pairs – four wires).

The final use of a repeater is to provide the opportunity for mixed cabling. In the IBM cabling guidelines it is recommended that STP be used as the main ring cable independent of the types of cable to be used for the lobes. In practice most vendors sell either a STP or an UTP solution: in the case of UTP the main ring is also UTP and not STP. Interconnection between these systems requires the use of a repeater; it is almost (but not quite) impossible to get RIN/ROUT ports that provide STP connectivity to type 3 MAUs and vice versa.

The most significant problem concerning mixed cabling is the full support of the automated wrap around facility. Surprisingly, the UTP standards are not the only problem in this area. Most Token Ring manufacturers have fault tolerant versions of their UTP systems (due to the use of active MAUs to provide suitable cabling distances). However, very few have an STP equivalent. In passive STP based systems the wrap around can only be forced by manually disconnecting the faulty element, at which time the physical relays close and reconnect the ring. This means that it is impossible to provide automated wrap around in a system which has STP cabling. Furthermore, it should not be assumed that in UTP the wrap systems are interoperable between different vendors – in many cases they are not.

10.5.2 Cabling design rules with repeaters

As can be seen in Figure 10.18 there are three cabling domains (but only one token domain) that must be considered during the design process for this network. The location of the repeaters is determined by the distribution of the longest lobe lengths in the network. Remember that the repeater is being used to enable the network to support longer lobe cable lengths. Whenever the signal crosses a repeater it undergoes full regeneration and so from the point of view of the signal it can be considered as a permanently active NIA. The cabling system located between two repeaters is called a domain and the limitation of the maximum lobe lengths is specific to its domain: in general, each domain will have a different maximum lobe length (Bird, 1994).

The formal standard for the cabling design, with and without repeaters, is still not available in draft form, so the IBM recommendations currently act as the *de facto* standard. Using the IBM recommendations plus those of several rival Token Ring manufacturers, the repeater system rules can be summarized as:

- The maximum number of users and repeaters in an STP network is 260. Repeaters are sources of jitter in the same way as NIAs.

- The maximum number of users and repeaters in a 4 Mbps passive MAU UTP system is 72 and in an active MAU UTP with jitter compensation circuitry system is 260.

- The fibre optic link between the repeaters or MAUs must be less than 2000 m.

- The maximum distance between two UTP remote repeaters is 300 m and between STP repeaters it is 750 m. The recommended unrepeated maximums were 200 and 120 m respectively.

The distances between the repeaters are specified as the same for both 4 and 16 Mbps, thereby avoiding a profusion of different rules for the two systems. This means that the 16 Mbps repeaters require a little more signal processing (and cost a little more) to provide the necessary distances.

10.5.3 Typical architectures

The cyclic nature of the Token Ring and the fact that the architecture is already hub based mean that there are very few topological variations to be considered when designing the network. Figure 10.18 demonstrates the basic architecture adopted by just about all commercial installations.

In the cases where repeater hubs are employed, as opposed to just local and remote repeaters, the detailed physical configuration is as shown in Figure 10.19. In this diagram the repeater hub supports three MAUs, configured in a non-redundant manner. One of the repeater ports is being used as a lobe repeater – that is, it is regenerating the signal for that lobe only and so permits the full lobe length to be considerably longer than otherwise possible. All but one of the ports are copper units, type 1, and so the single fibre interface requires that the MAU connected to it has a fibre ROUT port (an active MAU).

Using the hub repeaters (either by themselves or as part of modular rack systems) it is now possible to construct networks with several centres, each of which may or may not provide fault resilience in their domain. The network still has only one token passing around it and so its performance capability is the same as if all the users were supported by one MAU – in other words, the Token Ring equivalent of Figure 10.12.

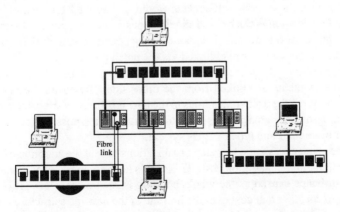

Figure 10.19 A typical Token Ring repeater network architecture.

10.6   Structured cabling

Structured cabling establishes data as the fourth utility and so it must be intrinsic to a building's architecture in the same way as water, gas and electricity. This means that the cabling infrastructure should be considered at the outset of any new building design and construction, and that if possible it should be retrospectively introduced to as many established buildings as possible. The reason for using structured cabling is the cost effective flexibility it gives to an organization in supporting its electronic data oriented users. This flexibility is provided by:

- Liberally providing PC/workstation connectivity ports throughout the whole of the building irrespective of whether or not they are of immediate use.

- Threading the cabling (based upon UTP due to its low cost and small bulk) back to centralized wiring closets which are themselves then wired together.

- Using a comprehensive patch panel system which permits any form of connectivity between the users and the network elements, including that of the internetworking relays.

- Using a cabling system, UTP, across which Token Ring, CSMA/CD and the copper distributed data interface LAN architectures can be supported without altering the infrastructure of the network. Such a cabling system can also support asynchronous systems such as 3270 terminals.

- Future proofing, by providing a cabling infrastructure capable of supporting new LAN MAC specifications. Particular examples of this are cell relay and Isochronous ethernet.

The basic infrastructure for structured cabling is shown in Figure 10.20. Here each floor is supplied with at least one wiring closet. The wall sockets are located throughout each floor and are connected as point links to the patch panel in the wiring closet. In most circumstances several wall sockets would be supplied for each office so that several connection points can be used simultaneously or to compensate for the location of various pieces of furniture. A backbone wiring conduit connects the wiring closets together and these wires are also linked via the patch panel.

In the wiring closet the user cabling enters the patch panel from one side and the network elements are linked from the other side. Rewiring the network then consists of moving the user connections to the new positions on the patch panel. Each connection across the patch panel is point-to-point and so it is possible for a single panel to support more than one type of LAN system.

The primary reason why many organizations balk at the adoption of structured cabling is the initial installation cost. This cost is not only in terms of money but also in the disturbance caused as the whole building is rewired for data. It is however, important to consider that cost over the lifetime of the new infrastructure – at least 20 years. The costing commonly quoted by structured cabling companies for a typical

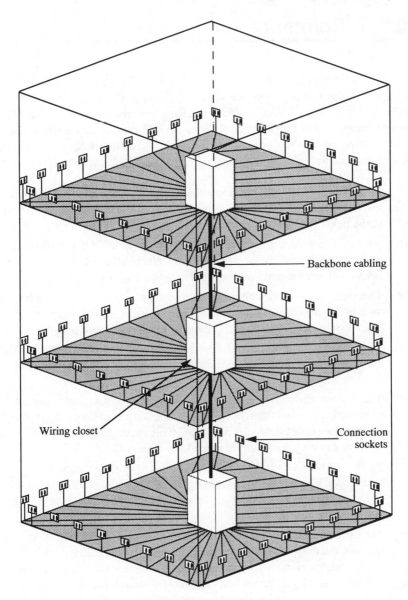

Backbone cabling

Wiring closet

Connection
sockets

Figure 10.20 A structured cabling architecture.

organization which uses the traditional wiring infrastructure is based upon the fact that it costs approximately £800 to move a PC/workstation from one connection location to another, takes two weeks to complete the move once it has been requested and that on average some 30–60% of all staff move office location per year. Given these figures it is claimed that the cost of structured cabling will have paid for itself in between three and five years. Clearly, over a twenty-year period it is a very cost effective solution.

10.7　Summary

The relationship between repeaters and their LAN type is extremely close and this is why the repeater specifications are included in the IEEE 802.3 and IEEE 802.5 standards. Most of the CSMA/CD and Token Ring NIA manufacturers and third party suppliers support a full range of repeaters, so the end user has an excellent selection from which they should be able to obtain an almost perfect match to their requirement at a very reasonable price. In summary:

- Repeaters connect together identical LANs to form a single physical network; that is, a single token or carrier sensing domain. The only difference permitted in the linked segments is their cabling type.

- Repeaters are used to produce networks which exceed the technological limitations imposed by the need for cost effective LANs. Repeaters supply LANs with greater geographical coverage and fault resilience.

- The types of repeater commercially available are local, remote, buffered, multiport, hub and modular repeater. The modern trend is to construct networks based upon combinations of multiport, hub and modular repeaters.

- Repeaters are responsible for full signal regeneration and retiming (as distinct from line drivers, which provide only signal regeneration). This includes the reconstruction of any preamble.

- The automatic partitioning facility of a repeater makes it particularly suited to constructing networks that can operate even when part of the cabling infrastructure has been catastrophically damaged. Failed segments are isolated from the network and only reintroduced when fully repaired.

- The use of repeaters means that it is possible to construct networks covering hundreds of kilometres and connecting thousands of users. Both are violations of the recommended cabling guidelines and so great care is needed not to 'accidentally' exceed them.

- The structured cabling architectures are based upon hub repeaters. Such systems, although expensive to install, are very cost efficient in the long term and provide excellent flexibility for reconfiguring the network, relocating users and for supporting different LAN systems on the same cabling infrastructure.

11

Bridges

11.1   Introduction

At some time or other the offered traffic load on a LAN will exceed both its original specification and that which it can effectively support. In some cases this excessive load will become apparent to the user through significantly increased response times, for example when accessing a file server. The solution is to break the network into smaller elements while still providing full connectivity across the whole network when required. A repeater will not supply such a solution and, indeed, its very nature may well have caused the problem in the first place.

A bridge is the internetworking relay element used to segment the network into separate logical LANs while still providing full connectivity across the whole physical network (Miller, 1991). The bridge achieves this by examining each frame it detects on the network and deciding whether or not the frame has to be forwarded onto the other connected networks: a bridge decides on whether or not data is to be forwarded whereas a repeater always forwards the data. Once again the functionality of a bridge is now well established and so the majority of the future developments will be concerned with modularization and increased management facilities.

11.2   Functions of a bridge

The bridge is protocol independent above the LLC and, as such, it operates on MAC frames; this does not preclude operations on higher layer protocol data items but this would be a specialized feature. The other important point to note is that bridges can support full WAN connectivity: they are not limited to intermediate fibre links that support the full bandwidth requirements. This means of course that the performance of a bridged network is not solely determined by the functionality of the bridge but also by the carrying capacity of the intermediate network and the native loading on the other linked LANs (Held, 1993).

11.2.1 Data filtering

The first and most important function of a bridge is its ability to filter the data received from each of its connected LANs. All bridges are connected to at least two LANs and so in the case of a CSMA/CD network the bridge is receiving data at 20 Mbps. This is equivalent to 29 762 minimally sized frames per second (each frame is 512 bits long plus 64 bits of preamble and 96 bits of interframe gap): the bridge must be capable of deciding whether or not to forward 29 762 frames per second. Similar statistics can be

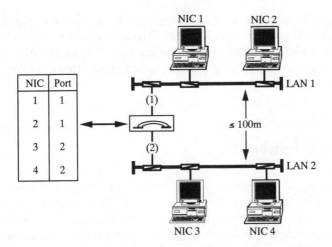

Figure 11.1 Data filtering and forwarding in a bridged network.

determined for the 4 and 16 Mbps Token Ring systems with a worst case of 45 454 and 181 818 frames per second respectively (a minimum frame size of 176 bits). The filtering rates for bridges are normally quoted as packets per second (pps) and in the case of CSMA/CD systems this is with respect to the 672 bit minimum packet size. It is always important to establish whether the quoted figures are per port or an aggregate for the whole bridge. Manufacturers always quote their performance figures in the most flattering way, so it is important to establish how these have been derived.

Consider the network shown in Figure 11.1. Here, two CSMA/CD LANs are linked via a bridge and so it must filter 29 762 frames per second. The filtering of the frames is normally based upon the destination address field in the frame (this is not true for the source routing bridges used in Token Ring). The bridge constructs the address map shown in the diagram (how this is constructed will be discussed later) and compares the destination address against the equivalent entry in the table. If the LAN table entry for the destination address indicates a port which differs from that on which the frame was received then the frame is forwarded, otherwise it is discarded. In CSMA/CD systems the destination address is the first field in the frame, so the filtering can be processed while the rest of the frame is still arriving at the bridge – that is, a minimum of at least another 464 bits. Given that the filtering rules are applied to the destination address it is important to ensure that the bridge is not located in such a position on the network that it is required to forward all information – this is a waste of a bridge. Instead, use the bridge to ensure that frames are restricted to those LANs that need the information.

An extension to the address filtering of a bridge is that of customized filtering, which can be used to operate on other fields in the MAC frames – including the data field. These filters are applied sequentially to the frames according to the logic rules defined by the bridge manager. In most cases there is a limit to the number of rules which can be applied to a single frame (usually sixteen rules) otherwise the filtering rate becomes too severely degraded. This filtering degradation is caused by the time taken to process each rule plus the fact that the data fields to which the rules are applied may occur anywhere within the frame – such as the final octet of the data field in a 1518 octet frame! When customized filtering is used then the quoted filtering rates do not apply and so the bridge can become a severe bottleneck.

11.2.2 Data forwarding

The second most important parameter that characterizes a bridge is its forwarding rate – the rate at which the filtered data is transmitted onto the target network. In the case of the network shown in Figure 11.1 the forwarding rate is notionally 20 Mbps because the bridge can pass the frames onto the target LANs at the carrying rate of those LANs. In reality, the rate is lower than this theoretical maximum because the target LANs will themselves have their own load and so the true forwarding rate is somewhat lower; the total load on the LAN must be less than 10 Mbps for the sum of the native and bridge forwarded information. Needless to say most suppliers quote the maximum forwarding rate, thereby assuming that the target network is unloaded.

If the intermediate network is not of equivalent capacity to the native LANs then the bottleneck is even worse. Consider the situation where two bridges are connected via a kilostream link (64 kbps). In this case the forwarding rate of the bridges is now 64 kbps for potentially 20 Mbps, clearly a problem. Each bridge has a finite buffer capability, typically thirty to fifty maximum sized frames; between 35 and 60 ms for a CSMA/CD system and 300–500 ms for Token Ring systems. When these buffers approach overflow the oldest frames are discarded. Frames are also removed from the forwarding queues if the time they have spent in the queues exceeds the maximum transit delay; this time has a maximum value of two seconds.

The result of buffer overflow and excessive frame delay means that a bridge can become a significant source of data loss. This means that in a bridged network the higher level protocols in the end-systems must provide a COS for at least one of the layers. If this is not the case then information will be lost, particularly under high loading conditions, and this loss is considerably more significant than that due to ambient electrical noise. It might seem that the solution is to increase the bridge buffer sizes or extend the frame holding time. The problem with this is that the resulting delays may then exceed the natural timeout periods supported by the protocols (a COS would still be required as losses will still occur, albeit far less frequently). The end-systems would then retransmit the data, thereby further loading the bridges with duplicated frames and so further degrading the bridge's capability.

The few benchmarks that have been performed on bridges have shown that they are capable of supporting a load of about 20% of the total throughput that can be supported by the LANs. This means that the bridge in Figure 11.1 should not be expected to forward more than 4 Mbps in total for both directions. If this loading is exceeded then the bridge may have to discard frames and so cause data loss.

11.2.3 Self learning

In Figure 11.1 the filtering table is fully populated. However, in a real system this needs to be determined by one of two methods: static or dynamic allocation. The static allocation system uses a predefined filter table which is loaded from some external device, typically a floppy disk. This table has to be manually distributed across the network to all of the bridges but it must be amended to suit the particular filtering rules required by each individual bridge. The entries in the static tables are unaltered by the bridge unless accessed by the bridge manager and so any changes in the topology and/ or NIA distribution about the network require manual intervention to renovate the static tables. In some bridges it is possible to have both static and dynamic filter tables. In such systems the static addresses take precedence over the dynamic entries and so it is possible to establish protected address filter rules which will remain unaltered.

The dynamic allocation system uses a self learning algorithm which observes the traffic flow across the network and derives from it the NIA distribution. Initially the filtering table is empty. As frames are detected by the bridge their source addresses are stored in the filter table along with their incoming port number – in other words, the bridge learns the location of an NIA once it has sent at least one frame. As the NIAs send data, the bridges become aware of the true distribution of the NIAs across the network. Eventually the filter table will become populated, as shown in Figure 11.1.

The real advantage of the dynamic allocation method is its ability to automatically adjust to the relocation of NIAs. This adjustment is caused as soon as the NIA transmits from its new location, whereupon the new incoming port number is used to replace the previous entry. A further addition to this process is that of address ageing. If a frame from a source address is not detected during some defined period then that entry is removed from the filter table and is only re-entered when a frame is received from the NIA. Bridges typically have enough storage for between 2000 and 8000 address entries with each entry being valid for about 300 seconds.

The ageing process means that each node must regularly transmit or else its entry is deleted from the filter base. A problem arises from this technique when a frame arrives at a bridge and the bridge does not have an entry for the destination address of the frame. In this case the bridges act conservatively and passes the frame onto all connected LANs, thereby ensuring that the frame is received by the destination. A later response by this destination will then cause the missing source address to be entered into the filter table. All broadcast and multicast addresses are forwarded across bridges unless explicitly prohibited during configuration of the bridge by the manager.

11.2.4 WAN connectivity

The separation between repeaters is limited to the maximum distance sustainable by a single fibre optic cable. In some cases it may be necessary to connect LANs together over many tens, hundreds or even thousands of kilometres. The filtering capability of bridges means that it is possible to make use of a wider range of intermediate links that are better suited to WAN connectivity. The types of WAN connectivity available are:

- Fibre optic – which is limited to a maximum separation of 2 km but which can support the full bandwidth requirements for the linked bridges.

- Kilostream – a 64 kbps link using the X.21, V.35 and RS-449 interfaces which can be obtained from a public network supplier or can be used to form a private network. Distance is no limitation. However, the bandwidth restriction will cause severe bottlenecks under heavy loading conditions.

- Megastream – a 2.048 Mbps (equivalent to kilostream) using the G.703 and E1 interfaces. This substantially increased bandwidth should be capable of supporting all but the most heavily loaded of bridge networks.

- T1 and fractional T1 – the 1.54 Mbps and 56 kbps interfaces, respectively, particularly suited to transatlantic links.

- Low rate serial links – making use of the RS-232 or X.21 interfaces for speeds up to 19.2 kbps.

- FDDI – this makes use of the 100 Mbps FDDI as a backbone link and so the interfaces act as encapsulational devices, thereby treating the link in the same manner as a kilostream or megastream interface.

- ISDN – the advantage of ISDN is that variable bandwidth allocations are available (64 kbps–2.048 Mbps) upon request. Unfortunately, there can be a relatively long setup delay while the circuit is established. Broadband interfaces, such as cell relay, are also under development.

There are two concerns when employing any of these links: the access delay time and the propagation delay. The greater the physical distance, the longer the propagation delay and so the less efficient the data transfer across that link. In general it is recommended that the diameter of the bridged networks should not exceed 20 km, to ensure minimal propagation delays. The access times mean that dedicated point-to-point links are used so that no switching delays are incurred. This point-to-point nature of WAN bridge links is one of the architectural features that distinguish bridges from routers and the other mixed router/bridge architectures – that is, in general the data does not enter the WAN cloud at the source and leave at the destination after having been passed through several switching elements. One other difference between bridges and routers is the lower frame latency across the bridge, particularly in switching bridges.

11.2.5 Fault resilience and triangulation

One of the important uses of a bridge is in the construction of networks that are resilient to single point failures. Figure 11.2 shows a Token Ring network with two bridges connected in parallel across two MAUs. The advantage of this architecture is that

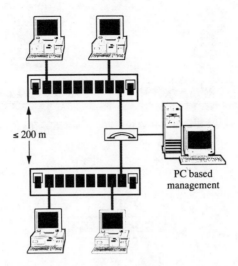

Figure 11.2 Fault resilient architectures using bridges.

should one of the bridges or their link cables fail, there is still another bridged route available between the two LANs. The problem now becomes one of providing a method by which only one of the bridges is actively passing data between the two networks at any one moment in time and which also ensures that at least one of the bridges is passing the data.

An extension to this resilience is the use of triangulating WAN links using remote bridges. Figure 11.3 shows three Token Rings linked by three bridges to provide a triangulated network architecture. The advantage of this approach is that each bridge is connected to the WAN network using two links and so in the event of a link failure communications can be immediately switched to the other. In many systems one of the connections is declared as the primary link with the other acting as a hot standby, but unfortunately such a solution is expensive particularly if the total load does not really justify three separate lines.

In such systems the filter tables contain the port number of the bridge associated with the destination NIA's LAN. When the bridge has located the port number the frame is passed to that port, in this case a WAN link. If a port fails, the secondary port is used and the intermediate bridge acts as a switching station for the re-routed data. These types of bridge use a simple adaptive routing system across their point-to-point links and so the failure of a single link does not separate the network.

11.2.6 Load balancing and triangulation

In the cases where the expected forward loading of the bridges is expected to exceed the bandwidth available across the WAN link then some form of link multiplexing is needed. Figure 11.4 shows two Token Rings connected by a pair of WAN links; link

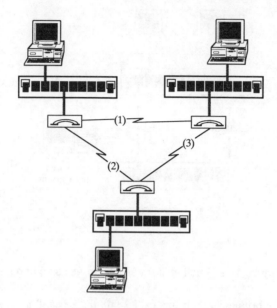

Figure 11.3 Triangulation using bridges.

1 could have a 2.048 Mbps capacity and link 2 a 64 kbps capacity. In this situation link 2 is used as the overflow link and the bridges would ensure that the best possible utilization was made of the high capacity link. A different situation could occur when both links have the same capacity. Here the bridges may actually split a frame into two fragments, send these concurrently down the two links and recompose the frame at the other end. This technique reduces the propagation delay across the link and requires minimal processing and data overheads for its implementation. It is also important to stress that this form of load balancing is supplied by only a few specialist bridge suppliers.

A combination of triangulation and load balancing is shown in Figure 11.5. Here the three CSMA/CD LANs are supported by three bridges. In this system, link 3 would be the primary connection between bridges 1 and 3 and would use links 1 and

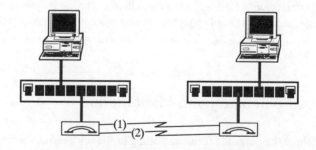

Figure 11.4 Load balancing in a bridged network.

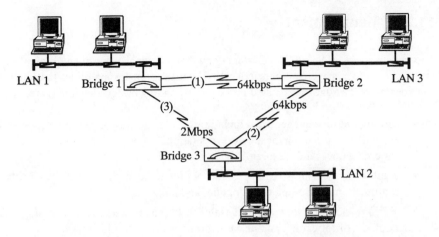

Figure 11.5 Combined load balancing and triangulation in a bridged network.

2 as the secondary route. Communication between the other bridges is supported by load balancing across the dual lines of links 1 and 2, providing an aggregate link capacity of 128 kbps. This architecture can now sustain a loss of at least two links, making the network more robust.

11.2.7 Data encryption and compression

In some systems the information being carried by the LANs is of a confidential or secure nature. While it may be acceptable for this information to be 'open' within the local confines it may be too sensitive for WAN access. In these cases some bridges provide an encryption facility for use across the WAN. The bridges encrypt the entire frame and transmit it across the WAN link, whereupon the receiving bridge decrypts the frame. The advantage of this system is that the whole frame is encrypted and so it is impossible to casually note for whom the information is intended, but the disadvantage is that the forwarding rate of the bridge is again reduced due to the processing overhead.

A further capability for some of the bridges is that of data compression. This is used to reduce the WAN bandwidth requirements and as a side-effect it also acts as a simple form of data encryption. Data compression is particularly useful when the LANs are transferring data of one particular type, such as video or graphics, whereupon it is possible to select a compression algorithm appropriate to the data type. Different compression algorithms are better suited to different data types, so much so that compression ratios of 50:1 are available when a good match is found. If no match is available then a ratio of about 2:1 is the best that can be expected, representing a 50% saving of bandwidth.

11.2.8 Management

The sensitivity of bridges to MAC frames and their contents makes them particularly important in the management of a network. The management capabilities that should be expected of a bridge (as is stated in the corresponding bridge standards) are:

- Configuration management – including the initialization, reset and closedown of all of the bridges on the network, operational parameter assignment, such as timeout values, and frame propagation control.
- Fault management – which is the ability to identify and correct bridge malfunctions, including error logging and reporting.
- Performance management – the ability to gather statistics concerning the numbers of forwarded and discarded frames for each bridge port.

The standard has nothing to offer on security, which is strange given that unauthorized access to a bridge which possesses a remote management capability could leave the entire network vulnerable. In most cases, access to this sort of function is protected by two-tier passwords, one at user level and the other at system level, the latter providing access to the wider management capabilities. Most manufacturers provide trap-door entry to password protected bridges. However, these are specific to each individual bridge and are normally only available to a manager after proof of purchase and access right have been established. Other secure features include the ability for the bridge to disable and re-enable itself at predefined times, thereby permitting a network manager to prohibit user access to the network outside normal working hours.

The management architecture for a bridged network is typically as shown in Figure 11.2, in which the management centre is linked to one of the bridges via a serial link. The better bridges interact with management software which is hosted by the workstation as opposed to within themselves. The latter approach needs just a terminal to access the bridges but invariably the response time is slower and the functionality more limited than that for a PC based system.

The standards stipulate that it should be possible to control all of the other bridges on the network from within one bridge. This means that the bridges must be capable of supporting a remote management functionality either out-of-band (making use of a separate management network) or in-band via the actual network itself. These techniques will be discussed in more detail in Chapter 14.

11.3 Types of bridge

The standard joke about standards is that 'there are so many to chose from' and never a truer word was spoken for bridges. The user's demand for flexible connectivity at the MAC level has forced the manufacturers to respond in a variety of different ways.

The standards committees are now attempting to unravel these different systems and to provide interconnectivity between the established bridges as well as providing for stable long-term options (Perlman, 1992).

11.3.1 MAC bridge

The media access control bridge (MAC bridge) is a relay element which connects together two similar NIAs – for example, it connects CSMA/CD to CSMA/CD or Token Ring to Token Ring. It does not support CSMA/CD to Token Ring connectivity. This connectivity creates separate access domains, thus two CSMA/CD LANs bridged as shown in Figure 11.1 consists of two separate carrier sensing domains, one on either side of the bridge. Similarly for Token Ring, the network shown in Figure 11.2 consists of two token domains, one on either side of the bridges.

In effect each access scheme is limited to its own domain. In the case of Token Ring this means that one token cycles on each side of the bridge. The bridge contains two Token Ring NIAs, one for each LAN connection; it should also be noted that this means that the bridge can become the monitor for one or both of the rings. In the CSMA/CD networks the equivalent separation ensures that the contentions on one side of the network do not propagate across the bridge and affect the other LAN. This separation either reduces the traffic loading on either side of the network because there are fewer nodes, or permits more nodes to be connected for the same loading on each of the LANs. The consequence of this separation is that when data has to be transferred from one LAN to the other the bridge has to participate in the normal access scheme (it has no advantage over the other NIAs on the network) and so its capability to transmit data is dependent on the loading of the target network.

11.3.2 Link and mixed bridges

The link bridge, originally termed the mixed bridge, is responsible for connecting different types of LAN in a manner that is protocol independent. This interconnection is provided by the LLC, hence the name link bridge. This form of bridge is known as a translation bridge because it translates the frames from one MAC format to another, such as CSMA/CD to Token Ring or Token Ring to FDDI.

In principle there are in fact two forms of link bridge: translational and encapsulational. The encapsulational link bridges take the MAC frame from a LAN and wrap around it the MAC header and trailer of the intermediate link. When the data reaches the destination LAN this outer header and trailer are stripped off and the original MAC frame is forwarded onto the destination LAN. This means that the source and destination LANs must be of the same type because the MAC frame has not been altered and an encapsulational bridge can only be used as an intermediate transport, for example the use of the FDDI as a backbone MAN link.

The difference between the encapsulational and translational bridges is readily demonstrated when considering the frame checksums. In the encapsulational link bridge the original checksum is unaltered and a second checksum is applied by the intermediate system. In the transformational link bridge the original header and trailer are stripped away and replaced by the new frame structure and header, and so only one checksum is used. When the frame reaches the destination LAN, the MAC frame is again altered to the corresponding form of that LAN's MAC structure and so a third checksum value is calculated.

It is generally agreed that only translational link bridges are acceptable in the internetworking of LANs (the encapsulation bridges are used in remote MAC bridging, for example with an FDDI intermediate network) and the functions that must be provided by such a bridge are:

- Bit and octet reordering – swap bits and bytes to compensate for reverse numbering schemes between different MAC systems.

- Frame length restriction – limit the frame size to a mutually agreed size. Recall that the maximum length frame for CSMA/CD is only 1518 octets whereas the Token Ring and FDDI frames can be considerably larger.

- Frame reformatting and checksum generation – change from one frame structure to another and recalculate the new checksums.

- Data buffering – compensate for significantly different data rates, between 4 and 100 Mbps, depending on the type of interconnectivity.

The internal organization of a link bridge becomes particularly intricate when considering the situation where there is an intermediate link between the two bridges. In this case the intermediate link must also be translational in nature. The local frames are transformed at the source bridge into the intermediate link format, forwarded across the intermediate link to the destination bridge and then transformed again into the formats required by the destination LAN. This approach means that the link bridges are only concerned with mapping between the frame formats of their local interface ports.

It should be stressed that at the current time and with the exception of the IBM mixed bridge the full operational features of link bridges have not been finalized. This is particularly true of link bridges separated by a third intermediate network.

11.3.3 Transparent bridge

The IEEE 802.1 committee has been responsible for the production and ratification of the spanning tree algorithm (STA) for use in local bridge architectures (IEEE 802.1D) and it is currently working on the equivalent standard for remote bridges (IEEE 802.1G). Both types of bridge are available for either CSMA/CD or Token Ring networks but the latter may also make use of the source routing bridges instead.

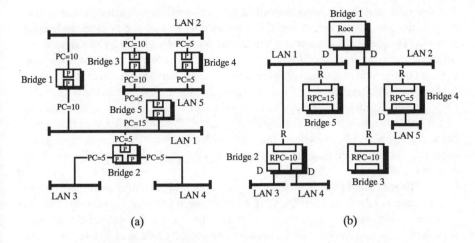

Figure 11.6 The spanning tree algorithm, before and after.

The primary function of a transparent bridge is that it undertakes all responsibility for the routing of frames across the network. Typically a bridged network could be physically connected as shown in the Figure 11.6a whereas the spanning tree would ensure that the frames crossed the network using the routes as shown in Figure 11.6b. Consider the operation of the STA given the physical configuration shown in Figure 11.6a (Halsall, 1992):

- The bridges must first elect the root – that is, the base from which the connectivity of the tree will be constructed. The bridge with the lowest 'bridge identifier' is selected (usually a management modifiable parameter), or if two bridges have the same identifier the one with the greatest number of ports is selected. If the bridges have the same number of ports then other criteria are used but if all else fails, the bridge with the lowest address is declared the root. In this instance assume that bridge 1 becomes the root.

- The root becomes the designated bridge for all of the LANs to which it is connected, namely LANs 1 and 2. The designated bridge classification means that the bridge will be responsible for forwarding frames between the LANs to which it is connected.

- A designated bridge now has to be assigned for each of the other LANs. Bridge 2 must become the designated bridge for LANs 3 and 4 (the only link to them) and so it will forward information from LAN 1 onto these other two LANs.

- The root now has to decide which of bridges 3, 4, and 5 will become the designated bridge for LAN 5. The arbitration method is based upon the path cost (PC) to LAN 5 from the root via each of the possible bridge links. Bridge 4 has the lowest PC and so this is selected.

- The bridges now forward frames across the topology shown in Figure 11.6b.

The description of the STA has been abridged. However, the end effects are the same. Each bridge has a root port, R, and if it is forwarding frames one or more designated ports D. The designated ports are the actual ports through which the frames are forwarded onto the connected LAN and the root port is that which is closest to the root. Ports are designated because a bridge could have more than one port linked to the same LAN, added fault resilience, and only one path should be used for connectivity to that LAN. The PC is a measure of the relative importance of a link. This is usually a measure of the link's bandwidth capability, with the lower PC being assigned to the higher capacity. The STA always selects the route with the lowest PC; that is, the highest capacity. The bridge management system should supply the user with the facility to control the STA.

The root port is that through which all of the bridge control frames are passed (bridge protocol data units, BPDUs). Communication between the bridges does not stop once the bridge configuration has been established. The bridges are also responsible for monitoring the state of the network and should a bridge or link failure occur then the network is reconfigured to bypass the failed components. This means that the bridges are continually communicating with each other, confirming that they are active and so on. The expected maximum loading on the network due to the STA is about 9.6 kbps, or 1%.

The background loading effect and the response time of the bridges to a topology change limits the number of bridges that should be used in a network. The recommended limit is seven bridges, which means that in the best case it should take the bridges between 14 and 21 seconds to reconfigure; the bridge timers for reconfiguration are normally a management definable option and can range between seconds and minutes. Router based architectures can expect routing table updates to be completed within 30 seconds and these will occur more regularly than the bridge equivalents.

Some architectures require more than seven bridges and so the use of spanning tree domains has been introduced to support these types of network. A domain is a collection of bridges which cooperate in the STA. This means that a network could consist of tens of bridges, each of which has been assigned to a particular domain and within which there are no more than seven bridges – a bridge must be a member of one domain only. The effects of the STA are localized to the domain and so the response time of the bridges to topological changes is as if there were only seven bridges. The problem now becomes one of assigning the bridges to the appropriate domain and ensuring that the network's fault resilience is supported collectively by the domains.

The above procedure is clear when initializing a network but what is the situation when a new bridge is introduced? Upon initialization all bridges assume that they are the root, whereupon they listen to the network and confirm their status. If the new bridge should indeed become the root (perhaps it has a lowest bridge identifier) then the entire network will undergo reconfiguration. The network is configured with respect to the root, so if the root is changed the network must be reconfigured and, naturally, no user frames will be forwarded while the network is undergoing reconfiguration; hence the need to minimize the reconfiguration time. It is also important to ensure that bridges do not keep asserting root responsibilities over each other, so newly enrolled bridges should be configured to enter the network passively. This also means that a newly active bridge could completely distort the operational configuration of a network, so secure installations must pay particular attention to unauthorized bridge entry

Once reconfiguration has been completed the bridges have to relearn the user distribution – that is, they must repopulate the filter tables with the new distribution information. The entries in the filter tables are aged as soon as reconfiguration occurs, so the repopulation process starts as a natural consequence of the reconfiguration.

At one time, it was considered that the use of the STA across a WAN architecture would impose too long a configuration delay and various alternatives were considered, such as adaptive routing and open shortest path first. The current thinking in the IEEE 802.1G standard is that the STA is perfectly acceptable with one or two 'tweaks' to address the problems of loops across the WAN. These modifications are based upon the use of remote bridge groups, subgroups, clusters and virtual ports. A remote bridge group is a set of remote bridges that are capable of communicating with each other over the intermediate system and a subgroup is a fully connected subset of the group. A cluster is also a fully connected subset of the remote bridges in a group and a virtual port is the logical point of attachment for a bridge to the intermediate system. The group and subgroup definitions are used to describe the static structure of the remote bridge architecture whereas the cluster is used to address their dynamic configuration. In the context of Figure 11.7, these definitions mean that all of the four bridges form a single group, that there are two subgroups of three bridges (bridges 1, 2 and 4, and bridges 1, 3 and 4) and several subgroups of two bridges. The clusters are formed as a result of the outcome of the STA and will ensure that the information does not loop around the network. The construction of the active topology for a transparently bridged network takes place in three steps:

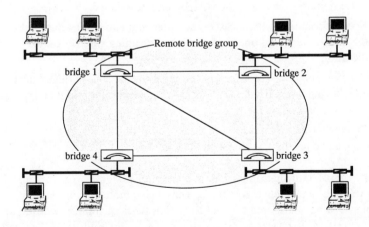

Figure 11.7 Remote bridging.

- Computation of the basic spanning tree – the STA is used to construct a strict tree of the LAN ports.
- Formation of the clusters – the virtual ports (those supporting the intermediate system) are configured to form the remote bridge clusters.
- Selection of the port states – the LAN and virtual ports are assigned to their operational state of forwarding or blocking.

These three steps integrate the operation of the STA across combined local and remote bridge architectures and ensure that data looping does not occur on either the local or intermediate systems. Some manufacturers, Retix for example, provide an additional feature whereby the 'unused' links on the spanning tree can be used to increase the available bandwidth between two LANs by triangulation and load balancing. These adaptive routing algorithms also ensure that data looping does not occur.

11.3.4 Source routing bridge

The Token Ring bridges are specified in the IEEE 802.5 standards, in which it is stated that source routing bridges will be used. The fundamental difference between source routing and transparent bridges is that in the former the NIA dictates the route that the data will take across the network. This technique means that the NIAs must be informed, either directly or indirectly, of a change in the topology of the network.

There are four different ways in which frames can be transmitted across a source routing network (Stallings, 1993):

- Null – no routing is to be used and so the source routing bridges will discard these frames, prohibiting them from being forwarded.
- Specific route (non-broadcast) – the frames contain routing information which the bridges read and operate upon when deciding whether or not to forward them.
- All routes explorer (broadcast) – this is a frame which all bridges must forward after having inserted within it the bridge number and the bridge and port number used for forwarding the frame.
- Spanning tree explorer (broadcast) – the method by which a frame traverses, once and once only, all rings on the network.

Two points are of immediate note: that source routing bridges make use of an STA and that information can be sent across the network using more than one strategy. In fact the bridges can be configured to react to certain types of frames in different ways. However, the IEEE 802.5 standard mandates the sending of frames using one particular method, as shown in Figure 11.8.

The network in Figure 11.8 consists of four rings linked by five bridges, so there are many different routes across the network. When a frame is to be transmitted the

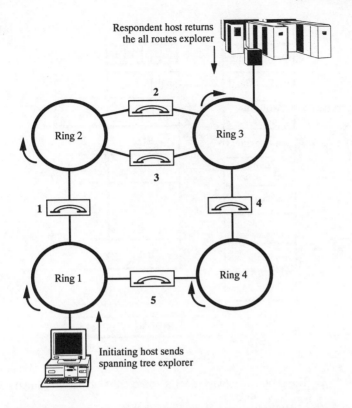

Respondent host returns
the all routes explorer

Initiating host sends
spanning tree explorer

Figure 11.8 Source routing bridges for Token Ring networks.

NIA must first determine its route. If this has not already been established then the NIA transmits a 'spanning tree explorer' frame (also termed a single-route broadcast frame) which ensures that every ring receives one copy of the frame (during initialization the bridges have employed the STA as defined in IEEE 802.1 to configure the network appropriately). This spanning tree configuration is used by the 'spanning tree explorer' frames only. In Figure 11.8 this broadcast frame eventually reaches the destination NIA, which receives the frame and responds with the 'all routes explorer' frame (also termed the all-routes broadcast frame). This frame is forwarded once by all of the bridges, each bridge inserting its route identification information, and so several versions of the original frame will arrive at the initiating host. The difference in the frames is the route they have used: one frame will have used bridges 4 and 5, another bridges 3 and 1, and so on.

The initiating host now selects one of the frames and uses the routing information within it to create the route for the original data frame. The standard makes no stipulation about how this selection will be supported but in most instances it uses the route of the first frame back (by implication this will be the fastest). The data is now sent using a specifically routed frame and the route destination is stored for future use.

There is one problem with this technique: where to place the routing information. The frame structure for the Token Ring was shown in Figure 7.3 and there is no

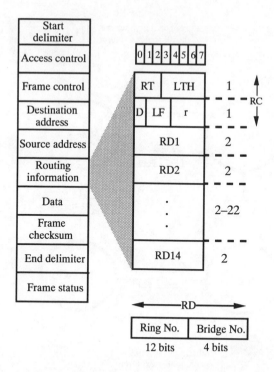

Figure 11.9 The protocol sublayers for a source routing Token Ring network.

routing field. This omission is historical; the concept of bridged rings was not considered in the original standards. The principle of NIA bridging control meant that the structure of the NIAs and their frames had to be altered, and this alteration had to be implemented in such a way that it was possible to enhance the original and installed non-standard NIAs.

Two changes were made to the frame structure, as shown in Figure 11.9. The first was to append on front of the user data a thirty octet routing field. This field consists of the routing control (RC) and route designators (RD). The RC contains the frame type identifier (RT), the cumulative routing field length (LTH), the direction field (D) and the largest frame (LF). The RD contains the ring number and the bridge number. Two RD fields are used every time a frame is to be forwarded by a bridge: bridge entry and exit points, and so only seven bridges can be traversed in a source routing network. The LF field is a coded representation for the largest frame that can be supported by that bridge. The LF always contains the smallest value that can be supported by any bridge on the route and so this is used in networks that must support mixed ring capabilities.

The second change was to highjack the first bit of the source address field. This bit is normally used to indicate individual or group addressing. Since the source must always be from an individual only, the bit can be reassigned. The function of this bit was therefore changed to indicate no routing (0) or routing (1); if routing then the

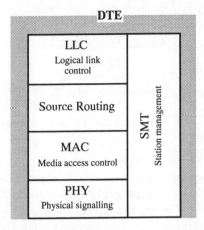

Figure 11.10 MAC frames for source routing token ring networks.

routing field would be present. The NIAs can now differentiate between routing and non-routing frames. The final problem was how to support the proposed frame modifications for installed NIAs. The solution was to structure the NIAs as shown in Figure 11.10, as compared to Figure 7.1 – that is, with the inclusion of a source routing sublayer. This sublayer extends the LLC field by appending the routing information to the LLC and modifies the source address. This sublayer is also responsible for coordinating route identification and for controlling the routing tables.

The advantage of this approach is that it is possible to renovate the older NIAs by releasing an upgrade to either the NIA driver or the LLC software and so remove the need for replacing the old NIAs. The new NIAs can support the source routing either in the NIA's firmware or as part of the LLC/driver software.

There may be a laudable intention behind a user oriented philosophy; however, any mistakes or omissions in the original specification can have wide ranging repercussions which strait-jacket the flexibility available for any modifications.

11.3.5 Source routing transparent bridge

From the point of view of Token Ring bridging the IEEE 802.1D and IEEE 802.1G standards must be reconciled with that of the IEEE 802.5. Naturally there is more than one way of supporting this reconciliation, so more than one solution exists; however, only one conforms to the emerging standard.

The solution originally provided by IBM is shown in Figure 11.11. In this network there are two distinct domains, one supporting transparent bridging and one source routing – the interface between them was supported by a single source routing transparent bridge (SR-TB). The advantage and disadvantage of this solution is that a single box must be used for the interface, so it is a relatively simple solution but this

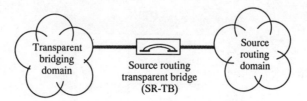

Figure 11.11 The IBM source routing transparent bridge scheme.

means that there is no bridge flexibility within each of the domains.

The standards committees are therefore adopting the solution shown in Figure 11.12. In this architecture it is assumed that both transparent and source routing bridges can be randomly distributed across the network. The source routing transparent (SRT) bridges are devices which support both source routing and transparent bridging depending on the type of frame: non-routing frames are bridged transparently and routing ones are source routed. This means their interaction with the surrounding bridges depends on the type of those bridges.

Fully interactive SRTs are now available and their long-term benefit to network designers is that they will provide interconnectivity between networks that have adopted one or other of the bridging techniques. This means that the future operation of a network will not be limited by the original design choices.

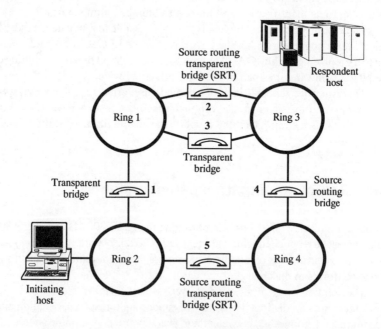

Figure 11.12 The standardized source routing transparent bridge scheme.

11.3.6 Local bridge

The local bridge is responsible for connecting two identical LANs, back-to-back; it is a two-port device only (cf. the local repeater). This means that there is no intermediate network or cabling and so the maximum separation between the LANs is limited to the native cabling distances on either side of the bridge.

Figure 11.1 shows a CSMA/CD network supported by a local bridge. Again, as is the case for the local repeater, the maximum separation between the two LANs is limited to 100 m. The equivalent network for Token Ring is shown in Figure 11.2. Here the two type 1 passive MAUs are linked using a bridge and so they must not be separated by more than 200 m (the length of the two lobe cables). If passive type 3 MAUs were used instead the maximum separation between them would be only 90 m.

In both systems the bridge is being used to break the network into two separate domains, each of which should benefit from a lower traffic load. The use of a local bridge in this way would be one of the first steps in compensating for an increased number of, or more active, users. The only restriction on the architecture is ensuring that the bridge isolates the network into its two logical user groups, thereby minimizing the amount of information that must be forwarded by the bridge. The typical cost for this form of bridge is between £1000 and £3000, depending on the functionality supported, for example management, customized filters and so on.

Interconnectivity between bridges from different manufactures is normally straightforward in the case of CSMA/CD. In the case of older bridges there will be all sorts of interconnectivity problems due to the many different draft revisions of the spanning tree standard and the fact that many of the original implementations were faulty. In the case of source routing bridges, care has to be taken to ensure that the bridges are using the same revision of the developing standard.

11.3.7 Remote bridge

Remote bridges are generally two-port devices used to connect two remote LANs using one form or another of WAN link: one port for the LAN and one for the WAN. The type of link used between the LANs is normally defined by its cost, with a 300 km megastream link costing in excess of £100 000, as well as the needed carrying capacity.

The IEEE 802.1G standard has undergone a considerable number of changes throughout its development. While the STA is still employed across remote bridge architectures, several proprietary solutions are also available such as adaptive routing from Retix, and the 'open architecture' is further threatened when some of the more specialized features of these bridges are considered, such as data encryption and compression. The intermediate system between the bridges is connectionless and as such is unreliable, even though some implementations will provide a proprietary reliable link (using the LAPB protocol for example), provided both ends are supplied by the same manufacturer. This uncertainty means that it is important to ascertain the potential connectivity problems when evaluating remote bridges, especially for Token Ring networks.

Figure 11.5 shows the remote bridge architecture for a CSMA/CD system and the equivalent Token Ring network is shown in Figure 11.3, with multiple WAN interfaces being used. The costs for each of the remote bridges range from £2500 to £6000 depending on the number and type of WAN interfaces, and so the unit pair cost ranges between £5000 and £12 000.

11.3.8 Multiport bridge

The name multiport bridge is the term given to a bridge that can support three or more interfaces (any combination of LAN and WAN interfaces); the range of WAN interfaces is the same as that for the remote bridges. A further restriction is that the multiport bridge supports one type of LAN, for example CSMA/CD or Token Ring. In most cases the actual port configuration of a multiport bridge is defined by the user and so can be tailored to fit a specific network environment.

Figure 11.13 shows a typical multiport bridge architecture for a CSMA/CD network. Here both the multiport bridges support five ports: three 10BASE2 links, a 10BASE5 link and a WAN link; each bridge supports four local carrier sensing domains. The WAN link is used to connect the two bridges, so in this configuration they are in fact remote multiport bridges. A Token Ring equivalent would replace the CSMA/CD links with Token Ring links. The typical cost for such a bridge depends on the actual port configuration, with the basic shell costing about £1000 and each port between £750 and £1500.

The advantage of a multiport bridge is that it is now possible to use a single relay box to act as a bridging hub as opposed to several two-port bridges all linked by a

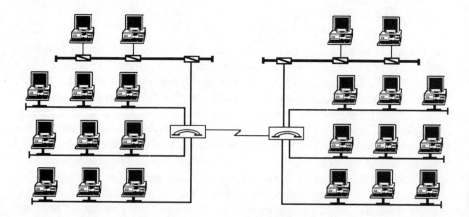

Figure 11.13 Multiport bridges in a CSMA/CD network.

backbone LAN. If several LANs are to be linked then this is a very cost effective solution. However, it does suffer from the disadvantage of creating a single point failure condition should the bridge's power supply fail.

11.3.9 Switching bridge

A switching bridge is a multiport bridge which is capable of switching a frame from one port of the bridge to another without having to wait for the full receipt of the frame, that is, on-the-fly. Under normal network loading conditions, this considerably reduces the frame latency across the bridge (particularly for long frames). A switching bridge still maintains the separate CSMA/CD and token domains but transmits a frame as soon as the destination segments become available instead of using the traditional store-and-forwarding approach.

An additional function now being supplied with switching bridges is that of full duplex switching. At present this capability is only available on UTP based systems in which both sets of twisted pairs are used to simultaneously transmit/receive information. Full duplex switching is provided through special switch interfaces and so the switch can be receiving information from a node while other information is being forwarded by the switch to that same node – each data stream is carried on a separate twisted pair.

Switching bridges are more commonly found in ethernet LANs, but they are now being developed for Token Ring networks. They support all of the appropriate, traditional bridge functions, such as source routing and transparent bridging, but the architectures in which they are used tend to be very simple, with a single bridge acting as a switching hub. The switches are based upon a high speed backbone and a variable number of interface ports, typically eight to fifteen being available, with the switching bandwidth increasing as the number of interfaces increase. A typical switching speed of 70 Mbps is available, but this is only achievable if there are seven pairs of segments across which data is being switched – that is, 10 Mbps across seven circuit switched links. The full capability of switching bridges is only achieved if the frames are evenly switched across the connected segments.

11.3.10 Modular bridge

The modular bridge is an extension of the multiport bridge systems. One of the attractions of this approach is that it is possible to locate all of the bridge elements in a single box, thus simplifying network management; both CSMA/CD and Token Ring bridges can be supported in the same modular bridge. However, no translation between the two is supplied. Each modular interface is capable of supporting several LAN links but it acts as a repeater for these connected LANs; in essence the modular bridge is a collection of modular repeater interfaces each of which are bridged together using the backplane. The interfaces normally used in a modular bridge are:

- The management interface to control the entire hub architecture. This may also support dual card redundancy and the ability to create separate network domains so that a single hub can be used for several separate networks.

- Multiport Token Ring and CSMA/CD NIAs which are capable of supporting one or more LAN segments.

- WAN link interfaces including kilostream, megastream, FDDI and so on.

Figure 11.14 shows a modular bridge architecture supporting separate Token Ring and CSMA/CD systems. The bridge is configured so that the 4 Mbps and 16 Mbps systems are linked to create a single physical network and the two CSMA/CD buses create a second but distinct physical network. The modular bridges can also support the usual range of WAN interfaces and so it is possible to fully extend the network. In most cases the hubs are capable of supporting up to eight interfaces with no more than six of these dedicated to LANs. The most recent hubs are based upon collapsible backbones which use proprietary switching algorithms for interface connectivity but these will eventually be replaced by cell relay switching. Collapsed backbone switching makes it possible to use a common channel to support different LANs both in terms of translation between and separation from each other.

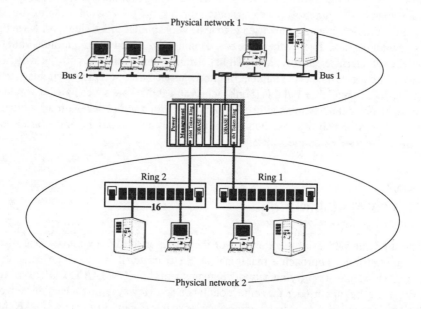

Figure 11.14 Modular bridges.

11.3.11 Bridge type comparison

The wide range of different types of bridge means that it is difficult to decide which bridges are best suited to particular networks. The main guidelines to consider are:

- MAC bridges link ethernet-to-ethernet and Token Ring-to-Token Ring only.
- Link bridges are used to connect CSMA/CD and Token Ring LANs.
- CSMA/CD networks always use transparent bridges whereas Token Ring networks make use of either source routing (predominantly) or transparent bridges (occasionally).
- Local bridges connect LANs together in a back-to-back manner whereas remote bridges make use of an intermediate network.
- Multiport and modular bridges are more complex forms of local and remote bridge, and are used to replace several individual bridge units.
- Switch bridges reduce the latency across the bridge and they are used to ensure that the bridge itself does not become a store-and-forward bottleneck.

The final choice of bridge depends on the network architecture that it must support, the degree of fault resilience required by the network, the number of extra features required by the users and network managers, and the cost of the proposed solution. The modularity of bridge design does mean, however, that it is nearly always possible to find the right bridge at the right price.

11.4   Uses of a bridge

Bridges are used in four basic ways:

- To provide extended connectivity between LANs.
- To improve the performance of a network.
- To restrict access to some part of the network.
- To supply fault resilience, thereby providing a robust and reliable network.

11.4.1 Extended connectivity

In some cases it is impossible to connect two LANs by using repeaters because the networks are either too far apart or the total number of users would exceed the recommended limit. A bridge is therefore the best solution for this connectivity because it is protocol independent, so any number of similar LANs can be interconnected without consideration of the higher layer protocols.

In Figure 11.15 two CSMA/CD repeater networks are linked using three bridges. If fault resilience was not a consideration then only the central bridge would be required; this bridge links the two multiport repeaters. The central bridge is connected to the repeaters using a BNC connector. Bridges contain NIAs and so do not provide internal termination, which means that T-pieces must be used when supporting 10BASE2 architectures. In principle this network could support 2048 users without exceeding the 1024 limitation imposed on a single repeater architecture.

An equivalent Token Ring architecture is shown in Figure 11.16. In this network it is important to note that:

- The two Token Ring domains operate at different data rates. This means that if the 16 Mbps ring wishes to put more than 25% of its load onto the other ring then this will be overloaded irrespective of its native load.

- The bridges are connected to lobe cables and the repeaters are connected to the main ring segment ports. Bridges are users of the network and so they can act as the ring monitor.

- Each ring has eight users: four workstations and four bridges.

The two token domains mean that this network can support a maximum of 520 nodes provided that each ring supports no more than 260 of them (the limit for a repeater based type 1 Token Ring network).

In both of the networks shown in Figures 11.15 and 11.16 the users would be unaware of which bridges were forwarding their data. Indeed, unless there is a significant distortion in the performance of the network caused by crossing the bridges (preventing this is a design aim), they will not even know whether their information is crossing a bridge. The advantages of this approach mean that any topological change of the network does not affect the users' perception of the network and so – within

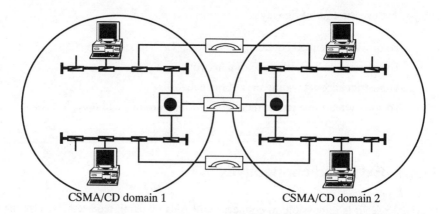

CSMA/CD domain 1   CSMA/CD domain 2

Figure 11.15 Network connectivity using bridges.

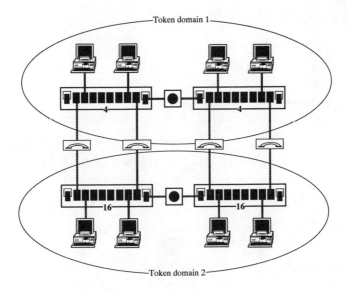

Figure 11.16 Bridge connectivity in Token Ring networks.

reason – the network can be altered without disturbing them. Again, from the user point of view it is irrelevant whether transparent or source routing bridges are used, just as long as the necessary connectivity is supplied.

11.4.2 Performance improvement

The primary function of the bridge is to filter information and to forward frames destined for users on the other LANs. This filtering breaks the network into two or more separate but connected networks across which it is possible to transmit information to any user. In general it is expected that the majority of the data is to be limited to the source LANs.

Figure 11.17 shows a switch (or switched) CSMA/CD network with three domains. In this system it is designed so that the file servers are available to their local LANs only; that is, the bridges should discard frames from the file servers. This system can be easily implemented because most file servers broadcast their presence as part of the service protocol and so the bridges must be instructed to discard all broadcast frames. Non-file server communication between the NIAs is still possible provided this does not entail frame broadcasting. In this network each LAN is predominantly supporting only two NIAs whereas if a repeater architecture had been used the loading on all of the LANs would have been due to all six NIAs.

The equivalent Token Ring network is shown in Figure 11.18. Again, the file servers support their local ring only; this network has four rings. Clearly each of the four rings could be of a considerably more complex architecture, supporting the full

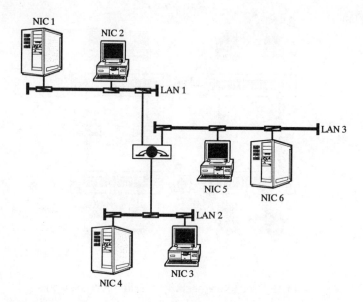

Figure 11.17 Performance enhancement for CSMA/CD networks using bridges.

260 users, thereby creating a network with 1040 users (impossible using repeaters only), but whose overall performance capability would be equivalent to a considerably smaller repeater network.

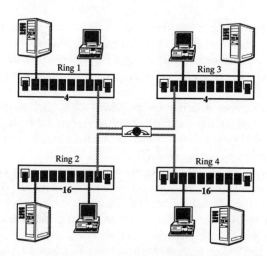

Figure 11.18 Token Ring performance enhancement using bridges.

11.4.3 Access control

The principle of access control was demonstrated in Figures 11.17 and 11.18, in which access to the file servers was restricted by the bridges, whose filtering discarded broadcast frames. This approach can be extended even further by establishing static filter tables which explicitly state where NIAs are located with respect to the bridge. The conservative action of a bridge always forwarding unknown destination frames onto all ports means that the blocking of particular NIAs must be supported by explicitly actioning the discarding of all frames associated with that particular destination address.

Access control of frames can also be augmented by using customized filtering. Recall that the internal structure of a frame is as shown in Figure 4.4. Customized filters can therefore be applied to the data content of the MAC frames in such a way as to coincide with the headers of the higher levels of protocol. If the formats of these protocols are known, as they usually are, then it is possible to filter frames according to some unique property of those protocols. For instance it would be possible to filter out all Novell NetWare frames by prohibiting frames which contain the LSAP address 'E0'; the filter would be required to analyse the first data octet of the frame; that is, the fifteenth octet of the frame.

Consider how this technique could be applied to the network in Figure 11.16. Assume that a Novell NetWare file server is on LAN 3 and that the other file servers are TCP/IP based. If the NetWare server contains confidential information then the bridges are configured to discard any of its frames, thereby prohibiting this data to leave the network. The TCP/IP frames will still have access to LAN 3 and so any TCP/IP based information is unaffected by the NetWare filters.

A favourite approach by some network designers is to use customized filtering to establish a 'firewall' around a particular part of the network. A firewall is used to prevent certain types of information from entering or leaving the protected zone. Unfortunately if the STA is being used and the active topology is reconfigured (due to the installation of a new bridge or the failure of one of the bridges) then parts of the protected zone may become compromised or even isolated from the rest of the zone. If a firewall is to be established then considerable care must be taken in ensuring that all possible bridge routes into the zone have the correct filter rules. In many cases it is simpler to disable the spanning tree for the bridges surrounding the zone. The failure of a bridge would cause the network to become disconnected – however, this was effectively the aim of the firewall in the first place.

11.4.4 Fault resilience

One of the essential aims of a network manager is to prevent the failure of the network, a failure being defined as any occurrence which prevents one or more users from using the network. The spanning tree and source routing capabilities of bridges mean that two or more bridges can simultaneously support the same connectivity, thereby ensuring that the failure of one of them does not cause the network to fail.

Figures 11.15 and 11.16 show architectures with fault resilience. In Figure 11.15 the three bridges are, effectively, in parallel, so any two of the bridges can fail without losing the network. This topology also ensures that the network is protected against the failure of one of the repeaters – it is, however, a relatively expensive solution. In Figure 11.16 the situation is even more extreme in that all four bridges are in parallel and so several elements must simultaneously fail to disconnect the network.

Clearly the trade-off for fault resilience is the cost versus the losses incurred should some or all of the network fail. In many instances only parts of the network require full protection and so it is these areas which receive the resilience. It is impossible to design a network that will never fail, no matter how much resilience is provided within it, but it is possible to make such a failure extremely unlikely provided that sufficient money is available. Conversely, most networks require some form of resilience and the rejection of this need due to expenditure is equivalent to not providing fire insurance because of the monthly payments.

11.5 Bridged network architectures

During the past five years a series of architectures have become adopted as the standard ways in which to link together CSMA/CD networks, and Token Ring networks. Although on paper some of these appear to be elegant solutions, in reality they can lead to long-term problems caused by the slow but insidious increase in traffic loading supported by the network.

11.5.1 CSMA/CD systems

The CSMA/CD architectures that are well suited to bridging have been well covered, so it is appropriate to discuss two architectures that have surprising consequences. The first is shown in Figure 11.19 in which the remote bridges are linked by a 1 km fibre. In many systems this link could be supported by a pair of remote repeaters, as shown in Figure 10.5. However, there is one situation in which bridges should be used. This is when the remote segment supports only a very few users in comparison to the many tens or hundreds on the other segments; this typically arises when a simple extension is made to the network to support some remote users.

If repeaters were used then the performance of the network should be the same for the whole network. However, this will not be the case where the user population is not evenly distributed about the network. The problem is caused by the remote users who are separated by the fibre link, which means that they experience the loading of

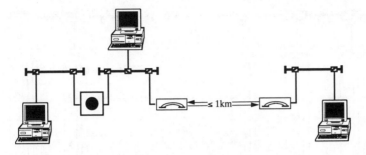

Figure 11.19 Bridging for small, isolated groups.

the network 'late' compared to the others. This lateness results in the remote users believing the network is idle when it is not and so they cause more contentions. The overall result is that a severely non-uniform distribution of users results in the average throughput per user being decreased except for the remote users, who experience a significant degradation in what they would expect – sometimes only 1% of their expected throughput (Tobagi, 1986).

The better solution is to use a bridge. The remote users are now grouped within their own domain, as are the other users. These two domains can now support the usual traffic loads and so the effects of the uneven user distribution are removed.

The physical location of file servers within a bridged network is of particular interest to many organizations. Consider the network shown in Figure 11.17, where the file server is located on LAN 2 but supports users on both LAN 1 and LAN 2. It would be incorrect to state that this configuration will not work. However, the point that has to be made is that the user will experience a slow but increasing level of performance degradation (increasing response times) as the utilization of the network grows. The reason for this is that the bridge is passing all of the traffic on LAN 1 onto LAN 2 (but not vice versa). The bridge's capability to forward information is dependent on the loading of LAN 2; as this load increases then the bridge becomes more likely to discard ageing frames.

The reason for the success of adopting this configuration in the first place rests on the fact that the average load on a CSMA/CD network is typically in the 5–10% region, which places the forwarding load on the bridge within the recommended limits of 20% of the total load. Unfortunately as the average load of the network increases then the forwarding load on the bridges may start to pass the recommended limit and the user response times will increase due to the error correction protocols recovering from frame loss. The moral of the story is that if this architecture is to be used then monitor the loading on the network closely and be prepared to move users to cause a redistribution of the load.

One of the most common architectures for two port bridges is that shown in Figure 11.20. The bridges act as pathways from the local LANs onto the backbone, thereby ensuring that the backbone only supports inter-LAN traffic. The bridges also ensure that the general backbone traffic does not flood onto their local LANs and so only pass information which is destined for one of their local users. The actual bridges

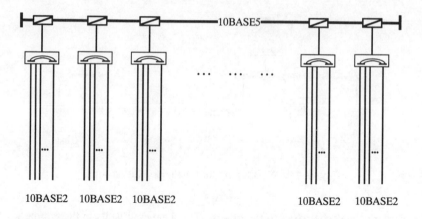

Figure 11.20 A backbone of bridges for CSMA/CD architectures.

can themselves be one of several types. In the simplest case these will be several local bridges supporting only one local LAN each. The next stage is to use multiport and switching bridges in which several local LANs are bridged together and so even less information is transferred onto the backbone. The most expensive solution is to use a modular bridge, in which the backbone itself is contained within the bridge and consequently a single box provides all of the required connectivity.

Once the local connectivity has been established the next problem is that of the WAN. Figures 11.21 and 11.22 show the typical architecture used to provide local and remote connectivity. Figure 11.21 shows four separate sites connected using remote

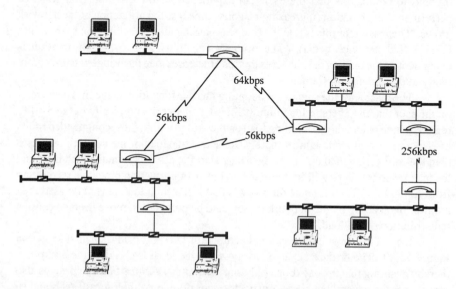

Figure 11.21 Local and remote bridging in a CSMA/CD architecture.

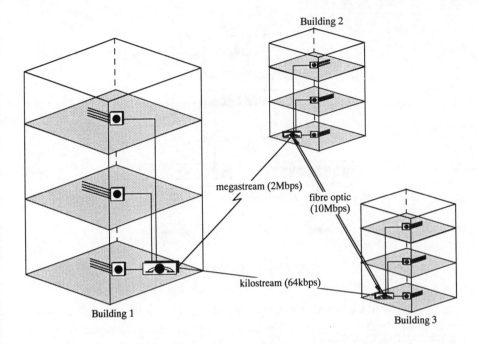

Figure 11.22 Bridging across remote building locations.

bridges. One site makes use of a local bridge and the others support single LANs only. Three of the sites are linked using a triangulation method and the use of the 56 kbps links imply that these are transatlantic connections (the use of the switches is a more modern approach to that shown in Figure 11.10). Figure 11.22 shows a three-dimensional representation of the WAN architecture. In each of the three buildings a switching bridge has been used to replace the separate local and remote bridges in each building. The three buildings are linked using triangulated remote bridging, each with a different carrying capacity.

11.5.2 Token Ring systems

Unlike CSMA/CD systems the bridged Token Ring architectures have the added consideration of supporting mixed 4 and 16 Mbps rings as well as transparent and source routing solutions. It is not possible to link mixed rate rings using a repeater. Most Token Ring bridges support source routing; however, from an architectural point of view there is no difference between transparent and source routing networks.

The linking of mixed rate rings using a bridge rapidly leads to the debate previously addressed for CSMA/CD networks; the location of file servers. One of the most commonly adopted Token Ring architectures is as shown in Figure 11.23. The

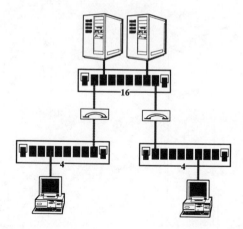

Figure 11.23 Bridges for linking mixed capacity Token Rings.

file servers are all located on the 16 Mbps backbone ring and the users are supported by their own local 4 Mbps rings. The networks are linked using bridges. Given this architecture the backbone ring can support at least four peripheral rings without any loss due to capacity considerations and the client/server relationship means that the peripheral rings should not become overloaded. The problems with this type of architecture arise when the backbone is actually supporting more than just four rings. In this case the backbone may become overloaded, particularly if the peripheral networks are heavily loaded, for example by intensive graphics manipulation, and it must be stressed that one of the reasons for using Token Ring is to support network intensive processing (CSMA/CD being completely unsuited to this type of activity).

A more sensible solution would be to put the file servers within the domain of the relevant peripheral ring and to use only a 4 Mbps backbone, or alternatively to make the file servers act as the bridge themselves. This latter solution means that the file servers support two Token Ring NIAs, one for each ring, and support all of the processing normally supported by a bridge as well as that of the file service; this form of solution is favoured by many workstation manufacturers and removes the need for separate relay elements. A similar solution can also be provided for CSMA/CD LANs.

Ignoring the debate concerning the location of file servers, the ring of rings architecture is particularly appealing because it is both simple and elegant. The network shown in Figure 11.24 demonstrates how each floor of a building can be supported by a local ring and that these rings are then interconnected using two backbone rings. If transparent bridges are used the STA must be employed to avoid looping, whereas the source routing algorithm will naturally ensure that looping does not occur. Here the backbone MAUs have been located on the central floor (normally they would be located in the primary wiring closet) and so they must not be separated by more than 100 m from each of the connected bridges (lobe cable lengths). The backbone MAUs can now support eight separate floors (assuming an eight port MAU),

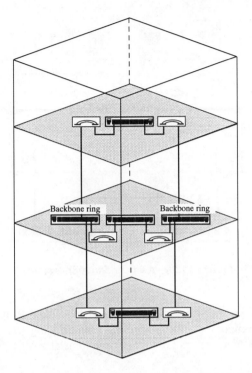

Figure 11.24 A Token Ring architecture supporting a single building.

or more if it has other daisy chained MAUs, and each floor can support upwards of some 250 users (allowing for bridges and repeaters).

11.5.3 Link bridge architectures

Recall that link bridges are used to support mixed LAN architectures, such as CSMA/CD to Token Ring connectivity. This means that the bridges must support some form of translational capability, whether from one MAC frame format to another or between a MAC frame and intermediate link frame. The growing trend for both CSMA/CD and Token Ring systems to be used in the same location is pushing the need for mixed LAN connectivity in a framework that is consistent with the established network architectures. This normally means that either the CSMA/CD or the Token Ring are required to act as the backbone onto which the other LANs are hung.

In Figure 11.25 a 10BASE5 system acts as the corporate backbone. The CSMA/CD LANs are linked to the backbone using a standard local transparent bridge whereas the Token Ring systems must use a link bridge; in this network the link bridges are actually enhanced file servers. This bridge translates the Token Ring frames into their CSMA/CD equivalent and forwards the frames onto the backbone for reception

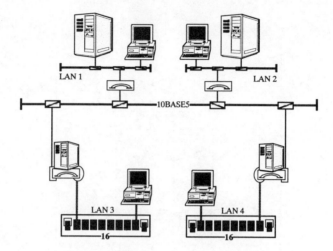

Figure 11.25 A link bridge architecture.

by other bridges. An added complication is that the Token Ring systems may be supporting transparent or more likely source routing bridging and so the link bridges must also act as SRTs as well as providing frame translations.

11.6 Summary

It is important to understand the differences between repeaters and bridges so that it is clear when and where to use each of the relays. Table 11.1 summarizes the capabilities of both these devices but the basic rule to be applied is:

- Use a repeater to extend the natural capabilities of the LAN and to overcome the limitations imposed by its component technology.
- Use a bridge when the LAN has to be broken down into more manageable groups, whether for fault resilience, security or performance considerations.

To conclude the topic of bridges it is important to recall that:

- MAC bridges are used to connect identical LANs in a protocol independent manner by constructing a logical LAN, from the physically linked LANs.
- The link bridge (for example, the IBM mixed bridge solution) is used to connect CSMA/CD and Token Ring LANs together in a protocol independent manner. Full link bridges are only just appearing, so be wary of problems with compatibility.

Table 11.1 A comparison between repeaters and bridges.

Comparison	Repeater	Bridge
LAN extension	Simple physical size extension.	Suited to separating the traffic flow across the network.
Change media	Simple to change media.	Media changes supported but should not be used for this solely.
Protocols support	Protocol independent above the physical layer.	Protocol independent at the LLC and above.
Topological flexibility	In CSMA/CD no more than four repeaters in serial. Effectively unlimited in Token Ring.	Limited to domains of no more than seven bridges.
Optimize management control	Transparent to frames and so no traffic control.	Support frame filtering capabilities.
Minimize management overhead	Just insert and switch on.	Can be self learning but may also require manual configuration.
Performance	Forwards frames at 100% utilization.	Filters frames at full utilization but will forward according to loading on the forwarding network.

- Local bridges are two-port devices used to connect back-to-back LANs and remote bridges are used to connect LANs via an intermediate network. Multiport, switched and modular (hub) bridges are extensions of local and remote bridges.

- The important characteristics of bridges are their filtering rate, forwarding rate, filter table capacity, WAN connectivity support and management capabilities. The range of support features such as customized filtering, triangulation and load balancing should also be considered.

- In general, CSMA/CD LANs employ transparent bridging (using the spanning tree algorithm) and Token Ring LANs use source routing. Transparent bridges for Token Ring LANs are commercially available but these have a relatively small market share.

- Bridges are used to extend the basic connectivity restrictions which may be encountered even after having used repeaters, to improve the performance of the network by partitioning the traffic distribution, to create fault resilient networks using frame based routing and to restrict access to the network using frame filtering control.

- Do not connect more than seven bridges together in any one domain and limit the total bridged distance to under 20 km. The spanning tree algorithm response time and source routing field sizes limit the number of bridges and the accumulated transfer delay limits the distance.

12

Routers

12.1 Introduction

Interoperability between two users is only possible when they share a common protocol. Repeaters and MAC bridges are responsible for interconnecting identical LANs (the same multiple access scheme) and so they are termed protocol independent – that is, independent of the protocols above the MAC layer. This means that in principle all information flow across the network is controlled by the MAC addresses only and so more sophisticated routing techniques must be supported by a higher level of protocol: the network layer.

A router is the internetworking relay which is used to connect different subnetworks that support the same network layer protocol. However, manufacturers use a variety of different routing techniques, giving rise to many different network layer protocols (Held, 1993). Routers do not provide protocol translation but the support of a common network layer protocol does provide mixed MAC connectivity (hence mixed subnetwork connectivity) through the natural process of encapsulation and unwrapping in layered protocols. The functionality of a router is limited to the capabilities of the network layer protocols it supports and so their future development will extend more towards adopting many of the functions provided by bridges.

12.2 Functions of a router

Unlike the repeater and the bridge, a router must actively communicate with the end system hosts and these hosts must, in turn, modify their operation when a router is present. The functionality of a router has therefore two main components: the efficient handling and routing of user data across the network and the effective network-wide maintenance of the addressing scheme (Perlman, 1992). Network layer protocols can be either connectionless or connection oriented and so both approaches must be supported by the appropriate routers. The OSI/RM mandates that a transformed X.25PLP service is used to provide the CONS – this transformation is provided by a two convergence protocols which convert the original X.25PLP interface into the OSI/RM CONS interface.

In an X.25 environment (and by definition a connection oriented system) the end-system is the DTE and the router is the DCE. This means that the transfer of information between the routers is not defined and so this is left to suppliers of the router-to-router link. Most router architectures are based upon connectionless network layer protocols such as IP, IPX, CLNP and so on, and so the following discussion will not consider the connection oriented protocols.

12.2.1 Routing techniques and protocols

Connectionless router networks must supply three basic services:

- Connectionless data transfer – the transfer of the source host's data across the router infrastructure to the destination host.
- Neighbour greeting – the process by which the hosts and routers identify each other, thereby enabling the local address tables to be configured appropriately.
- Routing – the process by which the routers cooperate to provide the packet store-and-forward transmission across the network.

It can be implied from these three services that one of the basic differences between a bridge and a router is that a bridge has no explicit communication with the hosts whereas a router must swap address information and packets with a host. Consider the network shown in Figure 12.1, in which CSMA/CD and Token Ring LANs are linked using two routers. Each device has its own unique address which contains its network identifier, host identifier and its MAC address; host address A.2.b defines host 2 on subnetwork A with MAC address b. The unique network address is therefore A.2.

Ignoring for the moment the presence of the routers then the normal mode of communication between host A.1 and host A.2 is:

- The network layer for host A.1 is told to send data to host A.2. The initiator now goes to its address table and retrieves the destination MAC address, b. The data is then sent to that MAC address.

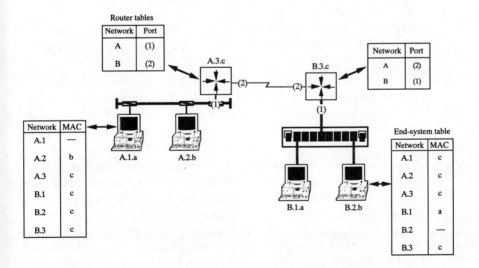

Figure 12.1 Router tables and their relationship to the network.

- The address mapping table between the network and MAC addresses must be either pre-configured or dynamically populated. In the dynamic allocation scheme a protocol is used by the hosts to identify other users on the network. This is called neighbour greeting.

Now consider the situation when the two hosts are located on separate subnetworks (routers can only interconnect networks with different subnetwork addresses). The first two problems encountered are that the MAC address systems on the two subnetworks will not, in general, be the same and that the information must be forwarded by the router. Therefore, if host A.1 wishes to send data to host B.1 then it must use the MAC address of router A.3, and not that of B.1; the use of the broadcast MAC addresses is not feasible because this would mean that every frame would have to be broadcast! Therefore, the network layer protocols must then be responsible for reconciling the presence of a router with an alteration of the addressing scheme. Different router systems establish their mapping tables in different ways and so only the OSI/RM and IPS approaches will be discussed. In an OSI/RM network the (greatly simplified) approach is:

- Whenever a router is inserted in a network it periodically sends a intermediate system hello (ISH) broadcast on each of its local networks and on each of its associated WAN links. At the same time every end-system periodically issues an end-system hello (ESH) which enables all local routers to populate their network/MAC address tables.

- The LAN based ISH is responsible for informing the hosts that a router is now present on their network. The WAN based ISH is responsible for informing all of the other routers of the newcomer's presence. When the other routers respond they provide information concerning the subnetworks which they support (hence the need for a set of unique network identifiers). While a router may only support a single subnetwork it might also be the only path through which access to other routers and their subnetworks may be obtained. In this case the user data will be stored-and-forwarded across the intermediate routers.

- The new router now has a mapping table of all of its local network addresses to MAC addresses and a table of the router identifiers to subnetwork addresses. The routing algorithms now re-evaluate the optimal routes across the network. This information is then propagated across the network, thereby ensuring that each of the routers has a consistent view of the optimal route topologies.

- The end-systems either send the information to the explicitly identified MAC address or to any identified routers. If the destination address is unknown and there are no routers then the information is broadcast to all end-systems. If a router receives a packet to forward, but knows of a more appropriate router to service the request then a redirect message is returned to the initiating end-system and this causes the network/MAC address table to be reconfigured with the new mapping.

In contrast the IPS approach is:

- In many cases the hosts are pre-configured with the network address of at least one router and the routers are pre-configured with the set of network layer addresses that are reachable on one of their links.

- The hosts identify the local addresses of the other hosts and the routers by using the ARP. The initiator uses this protocol to ask the destination node, and so the intermediate router, for its MAC address. The router intercepts this request and returns its own MAC address to the initiator (the router interception is possible because it knows which subnetworks can be reached through it).

- Routers use the ICMP to provide the redirect service and the only difference between this and the OSI/RM equivalent is that the host must then use the ARP to identify the MAC address of the newly identified router.

Once the routing tables have been established the relationship between them and the network's architecture is equivalent to those shown in Figure 12.1. The router table defines the relationship (or mapping) between the router's port number (of internal significance only) and the connected subnetwork addresses. The host tables define the mapping between the destination host subnetwork address and the MAC address for use on the local LAN. The table in host A.1 shows that all information intended for hosts on subnetwork B should be sent using the router's MAC address. The transmission of data between hosts A.1.a and B.2.b now entails:

- Host A.1 passes a transmission request to its network layer.

- The network layer retrieves the destination MAC address c to which the packet will be sent. The destination network address B.2 is placed in the network packet. This packet is encapsulated in the MAC frame and is then transmitted.

- All but the router's MAC will reject this frame. The router will recognize its own MAC address and will pass the frame's data up to the network layer. The network layer will strip off the network header.

- On examining the network header the router will note that the destination address B.2 is not its own A.3 and so will realize that the information must be forwarded. It uses its own tables for the subnetwork addresses and notes that packets for subnetwork B are sent to port 2. The packet is now encapsulated by the intermediate system and sent onto the other router.

- Router B.3 receives the packet from the intermediate system and retrieves from it the destination network address B.2. It notes that this packet is to be forwarded and so obtains the destination MAC address b from its own ES table. The packet is then encapsulated in the Token Ring frame and is transmitted onto the ring.

- The host B.2.b will receive the frame, strip away the headers and so on, and pass the packet to the network layer. The network layer inspects the packet and notes that the network address is for its own host and so passes the data up to the higher protocol layers. The data has been received by the correct end-system.

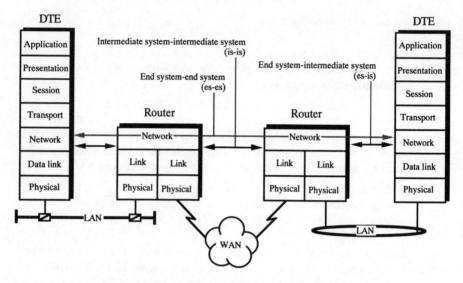

Figure 12.2 Routers and their classes of protocol.

From the previous explanation it can be seen that it is the network address that is responsible for ensuring that the data reaches the correct end user. The network address is a fundamental element of the network layer protocol and it is the only address which is mandated, by the standards organizations, as unique across all forms of subnetwork; in some cases an end-system may have several unique network addresses. The address maintenance and user communication requirements give rise to three classes of protocol which must be supported by a router:

- End-system to end-system (es-es) – this is the data passing protocol used by the hosts, such as IP, IPX or CLNP (data transfer).

- End-system to intermediate system (es-is) – this is the protocol which supports the host to router communications and is responsible for populating the end-system address tables with the router MAC address (neighbour greeting).

- Intermediate system to intermediate system (is-is) – which is the protocol that supports the router to router communications, and is responsible for populating the router address tables and establishing the optimal routing algorithms across the network. The hierarchical nature of router systems means that there are two types of is-is protocol: the intra-domain and inter-domain (routing).

The generic labels for these protocols are derived from the formal classifications used by the ISO, and so the OSI/RM CLNP (ES-ES) and Novell's IPX protocols are different implementations of the es-es class of protocols. The same rule applies for the es-is and is-is protocols. The relationship between these three protocols and the network's architecture is shown in Figure 12.2. It is important to stress that the routing algorithm is supported by the is-is protocol and so the performance capability of the end-system protocol is dependent on the efficacy of the intermediate system protocol. Two points should be noted when considering connectionless router systems and their protocols:

- In many systems the three protocol classes are in fact supported by just two physical protocols, one for data communication and one for addressing information.
- The physical protocols may well support a different class of service: the data protocol will typically be connectionless whereas the addressing protocols will normally be of an acknowledged connectionless service form thereby ensuring a reliable address maintenance scheme.

Clearly, the operation of a router is more complex than that of either a repeater or a bridge and consequently they normally require considerable configuration. Not only is their own configuration complex but in situations where routers are being introduced to the network then it is common for the current addressing system to need renovation to ensure that all of the subnetworks are uniquely identified. This renovation may well entail changing all of the host addresses throughout the entire network.

12.2.2 WAN connectivity

Routers are packet based store-and-forward devices which route data between LANs across some intermediate WAN. Originally they were used to provide LAN–WAN connectivity in which a common network service was provided but the user community's need for LAN-to-LAN connectivity across a WAN infrastructure took advantage of the router's capabilities and this approach accounts for most of the installed routers. It is important therefore that a router's internal architecture is flexible enough to support as wide a range of intermediate systems as possible. While it is inappropriate to expect a router to support several intermediate systems using a single interface it is common for each system to be supported by its own interface card which can sit on the router's backplane. Therefore, two important features to be considered when selecting a router are the range of available intermediate system interfaces and the number that can be supported at any one time. The range of intermediate systems that a router should be capable of supporting includes:

- Kilostream – a 64 kbps link which can be obtained from a public network supplier or can be used to form a private network. Distance is no limitation; however, the bandwidth restriction will cause severe bottlenecks under heavy loading conditions (cf. with bridges).
- Megastream – a 2.048 Mbps using the G.703 links which should be capable of supporting all but the most heavily loaded of routers (cf. with bridges).

- X.25 – the use of the full three-layer system with X.21 at the bottom. The problem with this approach is that its COS nature inflicts a severe delay penalty on the data communications.

- Fibre optic point-to-point link – the most commonly available multimode fibre is limited to a maximum distance of 2 km but it can support bandwidths in excess of 500 Mbps.

- Fibre distributed data interface (FDDI) – this makes use of the 100 Mbps FDDI as a backbone link and so the interfaces act as encapsulational devices, thereby treating the link in the same manner as a kilostream or megastream interface.

- ISDN links – the advantage of this network is that variable bandwidth allocations are available: 64 kbps–2.048 Mbps upon connection request. A disadvantage of this form of link is that there can be a relatively long setup delay while the circuit is established (cf. with bridges).

- Frame relay – the replacement for the LAPB based carrier systems to provide a bandwidth availability of between 2 and 45 Mbps. These types of interface replace the reliable data transfer services supported in the data link layer with a high speed data pipe.

- Switched multimegabit data service (SMDS) – the backbone MAN which is currently used to support data rates in the 34–45 Mbps region. The standard interface to these systems is based upon the distributed queue dual bus.

- Cell relay – one of the carrier systems undergoing specification for broadband ISDN architectures. The bandwidth availability for these systems is between 155 and 620 Mbps. At present many of the available interfaces are non-standard due to the incompleteness of the relevant standards.

- Satellite links – a variety of different such interfaces is available but the most significant issues to consider are the increased time delays caused by the up/down link time and satellite access protocols (0.25–0.5 s), the availability and cost of satellite time, and the point-to-point throughputs.

- Microwave – where line-of-sight communication is available, and when atmospheric conditions and safety considerations will not be a problem, then microwave links should be considered, especially when the data and voice systems must be integrated.

- Leased and dial-up analogue links – in cases where there will only be occasional use of a router it is sometimes more appropriate to make use of the telephone network (PSTN) for data transfer. Naturally the transfer rates are lower due to the access delay and limited carrying capacity but it is a very cost effective solution for very low volumes of data.

- Synchronous links – these will vary depending on the national carrier requirements and include the T1, X.21, X.32 and so on with rates up to about 4 Mbps.

The range of available interfaces is considerably more complete than for the equivalent bridge connectivity. This is to be expected since the router is a wide area access device (hence its support for flow control), unlike the bridge, which has evolved to support wide area access but which is still predominantly intended for localized access. In many instances the increased access delay and setup time introduced by routers is not a concern because the natural overheads caused by the increased number of protocols, protocol processing and manipulation cause the greatest increase in the delay time.

12.2.3 End-system protocols

The es-es protocols are responsible for user data transfer and as such are the commonly known layer 3 protocols which form part of the standard profiles. Each protocol must be explicitly supported if its associated profiles are to communicate through the router; in this case the relay is termed a multiprotocol router. In many cases an organization has need of three or four different es-es protocols typically originating from:

- TCP/IP – the *de facto* layer 4/3 protocols.
- Novell NetWare – the IPX protocol.
- DECnet Phase IV/V – Digital's proprietary protocol.
- XNS – the internetwork datagram protocol (IDP).
- UB XNS – again, this is IDP.
- Banyan VINES – Banyan's proprietary protocol.
- AppleTalk – Apple's proprietary protocol.
- ISO connectionless protocol (CLNP) and the enhanced X.25 for the connection oriented equivalent – the formal ISO network layer protocols.

The selection of the required protocols is simple once the user environment into which the router will be placed has been identified. The capabilities of a router should be restricted when security is important; for example, if a particular protocol is used for sensitive data, for internal use only, then the router should be configured to ignore such data, thus preventing its passage onto the intermediate network. A more extreme approach is to ensure the router does not support the protocol itself.

12.2.4 Intermediate system protocols

Intermediate system protocols are responsible for supporting routing devices, whereas end-system protocols support non-routing devices. In principle, a router based architecture can be exceedingly large because an integrated network is formed from the interconnection of the individual subnetworks. This in turn means that the routing tables can become large and unmanageable from the point of view of reliable and responsive maintenance.

The solution to this problem of scale is the introduction of a routing hierarchy based upon the segmentation of the network into router groups. The routing system is then supported by two types of routing protocol:

- Intra-domain routing protocols, which support router-to-router communication within the group, or domain.
- Inter-domain routing protocols, which support router-to-router communication between different groups, or domains.

Figure 12.3 shows the relationship between the intra- and inter-domain routers. In this system the routers in domain A could be further partitioned, with routers being allocated different responsibilities for communication within and between partitions. An example of this is the ISO approach, which permits the intra-domain routers to be split into level 1 and level 2 routers. The intra-domain router population is broken into subgroups, or level 1 communities, and communication between these communities is only possible using level 2 routers. This hierarchical partitioning reduces the range of connectivity across which the router must be concerned with optimal routing. This in turn reduces the time taken by the routing algorithms to determine the optimal routes across the network. Generally speaking the routing algorithms fall into two classes:

- Distance vector or Bellman–Ford algorithms, in which the routers send their entire routing information table but only to their nearest neighbours.
- Link state or shortest path first algorithms, in which the routers flood their routing information across the entire network but where the information is concerned only with the state of the links connected directly to the router.

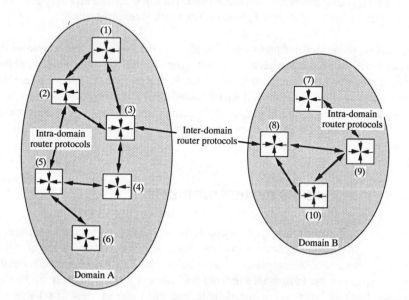

Figure 12.3 Intra-domain and inter-domain router protocol relationships.

The link state algorithms send small amounts of update information across the full network, whereas the distance vector algorithms send large amounts of information to a limited number of nodes. Both classes of algorithm have their advantages and disadvantages but in general they are both equally capable of supporting a typical router network. Each algorithm makes use of a variety of metrics to ascertain the capability of a route. Typically, these metrics are reliability, transfer delay, bandwidth availability, average loading on the link and router, and cost for using the resource. The algorithms differ in the way they evaluate the importance of these metrics and it is the sensitivity of this collation which reflects the algorithm's capability to effectively respond to a change in state of the network. The range of intra-domain protocols currently in use includes:

- Intermediate system–intermediate system (IS-IS) – this is the formal ISO standard for router to router communication. It is a link state routing protocol based upon the experience acquired by the DECnet Phase V development group and supports a variety of point-to-point and broadcast link networks. It also makes use of the level 1 and 2 router system to simplify the operation of the routing system. A 'dual' form of IS-IS is capable of supporting both IP and OSI profiles.

- End-system–intermediate system (ES-IS) – the formal ISO standard for host to router communication for the support of the CLNP. It is used by the routers and hosts to announce their presence (using the ISH and ESH, respectively) and then to maintain the MAC address to network address mapping table.

- Address resolution protocol (ARP) – the Internet protocol used by the nodes to identify the data link address of their neighbours – that is, hosts and routers.

- Interior gateway routing protocol (IGRP) – a distance vector routing protocol developed by Cisco for their routers and designed to support complex and large IP and OSI based networks.

- Routing information protocol (RIP) – the original IP intra-domain distance vector routing protocol. It is derived from the Xerox PARC universal protocol (PUP) and has in turn become the source for several other derivatives developed by Apple, Novell, Banyan, 3COM and UB.

- Hello – another distance vector IP based routing protocol but unlike RIP it uses network delay as opposed to hop count as its routing metric.

- Open shortest path first (OSPF) – a link state based protocol which has replaced RIP and Hello, and is derived from the IS-IS protocols developed by ISO.

- Routing table maintenance protocol (RTMP) – Apple's proprietary version of a modified RIP and used in the AppleTalk profile. The RIP modifications are related to addressing and other unique features of AppleTalk.

- Routing update protocol (RTP) – the Banyan proprietary version of RIP.

The range of inter-domain protocols includes:

- IS-IS inter-domain routing protocol (IDRP) – which is the formal ISO protocol for router to router communication between domains.

- Exterior gateway protocol (EGP) – which is the original IP profile domain to domain routing protocol.

- Border gateway protocol (BGP) – is the proposed IP replacement for the EGP protocol. Its most significant enhancements are that it can detect routing loops and supports intelligent routing.

A typical router profile is shown in Figure 12.4, in which the selected protocols are ES-IS for host–router and IS-IS for router–router communications. Note that the IS-IS protocol drives directly into the LLC protocol: it does not make use of CLNP as a bearer protocol. This is unlike the situation for IP systems which use RIP or OSPF. In both of these cases the protocols make use of IP as a bearer protocol, causing a further increase in the data and processing overhead, which is one reason why it is better to use the dual IS-IS protocol for IP profiles.

The point-to-point protocol (PPP) is used in Figure 12.4 because there are problems of compatibility between the routers when they are linked using serial lines. Although the serial link has a clearly defined interface there are several ways in which it can be driven to support the layer 3 protocols and in many cases different manufacturers drive the interface differently, causing compatibility problems. The solution to this problem has been the introduction of yet another protocol to act as the data link layer for routers using serial links, called the PPP. The PPP is the set of rules by which a common protocol is transported between routers across a serial link. Consider the architecture shown in Figure 12.4. Essentially, it consists of two routers that are required to support an OSI communications system based upon the CLNP. The PPP is used to encapsulate the CLNP and to define the ways in which the two routers will transfer between them the host CLNP data units.

The development of the PPP is not concerned with the definition of a single protocol. There are in fact many dialects of PPP – one for each of the protocols it must support. This means that PPP(TCP/IP) will support TCP/IP communications,

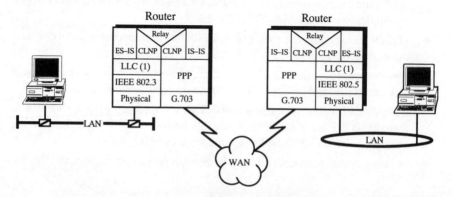

Figure 12.4 A typical OSI/RM router based network architecture.

PPP(CLNP) the CLNP, PPP(IPX) for Novell NetWare and so on. From the router's point of view the PPP is providing a similar functionality to the SLIP protocol (IP across serial links) for terminal servers and in so doing provides a more 'open' communications architecture.

From the user's point of view the existence and the functional operation of the intra- and inter-domain intermediate system protocols is irrelevant due to their transparent nature. The only issue of importance to the user concerning a router is whether or not the router protocols can maintain the routing tables quickly enough to ensure that the user data protocols do not timeout. In cases where the routing tables must be updated it is essential that this occurs within 30 seconds; this is the timeout period normally assigned to network layer data protocols, and if exceeded then the hosts will needlessly retransmit their information.

It is this time constraint which has resulted in the hierarchical layering of the routers. Although there are more individual tables to be maintained, these are of a considerably smaller size and so each individual update takes less time. The information can therefore begin to cross the network while the routing tables of the other unrelated domains are undergoing modification. It is therefore important for network designers to construct the router domains to reflect the ways in which the users make use of the network.

12.2.5 Tunnelling and encapsulation

Tunnelling is defined as the' function of transferring data units between host systems across an intermediate system when that intermediate system does not support the service needed by the data units'. A tunnel can be used to support layer 2 or layer 3 protocols. Layer 2 tunnels are used to support protocol profiles that do not have layer 3 protocols, such as LAT for Digital terminal servers and SDLC for SNA environments, whereas layer 3 tunnels are used to allow routers to forward information from protocols without being native routers for that protocol; this means that an IP router could support an IP tunnel to carry any other layer 2 or 3 protocol. From the point of view of LANs and routers this also addresses the problem of using a WAN to provide interconnectivity between two LANs when the network protocol used by the WAN (intermediate system) is different from that of the LANs (host systems). This definition gives rise to two different intermediate system architectures:

- Where the intermediate system protocol is identical to that used in the host systems – the Internet approach. In this situation there is no need to encapsulate the network layer data units in a second different layer 3 protocol, and the profile is structured as shown in Figure 12.4.
- Where the intermediate system protocol is different from that of the host systems – the hop-by-hop enhancement technique. In this instance the secondary layer 3 protocols are used to encapsulate the original network layer protocol.

Figure 12.5 shows a router architecture which is supplying an TCP/IP tunnel. In this system the end-systems are using the CLNP but the router backbone uses a TCP/IP protocol combination to forward the data units from router to router. The TCP/IP combination is used to ensure that reliable communication is supported between the routers (TCP is connection oriented whereas IP is connectionless).

A tunnel is the collective name given to the intermediate system's process of data encapsulation and unwrapping, and as such it need not only be applied to layer 3 protocols. Once a tunnel has been created then its availability is independent of the relationship between the data which is to travel through it and the information used to control its passage. This means that if separate configuration support is supplied then it is possible to establish tunnels based on layer 2 protocols, in particular SDLC, and so make use of proprietary systems as backbone networks. The routers have to be manually configured with the end point address mappings and their relationships to the tunnelled and tunnel support protocols, through which the data can then pass.

12.2.6 Data handling

The router's natural wrapping and unwrapping of the data (formally called encapsulation) in its various protocol layers is the essential feature for its reliable data transfer across different subnetworks. There are, however, several other functions that significantly add to the router's capability to handle data bundled in large amounts, of a sensitive nature or consisting of multiple levels of importance. These additions are:

- Data filtering – routers are point-to-point devices and while their own MAC sublayers are responsible for filtering out all but those frames addressed to the router there is still a need for further filtering. Not all valid packets, even of the appropriate protocol, necessarily need to be forwarded, so customized filters should be provided to support this filtering on user definable parts of the packets.

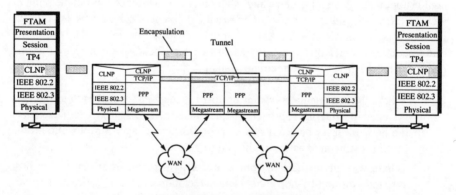

Figure 12.5 An IP tunnel.

- Data forwarding – sometimes it is important to be able to control from which ports the data packets will be forwarded. While the internal routing algorithms are normally responsible for the selection of the wide area link it is important to be able to assign links to particular data streams, for example to support time sensitive information.

- Data prioritization – in some cases, some classes of data will be more important than others, so it is advantageous to provide this with a prioritized service. Prioritization may be associated with classes of data, particular addresses or even the entry and exit point links.

- Data multiplexing – while it may not be appropriate to remove a link from the normal store-and-forward packet switching system and to reserve it for particular data traffic or services, it is often convenient to be able to reserve some of a link's bandwidth for special use. This reservation is normally supported using time division multiplexing with regular guaranteed access supplied on a periodic basis. This multiplexing then supports both the normal store-and-forward switching and the reserved bandwidth allocation.

- Data encryption – in some circumstances it is important that the data be protected from casual and intentional observation. This requires the use of data encryption, which is normally supplied by a data encryption standard (DES) chip. One of these is placed in each of the end-point routers and so all but the intermediate system headers are encrypted. The only problem is then one of ensuring that the encryption keys are themselves securely allocated.

- Data compression – high speed wide area links are very expensive and in many situations the use of data compression can reduce the wide area bandwidth requirements. Normally the compression algorithm is fixed independent of the data type and so only relatively modest bandwidth savings can be made, of approximately 50%; however, this still an important reduction.

It is important to note that unlike the case for bridges these functions are applied to the network layer protocol data units – that is, the packets. Bridges apply these functions to frames, so in some cases a packet may undergo several similar transformations as it passes across networks that include both bridges and routers.

12.2.7 Management facilities

Unlike repeaters and bridges, which in most cases require very little configuration and management interaction, routers (especially the more advanced versions) are very complex and normally require significant configuration – attendance at the manufacturer's training course is strongly recommended. Some of the more sophisticated routers are accompanied by automated configuration files and intelligent configuration support, which alleviate some of the difficulties, but it is still advisable to be fully trained before attempting to install any but the simplest of routers. There are two aspects that are particularly important when evaluating the management facilities of a router: its basic functionality and its integration with established network management systems. The management functions required of a router are:

- Configuration management – including the initialization, reset and close-down of local and remote routers. In particular it must be possible to control which protocols are and are not to be routed and the processing features that are to be applied to the data being forwarded by the router. In the case where the router also combines bridging capabilities it is essential to be able to define which links and protocols are to be bridged as well as routed.

- Fault management – the ability to identify and correct router malfunctions, including error logging and reporting, and to monitor the physical state and loading on the wide area links.

- Performance management – the ability to gather statistics concerning traffic analysis for subnetwork and link utilization, and numbers of forwarded packets and load analysis for each port. The network addresses associated with this information provide a mechanism for billing for access to the router and the wide area links.

All of the above functions are normally password protected using two-level security; user and supervisor. This ensures that the network cannot be accidentally compromised but further functions must be supplied if the router is to become a secure device. Services such as authentication are not yet available. However, many intra- and inter-domain protocols have allocated resource capabilities so that when the relevant standards and systems have been developed they can be readily adopted. The network management systems for which router integration should be considered are:

- Simple network management protocol (SNMP) – the *de facto* network management protocol originally introduced by the Internet developers.

- ISO's common management information protocol (CMIP) – the formal network management standard which is still undergoing ratification.

- IBM's NetView – the network management protocol used throughout the full range of SNA and SNA compatible systems.

- Digital's network control protocol (NCP) – the network management protocol used throughout the full range of the DNA and DNA-compatible systems.

The management architecture for a router can be similar to that shown for bridges in Figure 11.2, with the routers simply replacing the bridges. In many cases, however, the routers will report to some centralized network management system, which may or may not involve the use of a separate out-of-band network, and so they will be seen by the network manager as just another device on the network, albeit with a particularly interesting set of capabilities.

12.2.8 Architectural features

One of the key differences between the routers from different manufacturers is their internal architecture. This difference leads to several important functional additions which can be essential in some environments, for example those which need to be highly reliable. Some routers use a single processor which is responsible for all of the router processing and interface support whereas others use a fully distributed architecture in which each LAN/WAN interface is fully self supportive (several intermediate architectures are also used). The distributed approach makes it easier to provide:

- A hot-swap capability in which the router does not need to stopped or re-initialized when an interface is changed (the change could be a new or a replacement interface).

- A remote upgrade capability in which new versions of the router software are electronically distributed through the network itself. Each interface can then be upgraded without disturbing the others.

When purchasing a router it is important to ascertain the architectural nature of the router is consistent with the proposed environment. The distributed architectures and their interface cards are more expensive but they provide a more reliable architecture and support an environment which is easier to maintain without disrupting the users.

12.2.9 Additional facilities

Several manufacturers are providing various additional features so that their routers can be used as single device solutions. One particular example of this is the combination of router with terminal server. From the manufacturers' point of view this is a particularly important feature because it enables a router to support traffic that traditionally could not be routed because of timing constraints and the fact that most terminal servers do not have a network layer protocol, such as Digital's LAT protocol.

The terminal server/router (or trouter as it is sometimes called) encapsulates the terminal server's MAC frames (using the appropriate protocol such as SLIP for IP based networks) and transmits them across a dedicated link to the target LAN. Link dedication is used to ensure that the information does not suffer access delays. In some cases this link is in fact reserved bandwidth on a multiplexed channel; however, it is always dedicated to the terminal servers irrespective of the loading on the rest of the link's bandwidth.

A trouter architecture is shown in Figure 12.6, in which LAT terminals are used. On two of the LANs the traditional terminal servers are used whereas on the third the router itself is acting as the terminal server. In this case router 3 will either allocate a dedicated link to each of the other routers for sole use by the terminal server traffic or

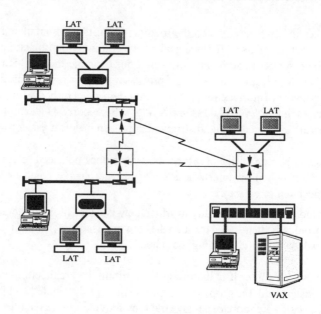

Figure 12.6   Routers with integrated terminal servers.

it will reserve, say, 9.6 kbps of bandwidth on each of its links, and multiplex the two traffic types (user and terminal) onto the one link. The latter approach is a more cost effective solution if the links have a significantly greater bandwidth than can be used by the terminals. The routers are still operating as usual concerning their normal routing functions, so the only change is the reservation of bandwidth for a particular function.

A second additional feature is that of translation between different terminal server protocols, such as LAT, Telnet and Triple-X. In fact, this is more of a gateway function because it involves protocol translation but many routers now provide this as an extension to their general terminal server support. This feature means that it is possible to use routers to provide an integrated support for terminal service irrespective of their host dependence, thereby creating an 'open' host access architecture.

In Token Ring based networks, routers are useful for overcoming the limitation in the number of source routing bridges that can be crossed (limited to seven). If a router is crossed then the total number of source routing bridges that can be crossed becomes fourteen – that is, seven each side of the router. This capability is made available because the router is responsible for mapping between the network layer and MAC addresses and so the subnetworks on either side of the router are independent with respect to their MAC addressing systems. Naturally, this principle can be extended so that the total number of source routing bridges traversed is unlimited provided that a router is inserted at the appropriate positions, although this will constrain possible paths across the network (cf. inter-domain routing).

12.3   Types of router

The two issues concerning the type of router required by an installation are the number of network layer protocols that must be supported, and the LAN and WAN interfaces needed. The commercially available devices fall loosely into one of two categories: low cost with the minimum functionality of two ports with single protocol support, or high cost based upon a modular architecture with tailorable configuration both in terms of the supported interfaces and protocols (Miller, 1991).

12.3.1 Basic router

The router is the generic term for a device which could also be termed a full/local router or a half/remote router. Unlike repeaters and bridges, the most common form of router is used for LAN-to-LAN interconnection across an intermediate WAN system (LAN-to-WAN-to-LAN). In general the router is a multiport device which supports several LAN and WAN ports. A typical router configuration is shown in Figure 12.7, in which a Token Ring and a CSMA/CD LAN are linked using two routers. The host protocols across the LAN architecture are the CLNP and IPX, so the routers must support both of these.

Routers are the most common way to interconnect CSMA/CD and Token Ring LANs; the natural encapsulation of the data in different MAC frames and the common thread of the network address being responsible for end-to-end communication. The

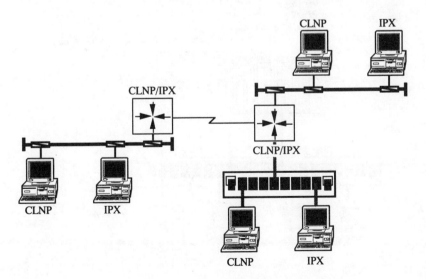

Figure 12.7 A half router architecture.

full range of WAN interfaces would normally be available and so it should be possible to link the LANs using any form of intermediate system. The cost of such a router would typically be between £3500 and £5000 (two ports only), each extra WAN and LAN interface costing between £500 and £1500.

12.3.2 Modular router

The low end of the market is supported by the two-port routers. The mid to high range is based upon the modular router or fully functional router device, in which a basic chassis is used to house many LAN and WAN interfaces. In some cases as many as thirty different links can be hosted in a single modular router. Although this arrangement provides a very simple management architecture it is susceptible to single point failure and so it is important to invest in a router with the appropriate fail-safe features, such as a hot swap capability.

Figure 12.8 shows a modular hub arrangement. Each of the interfaces in the hub supports a particular system and it is usual for there to be a sophisticated management interface used for configuring the router and for acquiring statistics about its performance. The cost of such a device is obviously very dependent on its actual configuration. However, the bottom of the range system would typically cost about £15 000 with the most expensive at about £50 000. The reason for the high cost even for the low end

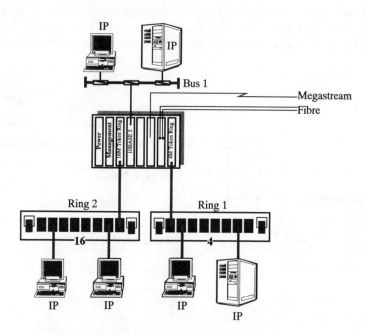

Figure 12.8 A modular router architecture.

devices is due to the internal architecture of the router, which is based upon a modular design supported by a very high speed collapsed backbone.

The latest generation of modular hubs are designed so that they can support a mixture of repeater, bridge and router architectures (Figures 10.18 and 11.17). It is then possible to support the hub using an integrated management system and so provide full performance statistics and fault resilience.

12.3.3 Single protocol router

The dependence of the router on the network layer protocols means that it is essential to choose a router which supports the necessary protocols. Most organizations make use of no more than four different protocol profiles and so normally only four different network layer protocols need to be considered. The low end of the router range consists of many routers which support only one network protocol; this means only one es-es protocol plus all of the associated es-is and is-is protocols. The router is opaque to other protocols.

A single protocol router architecture is shown in Figure 12.9 in which a full router is used to support the IP protocol across CSMA/CD and Token Ring networks. ARP is used to support the end-system/router address resolution and the SNAP is used to map the IP protocol to the IEEE 802 protocols. The distribution of unique IP addresses ensures that FTP users can communicate across the router. Protocols other than IP will not be recognized by the router (normally, they will not have the correct LSAP and certainly not the correct IP frame format and addresses) and so only IP information will be permitted to cross it.

The single protocol router can only be used in protocol specific environments and it is usually the case that these are vendor dependent devices (the actual protocol being proprietary to a particular manufacturer). In the longer term this sort of router

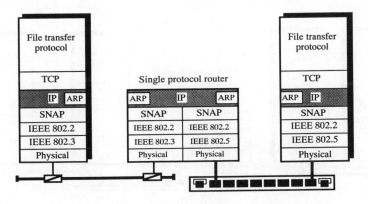

Figure 12.9 A single protocol router system.

can either become redundant (due to a change in protocol) or it can restrict the development of the network (not capable of supporting any change) and so its cheaper cost should only be considered as a short-term solution.

12.3.4 Multiprotocol router

The alternative to the single protocol router is the multiprotocol router. This router is normally purchased in one of two forms:

- Supporting only the protocols specifically required by the network.
- Supporting all of the protocols available to that router and providing a management facility to enable/disable the routing of specific protocols.

Defensive network design means that the second option is the more prudent choice because this provides a great deal of flexibility in the long term.

The important principle to remember when considering multiprotocol routers is that they do not support translation between protocols. The best analogy for a multiprotocol router is that of the international telephone system. The switching exchange provides physical connectivity between different countries but it is only possible to send information if the same language is used at either end of the link. The switching exchange provides the interconnectivity but does not provide translation.

A type of network which needs to use multiprotocol routers is shown in Figure 12.10. This network supports Novel NetWare and TCP/IP communities distributed across the network and so the router must support at least the IP and IPX protocols. The net effect is that the router has two concurrent pipes crossing it, one of which supports the IPX protocol (NetWare) and the other the IP protocol; no translation between IPX and IP occurs.

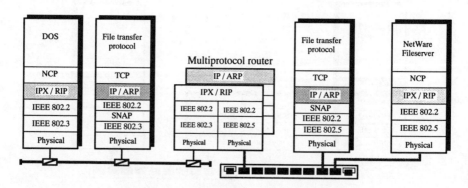

Figure 12.10 A multiprotocol router system.

In the cases where several routers are used in the network then NetWare and TCP/IP make use of RIP. At first sight it may be expected that the router would in fact make use of a single version of RIP to support both communities; however, this is not yet possible due to the slight differences in how the two implementations must operate. Development work to support single incarnations of each protocol is currently under way; however, any benefits to the user from this will only be apparent if the router's throughput becomes improved due to reduced routing table update times. The debate concerning the use of multiple or single incarnations of a common routing protocol is phrased in terms of 'integrated routing' or 'ships-in-the night' (SIN). The former refers to the single protocol being used to replace the different es-is and is-is protocols whereas the latter refers to the current situation, where each network layer es-es protocol has its own version of the es-is and is-is protocols even when two identical copies, each supporting a different es-es protocol, could be running concurrently in the same router (Perlman, 1992).

12.4   Uses of a router

Routers are the relays that are used to connect LANs to a comprehensive backbone WAN. This architecture can then provide mixed network connectivity, such as Token Ring to CSMA/CD; resilient and congestion free networks; and limited access to the network. While these uses can be provided by other internetworking devices it is only the router that can support them as a natural part of the protocols.

12.4.1 Mixed network connectivity

The layer 3 dependence of a router is equivalent to stating that its functionality is independent of layers one and two; that is, it is MAC independent. It is therefore the ideal device to support Token Ring and CSMA/CD connectivity; the different address systems of Token Ring and CSMA/CD are mapped together as a natural consequence of how the routers support their own network layer addressing.

A mixed network single protocol router architecture is shown in Figure 12.11, in which two Token Ring and two CSMA/CD LANs are linked using a multifaceted backbone WAN. Each LAN is supported by a single router; however, this need not be the case and in some environments there may be two, or more, routers supporting each LAN. In this example the user protocols are restricted to IPX and so strictly speaking only single protocol routers are required. The backbone consists of a mixed set of link types and capacities, and these would normally reflect the loading to be expected between the two directly supported LANs; it should be stressed that the traffic on these links will not be restricted to just the data from these local LANs. In fact the routers

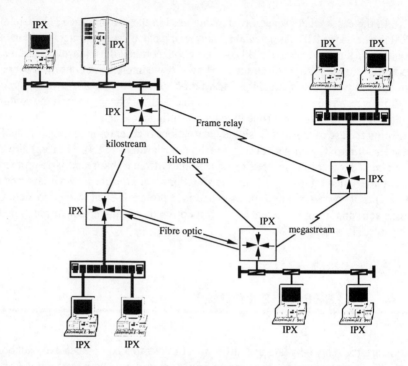

Figure 12.11 A mixed WAN connectivity architecture.

will distribute the full load across the WAN to provide a balanced delay/throughput characteristic for the network.

The advantage of this approach is that end-system communication is independent of the types of LANs supporting the users (unlike the case for MAC bridges). The routers ensure that the individual sites have flexibility in selecting their own physical architecture while still providing external interconnectivity. They also restrict external availability of information outside of the local LANs unless the correct access codes and so on are supplied within the NetWare protocol (in bridged networks this would only be possible using customized filtering).

12.4.2 High connectivity

A very important feature of routers is that they provide a very comprehensive congestion and flow control capability. In part this is needed because routers are true store-and-forward packet switching devices, which are supported by a highly connected backbone WAN. This highly connected WAN is used to ensure that a single link failure has minimal consequences on the network's capabilities and to provide a high capacity using relatively low bandwidth links.

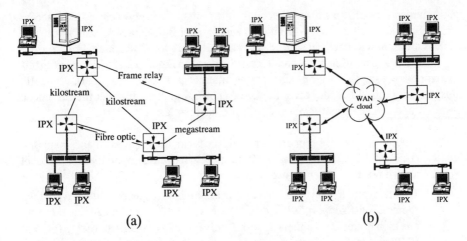

Figure 12.12 Physical and logical router representation equivalence.

Figure 12.12 shows the logical equivalence of a router network. The actual connectivity for the network is shown in Figure 12.12a and its logical equivalence is the network cloud in Figure 12.12b. This cloud represents the fact that the data enters the cloud at some point and leaves at another. The actual route taken by the data across the network is totally transparent to the end-system but also varies on a packet-by-packet basis – that is, packet switching. The network designer must ensure that this cloud has sufficient connectivity to minimize failure and to optimize traffic flow.

The routers will load the network evenly, thereby minimizing the congestion on a single link or route and so reducing the end-to-end delay while increasing the network's total throughput. If congestion occurs then the routing tables are reconfigured and the end-systems are temporarily choked so that the total load on the network is reduced. An update can take up to thirty seconds to complete, so it is important to establish how often such updates occur; good router systems only update when necessary – that is, when a device or link is added or removed due to either a network failure or performance enhancement, and the reconfiguration is restricted to the region of the network directly affected by the failure.

The extent of the backbone's connectivity is a reflection of the distribution of the end-system LANs and the amount of information that must be transferred between them. In general the volume of WAN traffic supported by the routers should be relatively low – less than 10% of the normal LAN load.

12.4.3 Access control

In many situations an essential requirement of a networking device is the capability to restrict access to the network. In the case of a router this is readily supported by the fact that a common protocol must be used by the end users and the router before any communications can take place. Secondly, the routers themselves can enforce access restrictions according to network address and/or other field contents, and, thirdly, the actual protocol will itself, in some cases, support some form of access limitation.

A typical multiprotocol architecture is shown in Figure 12.13. The users on this network are using either the XNS or the Internet protocols; that is, IDP and IP, respectively. The XNS file server is located on ring 2 and, the Internet file servers on buses 1 and 2. The salient features of this arrangement are:

- Router 4 need only support, or permit access to, the IP protocol and so no IDP (from XNS) traffic will load bus 2. Router 3 need only support the IDP protocol and so no IP traffic will load ring 2.

- If both users on ring 1 are to have access to their respective file servers then router 2 must support IDP and IP. If the IDP traffic is to be kept local to ring one then router 2 can either support IP only or it can be instructed not to forward IDP packets.

- In the case of bus 1, it may be that no external users are permitted access to the Internet file server. In this case the router must be instructed not to forward any of the local file servers' announcement packets. It must still permit access to the external IP file server. Support for IDP protocols is not required for the local LAN but at the very least an IDP tunnel is required to enable the IDP traffic from router 2 to be forwarded to router 3. It would be natural for this tunnel to be supported using IP.

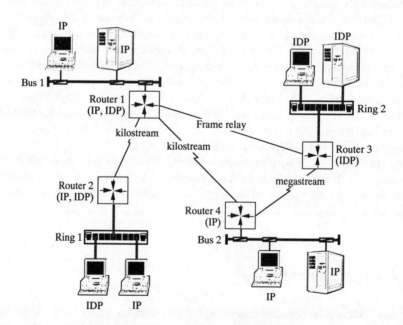

Figure 12.13 Access control using routers.

- From the point of view of packet switching across the WAN, all of the routers could be capable of handling both the IP and IDP packets provided they are encapsulated in some common intermediate protocol such as protocol tunnelling. This means that the routers can then evenly distribute the full network load across all of the WAN links, for example make use of the megastream link for communications between users on buses 1 and 2 as opposed to between just ring 2 and bus 2.

In this example the difference between the user and the intermediate WAN protocols is clearly shown. If an intermediate protocol was not used then it would not be possible for the routers to act as switching centres for packets of unknown protocols – in other words, the LAN traffic would only be forwarded by routers actively supporting the data's native protocol. In many cases it is also possible to configure the routers so that they can act as switching centres for a protocol while blocking the external packets' access to the local LAN and restricting the internal packets to the local LAN only. In this case a multiprotocol router would be switching protocols for which its local LANs had no requirement.

An environment that would make use of this architecture is one where several different organizations are submitting competitive tenders and so on to a common evaluation centre. The bidders need to be able to submit their tender to the evaluation organization but are keen to be assured that their bids will not be made available (intentionally or accidentally) to their competitors. The use of routers to isolate individual file servers while still permitting a general backbone switching architecture and access to some common facility is essential for the cost effective supply of such an architecture. Such a system could not be constructed using MAC bridges unless only one type of LAN was used, so the only realistic solution is to use routers.

12.5   Router network architectures

Unlike repeater and bridge architectures, there are very few fundamentally different router based network architectures. This is because routers provide a general connectivity capability, so there is no proliferation due to the idiosyncrasies of individual networks.

12.5.1 Typical architectures

The most commonly adopted template for router architectures is that shown in Figure 12.14. This architecture is a simple change to that discussed under bridging in Figures 11.22 and 11.24; the WAN connectivity is supported using routers as opposed to remote bridges but the LANs local to each building are unchanged. This approach allows the different buildings to select their own internal LANs but restricts their choice of network operating system.

In this example it can be seen that building 1 supports NetWare and OSI, building 2 XNS and OSI, and building 3 XNS and NetWare. The recommendation would be that each building use a multiprotocol router with three LAN ports and at least two WAN ports. Prudence for the future would recommend that the basic chassis should be capable of supporting at least twice this number of ports to provide for future expansion of the network. The network in Figure 12.14 would probably use TCP/IP as the intermediate system protocol, thereby providing a full packet switching system whose links can be efficiently utilized. It would be possible to replace the repeaters and router with a single intelligent hub but unless this hub was fault tolerant it could make the network vulnerable to failure.

Other typical architectures are as shown in Figures 12.6, 12.11 and 12.13. However, these are in fact merely detail changes to the same architectural template – in other words, the actual protocols and LAN components change but their router connectivity is still essentially that shown in Figure 12.14.

A different router architecture is shown in Figure 12.15; in this network LANs 1 and 3 support two routers. The routers ensure that the same information is not passed onto these LANs more than once – that is the routing tables, as constructed by the routing algorithms, allocate a single path for each LAN irrespective of the number of

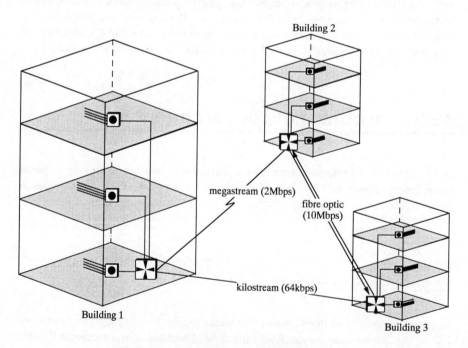

Figure 12.14 A typical router architecture.

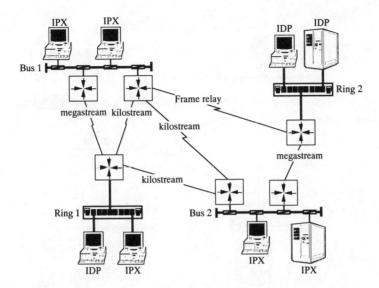

Figure 12.15 The use of multiple routers supporting each LAN.

routers connected to them. This approach is only possible if the routers can see each other and so they must be using a common intermediate protocol – if this is not the case then they must be manually configured to ensure duplicated packets are not passed onto a LAN. The reason for using multirouter links on a LAN is to ensure that the loss of one router will not cause a network failure. Although this is an expensive solution, it does provide increased network resilience.

12.5.2 Access and boundary routing

All of the router architectures presented thus far have used fully functional routers. Recently, two new architectures have been introduced, access routing and boundary routing. An access router is a 'stripped down' modular router and as such it normally consists of one LAN interface, two WAN interfaces (usually including ISDN) and two or three network layer protocols (always including IP). This creates a low cost router but one which can be used in any established router network and which still conforms to the traditional type of router architecture. In contrast boundary routers create a particular architecture.

A boundary routing architecture is shown in Figure 12.16, and the immediate difference when compared to access and fully functioned routing is that it uses a single central switching router to interconnect all of the peripheral, or boundary, routers (remote bridges can also be used as the boundary devices). The advantages of this approach are that:

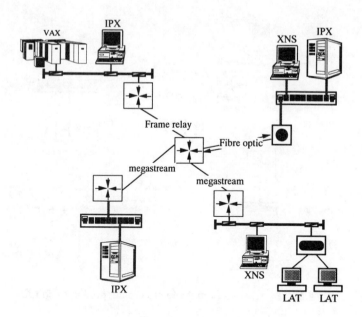

Figure 12.16 Boundary routing.

- Only the central switching router has to have more than two ports. Each boundary router has one LAN and one WAN port only and so it is relatively inexpensive to construct large networks.

- Each boundary router needs to support only those protocols that are used on its local LAN and no protocol tunnelling is required.

- The central switching router is responsible for inter-domain routing and so the routing algorithms will converge very quickly on the optimal routing path across the network.

Clearly, the main disadvantage of this approach is that the whole network infrastructure becomes disconnected if the central switching hub fails. Therefore, it is essential to make the hub fault resilient. In contrast, the access routing architectures are, in general, extremely robust but the individual routers are more expensive because they must house more WAN and LAN ports and provide features such as protocol tunnelling. Modular routers are capable of supporting dial-up access or acting as terminal server but both of these features are considered too expensive for a boundary or access router.

At present it is unclear under which conditions the two approaches are best suited – the proponents of each type claim their approach is the best for all cases. It appears that the boundary routing approach is targeted towards solutions where cost is a primary concern and where the architecture is suited to a switched hub infrastructure. If the usage of the network is likely to change then access routing provides a more flexible approach in the longer term but it is more expensive for large-scale networks.

12.5.3 Routers versus bridges

One of the problems most commonly faced concerning internetworking is choosing between bridges and routers. The current trend in the development of the new bridges and routers is for their functionality to become increasingly more common. The eventual result of this development will be to remove the need to decide which type of device must be purchased – a single unit will supply all of the required connectivity. However, until this point is reached a choice has to be made.

Table 12.1 summarizes the essential features to consider when choosing between bridges and routers. This table shows that:

- Bridges are used to link together like LANs to construct many logical networks from one physical network. Data frames are forwarded on a protocol independent basis across point-to-point links.

- Routers are used to interconnect different subnetworks to create a single network which supports specific network layer protocols. The routers create a resilient backbone network, which is used to support store-and-forward packet switching.

Table 12.1 A comparison between bridges and routers.

Comparison	MAC Bridge	Router
Network dependence	Like LAN to like LAN.	Link all forms of LAN.
Protocol dependence	Independent at LLC and above.	Network layer protocols must be common.
Bandwidth utilization	Fixed by spanning tree or source routing.	Optimized for loading across the whole network.
Data flow	Simple access limitation and filtering according to MAC address.	Network address dependent and can exert flow control.
WAN access	Typically single port access.	Can construct complex mesh of point-to-point links.
Management	Statistics about frames and bridge operation.	Statistics about specific protocols.
Performance	Suffers in heavily loaded environments.	As fast as bridges but can limit loading by sources.

12.6 Combination architectures

The distinction between bridges and routers has been considerably muddied by the introduction of bridge/routers, router/bridges, routing bridges, bridging routers and brouters. It is very difficult, and not necessarily relevant, to establish clear categorical differences between each of these but it is instructive to understand their historical development so that their intended capabilities can be appreciated.

The bridge/router and routing bridge are one and the same; it is an internetworking device which is derived from a bridge. The router/bridge and bridging router are also one and the same; this is based upon a router. The brouter is the name given by many manufacturers to their original bridge and router combinations, especially when they are non-standard devices. More recently, the term brouter has been applied to true hybrid devices which require only software reconfiguration to alter their operational capabilities from bridge to router to brouter.

Table 12.2 shows a superficial comparison of the bridge/router, router/bridge and the brouter. The bridge/router provides all of the bridging functions with routing capability across a limited number of ports whereas the router/bridge provides a full routing capability with bridging but usually for a higher cost. The brouter is a true hybrid, capable of being any form of bridge and router combination. However, in many cases its use limits the architecture to a single vendor solution.

Table 12.2 A comparison between bridge and router combinations.

Comparison	Bridge / Router	Router / Bridge	Brouter
Origins	Bridge manufacturer.	Router manufacturer.	Independent manufacturer.
Functionality	Bridge dominated but will route specific network layer protocols.	Router dominated but bridge protocols which do not support a network layer protocol. Complex layer 2 translation and SNA connectivity.	Proprietary systems which act fully as bridge, router or a true hybrid.
Interconnectivity	To standardized bridges and routers.	To standardized routers and bridges.	In general, proprietary based systems only.
Architectures	Bridge based and so tend to be two-port with single processor architecture.	Multiple ports with each port supported by its own processor.	Software configurable to bridge/router/brouter support. Tends to single processor architectures.
Performance	Full rate bridging but tends to support lower routing rates.	Routing and bridging capabilities supported at the full rates.	Full rate bridging but tends to provide lower routing rates.

12.6.1 Bridge/router systems

A typical bridge/router based network is shown in Figure 12.17, which also includes local and remote bridges. In many cases the bridge/router is capable of supporting only Token Ring or CSMA/CD LANs because the bridge manufacturers were originally based on one or the other of these. Figure 12.17 shows a CSMA/CD based architecture in which the bride/routers are capable of routing the IP and XNS protocols. LAT will always be bridged in its native form.

The reason for adopting this approach would be based upon the fact that the local and remote bridges would almost certainly have been used in an earlier form of the network. The original network would probably have consisted of three separate LAN structures based upon buses 1 and 2, buses 3, 4 and 5 and finally buses 6 and 7. A decision is made to interconnect the whole network and so it is important to keep the bridging of the original LANs but to limit the network-wide flow of information. The solution is to use the bridge/routers as backbone routers between the three domains but to use them as bridges within the domain. This means that the three domains keep their autonomy and only protocol dependent information passes between the routed LANs.

The adoption of the bridge/router would be the cheapest solution and would almost certainly derive from the fact that the original bridge manufacturer would have new products available to extend their previous solution. This means that there would be very little difficulty in upgrading to this solution, both in terms of the small amount of retired equipment and incompatibility problems.

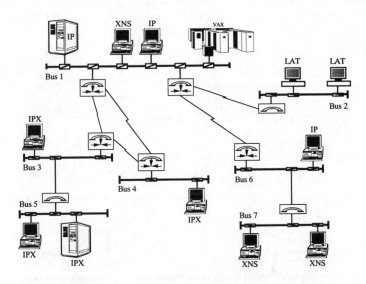

Figure 12.17 A typical bridge/router architecture.

12.6.2 Router/bridge systems

A different problem is that shown in Figure 12.18. Here the network would have originally been based upon a router architecture. This could not have supported the terminal traffic (LAT and SDLC) and so separate modem lines would have been required to provide the remote mainframe access. The functional extension of routers includes dedicated bridging across multiplexed links and so these new cards convert the routers into router/bridges. It is now possible to remove modem links and so on, with the bridging of the LAT traffic and the tunnelling of the SDLC traffic, thereby providing remote Digital and IBM mainframe access via the router/bridge network.

One of the strengths of the router/bridges is the rich set of functions which can be applied to the data link layer protocols as a part of the process of encapsulating and unwrapping them. Three of the most important features are MAC translation (cf. translation bridges), data link protocol translation and the extension source route bridging. The functions performed by each of these features are:

- Translation bridging – the interconnection of different subnetworks which use profiles that do not have a network layer protocol, for example NetBIOS. This means that hosts on ethernet and Token Ring LANs can be linked even when they use non-routable protocols.

- Data link translation – this is normally used in SNA applications where SDLC/LLC2 translation is required or where data link switching (DLSw) is needed.

- Extended source route bridging – this is used to overcome the seven bridge hop-count limit encountered in source routing bridge architectures. Unfortunately this technique is only possible if there are no route loops in the architectures.

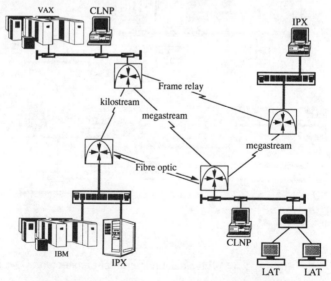

Figure 12.18 A typical router/bridge architecture.

Many of the additional features for router/bridges are a response to the problems of interconnecting SNA networks to the rest of the world, many of which are caused by the absence of routable protocols. These capabilities are well suited to router/bridges whereas they are inappropriate to bridge/routers due to their dependence on the MAC and LLC protocols.

12.6.3 Brouter systems

The final scenario for consideration is where the solution results in a brouter based architecture. In fact, in the early years of mixed interconnectivity a brouter based solution would have been the only option for all of the previous router and bridge combinations but would have resulted in a 'closed' solution. In some cases the brouter solutions are now more 'open'. However, care must be taken if this is a critical consideration. The modern brouter solution is usually adopted in 'green fields' environments where a completely new network architecture is being considered. The purchase of a general purpose shell that can be easily altered to be either a bridge or a router or a hybrid is very appealing for defensive design.

The architecture in Figure 12.19 assumes no previous connectivity. Brouters 1 and 4 would support the megastream link as a bridge for the LAT traffic and as routers for everything else. The other boundary brouters must act as single protocol routers because they are supporting mixed LAN connectivity. The attractive feature of this solution is that any future changes in the network's architecture or in the manner it is to be used will not cause the current devices to become redundant. In many cases the

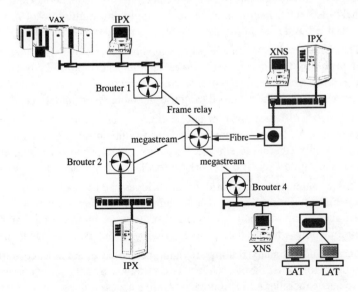

Figure 12.19 A typical brouter architecture.

changes will merely require an extension to the switching hub and the addition of new brouters for each new installed subnetwork. The brouters can be readily altered to suit their new demands, and this flexibility may well outweigh the disadvantage of being dependent upon a single manufacturer.

It is this approach that has produced the interest in boundary routing. The brouter is ideally suited to boundary routing based architectures because they need a flexible device that can be configured and reconfigured, in a cost effective manner, to act as either a central switching router, a peripheral router or a peripheral bridge. A fixed architecture device would provide too expensive and inflexible a solution.

12.7   Summary

In many cases routers are not fully 'open' devices because mixed vendor connectivity is difficult, due, in the main, to the different proprietary intermediate system protocols. The exceptions are the IP routers which are well tried and tested in environments such as the Internet itself. In conclusion, the important points to note concerning routers are:

- The router is an internetworking device which interconnects different subnetworks provided they use the same network layer protocol.

- Routers construct highly connected and resilient backbone networks which act as store-and-forward packet switching networks.

- Routers can provide back-to-back connectivity for subnetworks and can also make use of an intermediate system. Single and multiprotocol routers are available but no form of translation between protocols is supported.

- The characteristics to consider when choosing a router are the number and type of protocols that it can support, the number and type of LAN and WAN interfaces available, the types of routing protocol it can support and the response time of the routers during routing table reconfiguration.

- In general, different areas of application can be identified for bridges and routers. MAC bridges create fixed point-to-point links between similar LANs, for example ethernet to ethernet. Routers create packet switching environments to support specific network protocols independent of the type of LAN.

- Bridge/routers (or routing bridges) are bridges that have additional router like capabilities. Router/bridges (or bridging routers) are routers that support bridging of non-routable protocols. Brouters are hybrid bridge and router combinations which can perform as bridges or routers, or as true hybrids.

- Access and boundary routing are being promoted as the most cost effective solution for router based architectures, as opposed to the more common and expensive modular router approach. Unlike access routing, boundary routing is susceptible to single point failure of the switching.

13

Gateways

13.1   Introduction

It is impossible to anticipate all of the future requirements of a network and so at some time or another the issue of protocol incompatibility will have to be addressed. This is a very common problem for networks based upon proprietary systems, particularly when providing wider access. Interconnectivity between different protocols must be supported using a gateway – recall that routers provide interconnection between different systems that use the same network layer protocol. The gradual adoption of open systems means that, in principle, it should eventually become unnecessary to use gateways. In practice this will never be the case and, paradoxically, in the immediate future gateways will become more commonplace as they are used to support the interconnection of closed systems using OSI/RM based protocols.

Gateways are supplied in one of two forms: as a purpose built unit or in the guise of a workstation acting as a gateway server. In both cases the gateway consists of the appropriate network adapters (LAN and WAN based) and the software which hosts the end-system protocols and which translates between the two (Miller, 1991). In many cases a PC based gateway server is appropriate because this supplies a suitably cost effective solution without incurring significant performance degradation (the WAN access and transport protocols sustaining a relatively slow capability). Only in cases where there is to be a significant software processing overhead (IBM/Digital interconnection) is it necessary to purchase the dedicated but expensive (between £50 000 and £75 000) gateway solutions.

13.2   Functions of a gateway

The functions of a gateway are indistinguishable from those of the systems it interconnects; while this may seem obvious, it should be recalled that in the case of the other internetworking devices their functionality was largely independent of the interconnected architectures. This close dependence means that each type of system interconnection requires a specific gateway, fewer of each type are required and so they are considerably more expensive than their counterparts even though they provide a relatively limited range of capabilities.

13.2.1 Protocol conversion

The fundamental functional responsibility of a gateway is to interconnect different protocol profiles – in other words, to translate between them. All of the other internetworking devices require a degree of commonality at the lower levels of the

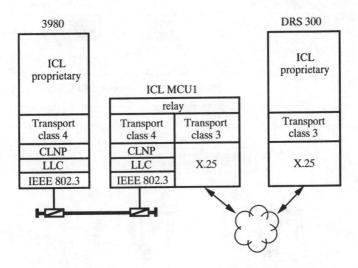

Figure 13.1 A transport relay providing protocol conversion.

profile, but for a gateway only the topmost layer needs to be common: a gateway cannot provide interconnection between an electronic mail system and a terminal handling system! There are three ways in which a relay can support a protocol:

- Remote service protocol encapsulation – in which the data from the remote system is encapsulated by the protocols of the local service. This encapsulation is stripped away as the data is passed up the local end-system profile until it is presented in its native form to the applications layer.

- Local service protocol encapsulation – in which the data from the local system is encapsulated by the protocols of the remote service. This is the same process as for the remote service encapsulation but from the local service data's point of view instead.

- Protocol conversion – in which the actual data content is reorganized by the relay device. This reorganization ensures that the appropriate information is stored in the correct position of the messages. Simple encapsulation is only possible if the service between the end-systems follows the same rules, for example no CLS/COS interconnection.

A gateway is the only internetworking device that can support all three forms of interconnection (bridges and routers support an appropriate form of encapsulation only). An example of protocol conversion, using a transport relay, is shown in Figure 13.1. Here an ICL transport relay converts between the class 3 and class 4 transport services. Recall that TP3 provides error recovery and multiplexing while TP4 also supplies error detection and recovery – TP4 is used with type C subnetworks (ones that provide connections where the residual error rate is unacceptable to the transport service user), whereas TP3 is used with type B subnetworks (ones that provide

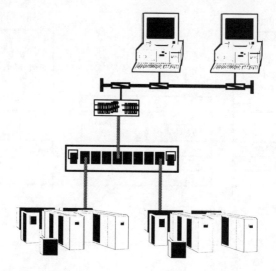

Figure 13.2 LAN connectivity for a gateway.

connections where there is an acceptable residual error rate but unacceptable rate of signalled failures). This gateway is responsible for mapping together the TP3 and TP4 services, so it must provide a connection oriented service for the two end-systems by coordinating the two individual connection oriented links.

In some cases a gateway must link together protocols supporting different types of service, such as COS to CLS and vice versa. In these circumstances it is particularly important for the gateway to maintain the COS half of the system because the end-system for the CLS half will not transmit any information concerning the maintenance of the virtual circuit. This type of problem is particularly important when a gateway is used to interconnect profiles that have different numbers of layers, such as an IBM mainframe using SNA/SDLC and PCs using ethernet and terminal emulation software.

13.2.2 LAN connectivity

In the case of LANs, the first gateways were required to connect a single type of LAN to a WAN infrastructure, such as Token Ring into the SNA world. The relatively recent introduction of network adapters for most ranges of computer hosts has now extended this requirement to include interconnection between mixed LANs. The IBM and Digital preferences for Token Ring and ethernet, respectively, immediately demonstrates why that is necessary. Unlike a router, where a common network layer protocol is required, a gateway will provide the necessary protocol translations, so this software will be responsible for driving the appropriate combination of NIAs.

The classical minimalist gateway architecture is shown in Figure 13.2. In this system the two mainframes support Token Ring adapters whereas the remote PCs have ethernet NIAs. In such a system the PCs would host a terminal emulation software package and its information would be encapsulated within ethernet frames. The gateway converts the frame into its Token Ring equivalent, which means that it must also be responsible for establishing the address mappings between the networks, and for establishing the service connectivity between the host mainframe and the remote terminals. In the case where the mainframes are without a network adapter then the gateway could support a direct interface into them or a FEP, for example using SDLC over a serial link.

13.2.3 WAN connectivity

The choice of WAN link is characterized by the capabilities of the end-system host processors and type of data link protocol to be used across it; the link does not need to be significantly faster than the slowest end-system, normally a host mainframe. In many cases these links need only have a 64 kbps capacity, with more of these being used if the aggregate data rate needs to be higher. Normally several sessions are concurrently active across a single physical link and so the data for each session undergoes statistical time multiplexing onto the link. Typically, this means that a 64 kbps link will in fact be supporting between 16 and 32 sessions and so each session would have access to 4–2 kbps, respectively. In practice, the gateways use a statistical multiplexing technique, and not time division multiplexing, whereby considerably more links (between two and four times as many) can be supported by the physical channel.

The network shown in Figure 13.3 shows two mainframes with their FEPs connected to the gateway via WAN links. The gateway also supports a Token Ring LAN on which there are two terminal servers. The terminals have access to the mainframes via the gateway and so a total of six concurrent sessions is required. If each terminal is set at 9.6 kbps then the maximum load on the link will be 54 kbps plus some margin of overhead for the protocols – 64 kbps is sufficient.

13.2.4 Service support

The essential feature here is the number of concurrent sessions that a gateway can, and is required to, support; each session must be explicitly supported by the gateway – that is, address resolution and service connection. A session could be responsible for supporting LAN-to-host access, a LAN-to-WAN service conduit or a LAN-to-LAN service conduit, and in each case it draws upon the finite resources of the gateway. The bandwidth available to each session is inversely proportional to the number of active sessions (time and statistical multiplexing being used to fit the session data flows onto the individual physical links), so it is important to ensure that the required aggregate bandwidth is supported by the total link capacity available.

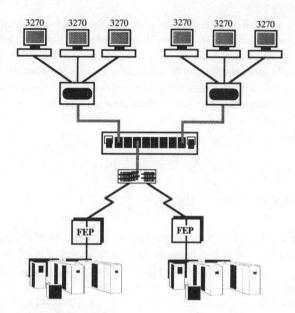

Figure 13.3 WAN connectivity for a gateway.

13.2.5 Management facilities

In common with all of the other internetworking devices, it is essential that the gateway is manageable. In many cases, the gateway is supplied as part of an integrated but proprietary network management architecture, for example NetView for SNA. While this is acceptable from the point of view of the proprietary architecture, it is unacceptable within an 'open' architecture, particularly when the proprietary management system accounts for only a small fraction of the total network management requirement. The type of information required from a gateway includes:

- Number of active sessions and the total traffic supported by each session.
- Number of session failures and the total number of sessions established during the lifetime of the link.
- The address maps across the gateways and a complete set of statistics as a function of each of these addresses.
- Capacities of each of the links and a record of the failure conditions for each of these links.
- Status of the gateway, a description of the available links, and the default and active internal configuration parameters.

It is important that this information is available both locally and at a remote network management centre, so it is essential for the gateway to support the appropriate network management standards and protocols (as discussed in Chapter 14). It is also essential that all of the management features are password protected so that the gateway cannot be 'accidentally' reconfigured or disabled.

13.3   Uses of a gateway

Gateways provide protocol translation between different network architectures so that a common service can be supplied to the users. In some cases this translation is necessary because different network cultures have to be linked (LAN based PCs with the traditional mainframe infrastructure) or because common services have been supplied using different proprietary implementations, for example electronic mail (Held, 1993). The situations for which gateways are required are:

- LAN-to-host (remote access) connectivity – whereby remote, dumb and intelligent devices can be supplied with access to the central host processors.
- LAN-to-LAN connectivity – in which common applications services have to be interconnected but where their network layer, or higher, protocols differ.
- LAN-to-WAN connectivity – to provide access for LAN based users to services that are native to the WAN, for example access to PSDNs such as X.25.

In each case the gateway, and any associated end-system applications software, provides an integrated link which is dedicated to that particular application. Generic gateways are not available because the range of services and architectures is too diverse to establish a cost effective core of functions. Instead, some functions have been appended to other internetworking devices such as routers, thereby extending their functionality and providing this in a cost effective manner.

One of the most significant problems when using a gateway is a loss of functionality. This loss is a result of the gateway supporting only the common services used on either side of the gateway. This means that any idiosyncratic features of a service on one side of the gateway will not be made available on the other side, and vice versa. An example of this loss of service is regularly encountered in electronic mail systems, in which some mail servers allow files to be appended to a message whereas others do not. Users on the 'wrong' side of the gateway would receive the message but not the appended file.

13.3.1 LAN-to-host connectivity

The original need for gateways was remote host connectivity wherein a remote terminal needed access to the corporate mainframe computer system. Although, this requirement still exists, it has now been joined by the need to provide LAN-to-host

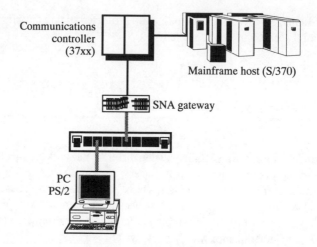

Communications controller (37xx)

Mainframe host (S/370)

SNA gateway

PC PS/2

Figure 13.4 LAN-to-host connectivity.

connectivity in which the terminal has been replaced by an intelligent NOS client and where the mainframe is the NOS server. In both cases the local environment is radically different from that to which the mainframe is connected and so a gateway is required to provide the necessary translation (Göhring, 1993). LAN-to-host and remote host access is normally supplied in one of three ways:

- Using a gateway which provides the protocol translation (software plus the appropriate network interface cards and drivers). The significance of this technique will decrease in the future as more integrated solutions become established.

- Using a router which provides an information tunnel for the remote host protocol (such as SDLC). This is the currently preferred solution because it can be supported as part of the wider internetworking infrastructure.

- As part of an integrated internetworking solution in which the global system protocols provide the necessary access capability. It is this type of approach which is being promoted by IBM in its advanced peer-to-peer networking (APPN) and was unsuccessfully advocated by Cisco in its rival form of advanced peer-to-peer internetworking (APPI) These types of approaches, once established, will become the standard host access technique.

An example of the LAN-to-host use of a gateway is shown in Figure 13.4. Here various NetWare based PC and PS/2 workstation clients need remote access to their mainframe server. To get this access they use an SNA/NetWare gateway which interconnects the Token Ring to the mainframe's control cluster or communications controller. Novell/ LAN/IBM host connection products provide a gateway in which NetWare/SNA software is used with an SDLC connection. The gateway is itself a PC or PS/2 with an appropriate SDLC interface.

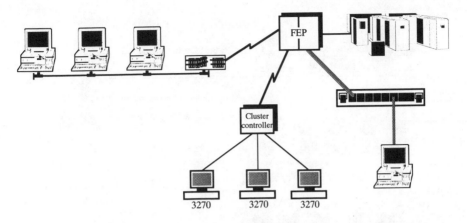

Figure 13.5   Remote host access for a 3270 terminal system.

The equivalent remote host access architecture is shown in Figure 13.5. In this system the three 3270 terminals are connected to the mainframe via the cluster controller and FEP. The ethernet based workstations must make use of a gateway which is responsible for interfacing the 10BASE2 network and the FEP's SDLC link. The workstations must host 3270 protocol emulation software, which makes them appear to the mainframe as 3270 terminals by encapsulating the terminal protocol in ethernet frames. In the case of the Token Ring based workstation the FEP supports its own Token Ring card, so a gateway is unnecessary – terminal emulation software is still required in the workstation.

13.3.2 LAN-to-LAN connectivity

During the initial stages of a network's lifetime it is almost impossible to predict how and for what the network will be used several years in the future. Therefore, the aim should be to provide a network which supports the immediate needs but which can be readily extended. The choice of applications and their support protocols is particularly sensitive to change but in the early life of a network it is unrealistic to expect users to be constrained by future possibilities. One very recent but now common concern is the choice of electronic mail system. In many LAN systems the mail facility is supplied by various means: as part of the word processor, and so on. It would be impossible to mandate a particular mail system and then expect all future internetworked systems to conform to it. Gateways are the natural solution to this form of problem, especially when considering delay insensitive applications such as electronic mail.

Figure 13.6 shows a typical architecture for LAN-to-LAN connectivity using gateways to establish a global electronic mail system. In this network several separate LAN systems are interconnected using an intermediate wide area network. Each LAN system consists of several different mail applications and the requirement is to provide

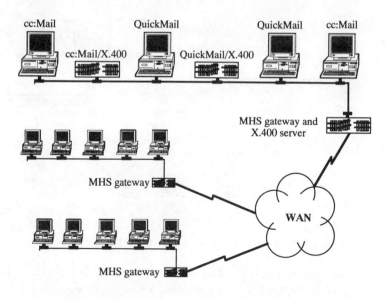

Figure 13.6 LAN-to-LAN connectivity for electronic mail access.

a global electronic mail facility. This is achieved by using gateways to provide the mail-to-mail translation. In Figure 13.6 each different mail system type has its own X.400 gateway (cc:Mail to X.400 and QuickMail to X.400) and there is an X.400 gateway server which provides access external to the LAN system. The basic principle is to use the X.400 MHS as the backbone mail system and to use gateways to translate each different mail system into X.400. The X.400 server on each LAN is then used to store the actual mail messages (both locally and globally) and is responsible for reliably forwarding the message to the appropriate destination.

The advantage and disadvantage of this approach is that a separate gateway function is required for each translation. This means that once the common backbone mail format has been established (typically an international standard such as X.400) then it is simple to introduce yet another gateway to cater for new local mail formats. Unfortunately, in some situations where there is a relatively large number of different mail systems in use, for example three or more, this can become very expensive. Each different translation does not necessarily mean a different physical gateway because in many cases it is possible to house the new translations within an already established gateway, for example by using a multiprotocol gateway (cf. multiprotocol routers). In Figure 13.6 this is the case for the remote LAN systems where there is only one gateway – this gateways supports the three separate functions of the other gateways.

Another example of this LAN-to-LAN architecture is shown in Figure 13.7 in which a mixed SUN/Apple network is constructed using LocalTalk, ethernet and a gateway. The SUN file servers are configured to support both NFS and AppleShare whereas the laser printer is available for all users of the network. A PC is connected to the network using an appropriate network adapter, such as a flash card. The advantage of this architecture is that it is possible to make use of the SUN workstations

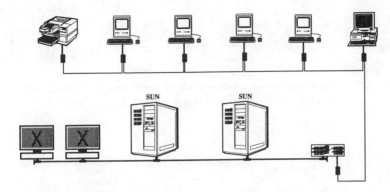

Figure 13.7   SUN/Apple LAN-to-LAN interconnection.

as the primary filestore, thus simplifying data organization and support across the network without compromising the peer-to-peer capabilities within each of the component systems themselves. The Macintosh and PC users of this network can now make use of the SUN workstations as remote hosts (using terminal emulation software), as file servers or as processor servers.

Gateways used in this way mean that it is not essential to achieve complete standardization within a LAN. From the users' point of view, apart from their own mail application preference they need not even know of the existence of other mail systems; the backbone standard is totally hidden from them, so it appears that everyone is using the same mail application. One problem with this hidden interconnection is that the gateways will only support common service features and so certain functions will, initially unknown to the users but soon learnt once the problems have been encountered, be lost across the gateway. For recently standardized applications (such as electronic mail), it is this gateway hopping strategy that has been adopted by the manufacturers so that users can migrate to these new systems in a cost effective manner.

13.3.3 LAN-to-WAN connectivity

The early predominance of PSDNs, such as X.25, for implementing distributed access WANs has resulted in a need for direct LAN-to-WAN connectivity; this must be supplied by gateway. In these types of networks the host consists of either intelligent workstations with their own network interfaces or dumb devices which make use of network access units such as terminal servers or PADs. A gateway is used rather than a router because of the difficulty in establishing a consistent addressing system across the LAN–WAN combination and because the gateway can provide translation between the different versions of the basic protocol, such as X.25 (80) and X.25 (84).

A typical example of a network architecture using LAN-to-WAN gateways is shown in Figure 13.8. In this system there are two uses for the gateways: the first is to supply ethernet access to the X.25 (84) hosts and the second is to support

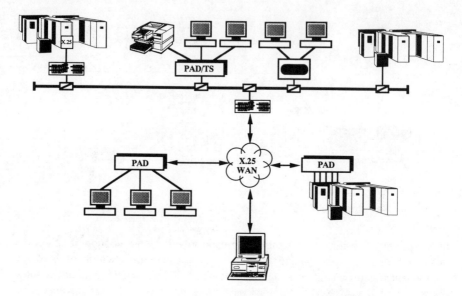

Figure 13.8   LAN-to-WAN connectivity using an X.25 network.

interconnection between the ethernet and the WAN – supported by the X.25 (80) version. The terminal server supports access to the ethernet based mainframe whereas the PAD/terminal server supplies access to the X.25 based mainframe (hence the mainframe's use of a gateway). The WAN based workstations and mainframe must all support the same X.25 version and the LAN-to-WAN gateway provides the appropriate conversion between the X.25 versions and the physical LAN and WAN interfaces.

13.4   The application of gateways

In many cases it is clear that a gateway is the only way to provide interconnection, for example mixed protocol interconnection, but a choice has to be made between a router and a gateway when considering remote host access support. In these cases the tunnelling capability of the router is well suited to the task, so if one is already available then it is the more cost effective solution. In other cases the most cost effective solution depends upon the actual networks and protocols involved, with, depending upon the required functionality, both approaches being equally costly. Once the need for a gateway has been identified the next stage is to decide what type of gateway is needed. The issues to be considered during this selection are:

- The type of networks that must be supported: LAN/LAN, LAN/WAN, WAN/WAN.

- Identification of the protocols used by your network and of those requiring translation.

- The number of network links to be supported: is routing to be a part of the interconnection system?

- The host computer systems needing support and the identification of any associated special interface boards.

- The number of concurrent sessions to be supported by the gateways and the corresponding buffer storage to compensate for speed mismatches and so on.

In principle, the above approach is well founded, however, in reality there is a limited choice. Once the basic interconnection need has been established – that is, the types of network (SNA, DNA, AppleTalk, ethernet and so on) then the choice is usually between two or three vendor dependent solutions.

13.4.1 IBM and Digital connectivity

Two of the most prevalent data communications oriented WAN architectures are Digital's DECnet and IBM's SNA. Typically, many organizations have used Digital processors for engineering processing and IBM mainframes for intensive data trans-action. This has generated a large demand for products to provide connectivity between both types of networks and processors. The two basic approaches for DEC/IBM interconnection are shown in Figure 13.9, in which there is direct connection using a full gateway or indirect connection using two half gateways and an intermediate network (X.25 in this example). The intermediate network approach is particularly suitable when such an infrastructure is already available and so the backbone is being used to support several different types of interconnection. Digital (note, not IBM) has three DECnet/SNA gateways which provide direct connection:

- A VMS/SNA software only solution.
- A channel-attached version for high-speed interfaces.
- A synchronous version for connection through an SNA network.

The VMS/SNA software approach is capable of supporting 16 concurrent sessions across a single 64 kbps link. This approach uses a VAX station as the gateway, so the physical links must be interconnected via the VAX processor bus – the SNA FEPs require access to the VAX via an SDLC interface card. The DECnet/SNA gateway for channel transport (CT) is a piece of software which runs on a dedicated processor (DEC ChannelServer) to provide a high-powered gateway between DECnet and SNA networks, as shown in Figure 13.10. The CT solution connects users anywhere in the DECnet or SNA networks and provides a 2–4 Mbps data link for up to 255 concurrent sessions.

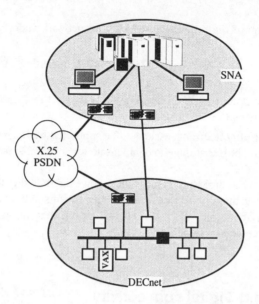

Figure 13.9 IBM and Digital proprietary systems connectivity.

The third approach is the DECnet/SNA gateway for synchronous transport (ST), as also shown in Figure 13.10. This is a piece of software which runs on a dedicated processor (DEC MicroServer) to provide a gateway between DECnet and SNA networks which supports up to 128 concurrent sessions across a data link of 256 kbps (both the CT and ST gateways appear as PU type 2 devices to SNA). The ST gateway is linked to an SNA FEP, using the SDLC protocol, which accounts for the slower throughput capability when compared to the CT solution.

One common use of gateways in the DEC/IBM interconnection is to permit remote workstations to gain access to their natural hosts via a different network environment; in Figure 13.10, this is reflected by the PCs which are hosting MS-DOS. Communication to their remote IBM mainframe host requires the use of an ethernet LAN, with its DECnet multiport repeater, which supports the ST and CT gateways. The DEC stations can also use this architecture to access their remote VAX host. If the DEC station wished to communicate with the IBM mainframe then it would have to use an MS-DOS emulation package, such as a DECnet-DOS 3270 Terminal Emulator.

Each of the DECnet/SNA interconnection approaches should be used in the following situations:

- VMS/SNA for low-volume traffic for access from a VAX processor to SNA.

- The ST gateway for full-function internetworking with significant traffic flowing across the Internet, for interfaces to IBM mail and document management services and for IBM 3270 terminals to obtain access to DEC systems.

- The CT gateway for very high volume and fast response times for users who can be served through a DECnet LAN.

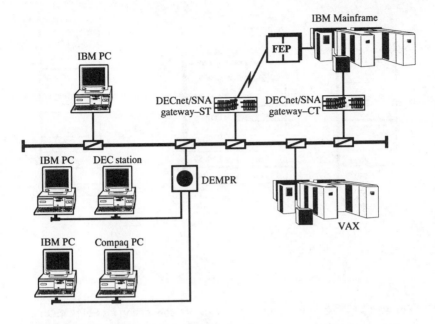

Figure 13.10 DECnet and SNA interconnection for remote host access.

The indirect interconnection of DECnet and SNA systems is readily supported by X.25 when the Digital approach is used, as shown in Figure 8.8. Here the hop-by-hop enhancement internetworking approach is used to link first with a DNA subnetwork and then with the SNA subnetwork. The IBM approach would have required the DEC systems to use the SNA as a backbone architecture (for example using the X.25/SNA interconnect approach, XI gateway) and operate with software which acted as the gateway. The IBM approach to open architectures is discussed in depth by Cypser (1992). The equivalent gateway structure for the direct connection approach is shown in Figure 13.11. The two protocol stacks in the gateway reflect each of the end-system profiles (SNA and DNA) and provide the switching between the physical subnetworks; note that the Digital host must also support the appropriate SNA application interface, such as 3270 terminal emulation software.

13.4.2 TCP/IP interconnectivity

In the TCP/IP context the term 'gateway' is used to represent any internetworking device which provides connectivity between subnetworks – in other words, it encompasses both routers and gateways as defined and used herein. TCP/IP is both a LAN and host architecture and so in such cases it is not necessary to use a gateway to interconnect hosts and LANs. TCP/IP gateways are required for:

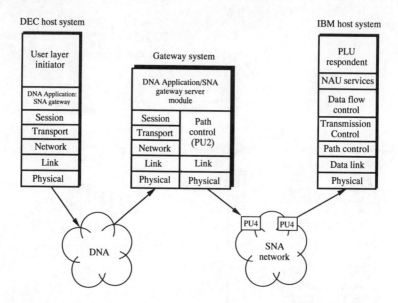

Figure 13.11   Hop-by-hop enhancement interconnection for SNA/DECnet.

- Interconnection and direct service access between TCP/IP and proprietary networks such as SNA.

- To provide a TCP/IP supported tunnel between two other network architectures – this was the approach proposed by Cisco and its unsuccessful APPI solution for SNA access.

The increasing number of integrated TCP/IP services within otherwise proprietary architectures means that in a growing number of situations there is no need to use a TCP/IP gateway. Such an approach has been adopted by both Digital and IBM. As part of their strategy to provide internetworking functions to a variety of networks, IBM provide support for TCP/IP on MVS and VM hosts which supply:

- File transfer to other TCP/IP hosts
- Sending electronic mail using SMTP
- Remote log-on to another host with TCP/IP TELNET server support
- File server support for the NFS access, such as PC-NFS based systems and SUN workstations
- Interconnection with TCP/IP on another IBM host across an SNA network.

A larger proportion of Digital LANs are interconnected than any other type of proprietary LAN, with only TCP/IP supporting a comparable number of installations. DECnet phase V, or Advantage-network, has a triple stack emphasis of OSI, DECnet and TCP/IP, with OSI being seen as the interconnection architecture between DECnet and TCP/IP. Originally, TCP/IP was to be excluded from DECnet phase V. However, its widespread popularity caused a rethink by Digital and so gave rise to the multistack strategy now being promulgated. Clearly, Digital's commitment to, and the increasing adoption of, UNIX and TCP/IP by the industrial and commercial communities has created a substantial market which cannot be ignored, so TCP/IP/DECnet gateways for UNIX/VMS connection will be available for the foreseeable future.

13.4.3 OSI/RM connectivity

It is important to note that the OSI/RM has no formal standard for a gateway but there is a clear implication that all such systems will consist of a complete seven-layer profile; that is, a gateway is an end-system. Clearly this is not possible in the cases where the profiles do not conform to the full OSI (such as X.25 or SNA) and where an OSI backbone network is required. The strength of OSI gateways is that their sophistication is such that they can be used to interconnect almost any type of proprietary architecture. While the mapping between the OSI and a proprietary system may not be simple, the complexity is reduced to one of mapping the layering and functionality of the proprietary system onto the equivalent layers and functions supported within the OSI.

It is possible that OSI gateways could become the standard mechanism for creating usable 'open systems', as reflected by the new X.400 infrastructures. This is the only cost effective approach for an organization that does not require the wholesale replacement of its established network architecture. OSI gateways will be linked to create an OSI backbone network across which all of the other network systems can be interconnected. These gateways will then be used to convert between the local 'closed' architectures and the global 'open' network, thereby providing the best of all worlds: a network optimized for the local environment but which still has access to the external global network using internationally agreed communications standards. This approach is particularly important where the performance criteria for the local network exclude the adoption of 'heavy' profiles such as those of the OSI. IBM have addressed this while considering the interworking of SNA with other profiles (Janson, 1992)

The proposed use of OSI gateways could, in the longer term, lead to a position of confusion concerning TCP/IP. One of the reasons why many organizations are migrating to TCP/IP as their underlying backbone architecture is that it will provide a very useful base from which further migration will be possible, for example to OSI. However, TCP/IP is not only an internetworking architecture but also a host architecture and so many organizations are also converting to TCP/IP within their host systems. This conversion does not necessarily reflect the optimal approach for the local system and any future migration will almost certainly result in a further erosion of the suitability of the local infrastructure to the host needs. This means that the adoption of TCP/IP for the host profile may, in the long term, not be beneficial to the performance capabilities of the end-system and is certainly not a requirement for the provision of a coherent migration path to other internetworked profiles.

13.5   Summary

Gateways complete the family of internetworking devices. The general rule of thumb is that if the required interconnectivity cannot be supplied by any of the other devices (repeater, bridge or router) then use a gateway. The reason for this principle is that gateways tend to be slower and more expensive than their counterparts, and their development from the mainframe market has not yet resulted in high performance systems which fully exploit the capabilities of LAN based architectures. In conclusion:

- Gateways are responsible for protocol conversion and depending upon the extent of the translation can range between £1000 and £75 000.

- Gateways are used to provide three classes of connectivity: LAN-to-host (remote access) for terminal access, LAN-to-LAN for LAN based service access and LAN-to-WAN for WAN based service access.

- The classical use of gateways in mixed vendor environments is to provide interconnection between the IBM and Digital proprietary architectures; that is, SNA/DECnet. This usually permits ethernet based PCs to remotely access IBM mainframes.

- The essential features of a gateway are the LAN and WAN interfaces it supports, the number of concurrent sessions that can be active across it, the management interfaces to it and the specific application it supports.

- Both TCP/IP and OSI gateways are supported by IBM and Digital. These provide one way of mapping between their proprietary systems but they can also be used to supply a backbone network for transporting data from one environment to another.

- Gateways are not generic in nature and so it is not possible to take a gateway from one application environment and use it in another completely different environment. This form of reuse is very common when using other types of internetworking device but it is not possible using gateways.

14

Network Administration

14.1   Introduction

Network administration has been identified as the key activity where there is most scope for improvement in efficiency and effectiveness, and where significant cost savings can be made; effective network management is central to this expectation. Network administration consists of system administration (providing user support) and network maintenance (supporting the network itself). It is generally recognized that network maintenance consists of:

- Preventative – monitoring and restructuring the network to prevent future problems such as cabling failure and excess loading.
- Corrective – fixing problems that occur on a day-to-day basis.
- Adaptive – changes to the network to provide extra functionality and services.

A key facet of network maintenance is network management. Network management provides the information and the control facilities by which the network can be maintained (Kauffels, 1992). If a network has no network management facilities, such as remote control of the internetworking devices, then it makes it considerably more difficult to identify potential and actual problems in the network. The cost of network administration is some 60–80% of the total lifetime cost of the network and consequently the most significant cost saving attempts should be made in this area – that is, the provision of the right management tools and an attitude of 'design for maintenance' at the outset of network procurement and installation.

The original demands made of internetworked systems were described in Chapter 1, Figure 1.3 in particular, but these are now developed further with the introduction of integrated systems network management; this becomes an essential element of the internetworked architecture, as shown in Figure 14.1. In fact, the adoption of new internetworking strategies will be dependent upon their capability to support an appropriate network management infrastructure. This is because:

- The factors pushing for integrated and internetworked systems are also creating the demand for integrated systems management. This means managing the whole community of processors and networks together as a single system.
- Many vendors realize that their future ability to sell their systems will depend upon their ability to provide systems that can manage the total network of systems including any associated subnetworks.
- Many companies are now competing to introduce their own network management architecture into the world of large interconnected networks and to establish their systems as the basis from which to manage all of the linked networks and systems.

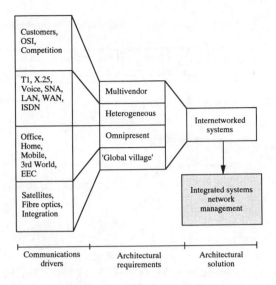

Figure 14.1   Integrated systems network management.

14.2   Administration objectives

Typically, vendors will provide some form of remote management capability with their products and it is often possible to connect this to a single network management centre (NMC). This is supplied because internetworking devices are frequently the cause of network problems, for example configuration, compatibility or performance issues, and therefore, need careful management. Sometimes these products provide interfaces into other all-embracing network management architectures (such as NetView), so that alerts and controls can be managed from a single screen. However, when this cannot be provided, these products are then frequently grouped into a single room, so that operators can see the status of each component on the network.

The management connectivity typically required of an NMC is shown in Figure 14.2. An integrated NMC must be capable of controlling all of the remote internetworking devices (local and remote bridges, routers and gateways) and the network adapters (Token Ring and Ethernet) in a seamless fashion. If this is not possible, then in the worst possible case a separate NMC must be used to support each different type of device and unless a common network management protocol (either proprietary or standardized) is used then similar devices from different manufacturers will also need different NMCs; effective network management is impossible in such an architecture.

There are two categories of network administration activities:

- The 'daily functions' required for the routine day-to-day operation of the network.

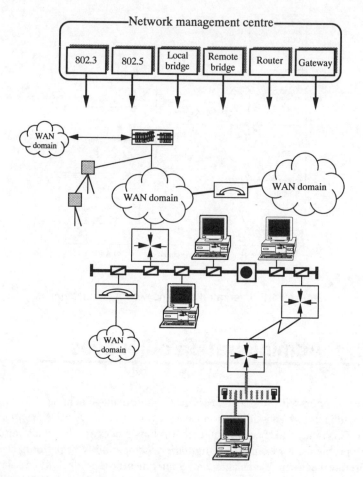

Figure 14.2   The problems of managing complex network architectures.

- The 'strategic functions' required to ensure that a network continues to meet business needs in a controlled and cost effective manner.

Network management tools generally support the first group but not the second. This is because the 'strategic functions' have long-term implications and require the capability to store and process large amounts of information over a long period (typically years). It is also useful to distinguish between 'network management' and 'system administration'. System administration is concerned with activities such as user registration, help desk support and user file directory services whereas network management is concerned with the control of the communications facilities. The emphasis for internetworking is in the context of network management but it is important to recall that both system administration and network maintenance are needed for network administration. The day-to-day functions require:

Table 14.1 The functional categories for network management.

Function	Category	Real-time	Design	Administrative
Fault management	Day-to-day	***	**	*
Change management	Day-to-day	***	**	*
Performance monitoring	Day-to-day	**	**	***
User support	Day-to-day	***	*	*
Accounting	Day-to-day	*		***
Planning and design	Strategic		***	
Security	Strategic	*	***	**
Vendor relations	Strategic	*	*	***
Cost control	Strategic		*	***

- Fault management to make sure that the network carries on running no matter what – a network which is faulty can cause the loss of many man days of effort.

- Change management, which involves installing new users and enhancing the network, for example by introducing new printers and so on.

- Performance monitoring so that any deviation from the normal performance can be investigated for faults or seen as a need for more capacity.

- User support and registration. Registration ensures that the system can differentiate between authorized and unauthorized users.

- Accounting to make sure that costs are controlled and that accurate internal billing can be provided.

The 'strategic functions' have a more long-term effect on the quality of the networking system. However, if these are not properly addressed as part of the role of preventative support then there is a significantly increased likelihood of an eventual catastrophic failure. The 'strategic functions' are:

- Planning and design to provide controlled growth. The alternative is panic buying and installation followed by a leisurely time to rue the decisions made.

- Security, which is becoming a concern for internetworking. This includes protecting the network against viruses, the worst of which are yet to come.

- Vendor relations to ensure that you get the best prices and service. Poor support maintenance will eventually cause a system to grind to a halt. Everything needs to be looked after and this should be planned and controlled.

- Cost control, which is essential if the network is to be seen as providing the business with a competitive edge.

Table 14.1 categorizes the different network administration functions according to their importance (three asterisks indicating a significant relationship, two asterisks some relationship and one asterisk little relationship). The three categories are:

- Real time, which accounts for less than 50% of the management task and is concerned with reacting to the network's changing operational requirements.

- Design, which is concerned with translating the planned changes of the network into the operational reality, thereby providing a controlled network evolution capable of supporting the changing needs of the users.

- Administrative, as distinct from network administration, which is concerned with supporting the organization of the network, from the user's perspective, and ensuring its long-term stability.

The 'planning and design' activity is that which is most likely to suffer due to lack of time and available effort. Ironically, it is often that oversight which causes many of the eventual problems – network overloading, ignorance of the true network architecture, and so on – and so it is essential that 'planning and design' is properly supported. The reason why effective planning is so important is because it:

- Requires an accurate knowledge of the current state and usage of the network.

- Needs consultation with the user community to ascertain their future needs.

- Produces a development plan of the network architecture and services so that it can support those future needs.

- Provides information such that the network support team can negotiate new purchases at their most economic price.

- Provides time to upgrade the network so that there is never a degradation in its performance and to plan the upgrade itself to ensure that this occurs at an appropriate time and without significantly affecting the users.

14.3   Current management systems

In many cases the LAN network management systems are derived from their WAN counterparts. Consider the network architecture shown in Figure 14.2. In this network the WAN domain managers use their own set of systems, for example, SNA systems engineers managing the network using NetView and, depending upon the sophistication of the LAN/SNA gateway, NetView may, or may not, be able to 'see' the gateway. The Token Ring users require their own management domain because they are in their own building (remote from the main office) and they need to manage their own printing and file store resources (which have very little to do with anyone else). The ethernet users in the main office are spread across a number of segments on different media, but

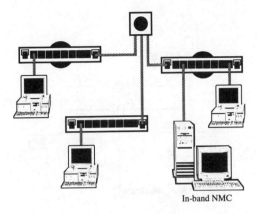

In-band NMC

Figure 14.3 In-band network management architecture.

they share data and services equally. They therefore need to be part of a separate domain which manages their interests. They also have responsibility as a backbone network for the remote Token Ring users – so they are likely to take a wider role in managing the full network. An integrated management facility would simplify the problems for the network manager but this can only be possible if different manufacturers use an agreed set of network management protocols and services.

14.3.1 LAN management systems

One of the first architectural choices to be made when creating a LAN management system is whether an in-band or out-of-band structure is to be used. The essential difference between these is that the in-band system makes use of the actual network itself for the transfer of management information whereas the out-of-band system makes use of a second external network.

An example of an in-band based network management architecture is shown in Figure 14.3. The NMC acts as another user of the network except that the information being transmitted is not to users but is to the network infrastructure itself – that is, the MAUs, network adapters, repeaters, bridges and so on. In contrast, the out-of-band approach uses another separate network to support the transfer of the management information – as shown in Figure 14.4. As can be seen in this network a second daisy-chained network has been used to link together the MAUs and the repeater. In the case of the in-band system it is also possible for the NMC not to have its own network adapter but to make use of a local internetworking device. In this case the NMC would be connected to the relay via a serial or parallel interface and would drive the relay to send and receive the management information to and from other relays.

The advantage and disadvantage of the in-band approach is that only one network is required. During normal operation this is an ideal configuration. However,

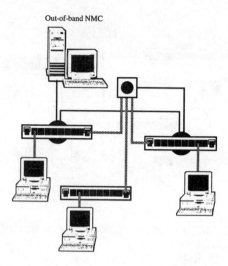

Out-of-band NMC

Figure 14.4 Out-of-band network management architecture.

if part of the cabling system becomes damaged then the network management system also becomes compromised and at a time when it is most needed. By contrast, the out-of-band approach is immune to failures of the primary network. However, its own architecture must be reliable and must have the same geographical coverage. The management system does not need high speed links and so the cost of the two networks are not comparable; even so, this second network has to be designed, installed and maintained.

14.3.2 Simple network management protocol

Communication across the network management system is supported by specific network management protocols and once again the TCP/IP community has established the industry standard. Originally, the simple network management protocol (SNMP) was intended to provide network managers with centralized control and observation of their TCP/IP based networks. Since then SNMP has been installed in many internetworking devices, and is now employed in many non-TCP/IP based networks – however, in most cases the NMC is housed in a UNIX box. The cause of this success is that once again the TCP/IP community has responded quickly to an important need and has produced an efficient and effective protocol to support network management (Rose, 1990). From the manufacturers' point of view the formal standardization efforts will take several more years before complete implementations are readily available and so SNMP provides them with a tried, tested and almost free technique which is ready for implementation and installation in their own products.

The network management architecture for SNMP follows the classical struc-

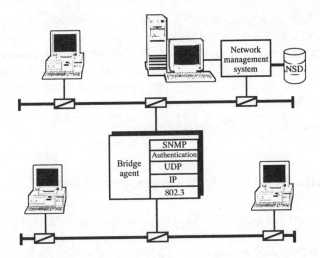

Figure 14.5 SNMP network management architecture.

ture of centralized NMC and remote agents, as shown in Figure 14.5. The agents respond to requests and instructions from the NMC and the resulting information is stored within the network statistics database (NSD). In each of the agents there are a collection of management information bases (MIBs) – more of these later – which store all of the appropriate local information concerning the device. SNMP is the protocol which provides the transfer of information between the NMC/NSD and the remote MIBs. Normally, the SNMP profile makes use of a connectionless service using the UDP/IP combination but TCP/IP is also available for use across unreliable networks, namely WAN links.

The control of an SNMP network involves the NMC in polling the remote agents and collating all of their responses in the NSD. SNMP supports this polling by providing three control primitives:

- Get – which enables the NMC to obtain information from an agent's MIB.
- Set – which enables the NMC to modify a value in an agent's MIB.
- Event – which enables the agent to inform the NMC of an alarm condition.

By using these three primitives it is possible to provide a simple but effective network management control system. The most recent release of SNMP, SNMP version two, has extended the range of control functions and has provided a superior data handling capability to reduce the number of instructions required to support standard network functions, such as read the entire contents of an address table. It has also added an authentication layer which is used to ensure that only authorized users can have access to the management features.

The long-term stability of SNMP depends on whether or not the major systems manufacturers (IBM, Digital, and so on) become committed to it and its compatibility with the OSI/RM standards when they are completed. In the short and medium term the TCP/IP based nature of the SNMP has meant that the major manufacturers have already begun to support it. In the longer term, there are several techniques being considered as possible ways in which SNMP and the OSI/RM protocols can be combined to provide a commercially acceptable solution for network management.

SNMP is the only available non-proprietary network management system and this, combined with its *de facto* standard status, means that at present it is the only sensible solution for the management of multivendor networks.

14.3.3 IEEE 802.1B network management and HLM

The LAN management architecture is currently undergoing definition by 3COM and Microsoft as part of the IEEE 802.1B committee effort. Their work is formally called the heterogeneous LAN management (HLM) architecture and will integrate the management of all LAN networks adapters. This management approach is based upon the station management (SMT) currently employed in both FDDI and Token Ring network adapters – the first ethernet cards to support this will soon be available from 3COM. Using this system it will be possible to:

- Establish default network parameters and have the network adapter interrogate the NMC for them.

- Let the NMC remotely disable network adapters that do not have the correct access privilege.

- Have the NIAs periodically report their status and performance statistics so that a separate performance monitoring system is no longer required.

Each host is internally organized as shown in Figure 14.6. The important feature is that the SMT entity has access to the LLC, MAC and PHY, and it reports the appropriate information to the remote NMC using a management protocol. The NMC itself must also be supported by the LAN management protocol. The SMT is an integral part of the operation of the network adapter (consider the operation of source routing in Token Ring systems) and as such the common functions must be fully supported by all types of network adapter. If this is not the case then there is no common basis on which to establish network-wide control of the network at the MAC level.

14.4   OSI/RM network management

Initially the standardization interests were purely concerned with the services and protocols used in communications. While these are obviously very important, the operational support of a fully conformant OSI/RM profile needs an appropriately

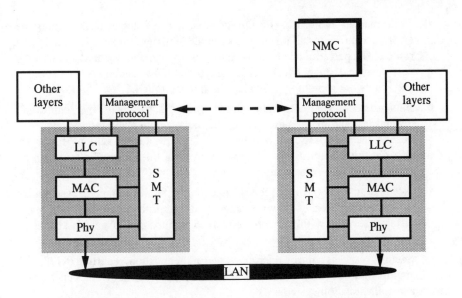

Figure 14.6 Internal management organization of a LAN adapter.

sophisticated management infrastructure is available to support the network – this would be the only method by which functions such as network configuration could be controlled. The protocol is relatively simple – management is not. Fortunately, the growing recognition of these facts by suppliers and standards makers has resulted in a substantial effort devoted specifically to network management and the creation of manageable networks.

The underlying architecture for the OSI/RM network management system is similar to that used by the Internet and its SNMP (Piscitello, 1993). Each device needs a management entity, or agent, and these entities must communicate with the NMC. The differences between the Internet and OSI/RM are reflected in the protocols which support the communication between the manager and the remote management agents, and these differences are a reflection of their different approaches to networking.

14.4.1 Management functions

The OSI/RM now has a network management addendum and this states that the main facets of management are:

- Configuration – initializing the network, enrolling new members, controlling the topology, keeping the equipment inventories and so on. The configuration facilities permit the manager to control the initialization, termination, enrolment and topology of the network.

- Performance – monitoring the throughputs, delays, detected packet and frame errors, and so on, for all layers of communications and for individual links and routes. The performance facilities allow the manager to remotely monitor the performance of the network. This is important if overloading is to be avoided and if network growth is to be planned and controlled.

- Fault – detection of fault conditions on the network, tracing of error sources and general test and maintenance aids. The fault facilities allow the manager to observe the state of the entire network and to have alert conditions displayed. Without this capability the task of discovering the cause of a fault can be difficult and time consuming.

- Accounting – the billing of users. Accounting facilities in open systems are very important because a wide range of different users can be using many different services within an internetworked architecture. Users must be billed for the use of any such service.

- Security – access control, encryption and authentication, reporting of break-in attempts and successes. This must also include key management for encryption and authentication systems.

14.4.2 Management architecture

The network management system has to be capable of supporting two types of management. The first is the vertical integration of the management processes contained within each node whereas the second is the horizontal integration which ensures that the NMC is fully aware of all of the distributed hosts (Langsford, 1993). Both of these viewpoints are supported by their own protocols and services.

Each of the stacks is structured as shown in Figure 14.7. The central column is the communications layers themselves with the left column being the timer task and the right being the system management entities (SMEs). The SMEs are responsible for the management of each of the local stack layers and for the collation of this with respect to the full stack and the global system management. The SME has an interface into each layer (and, when appropriate, each sublayer). The appointed NMC will have not only the local management application process but also the network management application process (NMAP), as shown in Figure 14.8.

The full OSI/RM network management architecture has two basic elements: the manager system management entity (MSME) and the agent system management entity (ASME), both of which are concerned with vertical integration of the stack's management – that is, they are specific versions of the SME. The MSME is the task which resides in the stack supporting the NMAP whereas the ASMEs (one for each host on the network) operate independently of any user process within the other hosts. The MSME and the ASMEs are in continual communication and report about the status of the network, providing information concerning the distributed performance, configuration, required billing, access status and fault status of the network. The NMAP is

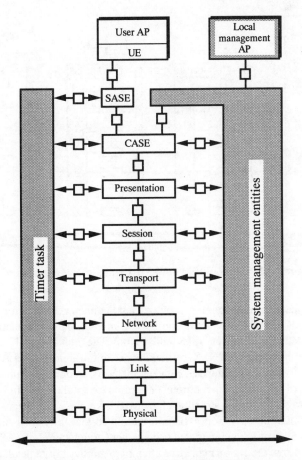

Figure 14.7 Internal management organization for a protocol stack.

directly supported by the management SASE (MSASE) which makes use of the common management information service entity (CMISE) to communicate with the remote agents, each of which uses the agent CMISE (ACMISE). The CMISE and ACMISE house the protocols that are responsible for the horizontal integration of the management of the different stacks and it is this functionality which provides management of the internetworked architecture.

Within a device the actual management protocols are only part of the network management architecture. These protocols are used to transfer management information describing the status of the device being managed, so the structure, organization and access rules of this information have to be clearly defined. The internal protocol architecture of a typical internetworking device (in this case a local bridge) is shown in Figure 14.9. The bridge contains two network adapters and so links together two separate ethernet LANs. The two adapters are linked internally using a MAC relay entity, which takes the information from one adapter, analyses it, and decides whether or not to forward the information. Above the MAC relay entity is the management

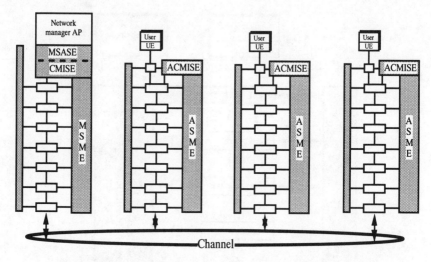

Figure 14.8 The OSI/RM network management architecture.

entity which houses the management protocol and the management information base (MIB). The MIB contains all of the appropriate management information such as performance statistics, filtering rules and so on. The management protocol can communicate in-band with the NMC by making use of the appropriate LAN segment: hence the need for the LLC interface between the MAC and management entities.

The use of the management protocol permits external entities to interrogate a relay's MIB, provided that the structure of the MIB is known. This means that device manufacturers must publish their MIB information so that the management system manufacturers can provide an integrated management architecture – the MIB architecture definition is now at version two. In an attempt to remove this dependence on MIB publication, the standards committees are establishing the concept of 'managed objects' which have inherent within them their data and access mechanisms. Each object will therefore have a well-defined management responsibility, including a standard access interface, and so there will be no need to understand the internal structure and organization of the MIB. In turn this releases the manufacturers from any historical compatibility dependence for their implementations.

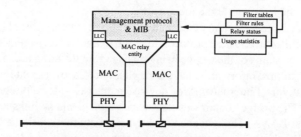

Figure 14.9 The heterogeneous LAN management architecture.

14.4.3 CMIS/CMIP

The definition of the OSI/RM network management system follows the usual procedure of defining the service and protocol separately. The protocol is called the common management information protocol (CMIP) and it supports the common management information services (CMIS); their relationship is shown in Figure 14.10. Both CMIS and CMIP are the common core which support the specific management information services (SMISs), in a relationship which is similar to that between the original application layer categorization of CASE and SASE. The SMIS and the corresponding system management information protocol (SMIP), or the SMIS/SMIP pair, support the five system management functional areas (SMFAs) which are, as described earlier, configuration, fault, performance, security and accounting.

While the functional standards have been completed, the world cannot wait for their implementation in a fully conformant OSI/RM stack and so several compromises have been established. The first of these was the creation of the common management over TCP/IP (CMOT) protocol which was proposed for use in TCP/IP based systems. CMOT was an attempt at reconciling the functionality of CMIP with the TCP/IP transport service; however, SNMP was still more popular due to its greater operating efficiency and so the CMOT proposals have now been stopped.

The second is the creation of the common management over the link layer (CMOL) protocol which provides the low level LAN management as demanded by the IEEE 802.1B HLM work. CMOL is the management protocol, as indicated in Figures 14.6 and 14.9, and as such provides the control for the network management system over the network adapters. In the interim it is also being proposed that SNMP should

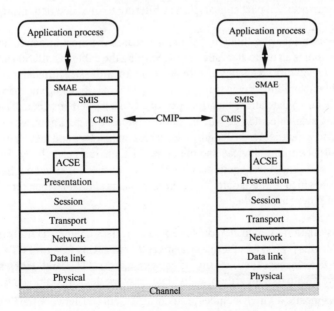

Figure 14.10 The CMIS/CMIP profile.

act as the CMOL equivalent. This provides a mechanism by which the future CMIS/ CMIP infrastructure can be integrated with the established SNMP, thereby providing a commercially sensible migration path between the current TCP/IP based approaches and the formally standardized CMIS/CMIP approach.

It is unlikely that any other new network management protocols will arise because they require a significant investment to produce, and the rapid development of CMIS/CMIP and the current dominance of SNMP make it commercially inappropriate. The latest trend is to integrate CMIP and SNMP, with CMIP being responsible for the interworking features and SNMP for the internetworking devices.

14.5   Installation and monitoring

Today's growing LAN market has spawned an increasing need for installation, diagnostic and monitoring test tools which can provide one or more of the following:

- Statistical information on network performance and resource usage
- Monitor traffic and error rate on a per station basis
- Quickly identify physical flaws in the channel
- User specified traffic generation to help with plans for future expansion; that is, simulated network loading
- User specified packet analysis and filtering to give detailed information.

It is however a sobering thought that in many cases the most effective and simplest diagnostic tool is an up-to-date site map specifying the cable installation and configuration of the network. This ties in with the trend towards 'structured networking' and the 'intelligent building' but in many installations there is either no site map or the copy is woefully out of date and is therefore practically useless. If an accurate site/network map is not available then it will be almost impossible to know which users are connected to which cable, the length of the cables themselves and the relative locations of the internetworking devices and the users. The site map can always be generated manually, so a lack of test equipment is not a valid excuse for either not having a map or for a map which is out of date. Once the site map is available, then three categories of test equipment are needed:

- Installation – which includes time domain reflectometers (TDRs), independent test units (ITUs) for ethernet systems and Token Ring testers (TRTs). TDRs are used to inspect the integrity of cables whereas ITUs and TRTs are used to investigate the integrity of individual network device components.

- Diagnostic – which includes protocol analysers and network traffic generators. Protocol analysers are used to analyse the flow of data across a channel and to inspect the structure of each frame whereas traffic generators provide the capability to investigate the effects of increased loading.

- Monitoring – performance monitors are used to inspect the data flow on the network and to produce sets of statistics describing its operation. These monitors are normally also capable of displaying the address maps of the network because each node sends its source address whenever it transmits data.

These tools are an essential part of a network manager's diagnostic 'armoury' and should be chosen carefully. In many cases these capabilities are supplied in an integrated fashion with the primary aim of helping the network manager to plan efficient resource usage and estimate network growth; some also provide troubleshooting facilities such as TDR functions. Unit sizes are usually desktop, although portable multitasking versions are becoming more popular and most manufacturers are also supplying PC-based board and software packages. Their typical functions include:

- Performance measuring – measurements of network usage and packets per second for each station and the network as a whole.

- Statistical analysis – including packets sent and received, total number of bytes sent and received, numbers of corrupted packets sent and received plus network totals. This often includes a statistical summary over variable time intervals, for example average load, peak load, error rates, and so on.

- TDR functions – this often supports a straightforward TDR test to assist in the identification of open or short circuits. Some may provide the testing of lower level communication functions using protocol based echo and loop tests.

- Traffic generation – user selectable traffic generation to assist in assessing the impact of new applications or additional stations. These typically provide information on load generated, packets sent and deferred transmissions.

- Packet analysis – most offer a range of packet-tracing facilities to assist in the identification of incorrect protocol software or bad packets. These usually work by capturing packets through filters and triggers (established via a user selectable screen display format). This permits packet decoding of a variety of protocols, such as ISO, TCP/IP, XNS, and so on.

14.5.1 Installation equipment

LAN cable testers, generally known as TDRs, are designed to detect cable faults along fibre, coax or twisted pair cabling: optical TDRs (OTDRs) are different from copper based TDRs. Correct interpretation of the TDR output can aid in identifying such things as poorly installed transceivers, abraded or kinked cable and non-conforming connectors. Optical TDRs are used by the fibre optics system installer, usually in conjunction with optical power meters, source emitters, bit error rate testers and variable optical attenuators. TDRs can provide graphical indications of features such as 'shorts',

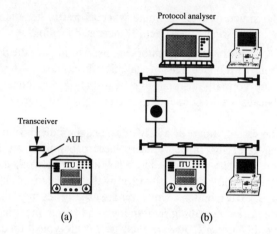

Figure 14.11 Testing and monitoring ethernet LANs.

'opens', water in a cable, cable impedance mismatches, crimped cable and damaged T-connectors by sending a test pulse down the channel and listening for the reflections back from the devices attached to the cable or from cabling flaws.

Apart from the cabling itself, it is also important to test the network adapters and cable connectivity devices. In ethernet systems this normally requires the use of ITUs and TRTs for Token Ring systems. The ITUs can be used to test transceivers on and off the LAN for bit-loss, SQE/heartbeat, collision oscillator, jabber protection and loopback test. The use of ITUs for off-LAN transceiver testing is shown in Figure 14.11a. More sophisticated testing, including round trip delay calculations, requires the ITU to be connected to the network, as shown in Figure 14.11b.

In Token Ring systems the hand-held TRT is predominantly used to investigate the operation of the MAUs and in particular their user ports. The TRT is used to ensure that the phantom voltage and electronic relay system operates correctly and as such it can also be used to investigate the operation of the RIN/ROUT ports of active MAUs. The TRT is inserted into each of the user ports of the MAU, as shown in Figure 14.12, but it should be noted that if the electronic relay is forced open on an operational ring then the network will start beaconing until the relay is closed. The more advanced TRTs support voice communications across the network, also crossing fibre links, making it possible to have cooperative testing by more than one individual.

14.5.2 Diagnostic equipment

Network diagnostic analysis is predominantly concerned with the use of protocol analysers. Protocol analysers can be used in a variety of ways to test the operation of the network or to determine where and why fault conditions are being detected. The types of diagnosis which can be supported by a protocol analyser are:

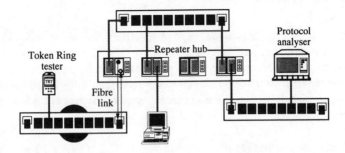

Figure 14.12 Testing and monitoring Token Ring LANs.

- The analysis of the content and order of data frames transmitted across the LAN, including automatic protocol decoding.

- Traffic generation to investigate the effects of increased loading on the network and to recreate the conditions that are suspected of causing network errors.

- The display of statistical information concerning the volumes of data transmitted across the network, the source/destination volumes and the time distributions of the loading.

The latest functional additions to protocol analysers include the use of expert systems to support network and protocol fault diagnosis, and the provision of computer based network simulation tools to compare theoretical capabilities with those being measured. In both ethernet and Token Ring systems the protocol analysers are connected directly to the LAN via the appropriate network adapter, as shown in Figures 14.11 and 14.12, respectively. In repeater based networks the protocol analysers have access to all of the traffic on the network whereas remote probes must be used in conjunction with the analyser when bridges and/or routers are present. In the case of Token Ring it is sometimes important to use a non-invasive analyser which does not participate in the token passing scheme. This is important because some error conditions will mysteriously disappear when an invasive analyser is used, for example when the cabling is too long, and so different types of analysers are required for different types of problems.

The typical price of a protocol analyser is between £10 000 and £20 000 (for a dedicated device), depending on the range of additional functions, such as combined ethernet and Token Ring analysis. This means that it may not be appropriate to buy such a piece of equipment but instead, to hire it when necessary; this is particularly important for small-scale networks. Software only versions are also available, costing between £400 and £2000, but these are slower than those with dedicated hardware and so they have a more limited functionality and can miss frames when the network is heavily loaded. In recent years the expertise needed to configure these hardware and software based systems has been reduced. However, it still requires a great deal of knowledge to take the results from a network and to use them to identify and locate problems.

14.5.3 Monitoring needs

Network monitoring covers a wide range of functions, including some of those also used during installation and diagnostic support. The primary difference between monitoring and the other management activities is the user emphasis as opposed to that of the network itself. Monitoring the network is concerned with ensuring that the user gets the appropriate level of service and consequently the types of LAN management tools needed for this are:

- Configuration management – utilities for creating graphical network topology, such as LANmap.

- Performance and fault monitoring – protocol analysers, such as Hewlett Packard's 4972A LAN Analyser and LANProbe.

- Accounting management – usually based on audit trails but there are very few products available, such as LANtrail.

- Security management – covers software supporting automatic log off facilities, software meters and automatic back-up facilities.

- User administration – provision of simple user interfaces via menu creation facilities and remote user software, allowing managers to access user screens.

The range of products available for network monitoring is limited when compared to that for testing and diagnosis. The reason for this is that it is still unclear what is actually required for good user oriented support whereas from the network point of view those requirements are very clearly known. It will be several more years before the level of support for the user is comparable to that of the network, so the network management team must employ manual methods for direct user support.

14.6   The management architecture

The current perception in the networking community is that LAN management is a bigger problem than WAN management. The reasons for this are that:

- Most LANs and LAN management tools are decentralized
- LAN management tools are highly specialized
- Performance is dependent on both networks and file servers
- Management across routers and gateways is very difficult, and can affect performance
- LAN management standards differ from OSI management standards today
- More LANs are interconnected.

14.6.1 The network management system

The cost of a network management system (NMS) varies between a few hundred pounds up to £50 000 for systems that are also capable of integrating the WAN elements. The functions normally expected of an NMS are:

- Performance management so that the network operates at its most efficient, including throughput measurement to indicate the loads on the links.

- Alarms which provide a visual register of fault or warning conditions and fault logging to provide a hard copy record of the network's history.

- Remote diagnostics/test so that the network can be tested from the NMC and remote configuration so that new users can be enrolled.

- Administration database to keep track of all the users and user accounting/ billing so that revenue can be earned.

Each internetworking device must also contribute to the NMS. These devices operate at very sensitive positions within a network and so it is important that accurate information concerning these is readily available. This information should include:

- The volume of traffic supported by the relay, such as the amount of information filtered and forwarded across a bridge.

- The sources of the information that crosses a relay, such as packets through gateways and routers.

- The topology of the network as understood by repeaters, bridges and routers.

- The state of the LAN and intermediate WAN links in the networks, such as repeater segments, bridge links and so on.

- The state of the relays themselves, for example in the case of bridges that operate the spanning tree algorithm.

- Data loss within the network – that is, the number of frames and so on that had to be rejected because of corruption, duplication or loss of communication.

There are, however, some consequences on the actual network itself whenever an NMS is installed and used. These effects are:

- The network performance is slightly degraded due to the fact that management information is being sent across the network itself.

- The performance of the user hosts is slightly degraded because there is extra host software (the management software) which is using up processing power.

- If the NMS is critical to the operation of the network then care must be taken to ensure that it also has a backup system.

If the use of a modular rack architecture is not possible then the two alternative management methods are the in-band and out-of-band approaches as shown in Figures 14.3 and 14.4. The range of approaches is further increased when an integrated or appended NMS is used, both of which are shown in Figure 14.13. In most installations an integrated approach is not possible (the normal exception is where a single vendor solution has been adopted) and so the NMS must be added to the established network architecture. While an appended solution is not an ideal approach (it is usually limited passive observation and not active control), it is considerably better than no NMS.

In Figure 14.13 a remote probe has been placed on each LAN structure – these are used by the in-band NMC and support the appended management architecture. The probes act as remote statistics gathering nodes which then report this information back to the NMC. From the NMC's point of view the bridges distort the true loading of the LANs and so a different probe must be placed on either side of any bridge. Repeaters act as transparent elements and so a probe will reflect the loading across all of the repeaters connected on any one side of a bridge. If there is a large number of probes then it is important to ascertain the data loading that these will make on the network, and it can also be advisable in some circumstances to put the NMC on a bridged off area of the network. It is then possible to filter off any unauthorized access to the centre.

If the internetworking devices themselves support management then it is usually possible to manage these by either an in-band or out-of-band method. In the case of the out-of-band NMC approach it is usually possible to control all of the similar but remote internetworking devices from the one which is directly supporting the NMC. This is possible in Figure 14.13 by one of two methods:

- Using the external network which links the two bridges – that is, make use of a separate network connected to the devices needing management.

- The bridge-to-bridge communication could in fact occur via the actual network itself; that is, in-band. In this case the bridge-to-bridge communication could

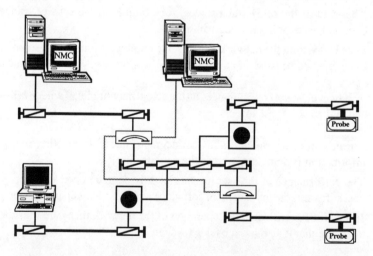

Figure 14.13 Performance monitoring using remote probes.

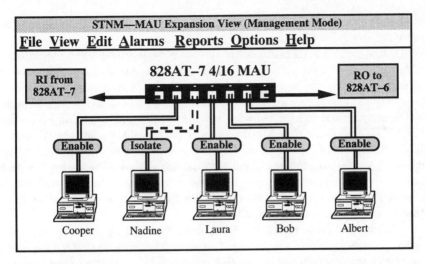

Figure 14.14   The network management centre display screen.

fail if part of the LAN architecture becomes disconnected due to failure, for example the central segment in Figure 14.13.

Clearly, the design and installation of an NMS is a significant element of the total network effort and in many cases it is concerned with the use of a network within a network. This means that all of the normal design considerations have to be analysed: reliability, security, connectivity, and so on. In return for this effort it should be possible to respond to problems and changes more effectively and to support the network with fewer individuals.

14.6.2 The network management centre

The NMC consists of a host environment, such as PC, and the management software. There are two approaches for hosting the management software:

- The software resides on the PC and communicates with the remotely managed devices either via the network or through a local connection to one of the internetworking devices.

- The software resides on the internetworking device and the NMC is either a dumb terminal or a PC hosting terminal emulation, connected via a serial or parallel interface. This approach is used by many out-of-band systems.

As a general rule it is wise to avoid the out-of-band systems in which the management software resides within the internetworking device only. The use of separate manage ment software on the NMC is preferred because this normally provides a wider range of services and quicker response to management commands.

More capable LAN management systems provide effective and simple to use window, icon, mouse and pull-down menu (WIMP) interfaces. These make it quick and easy to display the topology of the network and to ascertain its operational characteristics. One such interface is shown in Figure 14.14 – this is provided by the StarTek network management software, which can be hosted by a PC or PS/2. This 'window' shows a five-port MAU (this is not a commercially available MAU format) with the RIN and ROUT ports. The RIN and ROUT ports have their connection state shown along with the identifier of the appropriate linked MAU. The workstation ports show the five linked hosts. Four workstations are active and one is isolated; that is, inactive. This management facility requires that the MAU be powered so that it can transmit information to the attached NMC.

In an ideal environment the NMC consists of a large 'battle-map' which graphically represents the entire managed network. Most networks are too large to be viewed on a single screen and so the NMC must provide an effective system to scan across the network either by panning and zooming or by using a hierarchical windowing system. Onto this battle-map must be superimposed the status of the network devices and in well-designed systems it should be possible to interrogate any identified device on the network. The changeable nature of a network means that an essential feature of the NMC is the ability to create and amend the battle-map to reflect the changes made in reality. At present, battle-maps must be generated manually and it is still not possible to have automatic confirmation that the map is accurate; that is, assurance that there are no omissions or additions. This means that even with an integrated NMC there is still need of manual input and it is essential that this information is accurate and complete.

14.6.3 Proprietary architecture migrations

Several of the major computer and communications systems suppliers have announced or are further developing integrated multivendor network management architectures:

- Digital – the enterprise management architecture (EMA)
- IBM – the network management architecture (NMA) in the form of NetView and SystemView
- AT&T – the unified network management architecture (UNMA)
- Hewlett Packard – Open View.

The EMA is Digital's strategic management environment for their DECnet systems and it is designed to support heterogeneous systems in both a flat and hierarchical manner. In principle the EMA supports a series of open interfaces, third party control software and distributed processing. Unfortunately, the NMC, or the director as it is called by Digital, is only available under the VMS or Ultrix (Digital's version of UNIX) operating systems and so it cannot be considered a completely 'open' solution. In the longer term a further concern must be Digital's current reluctance (due to financial difficulties) to complete its commitment to OSI conformance which will cause problems for managing the new releases of the LAN network adapters.

IBM was the first communications manufacturer to address the issues of network management and so produced the NMA. Originally the core of the NMA was NetView (designed for the management of mainframe and related devices) but this has proved to be too limited to support distributed networks based upon LAN technology. In response to this and in an attempt to provide a more integrated and responsive network management architecture, IBM have proposed SystemView. SystemView is intended to provide support for OSI and TCP/IP based systems as well as SNA but unfortunately it is too poorly defined for the provision of a fully integrated solution. No doubt these difficulties will be resolved in the long term.

The UNMA is AT&T's proposal for the integrated management of mixed voice and data networks. It is this mixed voice/data integration which sets UNMA apart from OSI/RM proposals and other proprietary solutions. Within the UNMA the NMC is termed the 'Accumaster Integrator' and this is currently hosted by an AT&T 3B2/600 UNIX environment but future releases are planned on other UNIX boxes. From the European perspective the early UNMA systems will not be useful due to their American PTT emphasis and the fact that SNMP is not supported. It is only when the OSI/RM has been adopted that the UNMA will become a sensible option for European systems, at which point its integrated voice/data support will give it a significant advantage over all of the other similar systems.

Hewlett Packard's Open View is a decentralized NMS which incorporates a large number of different tools and utilities that conform to the appropriate standards. Open View is firmly oriented towards full standardization compatibility with the OSI/RM and *de facto* systems such as SNMP. It has a sophisticated conceptual definition but is flexible in its physical implementation; UNIX has been selected as the preferred host environment. It is generally accepted that Open View is an outstanding platform and once all of its proposed functionality has been completed it will be firmly positioned to become the predominate enterprise network management architecture.

14.7   Summary

Network administration is the single most important concern for the long-term stability of internetworked LAN systems. It consists of system administration (user support) and network maintenance (network support), with the latter incorporating network management. Originally, the inclusion of a network management capability in a LAN device was considered a 'frill' by vendors because they did not expect to recoup the investment made in its development. There has been a considerable change in emphasis as users have realized that good management tools can save them a considerable amount of time, money and frustration, and so now the need is to create an integrated network management system. Unfortunately the network administrators needs are considerably more sophisticated than the capabilities of the available systems, including those of a proprietary nature. The important points to note concerning network administration are:

- Modern networks need an integrated network management system, which must be considered at the planning and design stages of the network. Network management cannot be simply appended and so in most circumstances a long-term migration to such a system must be planned.

- Internetworking produces big problems for network management. All such networks must be managed but it is the use of relays which makes most networks unmanageable. This is because as yet there is no clearly established approach to which all manufacturers are firmly committed.

- The OSI/RM committees are standardizing the common management information service and protocol (CMIS/CMIP) for network management. For LANs this will take the form of the heterogeneous LAN management (HLM) architecture, which will be supported by the common management over the link layer (CMOL) protocol whose implementation will almost certainly be the simple network management protocol (SNMP).

- The SNMP, as used on TCP/IP networks, has become the *de facto* network management protocol and consequently many networking manufacturers supply SNMP interfaces with their equipment. The latest development activities are addressing SNMP/CMIP integration.

- Network administration involves activities of a daily (for example fault monitoring) and strategic (e.g. planning) nature. In many cases the strategic aspects become neglected and so the long-term stability of the network system becomes threatened because there is no clear understanding of the changing needs of the user or the network itself.

- The functional categorization of network management has been clearly established and is defined as performance, fault, configuration, accounting and security management. Each of these functions must be supported by the network management system within which a unique network management centre is the point of preferred information collection and collation.

- A wide range of installation, diagnostic and monitoring equipment is available to support the different functions of network maintenance. This equipment includes protocol analysers and time domain reflectometers, and while most of these are very expensive it is essential that the right equipment is available to support the support team. Failure to supply such equipment will result in a more unreliable network, and increased time wastage by users and support staff.

15

Internetwork Design

15.1   Introduction

The aim of a network is to supply its users with the necessary level of service; networks are not an end in themselves. This level of service must provide the user applications with a reliable and timely transfer of information, and at an acceptable cost to the user. This can only be supported and sustained if the network is manageable and easy to maintain. The fundamental objective of network design from the perspective of network support should be 'design for maintainability'. As discussed in the previous chapter, maintenance accounts for up to 80% of the lifetime costs of a network and so a cost effective network is one in which this cost is minimized. By definition, a well maintained network is one that supplies the appropriate level of service to the user and so the user should also expect 'design for maintainability'.

Network design is more of an art than a science, and it normally requires an insight and a pessimism which can only be developed through experience. It is unlikely that this state of affairs will change much in the future. This is because networks are complex and this complexity occurs in many different ways: the mathematical foundation for the detailed and precise analysis of network performance is not available; there is very little understanding of the problems and their causes in many networks even though they may sometimes be rectified by simple changes; all networks are different and each one supports its own unique set of users.

15.2   The design issues

There are many different types of network and many possible valid solutions for each starting requirement. The 'fitness-for-purpose' of a solution does not depend solely on the user's immediate needs but must also take into account the appropriate longer term issues such as reliability, security, and so on. Good design ensures that these longer term issues can be supported cost effectively while still supplying a degree of freedom within which, over time, it is possible to significantly change the original requirement.

For many network designers and engineers, cost is the central and starting tenet of their design. During the design phase, cost should be treated as an issue of secondary importance. This is because cost effectiveness must not create closed solutions and in many cases the cost effective solution is an acceptable subset of the 'ideal' solution. The advantages of tackling cost at the end are that:

- Several ways of achieving a particular cost limit can be considered once the 'ideal' solution has been designed. This is a refinement of the original design.

- The initial cost effective solution can be used as a platform from which the network can evolve towards the 'ideal' solution. This also provides for some flexibility in changing the original requirements themselves.

- Premature equipment redundancy should be minimized as the network evolves. Cost effectiveness at the start may produce significant waste in the longer term.

- All of the appropriate design issues such as reliability, fault resilience and so on should be thoroughly analysed and considered without cost prejudice. This makes it clear the extent to which the cost is dependent upon the functionality.

The principle of network layering, as reflected by the OSI/RM, should also be reflected in the design of the network. The design of a network takes place at many different levels: the physical topology, the logical topology, the functional architecture, and so on. This means that the different concerns of design should also be addressed at each layer of the network – for example, network management of the physical and logical topologies, fault tolerance of the physical topology and so on.

The following approach is indicative of a 'green-fields' site (new building). Although such an opportunity is rare, most of the information required for such an installation is also needed when changing a network. A more typical situation is one in which the network has to be extended and so there are a number of limitations defined by the established architecture. Extensions to the network must take account of these limitations but enforced changes are an opportunity to renovate the network.

15.2.1 User access

The differences between networks are a reflection of the users themselves. Different organizations use networks differently and so it is essential that the design process starts by establishing the intended use of the network; the word 'intended' was used to show that the actual usage will almost certainly differ from that originally predicted. The working practices that must be identified are:

- The types of applications and services the users will require, and the processing relationships between the users during the completion of a piece of work.

- The direct and indirect protocols required to support the user applications. Direct protocols support the data transfer whereas indirect ones provide support services such as name server access and so on.

- The expected user access time and duration of access. This should also reflect usage during shift working as well as normal working hours.

15.2.2 Connectivity

All of the users and network devices must be physically connected to each other. This requires cabling, the appropriate network adapters and the associated NOS drivers. The issues that need to be considered are:

- The number of users to be supported initially and the expected rate of growth in the number of users.

- The expected physical locations of the users, service facility rooms, the cabling ducts and the wiring closets. This should also include the location of extra access positions (for relocation and expansion).

- The preferred cabling type and infrastructure, and its relationship to what already exists. It is also important to ascertain the age of current cabling and the accuracy of the information describing it.

- The location and type of the network connection points, and the distance between these and the users' workstations. This will determine the length and type of the host connection cabling, for example AUI cables.

- The type of network adapters required from the point of view of the LAN and the host processor, for example, PCs, UNIX boxes, and so on. The NOS drivers are dependent upon the actual NOS and the network adapters but it is important to ensure that all of the version numbers are compatible with each other.

15.2.3 Performance capability

The most difficult aspect of the design process is capturing all of the performance related information and using this to derive the expected performance of the network. Another way of using this information is to anticipate the performance of a configuration and to use this to drive alterations in that configuration until the performance has reached an acceptable level (Verma, 1989). The information that must be obtained to establish the performance characterization of a network must include:

- The number of users on the network and their physical distribution across the area covered by the network.

- The anticipated applications of the network, message sizes normally attributed to these applications and their predicted utilization profile throughout the working day, week, month and year.

- A description of how the users will cooperate across the network – that is, the identification of the number and types of servers, electronic mail groups, documentation production groups, and so on.

The next series of parameters is concerned with the construction of the network, so the actual performance is particularly sensitive to these values:

- The type and length of cabling used throughout the network and the location of external noise sources.

- The number and carrying capacity of each of the LAN and WAN links.

- The type, number and location of internetworking devices.

In many cases the value of some of these parameters will be either unknown or just vague estimates. Even if is claimed that they are well known, treat them with some scepticism and assume that they are only 50% accurate at best. The worse that this can do is to provide a reasonable period of expansion during which it will be unnecessary to physically change the network.

In principle this collection of the parameter values is now substituted into the corresponding design equations and a simple judgement can be made as to whether or not the proposed configuration is suitable. Unfortunately, accurate versions of those design equations do not exist and most of their approximate equivalents are very complex and theoretical in nature, and so do not reflect the realities of actual networks. So, why bother acquiring the parameters in the first place? The first reason is that some of the equations can be used, provided the designer is skilled not only in their meaning but also in the hidden assumptions concerning their validity – these are outside the scope of this book and their use should only be attempted by someone who is a skilled network designer and mathematician. The second and most important reason is that they are useful guides during the application of general rules-of-thumb. These rules-of-thumb suggest that:

- Design the average load on an ethernet system to be between 5 and 10% of the carrying capacity of the network but permit much higher loads for Token Ring based systems. Optimal ethernet efficiency is achieved when the frame size is as large as possible and the network size as small as possible.

- The actual network load is approximately twice the user message load – in other words, the message and control overheads account for only half of the total traffic on the network.

- Use repeaters to physically extend the length of the network but be wary of poor node distributions across the network and of connecting too many users.

- Use bridges to improve the resilience of the network or to improve its performance. However, this is only possible if a bridge is limited to transferring only 40% of the maximum capability of the LANs supported by it.

- Use fibre optic cabling in electrically noisy environments and for all locally maintained wide area links. STP and UTP cables should be kept as short as possible and should not be placed close to fluorescent lights.

- Keep servers as close to their user community as possible and restrict the flow of information to areas where it is needed – use bridges and routers to filter out unnecessary data flows. Do not put all of the servers on a single backbone network because this makes them vulnerable to single link failures and subjects the backbone to the heaviest possible load.

- Be sure that the network adapters are capable of driving the host's data bus to its full capabilities and ensure that there is sufficient local RAM to buffer a burst of at least 10 ms of data. Also remember that for most NOSs the speed of the host workstation will have a more significant effect on the user's perception of the network than the carrying capacity of the network itself.

It should, however, be remembered that there are limitations on every design, such as:

- It is impossible to optimize a network for both minimal delay/response time and maximum throughput. A network has either a high throughput with high delay or low throughput with low delay.

- All networks suffer from noise and some internetworking devices are a potential source of information loss. Therefore, all reliable profiles must use a connection oriented service within one layer at least.

- The performance of a subnetwork is determined by the slowest component of that network. There is no point in having exceedingly fast remote bridges if the intermediate link is only capable of supporting a few kilobits per second.

Remember that network design starts with understanding the users and the way they will use the network. The performance of a network is a consequence of how the users drive a particular configuration of the network and so an alteration in either of these means that the other must also be affected. Regularly monitoring of the performance of the network (average response times, average network loads and so on) can be used to predict difficulties in the future and so it is important to develop an understanding of how the effects of these manifest themselves; unfortunately many of these manifestations are very dependent on the idiosyncrasies of each network, therefore it is essential to develop a historic perspective of the network.

15.2.4 Manageability

The case for network management was comprehensively discussed in the previous chapter and will not be repeated here – instead the implications for the design process will be considered. During the design process network management should be considered as an underlying theme for the particular make of devices used to supply a particular function of the network – that is, managed bridges as opposed to unmanaged ones. The only architectural consideration is that of whether the management system will be in-band or out-of-band. The latter requires the use of a second network which must also be designed, and that design must be subject to the same constraints placed upon it as those on the primary network, such as security, fault tolerance, management, and so on.

One important, but frequently overlooked, feature of a network management system is that it should be used to provide statistics for planning the development of the network. Network monitors need to be correctly located around the network so that performance statistics reflecting the entire network can be obtained and submitted to the NMC. These statistics supply accurate facts about the network and are invaluable when refuting accusations about, or supporting claims for, it. Without this type of information it is impossible to reliably plan and design the evolution of the network.

15.2.5 Fault tolerance

A fault tolerant network is one in which the architecture is intrinsically resilient to failures – that is, it does not provide special components that are only used when elements of the network fail (the implication in a fault resilient network). Fault tolerance is preferable to fault resilience because of its more cost effective use of resources and its integrated approach as opposed to 'add-on' philosophy. In all networks it is essential that the failure of a single component in a network does not cause total failure. This principle can be extended to cover resilience against a greater number of failures but this means that the network must be carefully designed and constructed. Simply adding more links and internetworking devices is not necessarily the right approach. Every extra component in a network makes the network more unreliable and so its resilience is increased by ensuring that these extra components provide 'cover' for each other, for example redundant links to provide alternative paths should the original links fail. There are several ways in which network resilience can be considered:

- Link duplication – provide a series of extra links to substantially increase the carrying capacity of the network so that it exceeds the required capacity and to ensure that all users arc interconnected by at least two routes. These links can then be used as part of the normal operation of the network and so the failure of a single link should not disconnect any part of the network.

- Internetworking devices – which can be used to provide protected areas of the network by producing firewalls against certain types of failure, such as using repeaters to restrict the consequences of a cabling failure. In some instances the need for resilience may be the only justification for using an internetworking device and in these cases the future expansion of the network is also simplified.

- Mirrored servers – to provide a single logical service infrastructure supported by a group of physically independent devices. The approach to this follows one of two ways: the provision of a 'cold' standby, which is manually activated to replace a failed device, or a 'hot' standby, which is automatically invoked should an appropriate failure occur. The main concern with these types of system is that of consistency, especially when concerned with file server duplication.

- Uninterruptible power supplies (UPSs) – these are capable of supporting a network for between a few minutes and a few hours. Their primary purpose is to protect the network from a 'brown-out', during which the power supply falls below its threshold settings for a few seconds, as opposed to a 'black-out', during which the power completely fails for a significant duration.

- Defensive design – which is more indicative of the designer's state of mind than by any physical realization. This requires the designer to assume the worse and design accordingly. It is also usual for this approach to result in systems that are relatively simple to expand because they already provide a basis from which many alternative features and architectures can be appended.

15.2.6 Security

Network security applies to the flow of information both internally and externally to the local system; in most cases the information is compromised internally and not externally, contrary to initial intuition, because the cabling system is more accessible. In this instance, the term security is extended to include protection from computer viruses because these also compromise the capabilities of the network and are a serious threat to the information stored and processed within it. The primary responsibilities to consider for a secure system are:

- Confidentiality – which means that the information must be secure or private. Privacy is obtained by simple encryption whereas for a secure system it is essential to use cryptographically secure encryption. The required level of encryption is determined by the sensitivity of the information and the duration for which it must remain confidential.

- Authenticity – which means that the destination can guarantee that the information came from the claimed source. Authentication is also closely related to the principle of non-repudiation in which a source cannot falsely disclaim transmission of a piece of information. Once again, these functions require cryptographically secure encryption methods but in this instance the coding is used to provide a unique digital signature as opposed to encrypting the information.

- Integrity – in which the information flow must be immune to insertions and deletions. This also includes protection against the resubmission of duplicated information, which could be used to create confusion and inconsistency within the network. This form of protection must be provided as an integrated feature of the protocols and must be capable of supporting time stamped message passing to ensure time related fidelity of the transfer of the information.

- Access – in which the availability of different network services is determined with respect to an access register. Such a system can be used to provide varying degrees of access to each service; for example, it may be possible to read information but not to print it. In most cases these systems make heavy use of password protection and access privilege tables which map the logical user to a physical location and so are dependent on the network adapter addresses.

- Key management – which includes the distribution and maintenance of the secure keys used for encryption and authentication, the creation and maintenance of the access and password protection system, and the integration of this with the full network management infrastructure.

From the point of view of virus protection it is important to consider that both accidental as well as intentional infection must be avoided. Prevention is better than cure. However, the current level of protection coupled with the pressures of access mean that in all but the most vigilant environments it is impossible to prevent infection completely. Protection against viruses must be based upon:

- Clean-room – this refers to the creation of a separate test network on which all new software installations are tested and analysed for potential infestation. Do not assume that new software fresh from the manufacturer is 'clean'; experience has shown otherwise. This same network can also be used as a general test-bed in which all network upgrades and so on can be tested before attempting them on the real network (this is particularly important when upgrading NOS drives, new NOS clients and/or servers and so on).

- Access limitation – in which the user has restricted access to the network. This limitation can take one of two forms: total prevention of access for external data sources or read only access to the servers. Total prevention entails the sealing of all external drives and the isolation of external network interfaces, for example routers. Read only access permits users to insert their disks but prevents them from storing this information on the network based servers. Clearly, both techniques have advantages as well as serious disadvantages.

- Continual monitoring – the installation and use of virus scanning software which is continually active and is independent of the user. These systems will scan all of the internal disks whenever a workstation is 'booted' and will scan external drives whenever a disk is inserted. Infected disks result in the ejection of the disk or in the workstation being disabled. Virus scanning software is an essential application for all workstations, whether or not they are networked.

Total control of the internal network is possible; however, it is impossible to exercise the same degree of control over the external elements, such as WAN links. In these cases the level of protection is determined by the services provided by the external supplier, so it is wise to provide further end-system to end-system protection such as encryption in the internetworking devices themselves. The final point to consider is that in most cases the addition of various secure features has very little effect on the performance capability of the network but does increase the 'boot' time of the workstations, caused by virus scanning, disk mirroring, access confirmation and the 'down-loading' of the user's work environment.

15.2.7 Topological flexibility

The most difficult aspect of design is structuring the network so that it can be endlessly expanded/contracted in any number of different ways, for example number of users, service range, security, and so on. Clearly, it is impossible to predict accurately how the network will evolve over a long period of time; however, it is important to minimize short-term redundancy and to ensure that a simple upgrade does not require a significant change in the network. There are several useful principles that should be adopted when designing a network for the long term:

- Divide and conquer – break the network into a series of hierarchical components and identify those parts that are clearly separated from the rest of the network, for example due to physical location, type of activity and so on.

- Use the appropriate internetworking devices to provide connectivity between the separate systems (gateways and routers) and hierarchical components (bridges and repeaters). It is accepted practice to try to use internetworking hubs and to house these in modular rack systems.

- Minimize one-off costs by allowing for substantial expansion, for example by using structured cabling. Do not equate provision for cabling access with necessarily supplying the full cable, for example use blown fibre cladding but only install the fibre when needed.

- The current consensus for good network design practice is the use of structured cabling (UTP), the provision of a fibre carpet for long distance (using SMF if possible) and external connectivity, the use of third generation hubs for user connectivity and the housing of internetworking devices.

- Assume that the application and service demands will alter (primarily growing) and so assume that a multiprotocol environment will be necessary at some time. This means considering multiprotocol routers, protocol independent bridging and mixed LAN architectures at the outset.

15.2.8 Costs

Telecommunications suppliers will provide a user with network access at a price that covers the cost of maintaining the network. This principle should also be used for internal budgeting systems, thereby forcing users and higher management to appreciate the costs associated with supplying their network. The full cost of a network should be determined by:

- Startup cost. This is associated with installing the network infrastructure and includes cabling, network adapters, internetworking devices and external connectivity charges.

- Fixed recurrent cost. The charges of items such as leased lines, test equipment and any other equipment or staff that are used on a fixed recurrent basis.

- Renovation costs. The replacement of equipment that has passed its expected lifetime – that is, when it is costing more to maintain than replace. This is independent of usage.

- Usage sensitive cost. This is determined according to the amount of time spent using the network, for example external access to PSDNs.

- Maintenance cost. The cost for service addition, reduction, rearrangement and repair. For example, if more users are to be supported do they need new cabling?

- Exit cost. Premature termination of external service agreements typically includes penalty clauses. Any alteration of a service range (supported applications) will have implications for user training, equipment and maintenance.

- Displaced cost. This is the difference between the new system and the old system cost. Included in this is the cost of retraining as well as that of increased/reduced numbers of personnel and equipment.

From the point of view of design, the aim should be to minimize the maintenance costs which means that the network should use equipment that provides local and remote management facilities. These types of equipment are generally more expensive; however, they reduce the maintenance overhead in terms of people and repair time and so are cost effective in the longer term. Another way of looking at the maintenance costs is to consider the effects on the organization during a failure of the network. In extreme circumstances such a failure could result in the loss of thousands – if not millions – of pounds; expenditure on an appropriate level of maintenance is not wasted money.

An appropriate level of maintenance depends on the physical size of the network, the degree to which it is resilient to failure and the extent to which it provides network management. Every network, even the smallest, needs a manager – that is, someone who is responsible for it. On average the network will require one person to support every twenty to forty users. The upper number is possible in networks that are well maintained, stable and have a low rate of change. The consequences of not having this depth of support are:

- Continual network failures and unacceptable delays in re-establishing the network (one to two hours).
- Premature ageing due to excessive loading and lack of performance monitoring, analysis and planning.
- Inconsistent network software, for example different releases of the network adapter/operating system drivers on the same physical network, resulting in network failure and user specific faults.
- Poor structural evolution of the network resulting in cabling and service 'spaghetti', and a complete loss of understanding of its true structure.

For these reasons cost should be considered as a secondary issue and the justification of the cost for an architecture should not be restricted to the installation phase only.

15.3   Design, installation and support

Once the design requirements have been captured, the next stages are to complete the detailed design, install the network and finally provide operational support. While there is no clearly established methodology for network design, it is essential that the problem is approached in an organized manner and that all of the operational support issues are clarified during the design process – in other words 'design for maintainability'.

15.3.1 The facts of life

Network users regularly complain about their networks and a series of surveys carried out by Frost and Sullivan, and Ovum support these complaints:

- LANs are available for approximately 94% of the time – which means that they are unavailable for three weeks each year. These statistics are derived from reviews which show that a LAN fails approximately 20 times per year with each failure lasting an average of seven hours.

- 73% of users experience network failures and for approximately 20% of these the failure lasts for at least ten hours.

- 70% of all network failures can be attributed to one of two causes: poor cabling installation and devices being incorrectly switched off.

In the above statistics a failure is defined as any network event that caused a user to be incapable of doing their job, and as such included software and hardware problems of the network and the host PCs and workstations. However, there are several good reasons why this poor level of service is produced; in most cases it is the diversity of users' demands which produces this poor service and this is itself a reflection of the difficulty in establishing an integrated network based upon different systems from different manufacturers. This is reflected by:

- 87% of organizations operate three or more different protocols on their networks and so each of these must have a comparable level of service.

- 75% of organizations have a mixture of IEEE 802.3 and IEEE 802.5 LANs, and interconnection between these is dependent upon the use of routers.

- It is claimed by Dataquest and others that between 50% and 80% of all PCs will be networked by 1995 and so the demands to be placed upon the network support staff will increase significantly.

- KPMG have calculated that the maintenance costs (including hidden costs) are £6000 per year to support a 486 based PC. If this level of investment is not being provided then the level of service drops accordingly.

Unfortunately, there are many anecdotes of poor practice in designing, installing and using networks, including:

- Fibre optic cabling installers who have been seen casually sanding the end of the fibre before inserting it into its connector.

- Cable installers who have used hammers to bend cables at 90° around doors.

- Users who casually disconnect the thin coax cables from their T-pieces and leave the cables open.

- Support staff who provide new network drivers for only part of the network and then cannot understand why transient problems affect certain users only.

As far as networks are concerned the network support team cannot expect any 'pats-on-the-back'. If a network fails then they are condemned for not supplying a decent system, whereas when it works the users want to know why it cannot do more. The problem is further compounded by the fact that a successful network attracts more users, who have different needs, which causes changes to the network and so the process repeats itself until it is no longer a reliable network, and then the users really start to complain.

15.3.2 Design approach

The lack of an established network design methodology means that the problem has to be approached using common sense and a degree of caution. The approach described here is not a methodology but is a framework within which many of the issues for designing the network can be considered and builds upon a technique advocated by Walford (Walford, 1990). The responsibilities of each of the five stages shown in Figure 15.1 are:

- Requirements – to obtain the requirements of the network from the current/ future users, the physical layout constraints and the network support team. A requirements specification is produced at the end of this phase (making use of annotated building plans) and it is against this that the implemented system will be compared to determine whether or not the network is suitable.

- Service architecture – which is used to establish the functional relationships between the client users and their servers. The end product of this phase is a connectivity matrix between the different users, which is used to represent the physical connectivity that the network must provide.

- Logical architecture – is used to determine which LANs are required and the internetworking devices needed to connect these. At this stage the potential locations of wide area links have been identified but these are not confirmed. The protocol architecture is also produced to finalize the actual protocol profiles and LANs, and this is used to predict the expected loading.

- Physical architecture – is used to complete the design by mapping the logical layout onto the physical layout. It is at this stage that all of the wide area links must be located and the appropriate changes to the internetworking devices are also made, for example the change from a local bridge to a pair of remote bridges linked using a kilostream. This architecture is amended to suit the equipment that can be supplied by the selected manufacturers.

- Operational support – which is responsible for producing all of the long-term support plans and activities pertaining to the operational lifetime of the network. This includes the development of the audit plan, equipment retirement policy, disaster recovery plan, and so on.

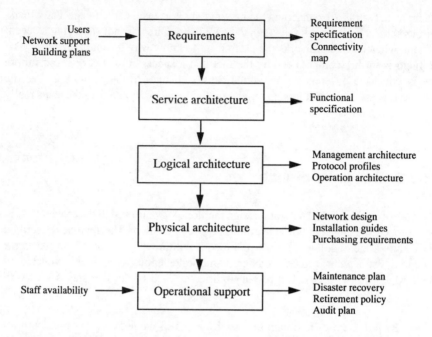

Figure 15.1 The typical activities for designing a network.

Each of these stages is dependent on the previous stages and so any mistakes discovered at a lower level will have to be examined to determine whether or not they are caused by problems at a higher level. It is this iterative technique (used in most engineering design problems) that provides the design process with the flexibility necessary when it is impossible to determine in absolute terms whether or not a design is correct.

Requirements

The first step of any methodology is to capture the requirements of the system to be designed. In the case of a network the requirements must be obtained from the user and the network support team. The following points are of particular interest and should be obtained as requirements:

- General – what are the performance constraints on the network?
- Application services – what type of information is to be transmitted along the network and how is this best supported?
- Wiring and transmission – how is the system cabling to be installed? What noise considerations are there and how can the system safety be ensured?
- Device interfaces – what devices have to be connected to the network? What are their protocol requirements?

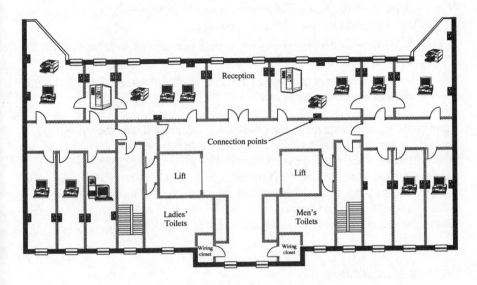

Figure 15.2   A typical building plan and computer layout requirements.

- Internetworking – how will the network be extended and linked to other networks? What types of networks must be linked together?
- Call management – what link services will be supplied to the users and how will access to them be controlled? Who will be responsible for initializing the links and for ensuring their availability?
- Network management – how will the network be managed? What are the automated and manual demands of the management systems?
- Strategy – how is the network to evolve? What are the longer term aims of the systems that are to be supported by the network?

In many cases the users will not be able to express their needs in sufficiently clear terms and so they will need prompting, and confirmation of your interpretation of their requirements will be needed. Remember that these are the initial requirements of the network, and the designers will have to extrapolate from these to cover any possible future development needs of the system.

Once the user requirements have been obtained the next stage is to establish the physical constraints placed upon the network – that is, determine where the workstations, printers, and so on are to be located on the building plans. In many cases these locations will be subject to considerable alteration in the long term and there are other factors to be considered. A typical map of one floor within a building is shown in Figure 15.2, in which all of the rooms, the computer equipment and the required connection points are clearly marked. The real applications of this plan are to:

- Locate all of the network connection points within the building – each room should have at least two connection points.

- Mark where all the primary wiring centres, servers and workstations will be located initially.

- Show the real distances between rooms and so on within the building (all plans should be to scale).

These maps, together with the user requirements, define all of the network's requirements. One aim of the design should be to construct a network within which changes to either the user's service needs or the physical location of the equipment should not cause any restructuring of the network infrastructure – that is, it should be unnecessary to add further cabling. It will not be possible to construct the final network until the building layouts have been obtained and in the case of newly constructed buildings the cabling infrastructure should be planned with the rest of the building's utilities.

Service architecture

The service architecture describes the relationship between the user workstations and their servers but makes no imposition on the physical structure of the network or the locations of these servers. There are many different types of servers to be considered:

- File server – which is the remote file store. The NOS creates an environment in which the user perceives the file server as another local disk store equivalent to an internal hard disk.

- Process server – a remote processor bank which is used to support dumb devices, intelligent X-terminals, and as a processor farm for PCs and workstations. In many systems the file server and process server are supplied by the same physical system.

- Print server – the printer facility which is responsible for spooling documents onto the appropriate printer. Print servers free the client workstations from waiting for the completion of printing before the users are free to carry on with other activities and allow users to efficiently share mixed printer resources.

- Name server – which allows users to locate and identify network objects. Typical examples of this are the X.500 directory and the domain name system (DNS) or the Internet.

- Management server – the network management facility which is used to control the user's access to the network. In many cases the user environment is loaded across the network from the management server once the appropriate authorizations have been received.

- Gateway server – this is used in the mainframe community where users require access to a remote host. The gateway server is responsible for supporting all of the sessions that require access to the host.

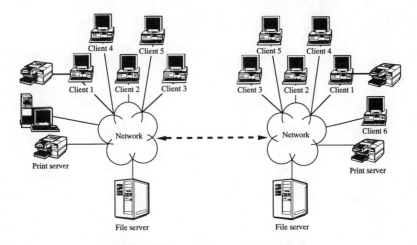

Figure 15.3 The service architecture.

An example of a simple service architecture is shown in Figure 15.3, which is based upon the physical layout presented in Figure 15.2. In this structure two separate client/ server architectures can be identified, each with its own file server and print server. The need to provide network management implies that the network must supply physical communications between the servers and their clients and that they must all support the same NOS – that is, use the integrated management features of the NOS. In many cases a workstation will be a client of more than one file server, and so the service architecture will consist of several linked regions: one region for each server and separate regions for multiple server links. In the case of two servers this would create three service regions: one for each server and one for hosts that required access to both servers.

The service architecture is a more formal representation of the required user connectivity and can be used to determine the traffic loading created by each of the service structures. From this architecture it is possible to generate a connectivity requirements matrix and to establish the network capacity needed to support the user traffic. It is also an indicator of the way in which the network should be logically and physically constructed.

Logical architecture

The logical architecture breaks the network into its component subnetworks and identifies the internetworking devices used to connect these. The intention is to identify the LANs required to support the different server systems and to determine which of them must be interconnected to provide the necessary level of service and how this should be done. It is at this stage that the fault tolerant and management aspects of the network must also be considered; in both cases extra components may have to be used to provide the logical network with the required functionality.

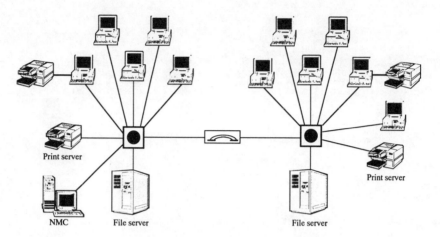

Figure 15.4 The logical architecture.

Figure 15.4 shows the logical architecture of the service architecture shown in Figure 15.3. In this system, each of the server systems is supported by a repeater and these are interconnected using a bridge. The bridge provides connectivity between the two systems but minimizes the amount of traffic passed between the two networks. It is also possible to link the two repeaters together directly but this would result in increased loads on the network and would make the user response time slower. The second part of the logical architecture is to determine the protocol – this is used to formally identify all of the protocols needed within the network. The protocols that must be identified are those which support the:

- Client/server and end-system applications.
- LAN MAC and cabling infrastructure.
- Internetworking devices, especially those related to the es-es, is-is and es-is within the network layer.
- Transport service.

The protocol architecture for the example network design is shown in Figure 15.5. In this network the 10BASET signalling and cabling system is used with the ethernet LAN. The client/server architecture is based upon Novel NetWare, which means that the printers must also support NetWare drivers.

Physical architecture

The physical architecture is the result of mapping the logical architecture onto the physical layout of the building. This process must consider the stretching of the logical architecture to fit the physical layout and so must consider the use of extra repeaters and cabling. Once this mapping has been completed it is then possible to produce the

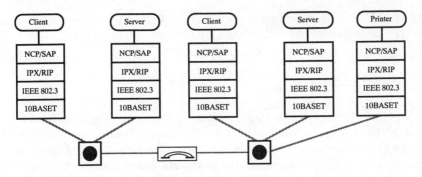

Figure 15.5 The protocol profiles of the logical architecture.

detailed installation and purchasing guides; these should differentiate between the infrastructure needs and the per room based costs.

Once the initial physical architecture has been produced and the corresponding suppliers have been identified, there is one further refinement of the design. This refinement is responsible for optimizing the suitability of the suppliers' equipment to the preferred design. In some cases it would be possible to use an integrated modular hub to house repeater/bridge/router combinations, whereas in other cases these may have to be supplied as individual devices. This means that the final physical architecture should be able to exploit the best technology available without being unnecessarily restricted by the limitations of the original requirements.

The physical architecture of the example network design is shown in Figure 15.6. In this layout it is assumed that the building has structured cabling and that all of the cables feed back to the two wiring closets; these are also connected using a UTP

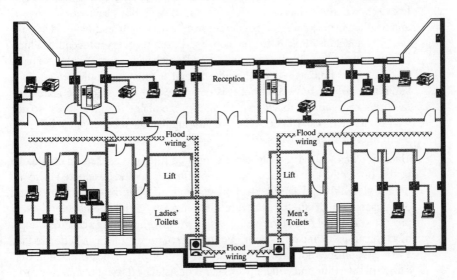

Figure 15.6 The physical architecture.

(all of the UTP cables must therefore be less than 100 m). The individual workstations and printers are connected to their nearest connection point using UTP.

Operational support

A series of operational support procedures have to be developed and in an ideal situation these would be available as soon as the network became active. However, in reality they are normally either developed during the early stages of the network's operation or are never established. The procedures which should be developed are:

- Help desk – do not assume that the users will understand how to use the network or the applications on the network. They will require continual support and advice on how to use the network, especially when an alteration is made to the service or applications it provides or when new users are enrolled.

- Test network – new services or devices should not undergo initial testing on the primary network. Instead a small but representative test network should be installed (this should also be physically separate from the primary system to ensure that there can be no contamination of the primary network), which should have all of the features and services supported by the primary network. Alterations to the network can then be tested in isolation and their impact on the network can be evaluated before implementation on the primary network. This approach will not prevent all of the possible problems when installing new systems and so on but will stop many of the more evident ones.

- Disaster recovery procedures – the consequences of a catastrophic failure of a network could result in significant losses of revenue. There have been several instances where fire has completely gutted the operations centre of a network and resulted in the total failure of the entire networking infrastructure. The only protection against this is to develop a disaster recovery procedure which assumes several levels of system failure and which has a recovery plan for each of them. The final aspect of the plan is that it must be implemented, in a simulated failure, to ensure that it is complete and that all of the necessary facilities are available to achieve the aims of the plan – in other words, do not wait for a real disaster to occur before proving that the recovery plan will – or more likely will not – work.

- Backup plans – all of the file servers must be formally backed up on a daily basis. In fact the grandfather, father, son principle should be adopted to cover monthly, weekly and daily protection, respectively. It is important that at least one master set of all the software distributed by applications suppliers is protected and kept free of viruses. It is also worthwhile having a complete copy of a typical server and client configuration stored for remote distribution so that a workstation does not have to be constructed directly from the distribution kits. This will save time and will help to ensure consistency throughout the network. Multiple copies of the backup must be taken and these must be kept in separate locations so that a single accident cannot destroy all of them.

- Maintenance plans – ensure that all of the maintenance activities are appropriately staffed and timetabled so that the users suffer minimal disruption. Again, the process of planning will highlight many of the deficiencies in the network and staff availability and capability. These plans should also include training schedules to ensure that the staff are fully conversant with the systems and techniques they are supporting.

- Service level agreements (SLAs) – these are the service contracts between the network administration team and the user community, as represented by the line managers. The SLAs describe the range, type and limitations of the services that will be provided for the users. These agreements establish the ground rules for both the users and the network administrators.

- Operational records – all aspects of the network's configuration, performance and events should be recorded electronically and on paper. This information should be analysed regularly so that potential problems can be anticipated and corrective action planned and taken. This information should also be used to plan the development of the network and to help avoid embarrassing design mistakes.

- Annual audit – the network should be formally audited once per year. This audit should cover every aspect of the network (cable inspections, network adapter testing and so on) and is the process by which the current status of the network is formally compared to that of the previous year. The audit should be planned and should cause minimal disruption to the normal operation of the network.

- Retirement policy – the network will age as its devices wear out, its links become overloaded and its functional features become limited when compared to those of the new devices. Devices that have a high failure rate should be replaced instead of being continually repaired. All devices should be retired at an appropriate time, so a cost plan supporting this approach must be produced. A regular retirement policy should ensure the continual renovation of the network but care is needed to avoid network inconsistency due to device incompatibilities.

- Right-sizing policy – the network will be expected to grow as new services and users are supported. However, at some point it may be important to consider reducing the capabilities of the network as part of a process of division and down-sizing. It is important to remember that the size and capabilities of the network must be tuned to the needs of the users otherwise excessive costs will be incurred in supporting it.

It is important to stress that the extent of these procedures should be appropriate to the size of the network. Small networks, under ten users, require a considerably less sophisticated set of procedures than a network with several hundreds or thousands of users. However, the activities these procedures address are fundamental to the well-being of every network and so it is essential that they are considered for every network. The major problem with these procedures is that they require time and staff effort to produce and in many cases they act only as an insurance policy – it is when things go wrong that they are shown to be necessary. Insurance policies are very important.

15.3.3 Validating the design

Once a design has been completed it should be validated against the requirements. It is not possible to do this precisely using a mathematical approach, so alternative schemes have to be considered. These fall into three categories:

- Simulation – the construction of a computer simulation of the network using a specialist discrete event simulation language. These types of language reduce the development period for the simulation by providing a wide range of standard libraries which can be used for building models of specific networks.

- Modelling – the construction of simple mathematical models, which can be used to examine particular aspects of the operation of the network. Care is required to make the model sufficiently, but not overly, complex.

- Benchmarking – the construction of a scaled test system whose performance can then be measured. The network can then be scaled up and the benchmarking process repeated. The advantage of this approach is that as part of the maintenance activity the final system will have to be repeatedly benchmarked, so this method promotes advanced preparation of the systems needed to provide that information.

The creation and continual modification of documentation describing a network is the most unpopular activity of network design and maintenance. It is, however, essential and many problems in networks can be blamed upon misunderstandings of the structure and operation of a network caused by poor documentation. An important element in that documentation is a record of the tests made on a network. A complete record must be kept of all of the tests completed on the network along with the results of those tests. The history of the network can then be displayed by viewing the changing responses of the network to the series of standard tests – this will show degradation in the network's capabilities due to increased nodes, topology changes and cabling faults.

15.3.4 Design to installation

The process of implementing a design must be rigorously controlled. Undiscovered faults created during installation will not only cause severe problems throughout the lifetime of the network but will also be considerably more expensive to correct at a later stage. There are several legal issues which need to be agreed with any supplier before installation should begin and payment should only be made subject to confirmation of completion of all the appropriate deliverables. It is useful if a technical member of the network support team can actually be involved with the installation team, who is responsible for confirming that all of the necessary procedures have been completed (cf. building surveys made at the completion of each phase of construction). The general principles to be followed during the installation of a network are:

- Test every piece of equipment before it is installed (component testing). A significant amount of new equipment is faulty when it is delivered: never assume that because it is new it must be fault free.

- Test the integrity of all cabling on the network, with and without any physical taps. It is important to make TDR/OTDR print-outs as one of the contractual deliverables. All of the cables must be uniquely tagged, at both ends.

- Incrementally test the operation of a network (build testing) – in other words, do not install it and then start to test its correct operation. The quicker a problem can be identified then the cheaper it is to correct.

- Every piece of equipment and cable should have an accompanying log sheet recording all of its details, including installation and test dates. These records should be collated in one central volume which acts as the configuration register of the network.

- A record must be kept of the test configurations of the network and the test equipment. If it is not possible to purchase every piece of test equipment then its type and operation must be clearly recorded so that if necessary the device can be hired at a later time.

Remember, fully document the installation of the network. Poor documentation at this stage will result in a poorly documented network throughout the rest of its operational lifetime. Make all external contractors responsible for producing this documentation and review this to ensure that it is of the appropriate level of quality – the documentation must be a contractual deliverable.

15.4   The commercial issues

From the financial point of view, the commercial issues are of equal importance to the technical ones. The commercial decisions include deciding on the extent to which external support is needed for designing and installing the network and the selection of the suppliers and their equipment. A commercially attractive solution does not mean choosing the cheapest on offer – remember that the major costs are incurred after a network has been installed and so the long-term perspectives of upgrade compatibility, renovation and retirement, and staffing requirements must also be considered.

15.4.1 Internal and external support

The first decision to be made, before the design has begun, is what level of external support will be required. Both extremes are unsound (totally internal or external) because the in-house team has important knowledge and an external team will have a more detached view of the requirements. At the very least, an in-house approach should make use of external consultants to evaluate their proposed solution and an external approach must use the in-house specialists as their consultants.

The most difficult decisions are not those related to the design but are associated with selecting the suppliers and installers. Badly manufactured equipment and poor installation will very quickly undo even the most ideal of solutions. The approach to this problem depends upon the size of the network:

- Small networks (a few thousand pounds) – normally, these will be quoted for on an individual basis because it is not worthwhile competing for this type of work as part of a competitive tender. Small third party suppliers are best suited to this type of work because they will normally use well-established products from reputable manufacturers and will charge reasonable mark-ups.

- Large networks (several hundred thousand pounds and upwards) – these should be subject to competitive tenders, with the technical and financial proposals being submitted on independent documentation. The financial aspects should not compromise the technical evaluation of the proposals; in many cases the negotiation process can significantly alter the price without affecting the technical elements of the proposal. The design houses of the major suppliers are best suited to this form of submission because they will have access to the equipment at cheaper rates than third party suppliers and so should be capable of supplying a more cost effective solution (they will of course bid on the basis of their own equipment).

- Medium networks – the low end should still consider single proposals whereas the high end should move towards a competitive tender between several third party suppliers. In this region it is more likely that the design and installation will be completed by an in-house team and so any external support would only be on a consultative basis for advice on potential suppliers and reviewing the proposed solution itself.

It is essential that a LAN supplier has a clear understanding of the problems concerned with internetworking and is well aware not only of the capabilities of their own product range with respect to this but also of their future conformance with the various standardization efforts. Most suppliers have their own proprietary versions of functions currently undergoing standardization and so it is essential to ascertain the extent of the incompatibility between other suppliers and the upgrade paths that will be provided by the supplier as the standards become established.

15.4.2 Recognized suppliers

It is noticeable that during the past two years there has been a significant rationalization of network device manufacturers, with many smaller companies being acquired by their larger competitors and a general decline in the wealth and stability of the major systems manufacturers. This has been particularly evident in the ethernet market where both 3COM and Retix have either acquired or established close selling agreements with companies in the Token Ring markets. The major suppliers of networking and internetworking devices are:

- Network adapter suppliers – the major suppliers of ethernet adapters are 3COM (28%), SMC (23%), Eagle/Novell (15%) and Intel (12%). For Token Ring the market is considerably more polarized, with IBM (78%), Proteon (7%), Olicom (4%), Madge (4%) and SMC (4%). A total of 3.9 million ethernet adapters and 2.7 million Token Ring adapters have been sold.

- Repeater suppliers – the leading ethernet repeater suppliers are Digital, 3COM and Cabletron. The leading repeater manufacturers for Token Ring networks are LANNET Data Communications, RAD, Andrew and Olicom.

- Bridge suppliers – NIST benchmark tests found that the Retix local ethernet transparent bridges were the fastest. Cabletron and 3COM provide a wide range of ethernet bridges. Retix, RAD and Vitalink supply both ethernet and Token Ring bridges whereas Andrew and Madge are limited to Token Ring.

- Router suppliers – the dominant supplier is Cisco (51%) with Wellfleet (9%) and Digital (7%) being the other two major suppliers. Retix has recently entered this market and has become a leading router supplier. Cisco have adopted a software approach and make heavy use of TCP/IP whereas the others use a more fixed hardware architecture solution.

- Gateway suppliers – both Eicon and Rabbit are major suppliers of Novell/SNA gateways, with Digital supplying the majority of the DECnet/SNA gateways.

- Hub system suppliers – Synoptics are the dominant hub supplier but they supply only LattisNet, which is a proprietary architecture. UB, Chipcom and Cabletron are the other major hub manufacturers with a wide range of intelligent hubs supporting mixed ethernet/Token Ring systems and containing mixed configurations of repeaters/bridges/routers.

- Test equipment suppliers – the dominant supplier of test equipment is Hewlett Packard, who supply a wide range of expensive but highly reliable and robust units, including link testers and protocol analysers. Other suppliers are Spider (protocol analysers), Tektronix (TDRs) and M-trade (hand-held test units and PC based monitors).

- Network operating system suppliers – the dominant PC NOS is Novell's NetWare (55%) with SUN's NFS dominating the UNIX environment.

- Protocol architectures and applications suppliers – Retix specialize in the provision of OSI based solutions. Microsoft are the world's largest software manufacturer and supply a variety of network based office applications, operating systems and network management systems.

- Network management system suppliers – as yet there is no single non-proprietary system but NetView is dominant for IBM based systems.

The DATAPRO International series of surveys on LANs and Internetworking is an excellent source of information concerning the capabilities and costs of devices from a comprehensive lists of suppliers and manufacturers (Datapro, 1994).

15.4.3 Standardized and proprietary solutions

When considering which pieces of equipment to buy for building the network there are three issues that must be clarified:

- The degree to which the network will be 'open' or 'closed'. There are three basic approaches , reflecting the 'open systems' philosophy in which all of the end-systems conform to the standards, the 'isolated system' in which a local solution is adopted and from where there is no connection with the outside world and the 'closed' solution in which the isolated approach is augmented with the appropriate 'open' gateways.

- Whether the implementation is to be supported by a single vendor or mixed vendor approach. Integration is a problem with mixed vendor solutions but provides protection against the financial collapse or intransigence of a vendor when technical difficulties, or other problems are encountered. Single vendor systems are more reliable in terms of interconnectivity but the long-term stability of the network is dependent upon the vendor providing device compatibility as its product range evolves.

- The degree to which the historic development and current state of the network is permitted to affect the future form of the network. The migration path from the current to the proposed system must be addressed and it is also important to consider how the future development of the system is expected to proceed so that future migration problems can be anticipated and minimized.

While each of these issues can be independently expressed their solutions are very closely related; for example, the preference for a mixed vendor solution implies that an 'open systems' architecture is required so that the problems of integration can be minimized. This means that:

- The 'closed system' approach minimizes the local changes and provides an architecture in which the different systems can be radically different provided they support the appropriate open systems gateways. Many of the current standards are still in draft form only and so these will be altered – in some cases this will involve significant changes, for example, 16 Mbps Token Ring.

- Very few manufacturers provide all of the devices and services needed to construct a network and those which do normally provide a proprietary solution. Third party resellers provide a wider range of systems but once again integration can be a problem.

- A network's history should not be allowed to dominate the design process; however, this cannot be used to justify its wholesale replacement. Instead the new network components should be linked to the older elements, using the appropriate internetworking devices, and a retirement policy should be considered to promote the renovation of the older parts of the network.

Irrespective of all the issues of migration, openness and so on, there is one inescapable fact that must always be remembered: real systems can only be built from devices that can be purchased. If it cannot be bought then it cannot be used.

15.5   Internetworking case studies

The most effective way to demonstrate some of the issues and their solutions when designing a network is to examine some simple case studies. Three such case studies have been chosen to reflect the most common environments:

- Startup and growth – a network that is required to support a newly established company occupying a single office. The network grows as the company expands and so it is inevitable that it carries within it the history of its development, for example functionally limited equipment.

- Green-fields and integration – an opportunity to design and install the ideal network, which is both perfectly suited to its immediate requirement and provides a suitably flexible architecture for future developments. The essential element here is to ensure that later developments do not disturb the integrated features of the network.

- Renovation and migration – in which a traditional point-to-point modem and dumb terminal network has to be modernized and converted to its LAN equivalent. The network then has to undergo a series of migrations as its functionality and range of services are extended.

In each of these case studies there are several possible solutions. The intention is not to show that the presented solution is the one preferred (in many cases it isn't!), but that it is the one more likely to be adopted given the historic perspective of the problem, the experience of the in-house designers and the money available to fund the solution.

15.5.1 Startup and growth

The classical characteristics of most startup networks are that they fit the immediate task in hand and little consideration is given to their development. Normally they are needed to support a small office environment and may even be used for technical support, such as computer aided design or small-scale software development. In most cases the ethernet system is selected because it is cheaper to install than an equivalent Token Ring network and has a higher awareness within the potential user community.

A typical startup network is shown in Figure 15.7, which would be used within a small office; it provides a file server and a printer and so is ideal for documentation production, database work and financial planning. The use of the repeater provides support for up to sixty devices (two linked 10BASE2 systems) and this can be easily extended by adding more repeaters or changing to a multiport repeater. Installing and managing this network is very simple, particularly if the NOS provides a rich set of features, for example the provision of access management, automated backup, disk mirroring, and so on. The classical fault with this system is the adoption of the older 10BASE5 ethernet cabling to support the file and print servers. This is unnecessary and, instead, thin coax should be used throughout or, if available within the workstations without extra cost, UTP with a 10BASET hub.

Naturally, the development of a startup network follows the expansion of the host organization. Typically, this includes more users being supported by the original network but eventually leads to support being required on other floors in the building – the number of nodes will grow from under ten to perhaps a few hundred. The classical approach to this expansion – and hence somewhat outmoded with the currently available equipment – is to install a backbone network to which all of the other networks are interconnected; the network shown in Figure 15.7 would therefore become as shown in Figure 15.8. In this network each floor is assumed to be autonomous, hence they each have their own file server and printer, and the bridges are used to ensure that the performance of each subnetwork is unaffected by the loading on the others (the use of a chain of repeaters would violate the design guidelines and would result in an overloaded network, causing excessively long response delays).

It is easy to see that the design approach consisted of cloning the original (and successful) architecture and using bridges to provide the link to the backbone. A more

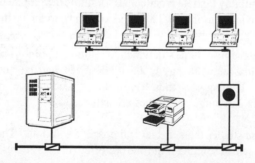

Figure 15.7 A typical startup network configuration.

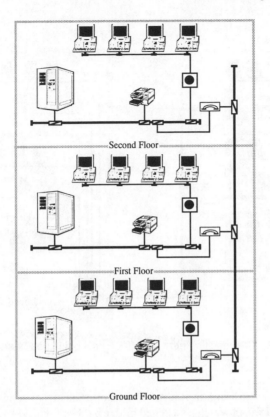

Figure 15.8 The classical architecture for a single building based network.

sensible approach would be to replace the local thick coax with thin coax, the local repeaters with multiport repeaters and the backbone/bridge structure with a fibre optic based multiport bridge or a switched bridge. This new solution would cost less to install and would provide a more flexible base for further developments.

The installation of this network would be complicated by the physical location of the backbone and its bridges but with the proper test equipment it should only take a few days to install it and make it operational; the installation of the client/server architectures could be completed quickly, provided a standard configuration disk was used as opposed to repeatedly generating the configuration from the distribution disks. This network would need to be managed and so all of the bridges should support a common management facility – preferably in-band so that a separate management network is not required. It should also be audited on an annual basis and someone should be assigned to act as the permanent and full-time network manager.

The next stage of development occurs as the organization acquires new but physically separate premises. At this stage the expansion of the network has to be carefully planned and controlled otherwise expensive mistakes will occur. It is important to use each expansion as an opportunity to rationalize and renovate the network – this is a more cost effective approach than casual renovation. The more

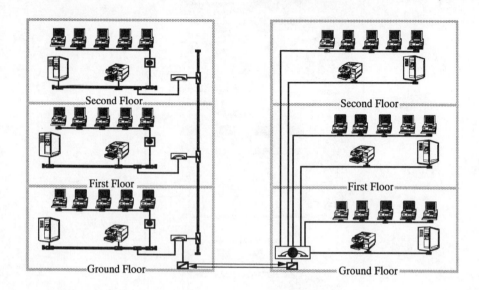

Figure 15.9 The resulting network after a new office has been acquired.

considered approach to designing the network is reflected in the expanded architecture shown in Figure 15.9, in which a switched bridge has been selected as the hub device for the 10BASET systems – if the hosts are further than 100 m from the switch then repeater hubs would be used. This achieves the same degree of connectivity as the repeater/bridge/backbone approach in the older part of the network but in a more cost effective manner. The major problem with this approach is that the complete network will be disconnected should the switched bridge fail – a temporary replacement of a multiport repeater could be used but this would result in a significantly degraded performance on the network, with it becoming one or two orders of magnitude slower.

The original network has not been renovated but one of the bridges has been replaced by a three-port modular bridge so that an optical link between the buildings could be used (this assumes that the buildings are within 2 km of each other). The other area for criticism is that the new building has not been flood wired and so there will be increased difficulties when users need to be added or moved about the network. The complete cabling and installation of this network should take no more than three or four weeks of effort, provided the correct equipment is available – TDRs and so on. The management of this network is dependent on being able to remotely manage the switched bridge and unless this is possible then a separate management probe would have to be installed on each of the bridge's spurs. The network management team would have to be increased to at least three people, one for each building and one controller, and they would require a considerable annual budget to maintain the network at a suitable level.

15.5.2 Green-fields and integration

The opportunity to design and install a network without any initial restrictions is normally only possible when new corporate offices are built. This situation usually occurs when a startup company moves into its first purpose-built premises or when a larger organization decides that new accommodation is required for some particular activity. In both of these, relatively rare, cases the network support team can take advantage of their accumulated knowledge of the network's requirements and have an opportunity to design a network that is well suited to both their new offices and to the ways in which the users' applications operate across the network.

A green-field site is shown in Figure 15.10. The network was designed to provide remote access to an ethernet based VAX cluster. The VAXs are used to act as process servers for a major software development facility. The users access the network via their own workstations, which are also used to support the daily office needs of word processing, financial planning and so on.

The site consists of three newly constructed offices: a purpose built data processing centre, to house all of the mainframe systems and their data packs, and two offices to house the majority of the staff. Each of the office buildings has undergone flood wiring and so there are no connection problems, and the data processing centre is supported using 10BASE2 (the hangar like building being too large and open for reliable flood wiring). Each of the offices uses a group of 10BASET hubs (placed within the wiring centres) interconnected using a local switched bridge. The switched bridges are linked to the data processing centre via fibre optic links (assuming distances of under 2 km). The data processing centre has its own multiport bridge which is used

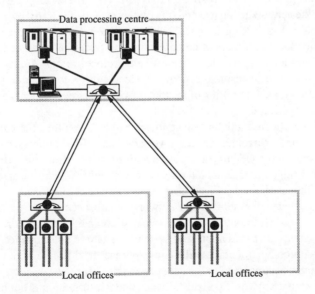

Figure 15.10 A green-field site and its accompanying network.

to link together the mainframe spurs and the network management system – each mainframe has its own spur, thereby ensuring that they are not saturated with irrelevant information.

The combination of the three repeaters and the switched bridge in each of the local offices could be replaced by an intelligent modular hub. This hub would supply all of the necessary connectivity, would also provide a simple upgrade policy by the addition of more interfaces to the hub and its failure could be rectified by using dual redundant interfaces. The major concern with this approach is that it would almost certainly mean that all of the future interfaces had to be supplied by the same manufacturer.

The network management infrastructure for this system would need careful consideration. The NMC must be integrated with the VAXs, the switched bridges and the structured cabling system itself. This would almost certainly entail several different sets of software operating within the NMC (one for the VAX management, one for the switched bridges and one for the hubs) and so could not really be termed an integrated system. The exception to this would be if all of the systems supported SNMP, in which case the NMC could collect all of the management information using just one piece of software. Clearly, a complete network support team is also required and this should be distinct from the general data processing centre support team who should be more concerned with running the computer systems and not the network infrastructure.

One of the threats to the integrated aspect of this network would be the discovery that a particular group require Token Ring support for some of their local work as well as retaining their remote access to the data processing centre. The aim would be to introduce the Token Ring LANs while maintaining the connectivity to the current data processing centre and providing this access from a single workstation. The ensuing network is shown in Figure 15.11, in which the Token Ring LANs are linked to the rest of the network using routers – the routers provide the translation between the ethernet and the Token Ring LANs. Within the Token Ring system all of the local traffic remains local and there is no contamination from the ethernet system. This initial configuration suggests that simple single protocol routers are required. However, it would be wise to ensure that upgrading to a multiprotocol router requires only a firmware alteration. Integration of the routers with the network management system must also be considered.

If the intelligent modular hub approach had be taken then there may be some problems with finding a router interface. Most modular hub suppliers have a full range of internetworking device interfaces, but not all of them. Router interfaces are less common than bridge and repeater interfaces and so enquiries should be made at an early stage about their availability.

The next development of the network would accompany further property acquisitions. Consider the situation when two new companies are acquired but in both cases their systems are based upon IBM systems – a natural consequence of acquiring companies with complementary skills and expertise. In this case both of these new companies must be connected to the data processing centre because this is where the corporate headquarters would collate its management information. The corresponding network architecture is shown in Figure 15.12, in which the two IBM based offices use

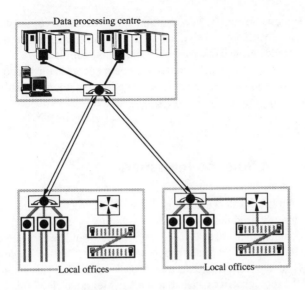

Figure 15.11 Extending the network by adding a different type of LAN.

a classical SNA configuration with an FEP and communications cluster supporting the terminals. The FEPs are linked to the data processing centre using a gateway which interconnects the ethernet system with the SNA's 64 kbps SDLC link. The gateway (a DECnet/SNA ST device) provides two forms of protocol translation: terminal access

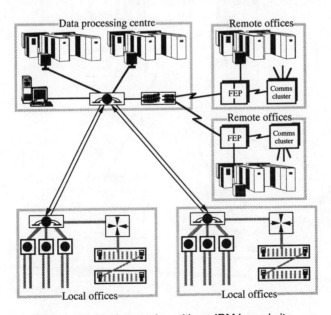

Figure 15.12 Integration with an IBM based site.

so that workstations hosting 3270 emulation software can have remote access to the mainframes and VAX/SNA translation so that the mainframes can communicate with each other. It should be noted that the Token Ring users can also have access to the IBM mainframes. Once again, the network management becomes further complicated and it is now impossible to provide an fully integrated system; consequently there will be IBM and non-IBM NMCs.

15.5.3 Renovation and migration

The final case study considers a network that was constructed before the use of LANs became a commonly used interconnection technique. A classical example would be a banking system in which the data processing centre would be connected to its remote offices using an X.25 PSDN and which would also use dial-up modems to provide remote access to the mainframes on an occasional basis. This approach remains suitable until the remote offices wish to install an integrated electronic office environment based upon LANs – a natural step with the introduction of networked PCs.

The resulting network is shown in Figure 15.13, in which one of the remote offices has been converted to a LAN based solution. The data processing centre houses the normal IBM mainframe configuration with the FEP housing X.25 and SNA SDLC

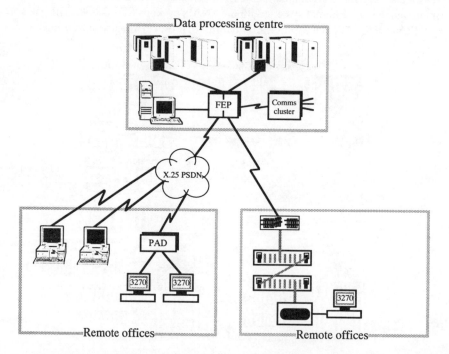

Figure 15.13 Upgrading a traditional PSDN based network architecture.

interfaces. The X.25 interface is used to support the offices that have not upgraded their communications network. In these offices the PADs act as terminal servers for the 3270 terminals and the PCs have their own X.25 interfaces. The upgraded offices have adopted the Token Ring LAN (what else from an IBM shop?) and use a terminal server to provide direct network access for their original 3270 terminals. All of their PCs would have Token Ring interfaces and would use terminal emulation software to obtain access to the remote hosts. Initially the gateway would be a modified PC and so would house the Token Ring and SDLC interfaces as well as the translation software. While this is a slow configuration it would still be quicker than the original X.25 solutions. These modifications provide the remote office with its own networked PC environment, still maintain access to the remote hosts and use a gateway that would fall under the normal IBM network management system, such as NetView.

The success of the upgraded systems would result in all of the other offices wishing to follow suit. This would entail a major renovation of the corporate communications system followed by a change in their working practices – that is, a more decentralized approach. The renovation process would almost certainly require the replacement of all of the X.25 and dial-up modem access systems with Token Ring LANs. A more sophisticated approach would consider the replacement of the PC based gateways with multiprotocol routers which also supported either SNA tunnelling (which would almost certainly use TCP/IP as the transport mechanism) or SDLC bridging. This would lead to the architecture shown in Figure 15.14. The routers would be used to supply access to the remote hosts but would also support a fault tolerant

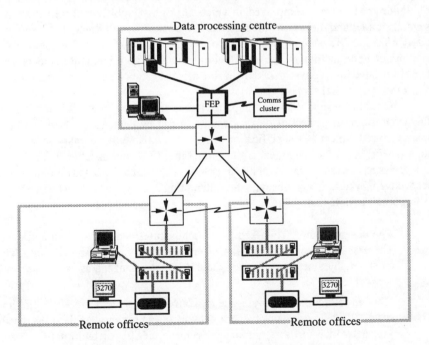

Figure 15.14 Totally renovating the network.

LAN-to-LAN communications infrastructure (using the routers as switching systems). This new architecture is well suited to further development such as the introduction of ethernet LANs, new protocol services and so on; thus in a relatively simple manner the original architecture has been transformed into its modern equivalent with all of the corresponding service enhancements.

The disadvantage of this new architecture is that the routers would not fall under the NetView management system and so a second NMC would have to be installed. The dependence of the routers on TCP/IP as the transport service would almost certainly mean that they would use SNMP. Until the formal network management standards have been completed and implemented within the proprietary systems, network management integration between mainframe systems and internetworked LANs will always be difficult.

15.6 Summary

Designing networks, particularly those that depend upon internetworked LANs, is a complex engineering problem. The lack of an established design methodology means that each organization approaches the problem differently and meets with varying degrees of success. It is important to use a logical approach, and usually the principle of 'divide and conquer' is employed, in which the original problem is broken down into several smaller and more tractable problems. One such way of doing this is summarized in Table 15.1, in which the design process has been broken into five stages. Each step builds upon the others, refining the design until the original requirements have been translated into a physical and realizable design accompanied by the definition of all of the operational support activities.

Once the design has been completed it must be implemented. It is at this stage that even the most perfect of designs can be ruined by devices that have not been manufactured to meet their specification or that are unreliable. A summary of the major internetworking device suppliers is shown in Table 15.2. In this table nine different categories have been examined and in most cases the companies listed dominate their respective markets. In conclusion, when attempting to design a LAN based system it is important to note that:

- The design of internetworked LAN architectures is an art and not a science. There is no single correct solution but many equally valid and invalid ones. The most suitable one depends upon the detailed needs of the users and network support team.

- 'Design for maintainability' is the most effective way to decrease the lifetime costs of the network. However, the network must provide all of the users' needs – the network is for users, not for justifying the need for a network support team.

- Network design starts by capturing the requirements (from the users and the

Table 15.1 The summary of the suggested design framework.

Phase	Activity
Requirements	To capture the requirements from the users and network support team and to produce the requirement specification of the network. To obtain the plans of the host buildings and locate on these all of the positions of the computer equipment and connectivity points.
Service architecture	To produce the relationship between the different servers (file, print, gateway, mangement, etc.) and their clients.
Logical architecture	To create the logical network structure which shows the different subnetworks and their interconnection, and the distribution of the service architecture. To finalize the selection of the protocols to be used to create the physical network.
Physical architecture	The physical network structure, which is produced by mapping the logical architecture onto the physical layout.The modification of the physical architecture to reflect the products available from the suppliers selected to implement the network.
Operational support	The creation of all of the support systems for the network including the disaster recovery plan, audit policy, etc.

network support team) and finishes by developing the operations support (disaster recovery plan, backup policy and so on). There is no well-established design methodology but the process must be completed using a logical approach and with sufficient time made available in which to complete it properly.

- At each level of the design process the following issues must be considered: users' access, connectivity, performance capability, manageability, fault tolerance, security, flexibility and cost implications. Each step in the refinement of the design should improve the overall suitability of that solution to the original requirements.

- Three important design principles have to be agreed before the design should start: the degree to which the system will be 'open' or 'closed', the preference for mixed or single vendor solutions and the extent to which the historic development of the network is permitted to influence its future development.

- Users will always complain about their network. If it is faulty they will complain of its unreliability, whereas if it successful they will complain of its lack of extra functionality and question why other users cannot have access to it. This is further compounded by the natural ageing of the network, so constant renovation and flexibility are essential.

Table 15.2 A summary of the major internetworking device manufacturers.

Item	Suppliers	Equipment
Network adapters	3COM, SMC, IBM, Proteon, Madge	IEEE 802.3 NIAs IEEE 802.5 NIAs
Repeaters	Allied Telesis, 3COM, IBM, Andrew	IEEE 802.3 IEEE 802.5
Bridges	Retix, 3COM, Andrew, RAD	IEEE 802.3 (transparent) IEEE 802.5 (source route)
Routers	Cisco, Wellfleet, Proteon, 3COM, Digital, Retix,	
Gateways	Eicon, Rabbit, Digital	IPX/SNA connectivity DECnet/SNA gateways
Hub systems	Synoptics, Chipcom, Cabletron, 3COM, Digital, UB	LattisNet IEEE 802.3 Net/One, Access/One
Test equipment	Hewlett Packard, Spider, Tektronix	Protocol analysers etc. Analysers, TDRs
Network operating systems	Novell, SUN, IBM, Digital, Microsoft	NetWare, NFS SNA, DECnet, Windows NT
Protocols and applications	Retix, Microsoft	OSI software Office applications etc.

16

Advanced Network Architectures

16.1   Introduction

There is no doubt that over the next five years there will be a significant increase in the range of communications equipment and services available to the user. Two areas will witness the greatest change: the WAN bearer and the nature of the applications support for users. Until a few years ago the range of technology for WANs was stable and well understood with little need for any further developments. This changed once LAN interconnection became dependent upon WAN bearers; the relatively slow speed of the WANs created an unwelcome information bottleneck. The problem was further compounded by the introduction of devices capable of concentrating the information from several LANs across the same WAN bearer. The response has been to rethink the WAN infrastructure and to create fast packet switch architectures which are capable of handling data rates in the 1–10 Gbps region.

The second development, that of service integration, has been in response to the user's need to handle a variety of different types of information: voice, video, graphics, and so on. This data handling has two important implications: the need to transfer the data across a single bearer infrastructure, thereby reducing the physical complexity of the system at the user's workstation; and the capability to manipulate these different types of data from within a single application so that the user can be more concerned with the content and not the processing of the information. The user can then concentrate on using the data formats most appropriate to the task at hand and does not need to consider how this particular information will be submitted to and transmitted across the network (Stallings, 1994).

16.2   Integrated services networks

Integrated services networks are concerned with supplying the user with the capability to seamlessly transmit different types of data across a single network infrastructure. The different forms of information that must be supported by such a service include: voice, data, video, graphics, music, text, television, high definition television and documents. The emphasis of such a system is on the user and supporting their needs, and this gives rise to two flavours of integrated service: 'isn' and 'ISN'. Contrary to the claims made by many manufacturers, their current systems support only 'isn', the integration of the bearer capabilities, whereas the full 'ISN', which incorporates the bearer and the application services integration, is still a few years away.

The general architecture of 'isn' systems is shown in Figure 16.1. The 'isn' bearer system is represented by the bottom two layers and the network switch interfaces. Different flavours of the 'isn' use different data link and physical layers but in most cases the data link layer is split into two sublayers. The data link core is responsible for fast data transfer whereas the upper data link supports supplementary

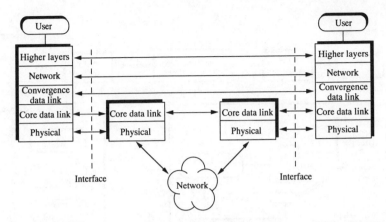

Figure 16.1 The scope of the integrated services networks architecture.

functions such as error correction and segmentation. The internal switches support the core services only and so this means that for reliable networks the end-systems must support the error correction services.

16.2.1 Integrated services digital network

The original integrated service digital network (ISDN) has now been renamed the narrowband ISDN (NISDN) because it is concerned with data rates in the 64 kbps to 2 Mbps region; the broadband ISDN (BISDN) is concerned with data rates in excess of 100 Mbps. The NISDN uses a series of differing channel capacities and the user is allocated a capacity according to their needs. The basic rate is defined as 2B+D which means that the user has a 64 kbps carrier for each direction (B) (a 64 kbps full duplex link) with either a 64 kbps (primary rate) or 16 kbps (basic rate) connection establishment channel (D). The European primary rate is 30B+D, or 2.048 Mbps, whereas the American primary rate is 23B+D, or 1.56 Mbps. The significant features of an ISDN architecture as shown in Figure 16.2 are:

- The network terminating (NT) 1 box supports the basic ISDN facilities and the NT 2 box is required if a PABX system is to be installed. Normally these two systems are supplied as an integrated NT 12 box.

- A series of standard interfaces has been defined according to their position within the architecture. These include: the R interface (V.24, X.21, and so on) for non-ISDN devices, S and T bearer service interfaces for ISDN devices, and U, or circuit switch interfaces for access to the exchange.

- Terminal adapters (TA) are ISDN equivalents to X.25 PADs whereas TE1 and TE2 refer to ISDN and non-ISDN devices, respectively.

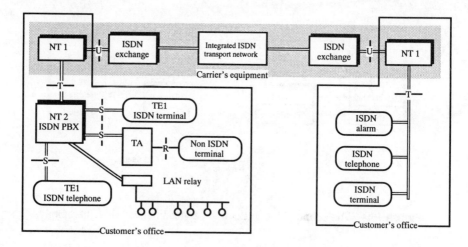

Figure 16.2 Integrated service digital network (ISDN) architecture.

From the point of view of internetworking the ISDN infrastructure provides a series of clearly defined access interfaces through which it is possible to obtain an appropriate data pipe capacity. These data pipes can then be used to support LAN-to-LAN connectivity – that is, bridges or routers with ISDN interfaces, remote terminal access using an ISDN PAD and voice communications.

In principle, packet switching under ISDN is supported either as a native function of the ISDN switch itself (through both the B and D channels) or through a PSDN interface using the B channel. The standards for ISDN native packet switching have only just been established and accepted in Europe and so at present all packet switching is through a PSDN system, normally X.25.

16.2.2 Integrated services local network

The integrated services local network (ISLN) is the LAN equivalent of the ISDN. There are several research and development ISLNs currently available for evaluation in several parts of the world, such as the Pandora system which is based upon the Cambridge Ring and provides an integrated voice, data, video and graphics transfer capability. Many of these multimedia systems are based upon sophisticated workstations, such as PS/2 and UNIX boxes but some of the most recent developments have seen these services become available on PC systems.

The services typically offered are the transmission of real-time video for videoconferencing or videotelephones. Other services include the distribution of graphics and images input from image scanners and so on. The user sees the distribution environment as a true multimedia system and the treatment of the different

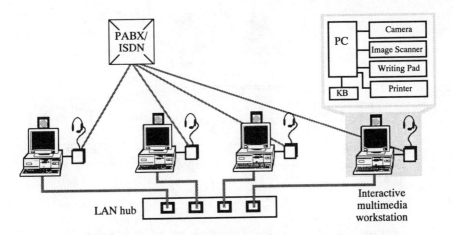

Figure 16.3 Integrated service local network (ISLN) architecture.

data forms is transparent to them. A typical ISLN architecture is shown in Figure 16.3, in which a LAN/PABX combination is used to interconnect multimedia workstations; the final form of the ISLN would require only one channel and not the LAN/PABX combination. These workstations supply voice access, a camera for video conferencing/ telephony, an image scanner for graphics input and a writing pad for hand drawn input. The integration of these systems is provided by the software residing within the workstation which synchronizes all of the information streams (Buford, 1994).

The next step is to use a single communications channel to support both the voice and data streams. The products for this integration are just becoming available at a reasonable price and the recent IEEE 802.9a standardization of the integrated services LAN (IS-LAN), based upon a 16 Mbps ethernet architecture (see section 5.4.9), will reduce these still further.

These types of systems will significantly alter the traffic loading characteristics currently experienced on LAN based systems. The overall loading will increase significantly but the general frame sizes will become smaller and the proportion of large file transfers will reduce in comparison to other service demands. These services will require greater bandwidth networks and guaranteed low transfer delays (severely stressing the network), and so the network architecture and the distribution of the users across this will require very careful design and monitoring.

16.2.3 The fibre distributed data interface

One of the continuing trends in networking is the increasing emphasis on fibre optic cabling. In many instances, fibre-to-the-desk is inappropriate but fibre is well suited to supporting backbone needs. The fibre distributed data interface (FDDI) is the formally ratified LAN/MAN architecture intended for use as a backbone network. This backbone architecture is shown in Figure 16.4, where access to the backbone is via

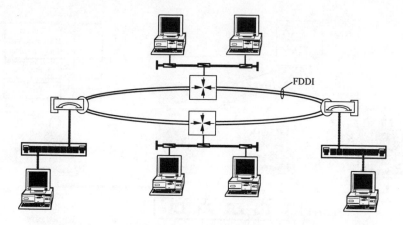

Figure 16.4 Using the fibre distributed data interface as a MAN.

translational bridges (link bridges) or routers. These access positions support individual LAN architectures, which could be ethernet, Token Ring or other FDDI LANs, and so this reflects the classical hierarchical design approach.

The FDDI is the ratified standard specification for 100 Mbps token-append networks based upon fibre optic cable links (some manufacturers are now calling this fast Token Ring). The topology is designed to be resilient with a dual contra-rotating ring architecture. The maximum perimeter length is 50 km (in failure mode this becomes 100 km) with each node being less than 2 km apart. If an 8 μm core fibre is used (as opposed to the more common 62.5 μm) this separation is increased to about 60 km. The FDDI is basically two Token Ring systems that can be linked should a failure occur on either one of them, thereby forming a single ring (Stallings, 1993). There are two classes of station for connection to the FDDI, as shown in Figure 16.5:

- Class A stations, which are linked to both of the rings and which take the form of a dual attachment station (DAS) or a dual attachment concentrator (DAC).

- Class B stations, which supply a link to only one of the rings and which take the form of a single attachment station (SAS), user nodes, or a single attachment concentrator (SAC).

The Class A stations can decide on which ring to send the data – file servers, bridges and routers tend to be of this type – with the Class B stations (SAS) connected to the FDDI via a Class A wiring concentrator (DAC). A SAC can support many SASs but it can only be attached to the main segments using a DAC. The tokens rotate around the two rings in opposite directions and if a failure in one of the point-to-point links occurs then the two nearest Class A stations disable that part of the ring. The stations then wrap the traffic back onto the other working ring, thereby re-establishing the integrity of the network but at the expense of doubling the effective propagation delay.

A schematic diagram of the generic FDDI MAC is shown in Figure 16.6. The MAC is split into two sections:

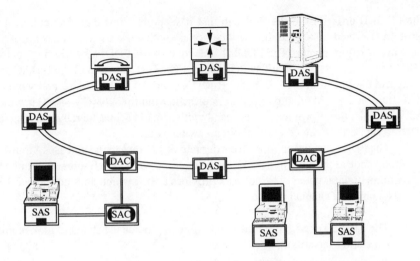

Figure 16.5 Primary and secondary rings in within the FDDI.

- The basic FDDI MAC which supports the standard FDDI functions and provides an interface to the LLC (another LAN MAC).

- The isochronous MAC (I-MAC) which supports the circuit switching service in the FDDI II and the hybrid multiplexor (the shaded area in Figure 16.6).

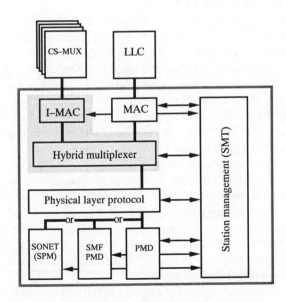

Figure 16.6 The MAC for FDDI I and II.

The FDDI II differs from the FDDI in that it supports a fast digital circuit switch capability (termed an isochronous service) for use with voice streams and some of the other ISDN requirements. The FDDI II adds to the basic FDDI a hybrid ring control (HRC); this supports the circuit switch service. The HRC consists of the I-MAC and the hybrid multiplexor (H-MUX); the H-MUX multiplexes the I-MAC and standard MAC frames. The I-MAC supports the circuit switch multiplexor (CS-MUX) in which each switch service is provided with a bandwidth of 6.144 Mbps, thereby enabling the FDDI to support sixteen concurrent circuit switched links.

The FDDI channel supports a carrier rate of 125 megabaud and uses a four-to-five group code to provide the 100 Mbps data rate, across which frames are limited to a maximum of 4500 octets. The network provides a BER which does not exceed 1 in 10^{-9}. The physical channel can be:

- The basic 50 or 62.5 µm multimode fibre to provide the standard maximum 2 km station separation.

- The 8 µm single mode fibre (SMF), or monomode fibre, for extended station separation (60 km).

- The SONET STS–3c physical layer mapping (SPM) for common carrier access (SONET is the CCITT's synchronous optical network standard discussed in Section 16.4).

The final part of the FDDI MAC architecture is the station management (SMT) entity and it is this feature which delayed the introduction of the full FDDI chip set. The SMT architecture is consistent with the aims of the IEEE 802.1B standard, which is discussed more fully in Section 14.3.3.

In general, fibre-to-the-desk is too expensive a solution but the high speed carrying capacity of the FDDI is attractive to network designers. The response to this challenge has been to develop an FDDI equivalent that can be used on copper based cabling systems. This has been termed the copper distributed data interface (CDDI) or, in the case of twisted pair implementations, the twisted pair distributed data interface (TPDDI). The intention is to develop a 100 Mbps LAN that can make use of the structured cabling systems currently installed to support the established LANs.

The implications of FDDI and the related methods on internetworking are uncertain. This uncertainty is not directly related to the technology or its capabilities but to the manufacturers' perception of what the networking market needs. This perception considers the FDDI to be a transient solution at best and with a useful lifetime of only another three to five years. The reason for this is the high expectations of the BISDN systems currently undergoing rapid research and development. These broadband systems have a considerably greater capability than the FDDI and will provide a more cost effective solution even in the LAN domain. Therefore, care should be taken when considering an FDDI solution because long-term support for such networks could be difficult and expensive.

A proposal for the next generation (after FDDI II) fibre based LAN is called the FDDI follow on LAN (FFOL). The FFOL reconciles the technologies of FDDI II and cell relay so that efficient voice and data switching is available across a BISDN infrastructure. It is intended to act as a high speed backbone for the interconnection of FDDI systems, cell relay and other established LANs, and is based upon an SDH/SONET carrier; it is not based upon token passing, as this was considered too limiting for gigabit networks. The recent developments in cell relay and fibre channel have delayed initial interest and it is a possibility that very little further discussion and development will take place.

16.2.4 Distributed queue dual bus

Apart from the FDDI, two other MANs are currently undergoing development: the switched multi-megastream data system (SMDS) and the distributed queue dual bus (DQDB). Bell Communications Research's SMDS specification is for a service supported by two classes of carrier: the USA NISDN (1.544 Mbps) and a higher rate of 44.736 Mbps. This provides a high speed connectionless packet switched service and uses the SMDS interface protocol (SIP) which is based upon the IEEE 802.6 DQDB MAN MAC. The intention is for the SMDS to act as a high performance LAN (including FDDI) interconnection, thus providing a LAN like packet switched performance and features over MAN and WAN distances. An SMDS service has just been introduced in the UK by BT but it has been available in the US for several years.

The original MAN specification was based upon the Australian PTT's dual bus with queued packet and synchronous switch (DB-QPSX) architecture. The DQDB, which evolved from the QPSX technique, has now been formally ratified and released as IEEE 802.6 and ISO 8802/6 (Stallings, 1993). The underlying architecture is that of a dual bus (normally fibre optic) with a distributed queuing multiple access scheme to support both CLS and COS data transfer, as well as an isochronous service (the latter provides a constant inter-arrival time). The multiple access mechanism is based upon a slotted access scheme in which a continuous stream of slots (53 octets each) is transmitted down each bus. The dual bus architecture has two possible topologies:

- Open bus, as shown in Figure 16.7 – two separate buses are used, one to transmit data in each direction. Each bus has a head-end (denoted by the solid circle) which is responsible for the generation of the slots. Each node is connected to both buses and can transmit/receive data onto/from both buses.

- Looped-bus topology – two separate bus are used as open loops with a single head-end being responsible for both links. Once again, each node is connected to both buses.

The DQDB is defined independently of the physical medium, with SONET and high speed G.703 interfaces being commonly quoted. These definitions are based upon an 8000 cycles/second bandwidth allocation scheme with multiple slots being issued every 125 μs. This cycle aligns the DQDB with SONET and the 53 octet slots aligns it with the cell relay based networks. The basic data transmission algorithm is:

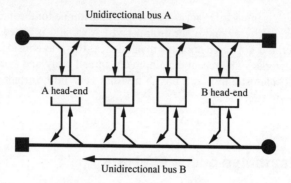

Figure 16.7 The DQDB architecture.

- The head-ends issue a continuous stream of slots on their respective buses. These slots are either free or they are reserved for an unspecified node.

- A node determines on which bus the destination node is downstream of it – the relative location of each node is determined during the initialization of the node.

- The node issues a reservation request to the head-end on the other bus. This means that the node must wait for an empty slot, which is then converted to a reservation request.

- When the node acting as the head-end for the other bus receives the request it issues a reserved slot. This slot will be detected by the waiting node (which has been keeping a count of the outstanding requests) and so it will then be able to transmit one slot of data (53 octets);

- The node can now request another slot.

One of the important limitations of the DQDB is that it is intrinsically unfair in that certain nodes on the network get preferential access. This is because nodes that are closer to the slot generator source obtain more opportunity to acquire channel access and those further away receive less opportunity. This unfairness has been alleviated by the use of a bandwidth balancing scheme in which nodes must delay access according to an access counting scheme. This unfairness is further ameliorated by the use of a three-level prioritization mechanism.

The DQDB has three sublayers, as shown in Figure 16.8, which are responsible for mapping the MAC frames onto the slotted data stream. Each of the three sublayers is responsible for:

- Common functions – the relaying of the slots between the physical layer and as a common platform for the higher layer services. It also provides head-end actions and configuration control.

- Arbitrated functions – media access control for the queue arbitrated services (COS and CLS data) and the pre-arbitrated functions (isochronous services).

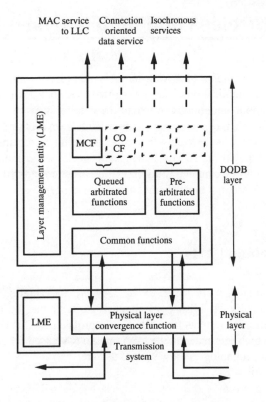

Figure 16.8 The DQDB MAC and its sublayers.

- Convergence functions – responsible for mapping the data stream to the 53 octet slot stream. This consists of the MAC convergence function (MCF) which maps the CLS data stream to the QA function (this is responsible for the segmentation and reassembly of the initial MAC frames), the connection oriented convergence function (COCF), which supports the COS data services, and the isochronous convergence function (ICF), which maps the isochronous service to the PA function.

DQDB networks will be available as both public and private services, similar to SMDS but unlike FDDI. Public networks will normally be used for long distance connectivity whereas the private architectures will be used on campus or in small cities. It is unlikely that users will have direct access to DQDB (due to cost) but instead it will be used to act as an intermediate network. Access to this will then be via bridges or routers, with router based access more likely. Router based access means that the DQDB network will be able to support the interconnection of mixed networks, for example, Token Ring, FDDI and ethernet connectivity. A DQDB network will also be able to support voice links and so a PABX could also be directly connected to it.

16.3 Wireless and mobile systems

There are a growing number of cases where it is either inconvenient or impossible to use cable based communications. The systems that commonly fall into these categories are those that support mobile users, where the cabling ducts are full or where the network infrastructure is of a temporary nature. With the exception of mobile systems, it is more convenient to use a wireless communications infrastructure so that a network can be assembled quickly and easily, and located exactly where required. In contrast, mobile systems require a completely different infrastructure and so the interconnection of these to LAN based systems becomes an area of concern.

16.3.1 Wireless LANs

Wireless local area networks (WLAN or LAWN), or cableless LANs (CLANs) became commercially established in about 1991 with the introduction of three important but different systems from BICC, Motorola and NCR (IEE, 1992). All of these systems, which originated in the USA, are now licensed for use within the UK and Europe. The technologies these system use are:

- Spread spectrum – this entails the use of the UHF radio frequency (the industrial, scientific and medical, ISM, bandwidth at 2.4–2.5 GHz), which is normally used when intra-building communications (room-to-room) are needed.

- Microwave radio – which is typically in the 5–19 GHz region. The higher the frequency of the microwave radio systems the more light-like their properties become. This means that the microwaves will not easily travel through walls and so are well suited to frequency reuse systems.

- Infrared light – which is in the 600–1000 nm region – that is, teraHertz. Infrared systems need line-of-sight connectivity because the signals cannot pass through walls and so on (except for windows). There is very little mutual interference caused by other systems operating in close proximity and only exceedingly intense sources of light (such as the Sun) can cause external interference.

Each of the three technologies is suited to particular applications such as:

- Exhibition hall connectivity – here the buildings have very high ceilings and so are well suited to line-of-sight links as provided by the infrared systems.

- Warehouse connectivity – where the ceilings may again be high but there may be no line-of-sight (storage stacking). In these environments the spread spectrum radio systems are ideal due to their ability to pass through objects and their immunity to multipathing effects caused by reflections.

- Cabling replacement systems – in some areas there are restrictions on cabling installation due to building regulations, for example, and so a wireless solution is essential. In these applications the microwave systems act as good cabling replacements because they have the same overall characteristics and can provide the high point-to-point data rates expected of cabling replacement systems. In many cases it may also be important for these systems to be interconnected to cable based LAN systems and so compatibility is required.

- Point-to-point connectivity – where LANs require extended connectivity, for example, using radio/microwave connectivity between bridges and/or routers.

- Portable connectivity – to interconnect shared devices such as printers, file servers, and so on, and where portability of the device is important due to the nature of the environment, such as on-site police, medical systems support. This also includes connectivity for notebook and palm-top computers, both of which have been identified as being the applications which will be responsible for the success, or otherwise, of the wireless approach.

- Factory/shop installation – to replace the dependence on fibre optic cabling but for use in potentially electrically noisy environments where low speed data collection and distribution is required. These systems will also be needed where cabling may be impracticable, for example where flood wiring is not possible.

There are two basic architectures for LAWNs: centralized and distributed. The centralized systems employ a relay beacon which is used to forward all transmissions. In Figure 16.9 the relay element is responsible for interconnecting the LANs; broadcast wireless communication is used to provide this connectivity. The advantage of this system is that it can be used to interconnect the standard LANs: ethernet to ethernet and Token Ring to Token Ring. In contrast, the distributed systems adopt a new MAC definition and so all of the users need the appropriate LAWN network adapter. Figure 16.10 shows such a system in which each node has its own wireless transceiver and where the transmissions are broadcast across the network. The advantage of this system is that, within the area of coverage of the system, the users can easily be moved without requiring any alteration to a cabling system. The standardization organizations have several areas of development:

- Spread spectrum LAWNs have been allocated the 2.4–2.5 GHz frequencies, as part of the ISM bandwidth. The UK has unilaterally assigned the 2.445–2.475 GHz region for spread spectrum LAWNs within the UK but these systems will have a limited period of licence once the standards have been ratified.

- The IEEE 802.11 committee which is considering many different architectural aspects to ensure consistency with the other LAN medium access control definitions. The IEEE 802.11 expects to present (optimistically) their final draft for ISO/IEC consideration by the end of 1994.

- The high speed LAWN proposal which is named HiPerLAN. It is intended that this system will provide a 20 Mbps carrying capacity in the 5 GHz region and will operate across distances of a few hundred metres.

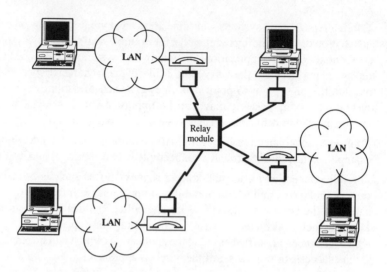

Figure 16.9 A centralized wireless LAN architecture.

- The European Telecommunications Standards Institute (ETSI) mandates the use of the digital European cordless telecommunications (DECT) standard in the 1.8–1.9 GHz region for 2 Mbps carrying capacity systems.
- The US development of spread spectrum LAWNs based on the 5.41–5.875 GHz and 902–928 MHz regions will not be permitted within Europe, unless the HiPerLAN specification is extended to incorporate spread spectrum. At present the telecommunications regulatory bodies are not addressing the deep micro-wave or the infrared regions.

The implications of wireless technology for LANs and interconnectivity are clear and considerable. A combination of the centralized and distributed systems will enable network managers to easily move networks and users within networks as well as

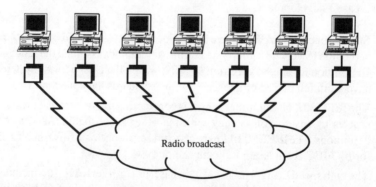

Figure 16.10 A distributed access wireless LAN architecture.

rapidly creating new networks to support temporary installations. LAWNs will also provide network connectivity in areas which before were inaccessible or where the installation costs were disproportionately large. It is, however, important to note that wireless communication systems are not intended to replace other techniques but are to be complementary and provide a value added service.

16.3.2 The personal communications network

The liberalization of the UK cellular radio telephone market has quickly established the UK as one of the leading users of mobile and cordless telephones. The aim over the next ten years is to establish the personal communications network (PCN), or the personal communications system (PCS) as it is referred to in the US, which will permit the use of mobile and cordless telephones at any place in the world. To this end the CCIR is developing a global standard called the future public land mobile telecommunications system (FPLMTS); the installed Pan European equivalent, also under development, is termed the universal telecommunications system (UMTS) and builds upon the established global system for mobile communications (GSM).

Both standards are based upon digital communications and so will require second generation handsets; most of the current systems use analogue technology. Once again two systems are in competition: the cordless telephone 2 (CT2) and the DECT. CT2 (which employs digital frequency division multiple access) supports call only access and so the DECT system (which employs digital time division multiple access) with its full two-way communications may well become the accepted standard. The situation is made even more complex by the American decision to standardize a system based upon CDMA (spread spectrum) from Qualcomm, and termed Q-CDMA.

A network infrastructure which could be used to integrate the mobile and LAN is shown in Figure 16.11. In this network the base stations are used to forward data between the handsets across the picocell (intra-building communications), microcell and macrocell infrastructures. LAN access is through an appropriate gateway into the host building and would be capable of supporting a limited number of mobile systems (cf. PADs and terminal servers). The base stations have a limited coverage and so the handsets must be capable of supporting handovers between different base stations while still mapping to the same end-system and without losing any information.

Pan European PCNs will produce networks that are at least an order of magnitude larger and more sophisticated than their current counterparts. While the PCN will initially be a voice only system, the longer term aim is to make use of the hand-held sets to support data transfer also (as proposed for the LAWN systems). In particular, it is envisaged that the new handsets will also support data access to remote file servers (cf. remote terminal access) whereas at present data transfer is limited to short text based messages. This means that the networks will have to support:

- A considerably larger number of users. The relatively low cost of personal access to such systems means that users will be able to access the network from

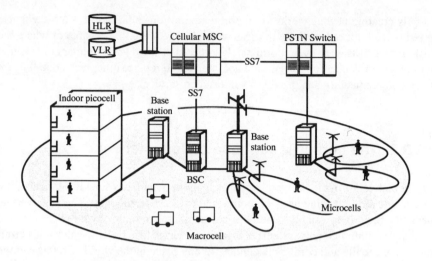

Figure 16.11 The personal communications network.

several positions, for example their own PCs and one or more hand-sets.

- The user will expect their environment to follow them and so, within reason, the system must be capable of supplying the required resources independent of the physical location of the user.

- Network management will become even more difficult with issues such as access accounting, security, performance loading and fault location reflecting continually changing user access patterns.

One possible area of conflict between Europe and the US concerns the use of CDMA technology for mobile communications. The US company Qualcomm has several CDMA based mobile systems undergoing trials in different countries, whereas Europe is still committed to TDMA approaches and is, in general, uncertain of the claims made about the CDMA systems.

16.3.3 Very small aperture terminal systems

One of the latest elements in a modern data communications based WAN is the satellite. A satellite provides both a physically large broadcast area (a footprint which can be many hundreds of kilometres in diameter) and a space switching capability so that the bandwidth can be physically moved to where it is required, for example Intelsat VI which is a geostationary satellite that supports some 120 000 telephone circuits covering Europe, Africa, and North and South America. The increased power density of satellite transmissions and their on-board processing capability means that the diameter of the receiving dishes can be reduced, thereby decreasing their cost and bulk.

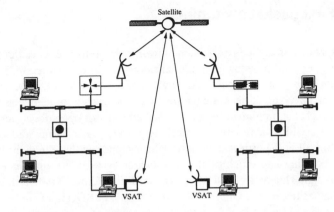

Figure 16.12 A VSAT communications network.

This is the foundation for the very small aperture terminal (VSAT) systems, in which the actual satellite dishes have a diameter of between 60 and 70 cm.

The advances in satellite communication technology have made VSAT based WANs an economic reality and so the next stage is to consider their application for LANs. The VSAT systems utilize low cost earth stations which provide an alternative to terrestrial data communications systems and offer several desirable properties, including distance insensitivity, and improved reliability and flexibility. A typical VSAT architecture is shown in Figure 16.12, where either gateways or routers are used to support the satellite connectivity. The remote PCs will require their own VSAT interface with the appropriate network drivers and adapters.

The consequences of VSAT technology on the internetworking architecture are not as severe as those for the mobile systems but include many of the same problems. One area of particular concern is that of network device fault location and replacement. The strength of the VSAT approach is that it supplies a very effective home-working environment which, while it is well suited to the user, will make fault location and repair in such networks considerably more difficult. It would therefore be essential that such systems have a fully integrated network management system.

16.4   New carrier services

There is a continual demand for increasing amounts of bandwidth. However, there are very few applications that require large bandwidths for prolonged periods. Therefore, high bandwidth systems need flexible multiple access techniques so that the bandwidth can be readily allocated to the users when and where required. It is the convergence of this need with internetworking that has created the pressure for new bearer technologies, which has in turn spawned a plethora of competing WAN technologies.

16.4.1 Fast packet switching

Fast packet switching is the generic name given to the bearer services developed to support the integrated broadband communications (IBC) infrastructure. In general such systems supply carrying capacities well in excess of 2 Mbps. The underlying principles for many of these systems are to adopt packet switching as the data transmission scheme, minimize the protocol overheads for operations such as error recovery and establish a flexible but well regulated bearer bandwidth allocation scheme so that all of the different systems can be supported by a single bearer.

The carrying capacities of the new bearer systems are unified under the synchronous digital hierarchy (SDH) which has a clearly defined bandwidth allocation scheme for capacities up to 2 Gbps (Partridge, 1994). The SDH is an internetworking interface for digital networks which defines a synchronous transport signal (STS) hierarchy in multiples of n = 3, 9, 12, 18, 24, 36, 48 of 51.84 Mbps. The STS level 1 is the basic 51.84 Mbps SONET carrier with the concatenated super-rate mapping STS-3c level providing a 155.52 Mbps SONET carrier. Multiples of the STS-3c carrier are used to define the synchronous transfer mode (STM) such that an STM level 1 is a 155.52 Mbps (STS–3c) carrier, with STM level 16 being the 2.48832 Gbps (that is, sixteen STM-1) carrier. Originally, SONET was just the CCITT's recommended 155.52 Mbps synchronous optical network. However, the term SDH/SONET is now used to show the equivalence of the two; the USA prefers the term SONET and Europe SDH. The multiplexing of information onto wide area optical networks will, in the short term, be based upon two techniques – the synchronous and asynchronous transfer modes, STM and ATM, respectively. STM assumes a common time reference and imposes a slot and framing scheme on the data whereas ATM is free running but enforces a cell structure on the data. STM systems are used for building optical circuit switching whereas ATM is used for cell switching; however, there are several hybrid schemes (using both STM and ATM) which are expected to produce systems capable of concurrently supporting both circuit and packet switching.

LAN internetworking devices will eventually replace the current megastream and kilostream services with frame relay (30–45 Mbps) and cell relay (45 Mbps and higher). These will provide fast switch access but will require a network layer protocol to provide a reliable network service – that is, frame and cell relay are data link pipelines. The future for X.25 in such an environment looks limited; however, there are efforts to produce a 10 Mbps X.25 service which may or may not make use of frame relay – the 45 Mbps carrier would provide a 10 Mbps data rate at the X.25PLP interface.

Frame relay refers to the technology responsible for the high speed switching of data frames and as such is concerned with information flow at the data link layer of the OSI/RM; formally it employs the NISDN standards (Smith, 1993). PSDNs, such as X.25, provide very sophisticated error recovery capabilities which are mandatory but which were originally created for relatively noisy communications links. Modern signalling techniques and fibre optic cabling have made many of these systems redundant and so frame relay is intended to provide a very high speed data pipe, which is unreliable but has a very low probability of error. The error recovery functions are then located in the end-systems.

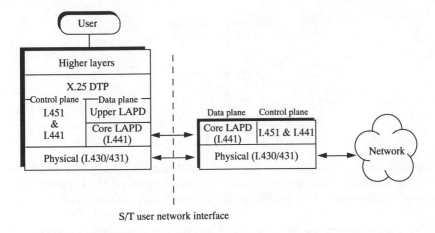

Figure 16.13 Frame relay and its support protocols.

The architecture for the frame relay systems is shown in Figure 16.13, where it can be seen that the actual technology is based upon the established ISDN systems. In keeping with the classical signalling nomenclature, the profile in Figure 16.13 is split into the control and data sections (in data communications there is no separation of these two functions). Both the control and data access is supported by the LAPD protocol across the D-channel but, in keeping with the X.25 approach, these standards only apply to the actual user network interface (ISDN type S and T). The error recovery system is located in the end-systems; in this example it is a part of the X.25 data transfer protocol (DTP) and consequently none of the switching elements are responsible for any error recovery. The X.25 DTP uses frame relay switching to provide a high speed data pipe between the end-systems; this is one way of creating a faster X.25 system.

16.4.2 Cell relay

Frame relay is considered a transition system for migration towards cell relay, whose most likely form of implementation uses the asynchronous transfer mode (ATM) technique. In ATM the data is broken into very short cells (53 octets in length with 48 octets of data and 5 of header) and these and other cells are then multiplexed onto an appropriate bearer. Cells are used so that mixed bandwidth systems can be readily supported without loss of efficiency, for example mixed voice and data networks. Once again ATM is seen as a low level bearer service upon which higher layers of protocol must be used to support the appropriate services (Händel, 1994).

One of the currently marketed LAN based architectures is shown in Figure 16.14 in which ATM switches (costing some £20 000 each) are interconnected using fibre based SONET links. The workstations are linked to the ATM switches using fibre links; the workstation interfaces cost between £1000 and £3000 each. The claimed advantage of using an ATM based switching system is that it is the most effective way

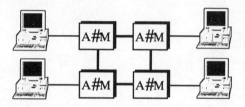

Figure 16.14   ATM switching for LANs.

of integrating voice and data transfer; while this may be true (some benchmark tests have shown severe efficiency problems with heavily loaded ATM switches) it is too expensive a solution at the current time. ATM switches fall into one of two categories:

- Access switches – these supply the user with an access interface to the ATM network, that is, the user-network interface (UNI). The standards bodies have established 51 Mbps as the interface data rate but some manufacturers are still hoping to force the acceptance of 25 Mbps. These lower data rate specifications are a reflection of the fact that most end-systems do not need 155 Mbps and so the access switch acts as a concentrator.

- Network switches – these are the ATM infrastructure switches which operate at the recognized 155–620 Mbps.

The protocol model for the BISDN based upon the ATM is shown in Figure 16.15. This shows that the BISDN has three layers, each of which is responsible for:

- The ATM adaptation layer (AAL) – which is responsible for preparing the higher layer frames (MAC frames for LANs) for encapsulation in the ATM

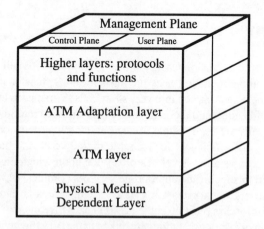

Figure 16.15   The BISDN model for ATM.

cells. There are several classes of AAL to reflect the different types of information supplied by the higher layer protocols.

- ATM layer – this is the actual cell switching system.
- Physical medium dependent layer – this is the physical carrier system and would be based upon systems such as SDH/SONET.

The AAL is further split into two sublayers: the convergence sublayer (CS) and the segmentation and reassembly sublayer. The CS is responsible for encapsulating the higher layer protocols to provide the appropriate address support. The SAR then takes this information and prepares it for encapsulation in the cells themselves; the SAR produces pseudocells which are 48 octets long. The ATM physical layer is also composed of two sublayers: the transmission control (TC) sublayer and the physical medium (PM) sublayer. The TC is responsible for cell construction – that is, the collation of bits into the 53 octet cell, whereas the PM is responsible for bit timing and interfacing to the channel itself.

At the current time there are five types of AAL, each of which is allocated according to the class of service required. These types and their service classes are:

- AAL 1, Class A, intended for isochronous or constant bit rate sources, for example voice.
- AAL 2, Class B, intended for variable bit rate audio and video sources.
- AAL 3/4, Classes C and D, intended to provide access for connectionless and connection oriented data services.
- AAL 5 for LAN traffic. It is also known as the simple and efficient adaptation layer (SEAL) and it is claimed to be a streamlined version of the AAL 3/4.
- The null AAL which is intended for non-isochronous connection oriented traffic. This assume that the data source already produces the basic cells, such as interconnection of DQDB to cell relay.

A proposed ATM based profile for the support of file access, in this case Novell NetWare, across connected LANs is shown in Figure 16.16. In this system two remote bridges are linked using an ATM switch. The ATM protocols are based upon the AAL 3/4 and the connectionless network access protocol (CLNAP), which are responsible for mapping the LAN MAC frames onto the ATM cell structure. These cells are then passed into the ATM switch system itself. Several ATM switches and interfaces are currently available (supporting PC and UNIX workstations); these will switch at either 155 or 620 Mbps and so can be supported by an appropriate SDH bearer infrastructure.

ATM has been identified as the key technology. It is the first bearer protocol that has gained widespread acceptance for use in BISDNs and so most of the major communications switching system manufacturers are rapidly developing their own ATM systems. This impetus is being followed by the LAN and internetworking manufacturers, who are looking at ATM based hub and intermediate networking interfaces, respectively. From the internetworking perspective this means that ATM interfaces for bridges and routers will be available shortly but there will be many multi-

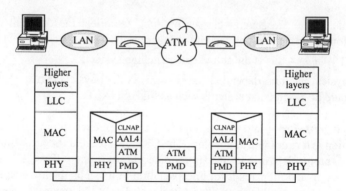

Figure 16.16   An ATM switch supporting bridged LANs.

vendor compatibility problems due to the lack of experience in implementing and using these systems. It is advisable to avoid such systems until the late 1990s, thereby letting the standards and technology stabilize and also letting prices decrease.

16.4.3 Photonic networks

Photonic networks is the term applied to very high speed optical networks which have carrier rates well into the gigabits region, typically 1–100 Gbps. This means that the bearer systems start to provide what appears to be unlimited bandwidth at relatively low cost and so concerns about network utilization efficiency become irrelevant. Instead the central design criteria becomes one of the selection of an effective and fair multiple access system. The essential element in the photonic network is the fibre optic cabling and the use of full optical coupling so that there is no electro-optic conversion until the signal needs to be processed by a network adapter. Suitable SMFs provide the necessary bandwidth (thousands of GHz) across long distances (tens of kilometres) and the 'unlimited' bandwidth is created when many of these are bundled together to create a single cable; such systems support bandwidths of thousands of teraHertz.

  As discussed earlier, the problem with very high speed systems is ensuring that the bandwidth is allocated where necessary and in particular to ensure that active nodes are not limited due to lack of bandwidth. In most time based systems each node has either a limited transmission period or else they must compete against each other to maintain their right of transmission. These approaches are particularly useful in bandwidth limited systems – that is, where the user population loads exceeds the capabilities of the network. If the bandwidth limitation is removed then it is possible to make inefficient use of it in return for other capabilities, for example access which is unlimited by the activities of the other users. For fibre based systems this form of access is supplied by WDMA and CDMA.

  The advantage of CDMA and WDMA is that the access time interdependence of the users is removed and the bandwidth is allocated to active users only. The consequence of this is that the receivers have to be more complex so that they can pick out the signals intended for them from the full entire bandwidth of the channel. In the case of WDMA the discrete wavelengths can be allocated according to a number of different criteria, for example related to the source or destination nodes, but one of the more recently proposed schemes makes use of wavelength switching. In wavelength switching the signal is transported by different wavelengths in the same manner as packet switching makes use of different physical links according to their availability. In such a system it is possible to adopt many of the established packet switching techniques and create analogous ones without needing a meshed architecture. The CDMA techniques are a combination of the TDMA and FDMA systems and are conceptually very difficult to appreciate. They make very inefficient use of the bandwidth, some 1–5% utilization, but provide unrestricted access to and use of the channel (irrespective of the load already on, or expected to be on, the network) and provide various other functions as an intrinsic property of the signalling system, such as privacy, noise resilience, and so on.

Photonic networks are between ten and twenty years in the future and so the only reason they are discussed here is to provide some perspective on how to create networks that will contain at least some of the elements common to those new systems. The clearest indication is that fibre optic cabling will have an even more significant role in such networks and consequently a 'fibre backbone' should be considered as an essential step in the enhancement of any network. This backbone should consist of many SMF cores – at least twice as many as you require for the system and its fault tolerance – thereby ensuring a reasonable potential for growth. In general fibre-to-the-desk is currently unnecessary and in the longer term this form of user access will be supported using fibre hubs on the backbone – hub technology is developing rapidly, so it is wise to purchase these as and when required and not to stockpile them for the future.

16.4.4 CATV based data networks

Within the UK, cabling companies are being awarded the franchises for community antenna television (CATV) services on a regional basis – the USA is several years ahead of the UK and Europe with respect to the installation of CATV. At present the CATV infrastructures are based upon a hierarchical star architecture with all but the smallest amount of bandwidth used for the distribution of the television signals. The return path bandwidth is unused except for the occasional retrieval of control signals.

The cabling companies are also supplying a telephone service and, in an increasing number of franchises, a primary and basic rate ISDN capability. Both the telephone and ISDN services are interconnected to the systems available from other suppliers, in the UK, for example, BT and Mercury. The cabling companies are now evaluating the potential for data communications across the return channel on the CATV infrastructure, that is, the path from the user to the head-end. Several multiple access schemes are being evaluated and in the USA some of these systems are now available commercially. The multiple access schemes under consideration are:

- Cell relay – this technique is being evaluated for all types of infrastructures, not just CATV, but at present the cost of the ATM interfaces is too prohibitive for this type of application.

- DQDB – the IEEE 802.6 committee is evaluating ways in which the DQDB MAC can be used on CATV and similar infrastructures;

- Broadband ethernet – these systems are already available commercially for CATV infrastructures and bridges, routers, terminal servers and transceiver concentrators can now be purchased.

The first generic information services, such as electronic mail, on CATV from the cabling companies will appear within the next two to three years but these will be available on the ISDN systems even sooner. This means that the user will have a greater range of telecommunications suppliers to choose from and if the current trends are maintained then the traditional suppliers will have to significantly reduce their costs to compete with the cabling companies.

16.5   Internetworking

During the next few years, network architectures will become both more complex and more simple. Their topologies will become more simple as they are reduced to hubs interconnected by a limited number of high speed links but on the other hand the hubs themselves will become more sophisticated and will support a very wide range of protocols. In some cases the hubs may also become the file servers. Eventually, the internetwork architecture, as shown in Figure 16.17, will be based upon a high speed backbone BISDN which will support:

- Satellite systems such as VSAT and the direct broadcast satellite TV services, including high definition TV.

- Networks which conform to different flavours of the OSI/RM, the Internet and proprietary systems. Gateways and routers will also be available between the different networks.

- The public and private NISDNs and ISLNs which will support local communities and will provide services such as multimedia communications.

- The mobile and personal communications systems, which are currently tied into the PSTN system on a country by country basis and which will form an integrated pan European network.

- The CATV data infrastructure across which it will be possible to access services such as video and music on demand, regional information databases, as well as providing an interactive multimedia teleworking environment.

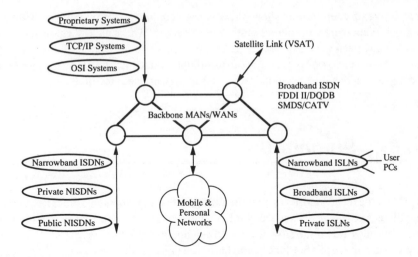

Figure 16.17 An integrated future.

At a more detailed level there will be a considerable evolution in the nature of internetworking devices and services. This evolution will be driven by the manufacturers, who will have to continually renovate their products in order to maintain their profit margins and to extend their usefulness to users. Significant changes in the relationships between the different manufacturers will also occur, with many of the smaller specialist companies being absorbed by the larger ones; this has already happened in the hub market. The issues of most significance will include:

- The router market will continue to expand, the bridge and repeater markets will remain stable but there will be a marked decrease in the use of gateways.

- Network management systems will increase in sophistication and will become integrated into the backbone and local architectures. Security will be the most significant concern, including resilience against the spread of viruses.

- X.25 will undergo a further evolution, it will always exist, and systems based upon fast switching (using frame and cell relay) will be introduced. This will permit X.25 applications to access the new bearer services.

- The new applications will be dependent upon the mixed traffic carrying capabilities of the broadband systems. It will be essential for the network to support integrated, interactive voice, data, video and graphics at the very least.

- Very high speed computer interface systems will be introduced to hub systems. These will include the high performance protocol interface (HIPPI) and fibre channel (FC) which will support bus interface speeds well in excess of 1 Gbps.

- The ISO/Internet uncertainty, in the rivalry between the OSI/RM and the TCP/IP family, will continue. The Internet protocols have been widely accepted by industry but these too are under threat from proprietary systems such as Windows NT and its infrastructure.

Irrespective of your point of view, there is one certainty – interoperability will be a major problem in networking for many years to come. The standardization activities have already been very successful – LANs are a powerful reflection of this – but the new range of technology is adding great uncertainty and so there will be many problems of compatibility as it is installed in established network architectures.

16.6   Summary

At present the most significant network infrastructure developments are related to the use of intermediate WAN systems for LAN interconnection. Current WAN throughput capabilities are far too slow for the current number of interconnected LANs. The only way to remove this bottleneck is to introduce radically different switching systems and to provide an integrated access infrastructure. In conclusion:

- The future user services will be supplied by the integrated services digital network (ISDN) and the integrated services local network (ISLN) architectures. These will supply mixed service integration (voice, data, video and so on) across an integrated traffic bearer system.

- All new bearer systems will conform to the synchronous digital hierarchy/ synchronous optical network (SDH/SONET). The SDH/SONET is a bandwidth plan that will eventually integrate all communication bearer systems.

- The new LAN/MAN technology will be fibre based and, initially, will take the form of the fibre distributed data interface (FDDI) or the FDDI II. In the longer term both of these will be superseded by cell based switching systems.

- Cableless, or wireless, LANs (CLANs or WLANs or LAWNs) are undergoing standardization and several new systems are being introduced. The new high speed CLAN will be called HiPerLAN and will support a data rate of 20 Mbps.

- New high speed carrier services based upon the frame and cell relay technologies will be introduced. The cell relay switching technology is based upon the asynchronous transfer mode (ATM). Other technologies include the distributed queue dual bus (DQDB) and the AT&T switched multimegabit data stream (SMDS) metropolitan area networks.

- The future LAN architectures will be based upon optical technology to supply almost unlimited bandwidths. Long-term planning of networks should therefore include the replacement of copper backbones by their fibre equivalents.

17

Final Thoughts

17.1   Networks

The past ten years have seen a huge shift in the ways that people work and the manner in which organizations do business. The gradual but increasing rate of growth in the use of personal computers (PCs) and local area networks (LANs) has produced a move away from the centralized corporate mainframe emphasis towards a distributed individual centred work environment in which users have more control over when and how they work. Unfortunately this shift has two important consequences:

- The potential profits available to companies offering distributed networking equipment are so large that this has attracted many different manufacturers to enter the market with their own proprietary systems or implementations of standardized systems. The user now has the problem of selecting the most suitable system from a plethora of available options.

- The adoption of a distributed approach still requires the interconnection of all the users and so a new range of devices are required to provide this connectivity. A further complication is that this interconnectivity can take place at several different levels of functional capability and so once again the choice of the most suitable solution is made more complex.

Added to these changes are the problems created by the rapidly changing technology and the conflicting attitudes of the people involved, the business managers, the network users and the network administrators. These two pressures completely define the underlying problems of networking and internetworking. Technology is changing and will continue to change at a very rapid pace (product development is typically nine months from concept to market-place) whereas it is unreasonable to expect a system to change as quickly.

The communications environment in the modern office is dominated by ethernet and Token Ring based systems, or more formally the IEEE 802.3 and IEEE 802.5, respectively. There is, however, a perceived need to provide increasingly faster networks and so in the last few years the fibre distributed data interface (FDDI) has been promoted as the high speed (100 Mbps) alternative to ethernet and Token Ring. It has only just started to establish itself commercially and it is now being threatened by the new cell relay technologies. Cell relay is already being advocated as the future technology for providing high speed (155–620 Mbps) LAN based switching as well as for wide area connectivity – if cell relay is as successful as predicted then it will remove the fundamental differences between local, metropolitan and wide area networks.

One of the underlying themes of the new technologies (this is especially true of LANs) is their conformance to the open systems interconnection seven-layer reference model (OSI/RM). The aim of such conformance is to ensure that new and different systems are vendor independent (resulting, at least in principle, in the end of the necessity of one-stop shopping) and that they can all be interconnected to produce an integrated network infrastructure capable of supporting all of the needs of the globally distributed user community. The success of this approach is reflected in the ease with which it is possible to change a network from one based upon ethernet to one which uses Token Ring. The adoption of the agreed international standards means that this change can be completed quickly by removing all of the ethernet cards and replacing them with Token Ring cards. The next and final change is to replace all of the ethernet drivers with their Token Ring equivalents and to bind these new drivers into the network operating system. In the case of Novell NetWare 386 and later releases such an upgrade, including card replacement, can be completed in under fifteen minutes per node.

One of the other aspects of this standardization is that in many cases it is also possible to change the physical cabling infrastructure (for example, from fibre optic to twisted pair) without changing the network adapters. The considerably lower cost of unshielded twisted pair (UTP) cable (some six times cheaper than fibre optic and coax) and the fact that American telephone cable is of sufficient quality to support data transfer has promoted the rapid development of UTP based versions of LANs; this interest has already stretched to the copper distributed data interface (CDDI), the copper based version of the FDDI, and even to cell relay across UTP.

The fate of network designers, engineers and support staff is similar to that suffered by all IT related personnel – a failure of empathy between themselves and higher management. The fault for this lies in both camps; higher management feels threatened (caused by their exposure to increasingly expensive and complex technical systems about which they have little or no understanding but upon which the welfare of their company depends) and betrayed (caused by the perceived failure of their technical staff to provide stable and reliable networks which provide the necessary capabilities but at a reasonable price), whereas the technical staff feel frustrated (caused by their inability to provide the requested level of service due to limitations on their budgets, thereby restricting the amount of equipment available for system testing and continual renovation) and misunderstood (caused by their impression that higher management do not appreciate the extent to which the network supports the current and future well-being of the company). Both points of view are equally true but both parties are equally responsible for these misunderstandings.

It is essential that higher management have among them at least one individual who is their technical expert in terms of IT – it is particularly important that this individual is not just a technical expert in the direct markets of the company but is also very aware of the wider aspects of the modern technologies available to help those markets. Likewise, it is essential that the network support and related teams are made fully aware of the financial constraints placed upon all elements of the organization and are requested to show how their proposals directly and indirectly affect the financial well-being of the company. In both cases this is only possible if a degree of mutual trust has been established and if a clearly defined set of professional procedures is used by the company with respect to the networking team.

One particularly sensitive but useful procedure is the creation of an internal accounting system which reflects the utilization of the network by the different groups within the company. This would include equivalent costs for moving an individual from one network location to another, connecting new users both physically and logically (entering user accounts and so on), charging according to link utilization and so on. This form of system is simple to create and implement (it should occur as a natural process of a well run network and company) and provides to all groups within a company a highly visible way of showing the use and importance of the network. The next step in the development of this system is to relate this internal cost and service to the equivalent increase in cost effectiveness, and so profitability, of the company; this is not easy and is susceptible to many misunderstandings but if a system can be agreed it provides the most effective way to show the strengths (high utilization for reasonable expenditure) and weaknesses (excessive expenditure relative to poor utilization) of the network.

Recall that in Chapter 1 it was argued that interconnected LAN systems were being used because of the combined pressures of the enabling technologies, the marketplace and the users' needs (see Figure 1.3). This means that the shape of the network is a consequence of events and not the cause. This is consistent with the three recurring themes in networking which unfortunately tend to become forgotten: networks exist to support users. If the technology does not exist then the network cannot be built and networks require cost effective investment. Both higher management and network engineers must always keep these in mind.

17.2   Internetworking

One of the most confusing aspects of internetworking is the conflict between the *de jure* standards (as typified by the OSI/RM and the IEEE), the *de facto* or industry standards (as typified by the Internet's TCP/IP) and the proprietary systems (Digital's DECnet, IBM's SNA and so on). In the long term, all networks should be expected to conform to the *de jure* standards, thereby replacing their *de facto* equivalents, which should be seen as transitory and should be used for supporting the migration from proprietary to OSI/RM conformant systems. Many people are now predicting that the migration from TCP/IP to OSI/RM will never occur. These predictions are founded on the belief that the OSI/RM will never be sufficiently mature and responsive for industry whereas the Internet protocols have already achieved that status, as reflected by the large number of commercially available products based upon the Internet protocols. A more cynical belief would be that the migration to the Internet protocols has been so traumatic for many organizations that yet another change would be too much for the users and the business managers to even contemplate.

The original aim of the designers of the OSI/RM was to impose a single networking philosophy and to support this with a heavily restricted range of network systems. Manufacturers have eagerly accepted the philosophy but have rejected the restrictions and so internetworking devices, or relays, have been created to link these different systems together. These relays fall into one of four categories:

- Repeaters (an OSI/RM physical layer device) – these are used to extend the physical capabilities of a LAN so that it can be used in environments which exceed the limitations imposed by the engineering technology, for example to connect more users, cover greater distances and so on. Repeater linked LANs must be similar, only their cabling systems can be different.

- Bridges (an OSI/RM data link layer device) – these are used to connect together two physical networks to create a logical network. In the case of media access control (MAC) bridges the LANs must be similar, whereas link bridges can connect different types of LANs. Bridges are used to improve the performance of the physical network by breaking it into several linked segments and by providing fault tolerance.

- Routers (an OSI/RM network layer device) – these are used to connect together different types of subnetwork to create a single network. The only restriction on the use of a router is that the different networks must use a common network layer protocol. Routers are normally used to provide reliable interconnection across a WAN infrastructure.

- Gateways (an OSI/RM transport layer to applications layer device) – these are used to connect networks which use different types of protocols but which share a common application need such as file access and transfer. Gateways provide protocol translation and are generally used to interconnect different proprietary network architectures, for example Digital's DECnet to IBM's SNA.

In general the functional complexity, and hence the cost, of these relays increases the higher up the OSI/RM they operate; the cheapest repeater costs about £400 whereas the more expensive gateways cost about £75 000. In many applications it is unclear whether to use a bridge or a router and this choice is being further complicated by the fact that the distinction between bridges and routers is becoming less clear as many manufacturers supply hybrid devices termed routing bridges, bridging routers and brouters, depending on their market roots. A further development is the introduction of the switch which is a low latency bridge. The general rule-of-thumb of a bridge manufacturer is 'bridge if possible and route if necessary' and for a router manufacturer it is 'route if possible and bridge if necessary'. Each design has to be treated on its own merits.

While it is relatively simple to envisage, in general terms, where internetworking devices should be used it is another matter to develop a network design methodology based upon sound engineering principles and which can be used to determine precisely when and where they should be used. Without such a methodology, it is impossible to design a network based upon the accurate prediction of its capabilities and the certainty that it can support the defined requirement; this is the position in which network designers currently find themselves. Instead, the design process becomes heavily dependent upon previous experience and the copying of what works elsewhere. Although this approach is successful it is not the basis on which to justify the expenditure of what may be thousands or hundreds of thousands of pounds. Given that there is no sound network engineering design methodology there are some rules-of-thumb that need to be followed:

- Use a logical approach and start by determining the needs of the users, the network support team and the physical constraints imposed by the installation environment.

- Assume that all of the performance constraints are unrealistically low and so provide a generous tolerance, for example at least 50%.

- Maintenance accounts for 80% of the network's lifetime cost so adopt an attitude of 'design for maintainability'. Be conservative and adopt a strategy of 'defensive design' – assume that if a failure can occur then not only will it occur but it will cause the most serious consequences possible.

- Ensure that the network can be managed, that it relies upon as few support staff as possible, that humans will abuse it in whatever manner is possible and that the average demands placed upon it will be significantly different from these defined during the requirements specification.

Recall, once more, that in Chapter 1 the classical corporate network was described as being based upon the use of packet switched data networks, such as X.25, and low speed modem links via the telephone network, which reflected the centralized manner of working on the corporate computing systems. The availability of cheap high speed networks based upon LAN technology has precipitated the adoption of decentralized working methods and as a consequence the imposition of corporate controlled purchasing has also been significantly relaxed. In turn, this has produced a wide diversity of installed networks and so the commercial effectiveness of an organization is now determined by its ability to interconnect all of these systems to provide an integrated network capable of reliably supplying the necessary information, to the right place, at the right time and in the right form.

17.3   The future

The future trends for networking are quite clear: bearer service speeds will continue increasing, the amount of available bandwidth will continue increasing and the rate of technological development will continue increasing. This means that the design and installation of even the newest network will be implemented using old technology and so the degree to which a network can be continually renovated will determine the extent to which it can provide the users with a competitive edge. From the users' point of view, the services which will be available at the end of the century will offer them, by today's standards, an extraordinarily rich set of integrated functions. Unfortunately, from the network engineers' point of view these services will almost certainly require extremely complex network architectures. This is because these new networks will:

- Be required to support hundreds of thousands of mobile users who will need transparent access to their own unique environment no matter where they are physically located. This means the same services must be supplied to the user whether they are in the office, at home, on a train, in an aircraft and so on.

- Be required to provide an integrated, interactive multimedia environment in which voice, video, data, text, graphics information is transported across the network in real time. The presentation of this information will have to be available to the user on their palm-top systems as well as at their workstation.

- Transparently interconnect the old and new technologies. Too much investment has been made in the present LAN systems for them to be cast aside and so a new generation of internetworking devices will be required to provide the needed connectivity. The fastest networks will be transferring information at about 2 Gbps whereas the original 4 Mbps Token Ring systems will still be operational.

- Still suffer from the problems of integrating standardized and proprietary systems. There is no doubt that most systems will conform to the OSI/RM but the wide range of permitted profiles does not remove the problem of integration. More importantly, manufacturers will be offering systems with appealing proprietary features which would only be supported by themselves, thereby perpetuating one-stop shopping.

Perhaps the most appropriate analogy for the treatment of networks is to consider an equivalent attitude towards a car.

A young man visits his local car salesroom and buys a new small car because it is reliable, functional and cheap. Within a few days he returns the car explaining how impressed he is but expresses concern that other cars are faster (citing the sports car of a close friend as a particular example). The salesman explains that the car cannot be replaced but that they can install a new 'super' engine, but at a cost. The young man considers the offer and eventually agrees to the modification. A few hours later he drives away in his 200 kmph car.

A week later the young man returns to the garage once again and explains to the salesman that the car is now too small (he now wants to take all his friends with him at the same time) and that he would like room for ten passengers. The salesman explains that this is possible but that it will take a few days to complete and will of course cost more money. The young man considers this new offer and eventually agrees to the proposal and takes a taxi home. A few days later he returns to the garage to collect his modified car. Upon seeing the car he expresses some surprise at the new middle section which has been inserted to accommodate the new seats but he is eventually pacified when the changes are explained to him. He pays and drives away, only to return some two hours later. The car now has a top speed of only 50 kmph – what has happened? The salesman explains about the extra weight, the consequent decrease in power to weight ratio and the resulting lower top speed but does propose a solution. Another new engine can be placed in the car and at quite a reasonable price. The exasperated young man reluctantly agrees to this suggestion and once again takes a taxi home. A few days later he returns to the garage to collect his car and this time he is elated at the speed of the car when taken on a test drive. He drives happily home.

Unfortunately the following day the car is badly damaged in an accident and all of the occupants (all eleven of them) are hospitalized for several days. The accident occurs when the car is travelling at full speed (200 kmph) on an open road, when the driver is forced to brake suddenly. The brakes, still those of the original car, are totally inadequate for the speed and weight of the new car, hence the near fatal accident.

The history of networking is littered with problems of every kind but most networks work correctly most of the time – recall the 94% figure. While it is true that the users' needs are quintessential in networking, there are times when these needs must be tempered for the overall benefit of the network and user community. However, the situation must be clearly explained to the users, in terms they can appreciate and with empathy, otherwise there will be continual conflicts between the users and the administrators. All modern-day organizations rely upon computers and communications; networks and internetworking are fundamental to these. Therefore, it is essential that they are designed, installed and maintained in a professional manner and that an adequate level of funding is supplied for this to be achieved.

References

Barnett R. and Maynard-Smith S. (1988) *Packet Switched Networks: Theory and Practice,* Sigma Press, p.274, ISBN 1–85058–095–2.

Bartee T.C., ed. (1989) *ISDN, DECnet and SNA Communications,* Howard W. Sams & Company, p.414, ISBN 0–672–22512–3.

Bird D. (1994) *Token Ring Network Design,* Addison-Wesley, p.270, ISBN 0–210–62760–4.

Black U. (1987) *Computer Networks: Protocols, Standards and Interfaces,* Prentice-Hall International, p.451, ISBN 0–13–166091–8.

Boggs D.R., Mogul J.C. and Kent C.A. (1988) *Measured Capacity of an Ethernet: Myths and Reality,* Digital Western Research Laboratory Research Report, Palo Alto.

Bridges S.P.M. (1986) *Low Cost Local Area Networks,* Sigma Press, p.182, ISBN 0–905104–86–2.

Buford J.F.K. (1994) *Multimedia Systems,* Addison-Wesley, p.450, ISBN 0–201–53258–1.

Bux W. (1981) *Local Area Subnetworks: A Performance Comparison,* IEEE Transactions on Communications, Vol. COM-29, October 1981, pp.1465–1473.

Bux W., Closs F.H., Kuemmerle K., Keller H.J. and Mueller H.R. (1983) *Architecture and Design of a Reliable Token Ring Network,* IEEE Journal on Selected Areas of Communications, Vol. SAC–1, November, pp.756–766.

Cheong V.E. and Hirchheim R.A. (1987) *Local Area Networks: Issues, Products and Developments,* John Wiley & Sons, p.190, ISBN 0–471–90134–2.

Chou W., ed. (1983) *Computer Communications: Vol I–Principles,* Prentice-Hall, p.449, ISBN 0–13–165043–2.

Cypser R.J. (1992) *Evolution of an open communications architecture,* IBM Systems Journal, Vol. 31, No. 2, pp.161–188.

Datapro International (1994) *LANs & Internetworking: Vols 1 & 2,* McGraw-Hill Communications & Networking Solutions.

Deasington R.J. (1986) *X.25 Explained: Protocols for Packet Switching Networks*, 2nd Edition, Ellis Horwood, p.131, ISBN 0–13–972175–4.

Flint D.C. (1983) *The Data Ring Main*, Wiley Heydon Publication, p.375, ISBN 0–471–26251–X.

Göhring H.-G. and Jasper G. (1993) *PC-Host Communications: Strategies for Implementation*, Addison-Wesley, p.362, ISBN 0–201–56894–2.

Göhring H.-G. and Kauffels F.-J. (1992) *Token Ring: Principles, Perspectives and Strategies*, Addison-Wesley, p.322, ISBN 0–201–56895–0.

Halsall F. (1992) *Data Communications, Computer Networks and Open Systems*, 3rd Edition, Addison-Wesley, p.772, ISBN 0–201–56506–4.

Hammond J.L. and O'Reilly P. (1986) *Performance Analysis of Local Computer Networks*, Addison-Wesley, p.411, ISBN 0–201–11530–1.

Händel R, Huber M.N.and Schröder (1994) *ATM Networks: Concepts, Protocols, Applications*, 2nd Edition, Addison-Wesley, p.230, ISBN 0–201–42274–3.

Hegering H.-G. and Läpple A. (1993) *Ethernet: Building a Communications Infrastructure*, Addison-Wesley, p.389, ISBN 0–201–62405–2.

Held G. (1991) *Understanding Data Communications: From Fundamentals to Networking*, John Wiley & Sons, p.546, ISBN 0–471–93051–2.

Hopper A., Temple S. and Williamson R. (1986) *Local Area Network Design*, Addison-Wesley, p.184, ISBN 0–20113797–6.

Hunter H. (1993) *Local Area Networks: Making the Right Choices*, Addison-Wesley, p.323, ISBN 0–201–62763–9.

Hutchison D. (1988) *Local Area Network Architectures*, Addison-Wesley, p.264, ISBN 0–201–14216–3.

IEE (1992) *Radio LANs*, IEE Colloquium, Ref. No.1992/04, May 1992.

Janson P., Molva P., Zatti S. (1992) *Architectural Directions for Opening IBM Networks: The Case of OSI*, IBM Systems Journal, Vol. 31, No. 2, pp.313–335.

Jones V.C. (1988) *MAP/TOP Networking*, McGraw-Hill, p.289, ISBN 0–07–032806–4.

Kauffels F.-J. (1989) *Practical LANs Analysed*, Ellis Horwood, p.334, ISBN 0–7458–0254–0.

Kauffels F.-J. (1992) *Network Management: Problems, Standards and Strategies*, Addison-Wesley, p.275, ISBN 0–201–56534–X.

Klienrock L. (1992) *The Latency/Bandwidth Tradeoff in Gigabit Networks*, IEEE Communications Magazine, April, pp.36–40.

Knowles T., Larmouth J. and Knightson K.G. (1987) *Standards for Open Systems Interconnection*, BSP Professional Books, p.338, ISBN 0–632–01868–2.

Langsford A. and Moffett J.D. (1993) *Distributed Systems Management*, Addison-Wesley, p.307, ISBN 0–201–63176–8.

Lynch D.C. and Rose M.T. (1993) *Internet System Handbook*, Addison-Wesley, p.790, ISBN 0–201–56741–5.

MacKinnon D., McCrum W. and Sheppard D. (1990) *Open Systems Interconnection*, Computer Science Press, p.254, ISBN 0–7167–8180–8.

Meijer A. (1987) *Systems Network Architecture: A Tutorial*, Pitman/Wiley, p.223, ISBN 0–273–02842–1.

Metcalfe R.M. and Boggs D.R. (1976) *Ethernet: distributed packet switching for local computer networks*, Communications of the ACM, Vol.19, No.7, pp.398–404.

Miller M.A. (1990) *LAN Protocol Handbook*, Prentice-Hall, p.324, ISBN 0–13–521378–9.

Miller M.A. (1991) *Internetworking: A Guide to Network Communications LAN to LAN; LAN to WAN*, Prentice-Hall, p.425, ISBN 0–13–365974–7.

Nowshadi F. (1994) *Managing NetWare*, Addison-Wesley, p.657, ISBN 0–201–63194–6.

Partridge C. (1994) *Gigabit Networking*, Addison-Wesley, p.396, ISBN 0–201–56333–9.

Perlman R. (1992) *Interconnections: Bridges and Routers*, Addison-Wesley, p.389, ISBN 0–201–56332-0.

Piscitello D.M. and Chapin A.L. (1993) *Open Systems Networking: TCP/IP and OSI*, Addison-Wesley, p.600, ISBN 0–201–56334–7.

Proakis J.G. (1983) *Digital Communications*, McGraw-Hill, p.608, ISBM 0–07–Y66490–0.

Rose M.T. (1989) *The Open Book: A Practical Perspective on OSI*, Prentice-Hall, p.651, ISBN 0–13–643016–3.

Rose M.T. (1990) *The Simple Book: An Introduction to Management of TCP/IP-Based Internets*, Prentice-Hall, ISBN 0–13–812611–9.

Schäfer W. and De Meulen H. (1992) *Systems Network Architecture*, Addison-Wesley, p.222, ISBN 0–201–56533–1.

Schwaderer W.D. (1989) *IBM's Local Area Networks: Power Networking and Systems Connectivity*, Van Nostrand Reinhold, p.294, ISBN 0–442–20713–1.

Shannon C.E. and Weaver W. (1980) *The Mathematical Theory of Communication*, 8th Edition, University of Illonois Press, p.125, ISBN 0–252–72548–4.

Smith P. (1993) *Frame Relay: Principles and Applications*, Addison-Wesley, p.268, ISBN 0–201–62400–1.

Smythe, C. (1990) *Spread Spectrum Local Area Networks*, Tutorial at IEEE International Symposium on Spread Spectrum Techniques and Applications, September 1990, King's College, London.

Stallings W. (1990) *Handbook of Computer-Communications Standards: Vol.2–Local Area Network Standards*, 2nd Edition, Howard W. Sams & Company, p.274, ISBN 0–672–22698–7.

Stallings W. (1990a) ed., *Local Network Technology – Tutorial*, IEEE Computer Society Press, p.495, ISBN 0–8186–0825–0.

Stallings W. (1993) *Local and Metropolitan Area Networks*, 4th Edition, Macmillan, p.550, ISBN 0–02–415465–2.

Stallings W. (1994) *Data and Computer Communications*, 4th Edition, Macmillan Publishing Company, p.875, ISBN 0–02–4154415.

Tanenbaum A.S. (1988) *Computer Networks*, Prentice-Hall International Editions, 2nd Edition, p.658, ISBN 0–13–166836–6.

Tobagi F.A. (1986) Multiaccess Protocols and Real-Time Communications in Local Area Networks, Proceedings of the Advanced Seminar on Real-Time Local Area Networks, INRIA, April, pp.1–21.

Verma P.K. (1989) *Performance Estimation of Computer Communication: A Structured Approach*, Computer Science Press, p.133, ISBN 0–7167–8183–2.

Walford R.B. (1990) *Network System Architecture*, Addison-Wesley, p.384, ISBN 0–201–52409–0.

Washburn K. and Evans J.T. (1993) *TCP/IP: Running a Successful Network*, Addison-Wesley, p.537, ISBN 0–201–62765–5.

List of Abbreviations

AAL	ATM Adaptation Layer
AC	Access Control
ACMISE	Agent Common Management Information Service Element
ACSE	Association Control Service Elements
ADSP	AppleTalk Data Stream Protocol
AFP	AppleTalk Filing Protocol
ALS	Acknowledged Connectionless Service
AMP	Active Monitor Present (Token Ring)
APDU	Applications Protocol Data Unit
API	Applications Programming Interface
APPC	Applications Program-to-Program Communications (IBM)
APPI	Advanced Peer-to Peer Internetworking
APPN	Advanced Peer-to Peer Networking
ARL	Adjusted Ring Length
ARP	Address Resolution Protocol (Internet)
ARPANET	Advanced Research Projects Agency Network
ASE	Application Specific Element
ASME	Agent System Management Entity
ASN	Abstract Syntax Notation
ASP	AppleTalk Session Protocol
ATM	Asynchronous Transfer Mode
AUI	Attachment Unit Interface
BAS	Basic Activity Subset (OSI)
BCS	Basic Combined Subset (OSI)
BEC	Backward Error Recovery
BER	Bit Error Rate
BGP	Boundary Gateway Protocol

BISDN	Broadband Integrated Services Digital Network
BSS	Basic Synchronized Subset (OSI)
CASE	Common Application Service Element
CAU	Controlled Access Unit
CCIR	International Radio Consultative Committee
CCITT	International Telegraph and Telephony Consultative Committee
CCRSE	Concurrency, Commitment and Recovery Service Element
CD	Collision Detection
CDDI	Copper Distributed Data Interface
CDMA	Code Division Multiple Access
CEC	Central European Commission
CIM	Computer Integrated Manufacturing
CLAN	Cableless Local Area Network
CLNAP	Connectionless Network Access Protocol
CLNP	Connectionless Network Protocol (OSI)
CLNS	Connectionless Network Service
CLS	Connectionless Service
CLTP	Connectionless Transport Protocol (OSI)
CLTS	Connectionless Transport Service
CMIP	Common Management Information Protocol (OSI)
CMIS	Common Management Information Service
CMISE	Common Management Information Service Entity
CMOL	Common Management Over Link
CMOT	Common Management information protocol Over TCP/IP
COCF	Connection Oriented Common Functions
CONS	Connection Oriented Network Service
COS	Connection Oriented Service
COTS	Connection Oriented Transport Service
CRC	Cyclic Redundancy Check
CS	Convergence Sublayer
CSDN	Circuit Switched Data Network
CSMA/CD	Carrier Sense Multiple Access with Collision Detection
CS-MUX	Circuit Switched Multiplexer
CSTN	Circuit Switched Telephone Network
CT	DECnet/SNA gateway for Channel Transport
	Cordless Telephone
DAC	Dual Attachment Concentrator
DAS	Dual Attachment Station
DAT	Duplicate Address Test
DB-QPSX	Distributed Bus Queued Packet and Synchronous Switch
DCE	Data Circuit-Terminating Equipment
DDCMP	Digital Data Communications Message Protocol (Digital)
DEC	Digital Electronics Corporation

DECT	Digital Exchange Cellular Telephone
DES	Data Encryption Standard
DFC	Data Flow Control (IBM)
DIX	Digital Intel Xerox
DLC	Data Link Control
DLPDU	Data Link Protocol Data Unit
DLSw	Data Link Switching
DNA	Distributed Network Architecture (DEC)
DoD	Department of Defense
DPSK	Differential Phase Shift Keying
DQDB	Distributed Queue Dual Bus
DS	Directory Service
DSE	Data Switching Exchange
DTAM	Document Transfer and Access Management
DTE	Data Terminal Equipment
DTP	Data Transfer Protocol
DUA	Directory User Agent
DXE	DCE/DTE
ECMA	European Computer Manufacturers Association
EDI	Electronic Document Interchange
EFS	End Frame Sequence
EGP	Exterior Gateway Protocol
EIA	Electronics Industries Association
ELAP	Ethernet Link Access Protocol (AppleTalk)
EMA	Enterprise Management Architecture
EPA	Enhanced Performance Architecture
ES	End-System
ES-ES	End-System-End-System
ESH	End System Hello
ES-IS	End-System-Intermediate-System
ETSI	European Telecommunications Standards Institute
FC	Frame Control
FCS	Frame Check Sequence
FDDI	Fibre Distributed Data Interface
FDMA	Frequency Division Multiple Access
FEC	Forward Error Correction
FEP	Front End Processor
FFOL	FDDI Follow-On LAN
FMDS	Function Management Data Services (IBM)
FOIRL	Fibre Optic Inter Repeater Link
FPLMTS	Future Public Land Mobile Telecommunications System
FS	Frame Status
FTAM	File Transfer, Access and Management (OSI)

FTP	File Transfer Protocol (Internet)
GKS	Graphics Kernel System
GSM	Special Group Mobile
	Global System for Mobile Communications
HDLC	High-Level Data Link Control (ISO)
HIPPI	HIgh Performance Protocol Interface
HLM	Heterogeneous LAN Management
H-MUX	Hybrid Multiplexer
HRC	Hybrid Ring Control
IAN	Integrated Analogue Network
IBC	Integrated Broadband Communications
ICF	Isochronous Convergence Function
ICMP	Internet Control Message Protocol
IDN	Integrated Digital Network
IDP	Internet Datagram Protocol (XNS)
IDRP	Inter-Domain Routing Protocol
IEE	Institution of Electrical Engineers (UK)
IEEE	Institute of Electrical and Electronics Engineers (USA)
IGES	Initial Graphics Exchange Specification
IGRP	Interior Gateway Routing Protocol
ILG	Inter Link Gateway
I-MAC	Isochronous Media Access Control
ING	Inter Network Gateway
IP	Internet Protocol (Internet)
IPC	InterProcess Communications Protocol (VINES)
IPS	Internet Protocol Suite
IPX	Internetwork Packet Exchange (NetWare)
IS	Intermediate System
ISDN	Integrated Services Digital Network
ISH	Intermediate System Hello
IS-IS	Intermediate System-Intermediate System
ISLAN	Integrated Services Local Area Network
ISLN	Integrated Services Local Network
ISN	Integrated Services Network
ISO	International Organization for Standardization
ISP	International Standardized Profile
IT	Information Technology
ITP	Intelligent Twisted Pair
ITU	International Telecommunication Union (UN)
ITU-R	International Telecommunications Union–Radio
ITU-T	International Telecommunications Union–Telecommunications
IVD	Integrated Voice Data

JTM	Job Transfer and Manipulation
LAM	Lobe Access Module
LAN	Local Area Network
LAP	Link Access Protocol (CCITT/ISO)
LAPB	Link Access Protocol Balanced (CCITT/ISO)
LAPD	Link Access Protocol–Channel D (ISDN)
LAPE	Extended Link Access Protocol (CCITT)
LAPM	Link Access Protocols for Modems (CCITT/ISO)
LAPX	Link Access Protocol Extended (CCITT)
LAT	Local Area Transport (Digital)
LAWN	Local Area Wireless Network
LEG	Link Extension Gateway
LLC	Link Layer Control (Logical Link Control)
LU	Logical Unit (IBM)
MAC	Medium Access Control
MAN	Metropolitan Area Network
MAP	Manufacturing Automation Protocol
MAU	Media Access Unit
	Multistation Access Unit
MCF	MAC Common Functions
MEG	Medium Extension Gateway
MHS	Message Handling System
MIB	Management Information Base
MIC	Medium Interface Connection
MLL	Maximum Lobe Length
MMS	Manufacturing Message Service
MOTIS	Message Oriented Transfer Information System
MSASE	Management Specific Application Service Element
MSAU	Multistation Access Unit
MSME	Management System Management Entry
MTBF	Mean Time Between Failures
MTBSO	Mean Time Between Service Outages (CCITT)
MTD	Maximum Transmission Distance
MTTSR	Mean Time To Service Restoration (CCITT)
NAK	Negative Acknowledgement
NAU	Network Addressable Unit (IBM)
NCP	Network Core Protocol (NetWare)
NEG	Network Extension Gateway
NFS	Network File Service
NIA	Network Interface Adapter
NIC	Network Interface Card
NISDN	Narrowband Integrated Services Digital Network

NIST	National Institute of Standards and Technology (USA)
NMA	Network Management Architecture
NMAP	Network Manager Application Process
NMC	Network Management Centre
NOS	Network Operating System
NPDU	Network Protocol Data Unit
NPSI	Network Control Packet Switch Interface (SNA)
NSAP	Network Service Access Point
NT	Network Terminator
ODA	Office Document Architecture
OSCA	Open Systems Cabling Architecture
OSI	Open System Interconnection
OSI/RM	Open Systems Interconnection Reference Model
OSPF	Open Shortest Path First
OTDR	Optical Time Domain Reflectometer
PA	Prearbitrated
PABX	Private Automatic Branch Exchange
PAD	Packet Assembler/Disassembler
PC	Path Control (IBM)
PCI	Protocol Control Information
PCN	Personal Communications Network
PCN	Personal Communications System
PDN	Public Data Network
PDS	Premises Distribution System
PDU	Protocol Data Unit
PHY	Physical Layer
PICS	Protocol Implementation Conformance Statement
PLP	Packet Layer Protocol (CCITT/ISO)
PM	Physical Medium
POTS	Plain Old Telephone System
PPCI	Presentation Protocol Control Information
PPDU	Presentation Protocol Data Unit
PPP	Point-to-Point Protocol
PSDN	Packet Switched Data Network
PSS	Packet Switching Stream
PSTN	Public Switched Telephone Network
PTT	Postal, Telegraph and Telephone Administration
PU	Physical Unit (IBM)
QA	Queue Arbitrated
RARP	Reverse Address Resolution Protocol (Internet)
RFC	Request For Comment

RIP	Routing Information Protocol
ROSE	Remote Operations Service Element
RPC	Remote Procedural Call
	Root Path Cost
RTSE	Reliable Transfer Service Element
SAC	Single Attachment Concentrator
SAP	Service Access Point
	Service Advertisement Protocol (NetWare)
SAR	Segmentation And Reassembly
SAS	Single Attachment Station
SASE	Specific Application Service Element
SDE	Secure Data Exchange
SDLC	Synchronous Data Link Control
SDMA	Space Division Multiple Access
SEAL	Simple and Efficient Adaptation Layer
SILS	Secure Interoperable LAN System
SLA	Service Level Agreement
SLIP	Serial Link Internet Protocol (Internet)
SMDS	Switched Multi-megastream Data Service
SME	System Management Entity
SMF	Single Mode Fibre
SMFA	System Management Functional Areas
SMIP	System Management Information Protocol (OSI)
SMIS	System Management Information Service
SMP	Session Management Protocol
SMT	Station Management
SMTP	Simple Mail Transport Protocol (Internet)
SNA	Systems Network Architecture (IBM)
SNAP	Subnetwork Access Protocol
SNAcP	Subnetwork Access Protocol (OSI)
SNDC(P)	Subnetwork Dependent Convergence (Protocol)
SNIC(P)	Subnetwork Independent Convergence (Protocol)
SNMP	Simple Network Management Protocol (Internet)
SNR	Signal to Noise Ratio
SONET	Synchronous Optical Network (CCITT standard)
SPDU	Session Protocol Data Unit
SPX	Sequenced Packet Exchange (NetWare)
SQE	Signal Quality Error
SRT	Source Route Transparent
SSCP	Systems Services Control Point (IBM)
SSMA	Spread Spectrum Multiple Access
STDM	Statistical Time Division Multiplexing
STM	Synchronous Transport Mode
STP	Shielded Twisted Pair

STS	Synchronous Transport Signal
SWP	Sliding Window Protocol
TA	Terminal Adaptor
TAG	Technical Advisory Group
TCP	Transmission Control Protocol (Internet)
TCU	Trunk Coupling Unit
TDMA	Time Division Multiple Access
TDR	Time Domain Reflectometer
TEG	Transport Extension Protocol
TFTP	Trivial File Transfer Protocol (Internet)
TOP	Technical and Office Protocol
TP	Transport Protocol
	Twisted Pair
TPDDI	Twisted Pair Distributed Data Interface
TPDU	Transport Protocol Data Unit
TRT	Token Ring Tester
UA	User Agent
UDC	Universal Data Connection
UDP	User Datagram Protocol (Internet)
UHF	Ultra High Frequency
UMTS	Universal Mobile Telecommunication System
UN	United Nations
UNA	Upstream Neighbour Address (Token Ring)
UNI	User Network Interface
UNMA	Unified Network Management Architecture
UOS	Unconfirmed Connection Oriented Service
UPS	Uninterruptable Power Supply
UTP	Unshielded Twisted Pair
VICP	VINES Internet Control Protocol
VMTP	Versatile Message Transfer Protocol (Internet)
VT	Virtual Terminal
WAN	Wide Area Network
WARC	World Administrative Radio Conference
WLAN	Wireless Local Area Network
XNS	Xerox Network System
XTP	Express Transfer Protocol
ZIP	Zone Information Protocol (AppleTalk)

B

Glossary of Terms

Acknowledged connectionless (ALS). This is a connectionless service (datagram) but it demands that the receipt of each frame is acknowledged. This form of service is used in real-time environments where acknowledgement of the data is used to confirm the completion of the data transfer or to provide a rapid link error detection capability.

American National Standards Institute (ANSI). ANSI is the American equivalent to the British Standards Institution. It is the coordinating body for standards implemented in the USA on a voluntary basis and is the USA representative on ISO. It is also responsible for its own standards on topics such as encryption and LANs.

Baseband. This is the transmission of information without the use of a carrier frequency. The data is sent using the natural bandwidth of the signal and so in the case of a digital signal inter-symbol interference can be a problem.

Bridge. The interconnection of two LANs at their data link layers requires the use of a bridge. Most bridges link only the same type of LANs, for example IEEE 802.3/802.3 and IEEE 802.5/802.5 (currently termed MAC bridges); however there are some which will provide IEEE 802.3/802.5 interconnection (being termed link bridges). The important features of a bridge are their data filtering and data forwarding capacities. There are local and remote bridges which support back-to-back LAN connections and long distance connection (almost unlimited) using an intermediate link (for example fibre optic, kilostream and so on) respectively. Remote bridges must be used in pairs.

Bridge/router (routing bridge). This is an internetworking device produced by a bridge manufacturer but which has some layer 2 (OSI/RM data link layer) routing functionality. This relay provides MAC frame routing capability so that load balancing and triangulation can be supported by the network. At present it is essential that all of the connected bridge/routers are supplied by the same manufacturer.

British Standards Institution (BSI). The BSI is the British voluntary standards organization and is the UK representative at the ISO. It is involved in all UK standards activity and failure to comply with the relevant standards can be used as a basis for legal prosecution, particularly if compliance is wrongly asserted by a supplier.

Broadband. The transmission of data using a predefined and closely controlled bandwidth. Normally this technique employs frequency division multiplexing, thereby ensuring that the concurrent data streams do not interfere. Radio and TV stations use this type of system when carrying the signals of the different channels.

Broadcast. The transmission of data to all (or at least most) of the nodes connected to the network. Typical examples of such networks are the TV and radio transmissions where the end hosts are receive only. Problems occur when any form of data or acknowledgement feedback is required from the receivers.

Brouter. This is a hybrid bridge and router device which is capable of being either a bridge, or a router or a brouter. Brouters normally make use of proprietary intermediate link protocols and so the ability to cost effectively change the role of the relay is counter-balanced by its vendor dependence.

Carrier sense multiple access (CSMA). CSMA is a restrained form of chaotic channel access. Nominally the users can transmit data whenever required (ALOHA systems); however, they must first sense the state of the channel. This sensing is to determine if any other transmissions are present. If not then transmission may occur, otherwise a backoff and wait algorithm is applied and the sense process repeated. This system is ideal for bursty traffic with few nodes; however, contentions (simultaneously active transmitters) do occur and these must be removed and resolved by the use of some appropriate backoff and retry algorithm.

Cell relay. The very high speed bearer systems (data rates in excess of 45 Mbps) are expected to carry their information in small packets, or cells. These cells provide the most efficient way of multiplexing different types of data onto the same channel, for example voice and data. The protocol being widely promoted to support cell based systems is called the asynchronous transfer mode (ATM) and this operates at 155 Mbps and 620 Mbps.

Circuit switched. The establishment of a common physical connection between two communicating devices. The important feature is that the same actual link will always be used whenever the nodes in question communicate with each other. Telephone systems are circuit switched.

Code division multiple access (CDMA). The separation of signals in signal space is known as code division multiplexing. The dimensionality of a signal is dependent on its duration and bandwidth and so by the careful construction of the required signals it can be arranged that there is no mutual interference – that is, orthogonal signals. The most important aspect of such a system is that all CDMA signals can co-exist simultaneously (in the time and frequency domains) and so this technique provides a means of allocating bandwidth as and where required.

Common management information service/common management information protocol (CMIS/CMIP). These are responsible for the integrated management control across OSI/RM based networks. CMIS is an application service which either supports the management SASE (MSASE) or provides the remote agent interface (ACMISE). CMIP is the peer communications protocol used to realize the service.

Computer network. A network which connects computer driven devices such as file stores and word processors. These are characterized by high point-to-point data rates, no tolerance to errors and minimal delay requirements. Sophisticated protocols are normally required to support these types of systems.

Connectionless. This is more commonly termed a datagram or fire-and-forget protocol. The basic principle is for the initiator to construct the data and then send it, without expecting a response from the respondent. Such a protocol is used when nodes send different data to many other nodes and it is particularly useful in environments where the ambient electronic noise is relatively low.

Connection oriented. This protocol form is based upon the virtual circuit principle. A connection, or link, is maintained between the communicating hosts. This link provides bi-directional communications between the hosts and so it is commonly used when two, or more, hosts have a significant amount of data to transfer over a prolonged period. If this is not the case then the hosts waste processing time and effort in maintaining idle links.

Copper distributed data interface (CDDI). This is a copper based version of the fibre distributed data interface. The current developments are investigating the transmission of data at 100 Mbps down shielded and unshielded twisted pair (STP and UTP, respectively). This would then provide high speed LAN connectivity down established structured cabled installations.

Data network. A network which connects human driven devices together, such as radio, television, facsimile, word processors, and so on. Typically, these sorts of networks are more tolerant because the end user (the human) is capable, when willing and necessary, of a considerable amount of interpretation of the delivered data, for example poor telephone connections.

DECnet. This is the generic term used by DEC to refer to their range of networking devices – including hardware and software. A central feature of DECnet is the distributed networking architecture (DNA) which refers to the protocol architecture used to provide communications between Digital/Digital and Digital/other systems.

Directory service (DS). The is the OSI application responsible for maintaining the address directories in both white and yellow pages form. The DS is also responsible for managing system-wide security, for example, key distribution.

Distributed network. This is a subset of the available computer networks, which is itself a subset of the data network. A distributed network is also one application of a computer network in which the operational capability shown to a user is a reflection of the entire network and not just that of the local workstation with some communications capability.

Distributed queue dual bus (DQDB). The DQDB is the metropolitan area network as defined by the IEEE 802.6 committee. It utilizes a dual bus configuration which is usually based upon a 155 Mbps fibre optic channel (the standard does not actually define a data rate and so this figure has been chosen for conformance with the synchronous digital hierarchy). The DQDB employs a slotted asynchronous transfer mode structure (similar to cell relay), which means that in the longer term it can be integrated into the broadband ISDN (BISDN) systems.

Ethernet. This is the market leader in terms of number of LANs sold. The Ethernet LAN is officially known as the IEEE 802.3 or ISO 8802/3 LAN architecture – Ethernet (as licensed by Xerox) is in fact subtly different from the formal ISO 8802/3 systems. Ethernet was introduced in the mid to late 1970s and supplies a 10 Mbps carrying capacity for applications that are not sensitive to real-time constraints.

European Computer Manufacturers Association (ECMA). ECMA is an organization dedicated to the production of standards for use in the disciplines of computing and communications. It is a standards and technical review group and not a trade organization.

Fibre distributed data interface (FDDI). The FDDI is the emerging standard for the LAN/MAN backbone. It is based upon a 100 Mbps fibre optic contra-rotating Token Ring (IEEE 802.5) system with both synchronous and asynchronous classes of traffic. It incorporates a dual ring architecture which provides fault tolerance to failures in nodes and the link, as well as providing a more sophisticated data transfer capability. A second version, FDDI II, is under development and this will supply an isochronous service for voice communications also, thereby providing a mixed voice/data system.

File transfer, access and management (FTAM). This is the application protocol for the OSI/RM file server. It presents the user with a logical database (held on the local and/or remote file server) and permits them the standard access rights and controls to that database, for example, open, close, read, write, erase, locate.

Frame relay. This is a temporary bearer system, based upon the current ISDN standards, which is being used to provide a faster X.25 service. It is used for data rates in the range of 2–45 Mbps and achieves a greater end-to-end throughput because it does not provide an error correction facility (cf. HDLC). Error recovery is left to the higher layer protocols.

Frequency division multiple access (FDMA). The bandwidth of the channel is segmented into sub-channels with guard-bands between each of these. These sub-channels are now allocated to users, either on a fixed (radio stations) or variable (satellite) basis. The advantage here is that several nodes can access the channel at the same time (albeit on a narrower bandwidth); however, a significant amount of bandwidth is wasted due to the essential guard-bands.

Gateway. This is the relay which is responsible for the conversion between different protocol systems to provide a uniform applications environment. The most common usage of gateways is for providing remote PC connectivity to a mainframe environment; in particular, connecting together a PC based Ethernet system with the corporate IBM mainframe which uses the SNA so that the PCs can gain remote access to the mainframe's file architecture.

Heterogeneous LAN management (HLM). The IEEE 802.1B committee is standardizing the network management architecture for LANs and this is termed the HLM architecture. It makes use of the station management entities (SMTs) housed in the network interface cards and the common management over the link (CMOL) to transfer the management information across the network. The HLM will form an integral part for the CMIS/CMIP architecture.

High-level data link control (HDLC). HDLC is the definitive data link bit oriented protocol for use on all packet switched data networks, as specified by ISO. It is the superset of protocols such as LAP, LAPB, LLC, LAPD, LAPE, LAPM and LAPX.

Initiator. This is the name given to the user/node which transmits the original data request. In connection oriented protocols confusion often arises due to the use of the terms transmitter and receiver. This is because both ends of the connection are transmitting and receiving and so the originator of the transaction is called the initiator.

Institute of Electrical and Electronic Engineers (IEEE). The IEEE is the American equivalent to the IEE. It is a world-wide professional organization and is heavily involved in the production of standards at a very detailed level. In the communications field it is particularly well known for its 802 standards as adopted by the ISO 8802 committees.

Integrated digital services network (ISDN). This is the provision of an end-to-end digital connection for the support of a wide range of services, such as voice, video, data, facsimile and so on. The primary aim is to provide a uniform set of standards for the transmission of digital information between networks. The ISDN is evolutionary in nature and will be subject to change as and when the new technologies become available. One of these changes will involve increasing the current maximum bandwidth support from just 2.048 Mbps (narrowband, NISDN) to in excess of 100 Mbps (broadband, BISDN).

International Organization for Standardization (ISO). ISO is the international organization responsible for the production of voluntary standards for use world-wide. It is concerned with many disciplines (not just that of communications and computing) and always views things from the user perspective. Only one representative from each member state is permitted (some 89 members) and the detailed effort is based around technical committees: TC97 is responsible for information systems.

International Radio Consultative Committee (CCIR). The CCIR is an ITU subcommittee responsible for the world-wide standardization of all aspects of radio communications. This committee has now been replaced by the ITU-R.

International Telecommunications Union (ITU). The ITU is responsible for all aspects of telecommunications from the United Nations' (UN) point of view. It was formed in 1865 and now comprises three sub-committees: the CCITT, the CCIR and the WARC. The ITU and its sub-committees are responsible for standardization from the suppliers' point of view and so it is not entirely consistent with the ISO approach.

International Telegraph and Telephone Consultative Committee (CCITT). The CCITT is the committee responsible for the production of recommendations concerning data communications, telephone switching, digital systems and terminals. Many of its members are drawn from the private and public sector, which reflects its predominantly supplier point of view. This committee has now been replaced by the ITU-T.

Kilostream. This was the original 64 kbps service supplied by BT of the UK. It has since then become a generic term for this carrier rate service and no longer implies a source from BT.

Local area network (LAN). A network which is geographically localized is commonly known as a LAN. Typically this type of network supports fewer than 200 nodes across a diameter of less than 2 km – these limits are more commonly only a few tens of nodes linked across a few hundreds of metres. The supported host data rates are in excess of 1 Mbps with delays in the order of milliseconds and with probabilities of error in the order of 10^{-9}.

Logical circuit. This is the name given to the local identification of a communications link between two devices; the actual link could be physical or virtual. In a telephone system the number memory function establishes a physical link using a logical number. This terminology is used to differentiate between global and local views of a system.

Manufacturing automation protocol (MAP). MAP is the protocol profile used by the car manufacturing industry. It is a real-time communications environment which uses the enhanced performance architecture (EPA) for the remote robot devices and the MiniMAP for the controller. The MAP/MiniMAP pair form the overall systems control for the peripheral EPA based devices.

Megastream. This was the original 2.048 Mbps service supplied by BT of the UK. It has since then become a generic term for this carrier rate service and no longer implies a source from BT.

Metropolitan area network (MAN). A MAN is a network which covers an entire city, but which is based upon LAN technology – that is, the interconnection of hundreds of LANs. In turn the interconnection of MANs gives rise to a WAN. Cable TV (CATV) is an analogue MAN and it is envisaged that the use of fibre optics and the FDDI/DQDB will provide the digital equivalent (DQDB is the only formally recognized MAN specification). The characteristic performance of a MAN falls between that of a LAN – high data rates but with relatively high delays!

Multicast. The transmission of data from one node to many, but normally a subset of the user population. Typical networks are for those supporting group work, such as conferencing, brainstorming sessions and diary systems. The advantage of this technique is that a set of users can cooperate with each other more effectively than with a series of point-to-point links but still have the feedback lost in a typical broadcast system.

Network. A network is the mechanism by which many data sources and sinks are interconnected. The network protocols are responsible for providing a fair and efficient access mechanism to the communications channel. The efficiency of these protocols determines the effectiveness of the network and gives rise to the many multiple access techniques. A network provides a service – this service must meet the users' (computers, humans and so on) needs.

OSI seven-layer reference model (OSI/RM). This model is the basis for the specification of the protocols for all open networks. An open network is one in which extension and interconnection is defined by a commonly agreed set of standards and is therefore vendor independent. This philosophy is being defined by ISO and is not concerned with implementation specific considerations. Vendors will, and do, base their implementations on this standard.

Packet assembler/disassembler (PAD). An intelligent workstation is normally required for using X.25, due to the requirement of packetization. The PAD is a device which permits dumb devices (such as a terminal) to use an X.25 network. It converts byte oriented devices into packet oriented devices.

Packet/message switched. The establishment of physical connection between two communicating devices but whose actual route is determined by the load supported by the network at the time of initiation. In the case of message switched the actual route across the network may change on a message by message basis whereas for a packet switched system it will be on a packet by packet basis.

Packet switched data network (PSDN). A PSDN is a network which supports the transfer of data using packet switching technology. It is commonly used on PDNs, in which case it is termed a packet switched public data network (PSPDN). The salient point is that high quality channels are provided for the reliable transfer of the information using carriers in the 9.6 kbps to 192 kbps region.

Photonic network. This refers to high speed optical networks. The carrier is typically in the gigaHertz region and is transmitted along an optical fibre. The more recent advances suggest that code division multiplexing may be more appropriate for these types of network due to its inherent bandwidth sharing capacity. The term photonic means that the information is carried by photons and not electrons (copper link).

Physical circuit. This is the actual tangible link which connects the communicating devices. All devices must be physically connected, either by wire, its equivalent, or the atmosphere, for communication to be possible. In a telephone system the wire constitutes the physical link with the telephone number the physical address.

Point-to-point. The direct transmission of data between two hosts. Examples of such networks are those based upon active transmission, such as fibre optic, switched systems and the telephone system (when operated is its most common form). This form of protocol is ideal when transferring data between restricted sets of hosts.

Protocol converter. This is the term applied to any relay which translates from one protocol to another to provide a common service feature. This conversion is performed on a one-to-one basis and so different protocol converters are required for different combinations of protocols.

Public data network (PDN). A PDN is a network which is supplied by a PTT or privatized PTT for general use. Many users pay for access to the system and can use it for private or public communications. The channels are usually high quality (hence for data transfer) and so are expensive compared to pure telephone links.

Public switched telephone network (PSTN). The PSTN is similar to PSDNs; however, the network is based upon the telephone system, which can be used for data and/or voice transfer. Data access to these networks is via modems which must support all of the coding and modulation systems necessary to ensure reliable communications.

Register insertion rings. The IEEE 802.9 committee is standardizing a LAN architecture for use in integrated voice/data (IVD) environments. This architecture is based upon the register insertion ring principle, which is a ring topology. Each node has its own data register which is inserted into the network whenever data has to be transmitted. The latest addition to this work is that of the 16 Mbps isochronous ethernet which supplies a 6 Mbps isochronous service (96 channels at 64 kbps) as well as the normal 10 Mbps data service.

Relay. This is the generic term for the processor which acts as the internetworking link. Relays are capable of linking networks at varying levels of protocol capability – that is, from simple signal regeneration (repeater) to full protocol conversion (gateway).

Repeater. The interconnection of two LANs at their physical layer uses a repeater. Repeaters act as sophisticated signal regenerators and are used to link together two, or more, LANs to form one extended LAN. Every signal is passed from one side of a repeater to the other. Repeaters are also used to connect LANs which use different media, for example UTP to coax, coax to fibre. There are local and remote repeaters (cf. bridges) and the latter must be used in pairs.

Respondent. This is the name given to the user/node which receives the initial request for data transaction. The respondent is capable of data transmission but is usually considered as acting in response to prompted action.

Router. The interconnection of two LANs through their common network layer protocol is supported by a router. Routers will support the linkage of any type of LAN as long as they use a common network layer protocol such as TCP/IP. The more sophisticated routers will support several types of network protocol concurrently but they do not normally translate between them. Routers are responsible for routing data between the communicating nodes and so provide a reliable communication network.

Router/bridge (bridging router). This is a relay provided by a router manufacturer but which supports some bridging functionality. This relay can be configured to act as a bridge for those protocols which it cannot route, for example Digital's local area transport (LAT). At present it is essential that all of the connected router/bridges be supplied by the same manufacturer.

Source route bridging. Multi-ring Token Ring architectures are normally linked using bridges which use the source routing technique. This is a rival technique to that of transparent bridging and provides a system in which the end user network interface cards dictate the route their data frames take across the network. Source routing is defined as part of the IEEE 802.5 standard. There are new bridges now available called source routing transparent (SRT) bridges which permit the construction of mixed bridge (transparent and source routing) architectures.

Source route transparent (SRT) bridges. SRT bridges provide interconnection between transparent bridge and source routing bridge domains. Unlike their fore-runners (SR-TBs) there is no need to have two separate domains and so SRT bridges can be placed at any position within the network architecture.

Space division multiple access (SDMA). This refers to the switching techniques –

that is, circuit and message/packet/character switched. The information traverses a physically different route depending on the appropriate parameters, for example, network loading or destination address. The network therefore becomes limited by its physical topology: the more links then the greater the traffic that can be supported.

Spread spectrum multiple access (SSMA). This technique is closely related to CDMA – SSMA is one form of CDMA. In essence a SSMA system utilizes a carrying signal which is responsible for ensuring that the data is placed within the signal space such that it is orthogonal (or as near as possible) to all the other signals present, or to be present, in that space. Common systems are frequency hopping, direct sequence, chirp and time hopping, all of which result in the legendary spread spectrum noise immunity.

Synchronous digital hierarchy (SDH). The SDH is an internationally agreed bandwidth allocation mechanism which facilitates efficient signal multiplexing. The basic bandwidth fragment is set at 51.3 Mbps and this is allocated in multiples of this bandwidth, thereby providing a hierarchy from 51 Mbps to 2 Gbps.

Synchronous optical network (SONET). This is the CCITT's 155.25 Mbps synchronous optical network architecture. The multiplexing of the information onto this will be based upon the synchronous transfer mode (STM or frame relay) and the asynchronous transfer mode (ATM or cell relay). The 155 Mbps carrying capacity of SONET means that not only is it well suited to acting as the backbone network of FDDI based architectures but that multiples of these can then be used to support the 2 Gbps architectures as defined in the synchronous digital hierarchy (SDH).

Systems network architecture (SNA). This is IBM's proprietary networking architecture which is used to support communications between all of their product range. IBM claim that they are extending the range of non-IBM based interconnectivity of SNA to include OSI/RM as well as TCP/IP; the latter is already supplied.

Time division multiple access (TDMA). In this instance the access scheme is provided by either physically or logically segmenting the channel access into time slots – either fixed or variable length. Each time slot is allocated to one user only and so no corruption can occur from other transmissions. The advantage is that the bandwidth can be utilized very efficiently; however, if there are a large number of users then there can be a relatively long delay between successive accesses from a particular node.

Token bus. This is the oldest form of LAN but it is now used predominantly in real-time control environments such as manufacturing. Its most common application is as part of the MAP profile, as championed by General Motors. The token bus system uses the token passing principle across a passive bus topology channel.

Token Ring. This is the LAN championed by IBM and commercially introduced in 1983. It is currently being defined by the IEEE 802.5 committees and will support both

4 and 16 Mbps data carrying capacities. The Token Ring is well suited to systems which produce large amounts of regular traffic and which may have real time constraints.

Transparent bridging. This is the technique defined by the IEEE 802.1 committee for the interconnection of like LANs at the MAC level. The concept of transparent bridging is based upon the fact that the bridges take full responsibility for 'routing' the frames across the bridged architecture. This means that the physical nature of the network's topology is totally transparent to the end-system network interface cards.

Transport relay. The protocol conversion between different transport service is supported by a transport relay. These are the simplest form of protocol converter. The transport relay does not need to translate between different physical subnetworks as this is already a part of the functionality of the transport service.

Triple-X. This is the collective term given to the protocols which support the PAD: X.3, X.28 and X.29. X.3 defines the functions and characteristics of the PAD, X.28 defines the control procedures for communication between a PAD and the attached device and X.29 describes the procedures between the PAD and the remote DTE (either another PAD or an X.25 PLP unit).

Value added network (VAN). The provision of extra services on top of a commercially available or public network is termed a VAN. The sale of an electronic mail system based upon, say, the ethernet LAN would be a VAN because the network would have been enhanced so that is more useful to the end user. VANs are the mechanism by which most organizations sell their network based products; the basic subnetwork is purchased from, say, Digital or IBM and then user services are added as appropriate to the target applications environment.

Virtual circuit. This is a connection in which the user perceives the existence of a dedicated physical circuit but which in reality utilizes a physical circuit which is shared among a set of users. Such a link can also encompass the internal buffers required to implement the use of several logical circuits. Frames/packets may (external virtual circuit and internal virtual circuit) or may not (external virtual circuit and internal datagram) cross the same physical route depending upon the actual implementation.

Wavelength division multiple access (WDMA). This is the optical network equivalent to frequency division multiple access. The different carriers are segregated according to wavelength (cf. frequency) and are transmitted along an optical waveguide that is, a fibre optic link. The transmitters and receivers are usually sets of LEDs.

Wide area network (WAN). Most public networks are termed WANs. Typically these types of networks connect thousands of nodes across thousands of miles, for example, the international telephone system. The data rates are typically 10 kbps with probabilities of error in the order of 10^{-6}. Data delays can differ significantly from a few tenths of seconds (telephone) up to minutes for some telex and facsimile systems.

World Administrative Radio Conference (WARC). This is the meeting, under the auspices of the ITU, responsible for world-wide bandwidth assignment to different service requirements.

X.21. This is the recommended physical layer standard for the X.25 protocol (the link between a DTE and a DCE). It is a digital specification and so a second standard, termed X.21bis, has been produced for interfacing X.25 networks to analogue switching systems. Both X.21bis and RS 232-C use the CCITT V.24 circuit assignments, but RS 232-C is the more commonly used physical interface.

X.25. This is the CCITT protocol recommendation for point-to-point packet switched communications. The OSI equivalent is the communications subnetwork; that is, the bottom three layers of the stack, which are termed the packet, frame and physical layers in X.25 terminology − X.25 is one possible implementation of the communications subnetwork. Many X.25 implementations now use the same cabling infrastructure as the telephone lines for the physical layer.

X.75. This is the CCITT recommendation for interconnecting PDNs. X.75 is the protocol used to send data between signalling terminal exchanges (STEs). The routing algorithm plan which is employed by the STEs using X.75 is defined by X.110. X.75 is very similar to X.25 with only the physical signalling and transmission aspects being different between them (G.703 is recommended). The addressing scheme used is defined by X.121 (as is the case for X.25).

X.400. This is the CCITT recommendation for the message handling system proposed in the OSI seven-layer reference model (the applications layer). This system is more commonly known as electronic mail whereas the formal OSI implementation is termed MOTIS. In essence X.400 mimics the postal system in that a message consists of an address and a letter. The letter is mailed using the address, or group of addresses in the case of a mail shot.

X.500. This is the CCITT recommendation for the directory service proposed by the ISO committees. This directory service is responsible for providing the address tables for all of the users on the network. It is the computer and data communications equivalent to directory services on telephone networks.

X.700. This is the CCITT recommendation for network management. The aim is to construct an integrated network management architecture encompassing the public, private, data, voice, local and wide area networking elements.

C

Networking Standards

C1 Standards organizations

C2 ISO standards

C3 ITU-T (CCITT) recommendations

C4 IEEE 802 standards

C5 Internet RFCs

C1 Standards organizations

ISO

Central Secretariat, 1 Rue de Varembe
1211 GENEVA 20, Switzerland

ITU-T (CCITT)
2 Rue de Varembe
1211 GENEVA 20, Switzerland

BSI

Head Office, 2 Park Street
LONDON W1A 2BS, UK

ECMA

Rue de Rhone 114
1024 GENEVA, Switzerland

IEEE

345 East 47th Street
NEW YORK, NY 10017, USA

CEN/CENELEC/CEPT/ITSTC
Rue Brederode 2, PO Box 5
1000 BRUSSELS, Belgium

C2 ISO standards

The ISO standards use the following status designations:

ISO   Published international standard. Stable.

DIS   Draft international (ISO) standard. Usually stable, but subject to minor changes. Will rarely have major technical changes.

TR   Technical report (ISO). Finalized, but not having the status of an international standard.

ADD   Addendum to a published standard. Stable.

DAD   ADD at a stage equivalent to DIS.

AMD   Amendment to a published standard. Stable.

DAM   AMD at a stage equivalent to DIS.

ISP   International Standardized Profile.

DISP   ISP at a stage equivalent to DIS.

Note that the equivalent CCITT recommendations are given where applicable. This list is not exhaustive and it is under constant revision.

The ISO standards referenced in this book are:

ISO 7498–1 (1984)	OSI Basic Reference Model
ISO 7498–1 ADD 1	OSI Basic Reference Model – Addendum 1: Connectionless data transmission
ISO 7498–2 (1989)	OSI Basic Reference Model – Part 2: Security Architecture
ISO 7498–3 (1989)	OSI Basic Reference Model – Part 3: Naming and Addressing
ISO 7498–4 (1989)	OSI Basic Reference Model – Part 4: Management Framework (X.700)
SO 8571–1 (1988)	FTAM – Part 1: General Introduction
SO 8571–4 (1988)	FTAM – Part 4: File Protocol Specification
ISO 8649 (1988)	Service Definition for the Association Control Service Element (ACSE) (X.217)
ISO 8650 (1988)	Protocol Specification for the ACSE (X.227)
ISO 9066–1	Reliable Transfer: Model and Service Definition (X.218)
ISO 9066–2	Reliable Transfer: Protocol Specification (X.228)
ISO 9545 (1989)	Application Layer Structure
ISO 9804 (1990)	Service Definition for the Commitment, Concurrency and Recovery Service Element (CCRSE) (X.851)
ISO 9805 (1990)	Protocol Specification for the CCRSE (X.852)
ISO 10026–1 (1992)	Distributed Transaction Processing (DTP) – Part 1: TP Model
ISO 10026–2 (1992)	DTP – Part 2: TP Service
ISO 10026–3 (1992)	DTP – Part 3: TP Specification
ISO DIS 13712–1	Remote Operations part 1: Concepts, Model and Notation (X.880)

ISO DIS 13712–2	Remote Operations part 2: Service Definition (X.881)
ISO DIS 13712–3	Remote Operations part 3: Protocol Specification (X.882)
ISO 8822 (1988)	Connection-Oriented Presentation Service Definition (X.216)
ISO 8822 AMD 1	Presentation Service Definition – Addendum 1: Connectionless-Mode Presentation Service
ISO 8823 (1988)	Connection-Oriented Presentation Protocol Specification (X.226)
ISO 8824 (1990)	Specification of Abstract Syntax Notation One (ASN.1) (X.208)
ISO 8825 (1990)	Specification of Basic Encoding Rules for Abstract Syntax Notation One (ASN.1) (X.209)
SO 8326 (1987)	Basic Connection-Oriented Session Service Definition (X.215)
ISO 8072 (1986)	Transport Service Definition (X.214)
ISO 8072 ADD 1	Transport Service Definition – Addendum 1: Connectionless-Mode Transmission
ISO 8073 (1992)	Connection-Oriented Transport Protocol Specification (X.224)
ISO 8602 (1988)	Protocol for Providing the Connectionless-Mode Transport Service
ISO 8208 (1990)	X.25 Packet Level Protocol (PLP) for Data Terminal Equipment
ISO 8348	Network Service Definition (X.213)
ISO 8348 ADD 1	Network Service Definition – Addendum 1: Connectionless Mode Transmission
ISO 8473 (1988)	Protocol for Providing the Connectionless-Mode Network Service (CLNS)
ISO 8878 (1992)	Use of X.25 to Provide the Connection-Mode Network Service (X.223)
ISO 8880–1 (1990)	Specification of Protocols to Provide and Support the OSI Network Service – Part 1: General Principles
ISO 8881 (1989)	Use of the X.25 PLP in Local Area Networks
ISO 9542 (1988)	End System to Intermediate System Routing Exchange Protocol for use in Conjunction with ISO 8473

DIS 10028 (1993)	Definition of the Relaying Functions of a Network Layer Intermediate System
ISO 3309 (1991)	High-Level Data Link Control (HDLC) Procedures – Frame Structure
ISO 7478 (1987)	Multilink Procedures
ISO 7776 (1986)	HDLC Procedures – X.25 LAPB-Compatible DTE Data Link Layer Procedures
ISO 8802–2 (1989)	Local Area Networks (LANs) – Part 2: Logical Link Control (LLC)
ISO 8802–2	LANs – Part 2: LLC – Addendum 1: Flow Control Techniques for Bridged LANs
ISO 8802–3 (1992)	LANs – Part 3: Carrier Sense Multiple Access with Collision Detection (CSMA/CD)
ISO 8802–4 (1990)	LANs – Part 4: Token-Passing Bus Access Method and Physical Layer Specifications
ISO 8802–5 (1992)	LANs – Part 5: Token-Ring Access Method and Physical Layer Specifications
DIS 8802–6 (1992)	LANs – Part 6: Distributed Queue Dual Bus Access Method and Physical Layer Specifications
ISO 8802–7 (1991)	LANs – Part 7: Slotted Ring Access Method and Physical Layer Specifications
ISO 9314–1 (1989)	Fibre Distributed Data Interface (FDDI) – Token Ring Physical Layer Protocol (PHY)
ISO 9314–2 (1989)	FDDI – Token Ring Media Access Control (MAC)
DIS 9314–5	FDDI part 5: Hybrid Ring Control (FDDI-II)
ISO 10038 (1991)	MAC Bridges (IEEE 802.1D-1990)
ISO 10039 (1991)	MAC Service Definition
IEC 907 (1989)	CSMA/CD 10 Mbps LAN – Planning and Installation Guide
ISO 9595 (1991)	Common Management Information Service Definition (CMIS) (X.710)
ISO 9596–1 (1991)	Common Management Information Protocol (CMIP) Specification (X.711)
ISO 9594–1 (1990)	The Directory – Part 1: Overview of Concepts, Models and Services (X.500)

TR 10000–1 (1992)	Framework and Taxonomy of International Standardized Profiles (ISPs) – Part 1: Framework
TR 10000–2 (1992)	Framework and Taxonomy of ISPs – Part 1: Taxonomy

C3 ITU-T (CCITT) recommendations

The ITU-T (CCITT) recommendations referenced in this book are:

I.430	Basic rate user-network interface – Layer 1 specification
I.431	Primary rate user-network interface – Layer 1 specification
I.441	ISDN user-network interface data link layer specification (LAPD)
I.451	ISDN user-network interface network layer specification
X.3	Packet assembly/disassembly facility (PAD) in a PDN
X.21	Interface between DTE and DCE for synchronous operation on PDNs
X.21b	Use on PDNs of DTE which is designed for interfacing to synchronous V-series modems
X.24	List of definitions for interchange circuits between DTE and DCE on PDNs
X.25	Interface between DTE and DCE for terminals operating in the packet mode and connected to PDNs by dedicated circuit
X.28	DTE/DCE interface for start–stop mode DTE accessing the PAD facility in a PDN situated in the same country
X.29	Procedures for the exchange of control information and user data between a PAD facility and a packet mode DTE or another PAD
X.75	Terminal and transit call control procedures and network transfer system on international circuits between packet switched data networks
X.110	International routing principles and routing plans for PDNs
X.121	International numbering plan for PDNs
X.135	Delay aspects of grade of service for PDNs when providing international packet switched data services
X.136	Blocking aspects of grade of service for PDNs when providing international packet switched data services
X.137	Availability performance values for PDNs when providing international packet switched services
X.200	Reference model of open systems for CCITT applications

X.208	Specification of abstract syntax notation one (ASN.1)
X.209	Specification of basic encoding rules for abstract syntax notation one (ASN.1)
X.210	Open Systems Interconnection (OSI) layer service definition conventions
X.211	Physical service definition of Open Systems Interconnection (OSI) for CCITT applications
X.212	Data link service definition of Open Systems Interconnection (OSI) for CCITT applications
X.213	Network service definition for Open Systems Interconnection (OSI) for CCITT applications
X.214	Transport service definition for Open Systems Interconnection (OSI) for CCITT applications
X.215	Session service definition for Open System Interconnection (OSI) for CCITT applications
X.216	Presentation service definition for Open System Interconnection (OSI) for CCITT
X.217	Association control service definition for Open System Interconnection (OSI) for CCITT
X.218	Reliable transfer: model and service definition
X.219	Remote operations: model, notation and service definition
X.220	Use of X.200 – Series protocols in CCITT Applications
X.223	Use of X.25 to provide the OSI connection-mode network service for CCITT applications
X.224	Transport protocol specification for Open System Interconnection (OSI) for CCITT applications
X.225	Session protocol specification for Open System Interconnection (OSI) for CCITT applications
X.226	Presentation protocol specification for Open System Interconnection (OSI) for CCITT applications
X.227	Association control protocol specification for Open System Interconnection (OSI) for CCITT applications
X.228	Reliable transfer: Protocol specification
X.229	Remote operations: Protocol specification
X.250	Formal description techniques for data communications protocols and services
X.400	Message handling systems: System model-service elements
X.500	The Directory – Overview of concepts, models and services
X.610	Provision of support for the OSI connection-mode network service

X.650	OSI – Reference model for naming and addressing
X.660	OSI – Procedures for the operation of OSI registration authorities: general procedures
X.700	Management framework for OSI
X.710	Common management information service (CMIS) definition
X.711	Common management information protocol (CMIP) specification
X.800	Security architecture for OSI CCITT applications
X.860	OSI – DTP: Model

C4 IEEE 802 standards

802.1	Overview and architecture
802.1A	Conformance testing methodology
802.1B	LAN/MAN management
802.1D	MAC bridges
802.1E	System load protocol
802.1F	Guidelines for layer management standards
802.1G	Remote MAC bridging
802.1I	MAC bridges: FDDI supplement
802.1–90/28	Generic managed objects
802.1–90/29	Systems management overview
802.1–90/40	IEEE 802.1 recent meeting reports
802.1–90/55	SMI Part 1,2,4 definition of managed objects
802.1–90/57	MAC group addresses for standards
802.2	Logical link control (4)
802.3	10BASE5 CSMA/CD
803.3A	10BASE2 CSMA/CD
802.3B	10BROAD36
802.3C	Repeaters for 10 Mbps
802.3D	Fibre optic inter-repeater link (FOIRL)

802.3E	1BASE5
802.3G/d8	AUI cable test
802.3G/d4	MAU conformance test
802.3H	Layer management
802.3I	System considerations for 10BASET
802.3J	Fibre optic CSMA/CD for 10BASEF
802.3K	Layer management for hub devices
802.3L	CSMA/CD twisted pair medium type 10BASET–PICS proforma
802.4	Token passing bus
802.4B	Enhancements for physical layer diversity – redundant media control unit
802.4J/d2.3	Fibre optic conformance test specifications
802.4L–14a	Factory RF channel modelling
802.4L–14b	UHF characterization in factory
802.4L–8a	Microwave oven interference measurement
802.5	Token Ring access method and physical layer specifications
802.5A	Station management revision
802.5B	4 Mbps over UTP
802.5E	Management entity specification
802.5F	16 Mbps operation
802.5G	Token Ring PICS proforma
802.5H	Acknowledged connectionless LLC
802.5I	Early token release
802.5J	Optional fibre station attachment
802.5K	Token Ring wiring guide
802.5M	Token Ring source routing tutorial
802.5M/d2	Token Ring source routing supplement to MAC bridges
802.6	Metropolitan area networks DQDB
802.6A	Multiple post bridging

802.6C	PLCP for DCI
802.6I	Remote LAN bridging
802.7	Broadband LAN recommended practices
802.8	Fibre optic CSMA/CD network approaches
802.9	IVD architectural tutorial document
802.9A	Integrated voice and data LAN
802.10A	Interoperable LAN security – Part A: Model
802.10B	Interoperable LAN security – Part B: Secure data exchange
802.10–89/14	Tutorials–3 network security tutorials
802.10–90/16	Plenary tutorial

C5 Internet RFCs

Requests for Comments (RFCs) are the working notes on the Internet and refer to the design, implementation, standardization and experimentation involving the Internet Protocol Suite (IPS). All of the Internet standards are released as RFCs but the majority of RFCs are working documents covering many different facets of the work involving the Internet.

Access to the RFCs is most easily obtained through the Internet itself. There are several RFC FTP server sites throughout the world and so all of the RFCs can be electronically retrieved in postscript or text formats (Washburn, 1993).

Index

M